THE CAMBRIDGE
COMPANION TO
COLERIDGE

EDITED BY
LUCY NEWLYN
St Edmund Hall, Oxford

CAMBRIDGE
UNIVERSITY PRESS

PUBLISHED BY THE PRESS SYNDICATE OF THE UNIVERSITY OF CAMBRIDGE
The Pitt Building, Trumpington Street, Cambridge, United Kingdom

CAMBRIDGE UNIVERSITY PRESS
The Edinburgh Building, Cambridge CB2 2RU, UK
40 West 20th Street, New York, NY 10011-4211, USA
477 Williamstown Road, Port Melbourne, VIC 3207, Australia
Ruiz de Alarcón 13, 28014 Madrid, Spain
Dock House, The Waterfront, Cape Town 8001, South Africa

http://www.cambridge.org

First published 2002

Printed in the United Kingdom at the University Press, Cambridge

Typeface Sabon 10/13 pt   *System* LaTeX 2_ε [TB]

A catalogue record for this book is available from the British Library

ISBN 0 521 65071 2 hardback
ISBN 0 521 65909 4 paperback

The Cambridge Companion to Coleridge

Samuel Taylor Coleridge is one of the most influential, as well as one of the most enigmatic, of all Romantic figures. The possessor of a precocious talent, he dazzled contemporaries with his poetry, journalism, philosophy and oratory without ever quite living up to his early promise, or overcoming problems of dependency and drug addiction. *The Cambridge Companion to Coleridge* does full justice to the many facets of Coleridge's life, thought and writing. Specially commissioned essays focus on his major poems, including 'The Rime of the Ancient Mariner' and 'Christabel', his Notebooks, and his major work of non-fiction, the *Biographia Literaria*. Attention is given to his role as talker, journalist, critic and philosopher; to his politics, his religion, and his reputation in his own times and afterwards. A chronology and guides to further reading complete the volume, making this an indispensable guide to Coleridge and his work.

LUCY NEWLYN is Fellow and Tutor in English at St Edmund Hall, Oxford. She is an authority on Coleridge and Wordsworth, and has published extensively on English Romanticism. Her publications include *Coleridge, Wordsworth and the Language of Allusion* (1986), *'Paradise Lost' and the Romantic Reader* (1993), and *Reading, Writing and Romanticism: The Anxiety of Reception* (2000), all with Oxford University Press.

CAMBRIDGE COMPANIONS TO LITERATURE

CONTENTS

CONTRIBUTORS

JOHN BEER, Peterhouse, Cambridge

JULIE CARLSON, University of California, Santa Barbara

DEIRDRE COLEMAN, University of Sydney, Australia

JOSIE DIXON, Palgrave, Macmillan

JAMES ENGELL, Harvard University

ANGELA ESTERHAMMER, University of Western Ontario

KELVIN EVEREST, University of Liverpool

TIM FULFORD, Nottingham Trent University

PAUL HAMILTON, Queen Mary and Westfield College, London

PETER J. KITSON, University of Wales, Bangor

JAMES C. MCKUSICK, University of Maryland, Baltimore County

PAUL MAGNUSON, New York University

J. C. C. MAYS, University College, Dublin

LUCY NEWLYN, St Edmund Hall, Oxford

MARY ANNE PERKINS, Birkbeck College, University of London

SEAMUS PERRY, University of Glasgow

All quotations from Coleridge's prose refer to *The Collected Works of Samuel Taylor Coleridge*, general editor Kathleen Coburn, Bollingen Series (Princeton University Press, 1971–). Individual volumes in the series have their own abbreviations, which are offered below. Unless it is otherwise stated, all quotations from Coleridge's poetry refer to *The Complete Poetical Works of Samuel Taylor Coleridge*, ed. Ernest Hartley Coleridge (2 vols., Oxford: Clarendon Press, 1975).

    This volume was already in press when the latest additions to the *Collected Coleridge* were published; I was unable, therefore, to incorporate references to Jim Mays's fine edition of Coleridge's *Poems*, or to bring references to the Notebooks up-to-date.

AR	*Aids to Reflection*, ed. John Beer, Bollingen Series 75 (Princeton University Press, 1993).
BL	*Biographia Literaria*, ed. James Engell and W. Jackson Bate, Bollingen Series 75, 2 vols. (Princeton University Press, 1983).
Church and State	*On the Constitution of the Church and State*, ed. John Colmer, Bollingen Series 75 (Princeton University Press, 1976).
CL	*The Collected Letters of Samuel Taylor Coleridge*, ed. Earl Leslie Griggs, 6 vols. (Oxford University Press, 1956–71).
C. Lects	*Lectures 1808–1819 On Literature*, ed. R. A. Foakes, Bollingen Series 75, 2 vols. (Princeton University Press, 1987).
CM	*Marginalia*, 5 parts to date, ed. George Whalley and H. J. Jackson (Princeton University Press, 1980–).

CN	*The Notebooks of Samuel Taylor Coleridge*, ed. Kathleen Coburn, 4 vols. to date, each in two parts (London: Routledge and Kegan Paul, 1957–).
CPW	*The Complete Poetical Works of Samuel Taylor Coleridge*, ed. Ernest Hartley Coleridge, 2 vols. (Oxford: Clarendon Press, 1975).
CT	*Coleridge the Talker: A Series of Contemporary Descriptions and Comments*, ed. R. W. Armour and R. F. Howes (Ithaca, NY: Cornell University Press, 1940).
EOT	*Essays on his Times*, ed. David V. Erdman, 3 vols. (London and Princeton, NJ, 1978).
EY	*The Letters of William and Dorothy Wordsworth: The Early Years, 1787–1805*, ed. Ernest de Selincourt, 2nd edn, revised Chester Shaver (Oxford: Clarendon Press, 1967).
Friend	*The Friend*, ed. Barbara Rooke, 2 vols. (Princeton University Press, 1969).
Howe	William Hazlitt, *Complete Works*, ed. P. P. Howe, 21 vols. (London and Toronto: J. M. Dent and Sons, 1930–4).
IR	*S. T. Coleridge: Interviews and Recollections*, ed. Seamus Perry (Basingstoke and New York: Palgrave, 2000).
KL	*The Letters of John Keats 1814–1821*, ed. Hyder Edward Rollins, 2 vols. (Cambridge University Press, 1958).
Lects. 1795	*Lectures 1795 On Politics and Religion*, ed. Lewis Patton and Peter Mann, Bollingen Series 75 (Princeton University Press, 1971).
Misc. C	*Coleridge's Miscellaneous Criticism*, ed. T. M. Raysor (Cambridge, MA: Constable & Co., 1936).
MY	*The Letters of William and Dorothy Wordsworth: The Middle Years, 1806–11*, ed. Ernest de Selincourt, 2nd edn, revised Chester Shaver (Oxford: Clarendon Press, 1967).
Phil Lects	*The Philosophical Lectures of Samuel Taylor Coleridge*, ed. Owen Barfield and Kathleen Coburn (Princeton University Press, 1949).
Prelude	William Wordsworth, *The Prelude: The Four Texts (1798, 1799, 1805, 1850)*, ed. Jonathan Wordsworth (Harmondsworth, Middlesex: Penguin, 1995).
Sh C	*Shakespearian Criticism*, ed. Thomas Middleton Raysor, 2 vols. (London: J. M. Dent, 1960).
SM	*The Statesman's Manual, Lay Sermons*, ed. R. J. White, Bollingen Series 75 (Princeton University Press, 1993).

SWF	*Shorter Works and Fragments*, 2 parts, ed. H. J. Jackson and J. R. de J. Jackson (Princeton University Press, 1995).
TT	*Table Talk Recorded by Henry Nelson Coleridge (and John Taylor Coleridge)*, ed. Carl C. Woodring, 2 vols. (Princeton University Press, 1990)
VCL mss.	Victoria College Library mss.
Watchman	*The Watchman*, ed. Lewis Patton, Bollingen Series 75 (Princeton University Press, 1970).
Wordsworth Prose	*The Prose Works of William Wordsworth*, ed. W. J. B. Owen and J. W. Smyser, 3 vols. (Oxford: Clarendon Press, 1974).

CHRONOLOGY

1772 Born at Ottery St Mary, Devonshire (21 October)

1782 At Christ's Hospital School, London

1792 Jesus College, Cambridge

1793 Attends the trial for treason of William Frend (May); enlists in the army under assumed identity (December)

1794 Returns to Cambridge; collaboration with Robert Southey; publishes *The Fall of Robespierre*; begins 'Religious Musings'

1795 Political lectures at Bristol; marriage to Sara Fricker; publishes *Conciones ad Populum*

1796 Tours the Midlands to sell his political journal, the *Watchman*; Publishes *Poems on Various Subjects* and moves to Nether Stowey; first son, Hartley, born

1797 Finishes his play, *Osorio*; William and Dorothy Wordsworth become Coleridge's neighbours; publishes *Poems, to which are now Added, Poems by Charles Lamb and Charles Lloyd*

1798 *Fears in Solitude* published; starts writing for the *Morning Post*; collaboration with Wordsworth and anonymous joint publication of *Lyrical Ballads*; second son, Berkeley, born in May; visit to Germany (September)

1799 Death of Berkeley (April); return to England in July; meets Sara Hutchinson (October); working for the *Morning Post*

1800 Moves to Greta Hall, Keswick, to be near the Wordsworths in Grasmere; second edition of *Lyrical Ballads* published

1802 Marriage starts to founder; publishes 'Dejection'; birth of daughter, Sara

1803 *Poems* (1803); Scottish tour with the Wordsworths

1804 Visits Sicily; becomes Acting Public Secretary in Malta

1806 Returns to Keswick; agrees to separate from his wife

1807   Moves between London, Stowey and Bristol

1808   'Lectures on the Principles of Poetry' at the Royal Institution; moves to Allen Bank, Grasmere; begins to publish his weekly journal, the *Friend*

1809–10 Publishes 28 numbers of the *Friend*

1811   Contributions to the *Courier*

1811–12 Lectures on drama and Shakespeare in London

1813   Coleridge's play, *Remorse*, is performed at Drury Lane

1814   Lectures in Bristol

1815   Dictates *Biographia Literaria*

1816   Publishes *Christabel* (three editions), *The Statesman's Manual*

1817   Publishes *Zapolya*, *Biographia Literaria* and *Sibylline Leaves*; lectures on poetry and drama (January–March)

1818   Publishes *The Friend* (3-vol. edition); lectures on literature and philosophy

1819   Meets Keats; occasional contributions to *Blackwood's*

1822   Henry Nelson Coleridge begins recording *Table Talk*

1823   Begins *Youth and Age*

1825   *Aids to Reflection* published

1828   *Poetical Works* (3 vols.)

1829   *On the Constitution of Church and State*

1834   Death at Highgate

ACKNOWLEDGEMENTS

Many thanks to Josie Dixon for inviting me to edit this book; and to the anonymous readers for Cambridge University Press who made suggestions in the early stages. Thanks also to Linda Bree for her many helpful observations, to Leigh Mueller for her careful copy-editing, and to Neil de Cort for seeing the book through the Press.

I am very grateful to Phil Cardinale for giving up his own valuable time to check the typescript and the proofs. Any mistakes that remain are of course my own responsibility.

My thanks to the Principal and Fellows of St Edmund Hall for a term's sabbatical leave, during which the bulk of the work was completed.

LUCY NEWLYN

Introduction

Since the early 1980s, major developments have occurred in the way British Romanticism is approached and understood. We now read the literature of that period (1789–1832) with a greater consciousness of its political, economic and social contexts. The impact on British writers of the French Revolution and ensuing political movements has been more thoroughly investigated than ever before. New historicist criticism has taught us to understand how market-forces influenced the production and enjoyment of literature. Women's writing (as well as the work of various male authors previously judged to be 'minor') has come very rapidly to the fore, involving significant shifts in how we think about the canon.

As a consequence of all these changes, it would be unthinkable nowadays to design a course on British Romanticism based around the work of six male poets, Blake, Wordsworth, Coleridge, Byron, Keats and Shelley; or even around a list expanded to include the great prose-writers of the age: Scott, Hazlitt, Lamb, Peacock and De Quincey. 'What about Wollstonecraft, Austen, Mary Shelley?', our students might legitimately complain if such a course were offered. (And what about Barbauld, Edgeworth, Godwin, Burke, Paine and Thelwall, one might rejoin; for the list of writers available for study grows longer every year.) The 'Big Six' go on being of vital importance, of course. But we now want to understand and appreciate their achievements historically and comparatively, not just according to the standards of taste which have made them classics for two centuries. This evidently entails diversification, both in the range of writers we teach, and in the disciplines and methodologies we draw on in our teaching. But it also calls for a reconsideration of the central figures who at one time constituted the canon. For, if the meaning of the word 'Romanticism' has shifted to accommodate a broader spectrum of texts and approaches, then it follows that the contribution made by each individual Romantic writer asks also to be reappraised.

What does it mean to read 'The Ancient Mariner' as a contribution to political debate in the late 1790s? What happens to our understanding of 'Frost at Midnight' when we place it in its original context, as one of three poems published in a quarto volume (1798) entitled *Fears in Solitude*? How true is it to say that Coleridge began as a radical and ended as a conservative? Do those terms apply to his idiosyncratic engagement with the politics of his own day? If we think of Coleridge not just as a poet and a critic, but as a journalist, preacher and lecturer, how does this affect our view of his overall contribution? Such questions are being asked daily, at a specialist level – in critical essays, scholarly articles and monographs addressing specific issues, genres and texts. But the answers are slow to filter into the classroom; for these scholarly materials are scattered, sometimes even inaccessible. Moreover, the level of research expertise required to process them (let alone to amalgamate the separate areas of interest) is high. Hence the need for a volume such as this, addressing the full range of Coleridge's works, and making accessible to students both their contemporary contexts and current approaches to them.

This need is all the more pressing because of the interdisciplinary nature of Coleridge's thinking. If his 'myriad-mindedness' is legendary, it is also responsible for the difficulty his writings pose – and have always posed – for readers. His massive contribution spans most of the species of knowledge available to nineteenth-century enquiry. It bears witness to a historical moment at which interdisciplinary thought still seemed possible. The word 'science', for Coleridge, meant knowledge in general. Theology was not to be separated from philosophy. Philosophy – properly understood – was a species of poetry. But the interconnections between different discourses were already becoming less transparent, as knowledge became professionalised and therefore specialised. Even Coleridge's contemporary readers found the threads of his thinking mysterious, baffling, frustrating. These difficulties were compounded by the tenacity with which he opposed (or seemed to oppose) the secular reading practices of his day. His lifelong mission to retrieve a vanishing spiritual authority was the register of his resistance to modernity. He voiced that resistance in a language which has seemed to many obscurantist and impenetrable.

Readers in the twenty-first century, approaching Coleridge for the first time, are faced with the daunting task of re-building intellectual connections obscure in their origins, and now lost. They are aided in this project by the magnificent (though still incomplete) *Collected Coleridge*, by the *Letters*, *Notebooks* and *Marginalia*, and by a corpus of critical commentary whose exponential growth since the early 1980s has been both exhilarating and bewildering. Some of the difficulties they experience in reading Coleridge are ones he foresaw. Secularisation has not only relegated the Bible to a thing of the past, but has rendered the idea of spiritual meaning opaque. Knowledge has become diversified in such a way as to make Coleridge's combination of eclecticism and erudition inaccessible, both in terms of its actual content and in the habit of mind it presupposes. The professionalisation of literary criticism (intensified, in recent years, by the advent of critical theory) has made academic discourse so specialised that it can produce volumes of disparate exegesis on a single Coleridgean text.

On top of all this, there is the difficulty posed for readers by the passage of time. Time has the confusing tendency of making the significance of public allusions seem irretrievable, by obscuring or removing the immediacy of political events. Simultaneously, it moves private allusions further under cover. This makes the task of accurately interpreting Coleridge's poetry almost as difficult as understanding his vastly and densely knowledgeable prose. Let us take as an example the mysterious first line of 'Frost at Midnight', one of his most anthologised poems:

> The Frost performs its secret ministry

Coleridge is here describing a cold night in February 1798. He goes on to picture himself seated by the fireside in his cottage at Nether Stowey, Somerset, alongside his sleeping baby (Hartley), to whom the poem is addressed. There is nothing at first sight even remotely political either in the intimate domestic setting or in the quiet meditative register. But even so, the first line carries a freight of historical and biographical, as well as symbolic, associations, which help to illuminate Coleridge's political perspective at this time. The year 1798 was the one in which, offered an annuity by Thomas Wedgwood, this radical young dissenter gave up the idea of becoming a Unitarian minister in order to devote himself to poetry. So in a sense that year marked the beginning of his so-called apostasy, his retreat from the public political stage. But he was still a 'marked man' as far as the Tory government was concerned. It was while living at Nether Stowey that he and Wordsworth were allegedly followed and watched by a spy in Pitt's employment, who was under the impression that the two of them were plotting treason. The word 'ministry' is therefore inescapably loaded: it evokes a personal and spiritual vocation which has been abandoned (not without guilt) for poetic retreat. But it also connotes a public office which has peculiarly menacing implications, at a time when dissenters were persecuted and no one was beyond suspicion.

Are some of these haunting resonances perhaps also present in the description of the melting frost which concludes the poem?

> Therefore all seasons shall be sweet to thee,
> Whether the summer clothe the general earth
> With greenness, or the redbreast sit and sing
> Betwixt the tufts of snow on the bare branch
> Of mossy apple-tree, while the nigh thatch
> Smokes in the sun-thaw; whether the eave-drops fall
> Heard only in the trances of the blast,
> Or if the secret ministry of frost
> Shall hang them up in silent icicles,
> Quietly shining to the quiet Moon.

In this patient descriptive catalogue, Coleridge preserves the smooth flow of regular iambic pentameter, breaking it only once with the dactyls and spondees of

> Smokes in the sun-thaw; whether the eave-drops fall

Notice how the rhythmic irregularity in this line causes one to halt at the word 'eave-drops', as though it marked a kind of dissonance. Notice, too, how close the word 'eave-drops' is to 'eavesdrop' – so much so that, when reading aloud, it is easy to make the slip. As well as the acoustic resemblance, there is a close etymological connection between the compound noun and the verb. It seems likely that Coleridge, fascinated as he was by the power of puns, was evoking the idea of a private rumination 'listened in on', a conversation overheard. The poem's mood has by this stage moved onto a plane of tranquil resolution; and yet, subliminally, there is a sense of privacy disturbed – perhaps by the reader, perhaps by a wary and watchful public world. Perhaps even by a spy.

In its preoccupation with the precious fragility of seclusion, 'Frost at Midnight' resembles Coleridge's 'Fears in Solitude', a poem which laments the destruction of Somerset's rural tranquillity by warfare. His more overtly political 'France: An Ode' deplores the invasion of Switzerland by France, and re-defines liberty in terms of the mind's harmonious interaction with the natural world. The volume in which all three of these poems first appeared in 1798 took *Fears in Solitude* as its title – indicating a strong thematic linkage between poems ostensibly different in their register and subject-matter. Private and public anxieties mingle and intersect in these poems. For a writer who felt so acutely his accountability as a citizen and po-litical subject, it could hardly be otherwise. Critics differ, however, about whether the accent should fall on a change in Coleridge's political complex-ion, marked by his retreat from the public arena; or on the re-channelling of his radical energies at a time when dissent was forced underground, and political protest had to be camouflaged. Kelvin Everest, in his foundational book *Coleridge's Secret Ministry*, noticed 'the urgency', the 'almost fugitive quality', in the epithet 'secret', seeing here a coded allusion to the poet's continuing radicalism. More recently, in *Minotaur*, Tom Paulin has shown how the poet's 'occult activism' is overlaid by the naturalising and spiritualising tendencies of his art – tendencies which increasingly characterised his conservatism.

Careful annotation and commentary can supply much of the specialist historical and philosophical information that is needed for students to piece together their own interpretations of Coleridge's richly allusive writing, helping them to reach their own conclusions about his politics and psychology. But without direction and cross-referencing between works, they are unlikely to see the full picture. It is intended that the chapters in this volume should bring together the astonishing range of Coleridge's intellectual concerns, restoring to his writings some of their more inaccessible meanings. The collective aim of contributors has been to place Coleridge's works in their original contexts, paying special attention to the readership they addressed and the reception they received. The chapters are designed to introduce students to important areas of debate in Coleridge scholarship today. They also contribute to a clearer understanding of Coleridge's relationship with contemporary writers, as well as his later influence on poetry, criticism, and literary theory. The volume is divided into three sections. Part 1 provides essential material for students: the topics chosen are deliberately canonical, representing the standard range of material covered in undergraduate courses; and the material is presented in a broadly chronological sequence. Readers can then progress to the more general chapters in Part 2 ('Discursive modes'), intended to reflect the full range of Coleridge's interests and achievements; and finally to Part 3 ('Themes and topics'), which focuses on areas of interest that engage scholars today in critical debate.

Coleridge would have approved wholeheartedly of a book intended as a 'companion' for his readers. The metaphor of companionship is deeply germane to his concerns. In a poem of 1796 addressed to Charles Lloyd 'on his proposing to domesticate with the author', Coleridge figures their future life together 'arm linked in friendly arm', either 'in social silence . . . seated at ease on some smooth mossy rock', or unlocking the 'treasured heart' in intimate exchange. This idealisation of friendship, anticipating his later collaboration with Wordsworth, was a crucial ingredient in Coleridge's figuration of poetry as a domain in which political ideals could be fulfilled. Domestic fraternity was seen as a more accessible and harmonious alternative to political fraternity, at a time when the French Revolution was anathematised by conservative ideology. Friendship also provided an ideal figure for the poet's relationship with his reader, when the reading public seemed anonymous, hostile and overpowering.

But friendship was not just a favourite figure for domestic and literary fraternity. It was the organising principle in a hermeneutic enterprise designed to unite writers and their readers. As I have elsewhere argued, Coleridge saw the bond of sympathy between author and reader in terms of a communitarian spirit, which had its roots in Christianity. The models for his reading circles can be traced back to pantisocracy and its seventeenth-century analogues, as can the spirit which motivates his literary dialogues and publishing ventures including the *Friend* itself. Just as the ideal of easy, intimate exchange was embodied in the idiom of the 'Conversation' poems, so in the *Friend* it was sublimated into a style designed to transform public taste. The spiritual community Coleridge sought early on in pantisocracy was later projected onto the idea of a 'clerisy' of dedicated writer–readers.

Coleridge's concern with finding (or making?) a like-minded interpretive community remained steadfast. But his career followed a by-no-means-straightforward trajectory (as Peter J. Kitson shows in chapter 10) from idiosyncratic radical to equally idiosyncratic conservative. At each stage in the development of his thinking, he found himself experimenting with a new kind of language. Each was adapted to speak to a different community, a different kind of potential 'friend'. In 1795 he was a democrat and a republican, a supporter of the French Revolution and Parliamentary reform, opposed to the repressive measures of Pitt's government, and committed to the abolition of property. The audience he lectured to in Bristol, and whom he addressed in his early political journal the *Watchman*, was very different from the small family circle who read his 'Conversation' poems in the years at Alfoxden and Grasmere, or the middle- and upper-class intelligentsia who read the *Friend*. Yet further removed from his early radical milieu was the audience he addressed in the *Lay Sermons* of 1817 (and, later, in *On the Constitution of Church and State*, 1829) when he had come to be an Anglican conservative, advocate of restricted franchise, and stout defender of the rights of property. William Hazlitt, the radical who had admired Coleridge as a Unitarian and Jacobin, saw his career in terms of political betrayal. He 'at last turned on the pivot of a subtle casuistry to the unclean side'. But Kitson takes on the challenge of tracing a more complicated pattern of thought, emphasising that neither Coleridge's early radicalism nor his later conservatism were straightforward adoptions of currently held opinions. There were threads of consistency in his always-evolving political thought. Throughout his life he was a Christian, a patriot and a commonwealthsman, no matter how much the meaning of those words shifted for him during his life.

Coleridge has sometimes been represented as an intellectual chameleon (Keats's image for the poet) who changed his colour – his mode of address – to suit the audience he was trying to persuade. This is not just because his politics evolved, but because his personality, which is always so central a component of his writing, was weak and vacillating. Increasingly addicted to narcotics, he suffered from what a modern behaviourist would call 'obsessive–compulsive' disorders. He was also unusually self-conscious, and overly dependent on the approval of others for his self-esteem – a man, as Julie Carlson (chapter 13) puts it, 'whose character and relations with others [were] construed by everyone, including himself, as weak, subordinate, dependent, and whose essential condition [was] lack'. Perhaps as a consequence of all this, the longing to be liked or loved was projected onto his readers with unusual intensity, and this may partly explain his experimentation with so many methods of communication. The restlessness with which he sought out new forms of expression, as well as new kinds of listener, has indeed led suspicious or hostile readers to the conclusion that he had no intellectual centre.

In the twentieth century, Coleridge was received as a great poet (a judgement based on a small handful of poems, among which 'The Ancient Mariner' is surely the most famous). He was also identified as the founding father of modern literary criticism, largely on the basis of his *Biographia Literaria* and the lectures on Shakespeare. His creative and critical output are traditionally represented as synonymous with Romanticism. But this was not how he was seen in his own day: Byron dismissed the *Biographia* in a single memorable couplet ('Explaining metaphysics to the nation / I wish he would explain his explanation'); while Hazlitt lamented the loss of a potentially great writer in the lazy vagaries of philosophical prose: 'He might, we seriously think, have been a very considerable poet – instead of which he has chosen to be a bad philosopher and a worse politician. There is something, we suspect, in these studies that does not easily amalgamate.' Hazlitt is at his prickly best, here, but we should remember that the idiom he abhors is one that Coleridge invented as a means to an end. *Biographia Literaria* is at least three things at once: an idealistic exercise in syncretism (the marrying of disciplines that were pulling apart); an experimental form of hybrid writing, in which prose aspired to the conditions of poetry; and an expedient piece of what journalists would call 'copy' – dictated at high speed, under pressure from his publishers. The Coleridge who harks back to earlier models of knowledge is also, and simultaneously, an avant-garde writer and a Grub-Street hack. Stephen Bygrave has claimed that at the time of writing the *Biographia*, he was addressing 'an audience he had not yet invented' – a plausible enough explanation for the hostile contemporary reception of this rambling biographical-cum-philosophical disquisition.

It is no accident that Coleridge's most famous critical work was dictated, not written. Some of his greatest insights, as Angela Esterhammer (chapter 9) reminds us, came in a form that was fragmentary, fleeting: letters, note-books, marginalia, table-talk. When he labelled 'Kubla Khan' a 'fragment', and described its original inspiration as irretrievable, he was acknowledging the centrality of evanescence to his creative imagination. The public lectures presented between 1808 and 1819 (especially those on Shakespeare, touchstones of critical acuity) were delivered *extempore*. Based on scraps of paper and annotated volumes that he brought into the lecture hall, they survive only because they were pieced together from his notes and the reports of several listeners. Coleridge's audience quite often felt frustrated by the 'immethodical rhapsodising' which characterised his prose-style as critic, journalist, lecturer. But the criteria of method and unity do not apply to his letters, marginalia and notes, which have delighted and fascinated his readers. Sara Coleridge described her father as 'ever at my ear, in his books, more especially his marginalia – speaking not personally to me, and yet in a way so natural to my feelings, that finds me so fully, and awakens such a strong echo in my heart, that I seem more intimate with him than I ever was in my life' (letter to E. Quillinan, 1850). Perhaps there is a 'dialogic' ingredient in the notebooks, akin to that in the marginalia, which mani-fests itself in their construction of an imagined reader. Perhaps they were written 'for' someone, even though not intended for publication. There is always a difficulty, with Coleridge's writing, of placing it as either 'public' or 'private'. The extemporaneous forms he favoured allowed him to make a stylistic feature of this slippery demarcation.

Just as improvisation was a key component of his literary style, so lecturing and talking were the media Coleridge was most comfortable with through-out his life. The figure of 'Coleridge the Talker' has aquired a mythological status; and closely connected with it is the figure of Coleridge the preacher (first as a radical enthusiast, and later in the conservative Anglican mould of *Lay Sermons*). We should not forget the importance sermons held for him, as models of discourse that were at once off-the-cuff and deeply seri-ous. He was, after all, at one time planning a life in the Unitarian ministry. His career is best seen not as a disruption of that early commitment, but as a continuation of it in various different forms. The first occasion Hazlitt heard Coleridge talk was when he delivered a sermon in Shrewsbury, in the memorable year of 1798. 'It seemed to me, who was then young', Hazlitt wrote in his wonderfully ambivalent tribute, 'as if the sounds had echoed from the bottom of the human heart, and as if that prayer might have floated in solemn silence through the universe'. Seamus Perry (in chapter 7) shows how Coleridge's use of this medium extends from his early lecturing in Bristol, through his literary lectures, and on into the dictation of *Biographia Literaria*. In practice, his special kind of eloquence is shown to work on its audience in much the same way as a passionate sermon or a moving theatrical performance does, casting what Hazlitt calls 'a spell upon the hearer', which 'disarms the judgement'. The negative consequences of this kind of captivation are satirised in Max Beerbohm's mischievous caricature, 'Coleridge, Table-Talking', where all present (except the speaker) are fast asleep. The mischief is appropriate – and not just to Coleridge as he was experienced by the pilgrims and devotees who gathered round him in the Highgate years. It applies also to the early Coleridge, for whom conversation was not always what it might have been. 'Frost at Midnight', his most famous 'Conversation' poem, addresses a sleeping baby; and listeners have only a shadowy half-presence in 'The Eolian Harp', 'This Lime-Tree Bower My Prison', or the 'Letter to Sara Hutchinson'.

The kinds of language Coleridge used in addressing his readers reflect an anxiety, a lack of steadiness, in his idea of an audience. Sometimes he turned his discomfort to aesthetic advantage – much as he transformed his lack of philosophical consistency into a dazzling display of eclecticism. In the 'Conversation' poems, for instance, his register is mixed, appealing simultaneously to different kinds of expectation. The idiom of these poems is traditional, in that they look backward to Miltonic blank verse and to the eighteenth-century loco-descriptive and meditative poetry of Thomson, Cowper and Akenside. Yet they also place a new emphasis on intimacy and informality, which is germane to the radical concerns of *Lyrical Ballads*. Coleridge admired what he called the 'divine Chit-chat' (itself an oxymoron) of Cowper's *The Task*; but his own poems in that idiom are shorter and tighter than Cowper's – less inconsequential, more meditative and deeper in psychological insight. The earliest of such poems were written contemporaneously with the political lectures in Bristol, and they show an unusual, sometimes disconcerting, blend of the 'public' and the 'private'. Paul Magnuson (in chapter 2) argues that (despite the domestic focus, and the scarcity of explicit references to national events) they can be seen as resonating with politics. Domesticity 'was not merely a private matter, not exclusively a matter of individual psychology'; for at this time there was an intimate connection between the constitution of the family and the constitution of the state. Once its allusions are decoded, 'This Lime-Tree-Bower My Prison' can be read both as a poem celebrating Coleridge's domestic friendship with Lamb, and as an epistle publicly inviting Lamb to stand in opposition to the government and to forms of radicalism of which Coleridge did not approve.

Magnuson's emphasis on the politics of Coleridge's poetry is a helpful reminder that (as we saw earlier, in the case of 'Frost at Midnight') his radicalism did not simply disappear when it went underground. The 'Supernatural' poems, even though their material appears to belong to the inner recesses of the poetic imagination, are equally open to historical interpretation. Tim Fulford (in chapter 3) traces the political origins of Coleridge's concern with superstition, showing how, in a series of poems beginning with 'The Three Graves', the beliefs of 'savage' and 'civilized' societies are seen as closely resembling each other. Coleridge's intention, in pointing out these resemblances, was to expose contemporary habits of mental enslavement, themselves the product of superstitious beliefs. 'The Ancient Mariner', although not explicitly a political poem, arose from Coleridge's radical opposition to slavery, and it makes his readers aware of their fatal attraction to the powerful, makes them 'share the terror, desperation, and desire of a man enslaved, in mind and body'. 'Christabel' uses the Gothic genre – where superstition and the supernatural were expected – to locate in the nobility the same kind of slavish and irrational desires that are seen elsewhere as characteristic of the lower classes. Coleridge's critique of chivalry and aristocracy is as important to this poem as it is to the earlier, more explicitly topical 'On a Late Connubial Rupture in High Life', where the Prince of Wales is scathingly attacked for his lax morals and hypocrisy.

Coleridge was always a political thinker. It is for his 'Conversation' and 'Supernatural' poems that he is best known in this century, but his reputation as a lecturer was established before he became a well-known published poet; and throughout his life he was also a journalist, a commentator on topical events. This is all the more surprising because he once referred to 'the luxuriant misgrowth of our activity – a reading-public', and became increasingly unpopular for his defensive and illiberal fulminations against journalists, newspapers and readers avid for sensational news. His own publishing ventures, most notably the *Watchman* (1796) and the *Friend* (1809–10) took a peculiarly interventionist shape, reflecting the practical spirit in which he approached the task of transforming public taste. Deirdre Coleman (in chapter 8) offers a comparative study of these two weekly journals, which have much in common despite the very different circumstances under which they were written, and the different audiences they had in mind. Reflecting Coleridge's ongoing preoccupation with friendship as the necessary starting point of social life, both journals involved 'the informal and often generous patronage of friends, together with subscription schemes that were designed to deliver a fraternity of like-minded supporters, bonded together in brotherly love'. Coleridge's early ideals of communitarianism, intimacy and fellowship were thus reconstituted, after the demise of pantisocracy, in an 'alternative society of the text'.

Like his politics, Coleridge's thoughts on religion are characterised by their mix of conservative and progressive views. He has been portrayed as a radical Unitarian, a mystic, a theosophist, an Anglican, and a muddled metaphysician who tried to marry the questioning spirit of philosophy with religious faith. Mary Anne Perkins (chapter 12) uncovers a thread of cogency and consistency in his thought, notwithstanding the vacillations in his emotional life (which made him search, at different times, for different kinds of 'answer' to underlying questions). Once he had moved from Unitarianism to a belief in the Trinity, the concept of 'Logos' became a seminal principle in Coleridge's system – or at least in his quest for system. In the Logos the principles of Being, of Intellect, and of Action were identified with 'the Father, the Word, and the Spirit'. Coleridge explored the meanings and associations of this synthesising principle through a vast range of materials in Greek philosophy and Christian thought. He was inspired by the idea of Logos as an intellectual principle – both a source of dynamic polarity and a medium of reconciliation. The idea of the Logos made sense of his belief that polarities can be synthesised, that 'Extremes meet'. It also provided the foundation for his belief in the animating power of language – poetic and symbolic language in particular. He always contradistinguished symbol from allegory: the former occupied a higher aesthetic and religious ground, connecting the human word with the divine spirit. The act of seeking interior meanings in words was for Coleridge a deeply religious affirmation, and he once complained that 'It is among the miseries of the present age that it recognises no medium between the *Literal* and the *Metaphorical*.' This failure, he believed, came about as a result of the gradual secularisation of literature and of reading practices – the demise of spiritual meaning. James C. McKusick (chapter 14) shows the centrality of symbol to Coleridge's religious and linguistic thought, and takes us into terrain that has proved rich for modern literary theory.

Coleridge's conviction that, whereas Wordsworth was 'a great, a true Poet', he himself was 'only a kind of a Meta-physician' began to consolidate into a necessary fiction from around 1802, when he habitually complained that 'abstruse research' was taking over his life. This picture of Coleridge, as a writer whose brief poetic career degenerated suddenly and irreversibly, was compounded by his contemporary reception. Writers such as Hazlitt, hostile both to his political apostasy and to the abstruser musings of his philosophical prose, mythologised the *annus mirabilis* at the expense of his later productions. Among the much overlooked poems of his mature years, some only recently brought to light, there is nonetheless evidence of Coleridge's sustained poetic versatility and craftsmanship. J. C. C. Mays (chapter 6) subjects the category 'later poetry' to critique, tracing a line of continuity from youth to maturity by looking outside the major anthologised pieces to Coleridge's occasional verse. He rejects the commonly held belief that Coleridge wrote latterly about personal failure, and shows how – even in poems such as 'The Pang More Sharp than All' and 'The Garden of Boccaccio' which revisit earlier themes – there is a process of restatement and enlargement. He emphasises the importance of allegory and emblem to Coleridge's poetic imagination: his later poems resemble riddles, 'naming not summoning, working through pictures not sound'.

So how might one summarise the achievement of this multifaceted writer, to whom even Hazlitt once referred as 'the only man I ever knew that answered to the idea of a man of genius'? Coleridge experimented with so many discursive modes that it is impossible to categorise his writing. The labels, 'poet', 'journalist', 'philosopher', 'critic', 'religious thinker' are, by themselves, woefully inadequate to describe either his status or the importance of his overall contribution. That he was all of these things rolled into one should not blind us to the fact that he himself had a sense of the hierarchy to which each discursive mode belonged. Journalism was at the bottom of an 'ascent of being', which moved upward through criticism, poetry, and then philosophy, finally to arrive at the apex, religion. In the Conclusion to *Biographia Literaria*, Coleridge claimed that he had tried to show how

> the scheme of Christianity, as taught in the Liturgy and homilies of our Church, though not discoverable by human Reason, is yet in accordance with it; that link follows link by necessary consequence; that *Religion* passes out of the ken of *Reason* only where the eye of *Reason* has reached its own *Horizon*; and that Faith is then but its *continuation*: even as the Day softens away into Twilight, and Twilight, hushed and breathless, steals into Darkness. (my italics)

Here as elsewhere, Coleridge's prose crosses over into poetry. Notice how the italicised words create through half-rhyme an effect that becomes almost incantatory as the passage progresses, each clause approximating more and more closely to a regular metrical pattern. Notice too how the symmetry of the last two clauses is emphasised by the repetition of 'twilight' on either side of a strong chiasmus. This gives a sense of closure, suggesting a grand union or synthesis between the faculties of reason and imagination. The closure is softened by the falling rhythm of 'steals into Darkness', just as the metaphor of twilight itself softens the transition from reason into faith. A less idealistic writer would have seen potential tensions (if not actual frictions) between the analytic and the intuitive; but for Coleridge the union of these was itself a matter of principle. He used all the resources at his disposal – as poet, orator, theologian – to cement them. Just as he saw friendship as the foundation of a cohesive society, so he sought for the spirit of amity which connected all the discourses available to him into a single system.

Coleridge's urge to totalise was without question the driving motivation of his intellectual life; but as Seamus Perry's examples vividly demonstrate, there was always a countermanding tendency in his personality and habits of mind. An obsession with particularities often caused his illustrations to swallow up his thesis, just as his chaotic bodily and personal life (increasingly the prey of marital unhappiness, illness and addiction) fractured and dissipated his mental coherence. A disjunction between theory and practice was a strikingly consistent feature of his life and work. He was a deeply flawed human being, whose lifelong idealism provided him with some kind of compensation for his failings and inadequacies. Friendship proved more problematic in relation to actual human beings than it did in relation to ideas about community. Its difficulties were borne out in a string of broken relationships (the one with Wordsworth among them); in the tension between collaboration and competition which characterised Coleridge's interaction with other writers; and in the unease – sometimes the disingenuousness – of his attempts to co-opt independent readers as 'fellow-labourers'. His investment in the spirit of friendship as a cohesive principle grew even stronger as he came to acknowledge the disappointments and limitations of human relations.

A combination of these two warring tendencies in Coleridge – towards unity and towards fragmentation – makes him the baffling, contradictory phenomenon he was, and is today. John Beer observes, in the concluding chapter of this volume, that Coleridge's afterlife has been so long and so vigorous because readers have tended to recognise in his often fragmentary and divided thinking 'self-contradictions of their own'. During the Victorian age in particular, he stood as an example of someone whose achieved assurance had emerged out of his very vulnerability. He appeared 'to have distilled a message for his times from his own restless thought and experience'. Readers in the twentieth century identified more strongly with Coleridge's ultimate failure to build a system than with his aspiration to arrive at one. John Beer himself concludes that his 'ultimate gift to human thinking lay in his capacity for thinking on more than one level', that 'at its best his mind positively recoiled from watertight formulations'.

And what of Coleridge's fate in the twenty-first century? For most readers, there will always be something essentially flawed in so quixotic a literary personality. But the contributors to this volume approach Coleridge's divided nature in a spirit of investigation, rather than of accusation. They share a respect both for the spirit of determination with which Coleridge 'tried to understand things in terms of absolute questions' (Kelvin Everest, chapter 1) and for his steadfast refusal 'to subordinate his critical faculties to dogma of any kind' (Mary Anne Perkins, chapter 12). He was a deeply idiosyncratic figure. Idiosyncrasy is usually both frustrating and fascinating, in almost equal measure.

I

TEXTS AND CONTEXTS

I

KELVIN EVEREST

Coleridge's life

Coleridge's life has proved difficult to narrate. Its events are hard to understand as a developmental sequence. Like Coleridge's personality, and like his writings, they disclose numerous facets in loose and disorganised connection. His drive to articulate a philosophy of unity, with its conspicuous successes and sometimes embarrassing failures, has its fundamental context in the great sweep of momentous political and social change in Britain and Europe during the period of his life. The moves from radical to conservative, from necessitarian rationalist to philosophical idealism and Anglican Christianity, were negotiated under external pressures which were, at once, sharply focused for Coleridge personally, and profoundly representative of the spiritual journey of an entire generation. This representative quality gives a particular importance not just to Coleridge's successes, but, perhaps even more so, to his failures and failings.

Coleridge was born on 21 October 1772 in the small town of Ottery St Mary in Devonshire. He was the youngest of ten children. His own memories of childhood recall a powerful sense of sibling rivalry; as a small boy he felt threatened by the competition of older and bigger children. This vulnerability was shielded in the character of an infant prodigy, gifted with special powers of articulacy, and nourished by an astonishing capacity and appetite for reading. He claimed to have read the Bible by the age of three. He kept the company of adults, content to parade his precocity and to be paraded, always treated as a special case, self-consciously unordinary, in every way more alive than others to the pleasures and the threats of a difficult world.

This sensitive temperament was subjected to powerful shocks following the sudden death of his father in October 1781, when Coleridge was still only eight years old. He was clearly much closer to his father, an educated vicar who wrote books, than to his mother. The shock of his father's death was the more acute for being associated in Coleridge's mind with the claims of another brother; his father had died on returning from a trip to Plymouth to deliver Coleridge's brother Frank to the navy as a midshipman, a journey

itself expressive of Mrs Coleridge's ambition for her children. Soon afterwards, Coleridge was sent, through the offices of a family friend, to attend
school at Christ's Hospital in London, and found himself suddenly quite
abandoned and alone in the harsh regime of a boarding school in the great
city, far from his country home. He arrived in September 1782. Family connections in London at first took him in, and he again found himself paraded
as a prodigy. But these acquaintances fell away, and he embarked in lonely
solitude on a school career which began without distinction, in the dull and
comfortless routines of the school. This trial had its consolations, in the form
of enduring friendships with school contemporaries such as Charles Lamb.
After a slow start Coleridge's intellectual talents were recognised, and nurtured, notably by the schoolmaster James Boyer, vividly recalled years later
in *Biographia Literaria* as a harsh and unforgiving presence, who yet instilled in Coleridge an understanding of the attentive discipline necessary to
the writing, and reading, of poetry.

In the years at Christ's Hospital Coleridge's inner imaginative life took
on a bookish intensity which deepened in contrast with the cold banality
of his school experience. The voracious reading broadened to include contemporary poetry such as the popular sonnets of William Bowles, and also
philosophy and theology. These topics became central to Coleridge's intellectual development; but, significantly, his interest was from the start not
controlled and assimilative, but bewildering and disorientated.

Towards the end of his career at Christ's Hospital Coleridge was elected
a 'Grecian', a recognition of his academic ability which marked him out
for university. Before duly matriculating at Jesus College, Cambridge, in
October 1791 Coleridge had met and become friendly with the Evans family,
with whose daughter Mary he formed a shy but strong attachment. This
inaugurated a long and messily unsuccessful history of relationships with
women, which provides a constant jarring counterpoint to the larger pattern
of Coleridge's repeated failures and frustrations in adult life. In Cambridge
Coleridge kept up Christ's Hospital friendships, and quickly made new and
interesting contacts. His undergraduate career at first showed high promise.
He attended meetings of a literary discussion group run by Christopher
Wordsworth, came to know interesting undergradute contemporaries including Porson and Wrangham, and in 1792 he won the Browne medal
for a 'Greek Sapphic Ode' on the slave trade. But this sign of political engagement also confirmed the emergence of a further significant dimension
in Coleridge's experience, as he found himself caught up in the great social
upheaval of the French Revolution, and its momentous transforming impact
on Britain and Europe. He followed events and arguments with keen attention. Coleridge's instincts within the turmoil of this pervasive international

crisis were, like so many of his generation, to favour the radical cause. Events in France appeared at first very much in keeping with native British radical traditions, and the sense of a dawning new age of freedom and equality was widespread, particularly amongst the educated young. Coleridge's radical affiliation found a local Cambridge context in the cause of William Frend, a don who was tried in 1793 for publishing a pamphlet which attacked the liturgy of the Church in radical terms. Coleridge attended the trial and applauded so enthusiastically in Frend's support that he himself began to attract the attention of the authorities. Frend was banned from the university. As the course of events in France turned sinister and bloody, and more particularly after the execution of Louis XVI, and the declaration of war by France on Britain early in 1793, Coleridge felt the new pressure of a youthful enthusiasm for the political ideals of 'Liberty'. Support for France was now potentially treason, and as the forces of reaction gathered so Coleridge found that his beliefs and ideas needed careful expression, and a guarded sense of audience. This consciousness of a threatening social and political community now gave external form to the inner demons and insecurities already at work in Coleridge's experience. His life began to lurch vertiginously into a chaos of sudden irrational decisions and unpredictable changes of direction and heart. Too shy to make progress with Mary Evans, he fell into a damaging routine of loose living, prostitutes and debt, lost his way at university, and in December bizarrely chose to enlist in the 15th Light Dragoons as a trooper under the stagey name 'Silas Tomkyn Comberbache'. He did not try hard for anonymity, and was soon rescued. But the episode sounds an ominous note in Coleridge's biography; regular collapse into craven dependency and transparent untruth was to become its only predictable constant.

Coleridge's early radicalism exposed him to all the forces of a society in severe crisis, as the long-building tensions inherent in agrarian and industrial revolution, with their emergent formations of social class, were brought suddenly to focus in the charged political atmosphere of the 1790s. His intelligence and depth of reading in the complexities of the situation, coupled with his ambition to play some part on the public stage, as an intellectual on the side of progress, meant that these great tensions in British society were played out with profoundly unsettling immediacy in his own career. But he was equally interested in the vexed relation between his consciousness and the unconscious drives and activity of the mind. The dual pressures he was subject to in these contexts make for the tormented shapelessness of his maturity, and are representative of underlying contradictions in the social experience of his class and generation.

The duality is tellingly imaged in a famous passage from the twelfth chapter of *Biographia Literaria*. Coleridge apologises for the abstraction and difficulty of his philosophical exposition by affirming that philosophy is simply not a discourse equally available, accessible and interesting to all men. He then introduces a metaphor to illustrate the different orders of knowledge and understanding which may be brought to bear in the attempt to understand our experience:

> The first range of hills, that encircle the scanty vale of human life, is the horizon for the majority of its inhabitants. On *its* ridges the common sun is born and departs. From *them* the stars rise, and touching *them* they vanish. By the many, even this range, the natural limit and bulwark of the vale, is but imperfectly known. Its higher ascents are too often hidden by mists and clouds from uncultivated swamps, which few have courage or curiosity to penetrate. To the multitude below these vapors appear, now as the dark haunts of terrific agents, on which none may intrude with impunity; and now all *a-glow*, with colors not their own, they are gazed at, as the splendid palaces of happiness and power. But in all ages there have been a few, who measuring and sounding the rivers of the vale at the feet of their furthest inaccessible falls have learnt, that the sources must be far higher and far inward; a few, who even in the level streams have detected elements, which neither the vale itself or the surrounding mountains contained or could supply. (*BL* I, 239)

The image gives very powerfully what was to become Coleridge's chief characteristic as a thinker, his constant effort to see the timeless, permanent dimensions in local and transiently immediate experience. But the image in *Biographia* is strangely ambivalent, for this metaphor also suggests the far extent of external causes in local events, thus evoking the transformations in ordinary social life brought about by vast cultural and political upheavals. And there is the further contrasting implication that there are deep and obscure psychological determinates of consciousness and personality, largely unexplored and indeed hardly imagined by most people. This doubleness is embodied in Coleridge's life and work. He lives out the contradictions of his social position as a radical intellectual of the middle class in the momentous context of the years in Britain which followed the French Revolution. His reactions to the stresses of this situation, including a move to the right in politics, and towards orthodoxy in religion, typify the intellectual destiny of an entire generation. But his struggle with the differently intractable problems of his own psychology, and more particularly his extraordinary effort to confront, interrogate and document that struggle in his writings, at once gives an internalised intensity to the social contradictions, and anticipates the intellectual arena of modernity.

After his rescue from the Dragoons, Coleridge returned briefly to Cambridge but soon embarked with his friend Joseph Hucks on a tour to Wales. They stopped *en route* in Oxford, and Coleridge met Robert Southey in June 1794.

The two fell immediately into an intimate friendship born of shared interests in radical politics and literature. Their excited discussions led quickly to 'Pantisocracy', an idealistic scheme to establish an egalitarian community on the banks of the Susquehanna river in Pennsylvania. The Welsh tour proceeded and Coleridge was taken aback by a chance meeting in Wrexham with Mary Evans, the more so since his enthusiastic dreams of a radical community with Southey had quickly come to include the presence of the Fricker family; Southey was already engaged to Edith Fricker, and Coleridge had become entangled in an attachment to her sister Sara. Under Southey's watchful eye this solidified into an engagement by the autumn. The connection with Southey drew Coleridge to Bristol, and by the end of 1794 he had given up his Cambridge career and taken lodgings with Southey and another pantisocrat, George Burnett. He had made a start on his first serious long poem, 'Religious Musings', but now his energies were mainly devoted to developing a career as a radical lecturer, and public lectures followed, on politics, revealed religion and the slave trade. Coleridge fell out with Southey in the summer of 1795, and pantisocracy was abandoned; but its legacy was to prove disastrous in Coleridge's private life, for after a period of guilty absence in London he acceded to Southey's ominously self-righteous pressure and returned to the West Country to marry Sara Fricker in October.

Following his marriage Coleridge began to publish his political lectures, and he formed a plan to produce a journal, the *Watchman*, which would take his independent radical commentary to a wider audience. A tour to the Midlands to attract subscribers brought him into contact with leading intellectual radicals, and confirmed his growing status as an outspoken young critic of the government and supporter of 'Liberty'. The *Watchman* began to appear in March 1796, and ran for ten numbers, appearing every eighth day to avoid the stamp duty that was payable on weekly publications. April saw the publication of a volume of verse, *Poems on Various Subjects*. These publications began to shape the public image of Coleridge as a fiercely principled intellectual whose disinterested views rested on the authority of an immense range of reading in philosophy, theology and political theory. But he was feeling the pressure of local hostility from reactionary opinion, which in slave-trading Bristol was formidable. His domestic situation was also closing in, with the birth of his son Hartley in September 1796, and mounting pressures to find somewhere to live, and something to live on. He was also coming under a new influence, that of William Wordsworth, whom he had first met in Bristol in 1795. Towards the end of 1796 this friendship rapidly deepened and the two young writers, together with Wordsworth's sister Dorothy, became very close. Acting perhaps on the example of their simple style of life, Coleridge made arrangements through his friend Thomas

Poole to move to a small cottage in the market town of Nether Stowey in Somerset, and was installed with his family by the end of the year. He now spent a great deal of time with the Wordsworths, and after a series of mutual visits they moved in to Alfoxden, a house in the Quantock Hills close to Nether Stowey.

Under Wordsworth's influence Coleridge's abstract intellectual interests were joined with a truly remarkable transformation of his talents as a poet. In the mainly quiet retirement of their life in the Quantocks the two poets exchanged ideas and practice, often in the course of long country walks. Wordsworth had already written a substantial body of verse by the time of his friendship with Coleridge, and it is obvious that his confident sense of vocation, and his powerful understanding of his own place in the historical development of English poetry, made a profound impression. But it is equally true to say that the influence of Coleridge was the catalysing agent which confirmed Wordsworth's greatness, bringing an awareness of the need for critical principles, and a new and greatly heightened understanding of the possibilities of a plain and understated style in lyric and blank verse writing. The poetry that Coleridge himself produced in the period of his intimacy with the Wordsworths in Nether Stowey constitutes perhaps his least disputable claim to greatness. The 'Conversation' poems were mainly written at this time, as were 'The Ancient Mariner', conceived as Coleridge's principal contribution to the collaborative *Lyrical Ballads*, and also both 'Kubla Khan', and the first part of 'Christabel'.

But this creative and comparatively settled period in Coleridge's life had its tensions. As the long crisis of the French wars deepened with Napoleon's rise to power and Britain's isolation from Europe, so the radical character of Coleridge's public image attracted more hostility, and also covert attention from government agents. Coleridge's friend John Thelwall was discouraged from moving to the area because of his political affiliations. Coleridge and Wordsworth were spied on, with official reports travelling back to government. Coleridge later made a joke of this, but the danger must have seemed real at the time. More personally, Coleridge was beginning to appreciate the powers of laudanum, the alcoholic tincture of opium. His young family grew with the birth of a second son in May 1798. Coleridge had named his first son 'Hartley' after the associationist philosopher who influenced his early determinist position. He now named his new son 'Berkeley' after the idealist philosopher, a choice which marks both the extent of his daily immersion in the abstract life of the mind, and the changing character of his intellectual position. An early rational materialism had led him towards Unitarianism in religion, but now he found the influence of idealist thinkers increasingly arresting, and unsettling, particularly as his quest for gainful employment was driving him to consider a post as a Unitarian lay preacher in Shrewsbury.

During a visit to Shrewsbury to demonstrate his abilities to the prospective congregation, Coleridge was unexpectedly offered an annuity of £150 by the young industrialist Tom Wedgwood; his instant decision to accept the annuity is memorably recorded in Hazlitt's essay 'My First Acquaintance with Poets'. Hazlitt had walked ten miles from his home in Wem to hear Coleridge, and was completely entranced by the eloquence and erudition of Coleridge's talk, although over the years his initial devoted admiration would turn to bitter and vitriolic disenchantment. The annuity meant that Coleridge was suddenly at liberty to pursue his philosophical interests, and he found himself drawn to study in Germany, at that time the centre of European intellectual life. The Wordsworths' lease was up, and they decided to join him on a trip to learn German and study its contemporary literature and philosophy. In September 1798, almost on the day that *Lyrical Ballads* was published, they sailed for Hamburg. Coleridge left his family behind.

The party called on the poet Klopstock, then split up, with the Wordsworths travelling south to Goslar, while Coleridge first studied German in Ratzeburg and then moved on to Göttingen. Here he encountered the major currents of German intellectual life. These embraced contemporary literature and literary history, the philosophy of Kant and his followers, the Spinozists, Eichorn's biblical criticism, and the latest speculations on the relation of mind and body, and questions concerning the definition of 'life' raised by developments in scientific medicine. Coleridge had already encountered something of these interests, variously mediated, through his Bristol circle, but his studies in Germany gave him an almost unique knowledge of the latest developments in European thought. This was to prove a mixed blessing. In the following years, as Coleridge became the most important and influential agent for the dissemination of German Romantic philosophy in England, he often found it difficult to maintain a clear distinction between exposition and plagiarism.

In February 1799 Coleridge's baby son Berkeley died. Coleridge did not get the news until April, but he nevertheless continued his stay in Germany, not finally arriving back in Nether Stowey until the end of July. This can hardly have helped relations with his wife, and the subsequent breakdown of the marriage perhaps has its origins in this selfish irresponsibility. But other forces were now at work to undermine any stability in Coleridge's life. The Wordsworths did not return to the West Country from Germany, but decided to settle in their native Northern England. Other important Bristol connections such as Humphrey Davy were gravitating towards London. West Country projects were soon laid aside as Coleridge began an essentially wandering existence which characterised his middle years. He joined Wordsworth and his brother John in October 1799 for a walking tour of the Lake District, and in the course of this visit met and fell in love with Sara Hutchinson, a childhood friend of the Wordsworths whose sister Mary was to become Wordsworth's wife. Coleridge's love for Sara Hutchinson became a constant distraction and unhappiness, an abiding obsession. It confirmed the blighting failure of his marriage whilst doing nothing to free him from its frustrations.

Coleridge travelled back to London and found work as a political journalist with the *Morning Post*, where his breadth of knowledge and grasp of the underlying issues in local events were well suited to the role of commentator on current affairs. The course of events in France, in subtle combination with the prevailing political climate in England, pushed Coleridge towards a patriotic anti-Napoleonic stance. The discomforts of this growth away from his earlier very public radicalism were intensified when he emerged as the target of satirical attack by the conservative *Anti-Jacobin* for the radicalism he was fast discarding. This kind of public contradiction was particularly awkward for Coleridge, who always felt uneasy in the presence of what he considered a hostile audience, and who thus increasingly found himself obliged to provide retrospective explanations for an earlier self whose commitments and loyalties he wished to disavow. Lacking the confidence and self-belief simply to articulate changed opinions, he came to rely on his eloquence to present his own development as internally consistent, but at a level of complexity which left most observers perplexed, if not sceptical. This tortured compulsion to revise his past in accordance with present imperatives was made the worse by its connection with Coleridge's increasingly relentless self-psychologising, particularly in his notebooks, which courageously pursued his nightmares and neuroses deeper and deeper into the sub-conscious. In the absence of a secure family, or any viable alternative in the always out-of-reach Sara Hutchinson, the attraction of laudanum, not to mention alcohol, grew stronger and stronger.

After a few busy months in London, Coleridge visited the Wordsworths at their new home in Grasmere, and in July 1800 he moved his own family to Greta Hall in Keswick. His plan was to emulate a Wordsworthian project of lofty commentary from the distance of a country retirement. But he found increasingly that he could not sustain such productivity. Although he continued his metaphysical studies, and managed some translations from the German, he was now publishing very little. The poetic gift that had blossomed so marvellously at Nether Stowey in 1797–8 now appeared virtually to desert him, although a long and anguished verse-letter to Sara Hutchinson was edited down, depersonalised, and published as the 'Dejection Ode' on

4 October 1802, Wordsworth's wedding-day. His family life was deteriorating, and his laudanum habit began to get very much more serious. In due course Southey and his family moved in to Greta Hall, and Southey effectively took over full responsibility for Coleridge's family, which now included his daughter, Sara, born in December 1802. Coleridge absented himself in the summer of 1803 on a tour of Scotland with the Wordsworths, but with failing health and increasingly serious dependency on opium a more absolute break was inevitable. He chose to seek a better climate in Malta.

Malta was an important naval base, at a difficult time for Britain in the war with France, so Coleridge's decision to go there was itself a kind of patriotic affirmation. Once arrived, he managed surprisingly well. The High Commissioner, Sir Alexander Ball, was impressed by Coleridge's abilities and conversational powers, and quickly developed a role for him in the administration of the island. Coleridge was able to travel, and to think through the intellectual progress he had now completed towards a Trinitarian orthodoxy in religion. His stay in Malta ended with news of the death of John Wordsworth in a shipwreck, but his return involved a protracted overland journey through a Napoleonic Italy that had real dangers for Coleridge, following his widely noticed attacks on Napoleon in the *Morning Post*. He finally arrived back in England in August 1806, after meetings in Rome with the poet Tieck and the American painter Washington Allston, amongst others.

Coleridge could not face returning to his family in the Lakes, and after a period of indeterminate wandering he settled briefly in London and worked as a journalist for the *Courier*. His articles on the war saw his position becoming not simply conservative but emphatically pro-government, alienating some amongst the dwindling band of his admirers. Coleridge also made arrangements to give lecture courses in London. These came to fruition in the autumn of 1807. They were hampered early on by Coleridge's increasing unreliability, but once he began to trust his own improvised fluency in performance then lecturing became a principal vehicle for his developing public personality. The marvellous talk could flow uninterrupted, finding its own shape, and unchecked by such niceties of print publication as documented sources or sustained argumentative coherence.

Relations with his wife deteriorated badly in the period following Coleridge's return from Malta. He avoided contact, although there were visits north to the Wordsworths, who were appalled by his changed appearance and troubled by his drinking and dependency on laudanum and the erratic behaviour which went with them. There was a strange crisis in his relations with Wordsworth when in December 1806 Coleridge apparently hallucinated that he had witnessed an explicit sexual encounter between Wordsworth and Sara Hutchinson.

An increasingly tortured mental life, savagely lucid in guilty and unflinching self-analysis, was now often joined with physical illness. He found comfort in the family of a Bristol friend, John Morgan, whose support became important in the dark middle years of his life. By the summer of 1807 he again gravitated north to the Wordsworths, this time with the intention of pulling his career round with the production of a journal, the *Friend*, which against all odds he succeeded in producing, mainly single-handed, over twenty-eight issues up to March 1810. The *Friend* is a quintessentially Coleridgean production. It is a philosophical journal committed to thinking through the basic principles and abstract issues which underlie ordinary experience and the commotion of social and political life. As such it embodies all that is most admirable in Coleridge's undaunted determination always to try to understand things in terms of absolute philosophical questions of origin and ultimate destination, and to identify and tease out traces of the transcendent in the everyday. But the *Friend* is also wilfully obscure, bittily disorganised, eclectically derivative and compulsively devious in its constant rhetorical manoeuvring to justify its own hurried incompleteness. And yet in spite of these formidable obstacles to success it found readers, and admirers, and certainly contributed through its successive revised editions to the development of English intellectual conservatism through the nineteenth century.

Once the *Friend* had been finally abandoned, Coleridge entered upon a period of depression, illness and addiction which brought him close to suicide. Sara Hutchinson effected a decisive break. He quarrelled disastrously with Wordsworth, after a mutual friend unguardedly reported some mortifyingly disparaging remarks made by Wordsworth in private about him. He found himself in London, keeping up appearances for old friends such as Lamb, but more and more reliant on the support of others. Morgan looked after him for a while. He turned again to lecturing, this time attracting a fashionable literary audience. But these lectures were very markedly dependent at times on recently published German work, notably by Schlegel, and, from this time on, the shadow of plagiarism is often seriously problematic in Coleridge's published writings. In 1812 he visited the Lakes for the last time, to arrange for a revised edition of the *Friend*. He did not call on Wordsworth, but a meeting did follow soon afterwards in London, and led finally to a reconciliation of sorts. Now and then Coleridge still proved capable of literary exertion. He produced occasional journalism, continued with his lecturing, and managed a revision of his drama *Osorio*, first written in 1797 in Nether Stowey but now successfully produced at Drury Lane in January 1813 as *Remorse*. But these encouragements were overwhelmed by a brooding sense of personal failure, an inability to discipline himself to the production of work on a scale which could properly articulate the undoubted power and extraordinary breadth of his intellect and talents. Wedgwood's annuity was withdrawn. His great support John Morgan was bankrupt and himself in need of support. Coleridge did his best to help, and spent a period in Wiltshire with the family. But towards the end of 1813 he fell into a state of total collapse while staying at an inn near Bath, able to do little more for months on end than contemplate what he felt to be the wreck of his life and ambitions.

His efforts with the *Friend*, however, and his lectures in London, together with the success of *Remorse*, had kept his reputation alive. Coleridge's notorious lack of will power and self-destructiveness were always bafflingly joined with a surprising resilience, and in the summer of 1814, at the age of forty-one, he began a painful but nonetheless startlingly energetic resurgence in his literary career. He was now more or less alienated from his contemporaries Wordsworth and Southey, and had disappointed the expectations of many who had known him as a brilliant young poet and lecturer in the 1790s. But a new generation had grown up, admiring Coleridge's published poetry and also those works, such as 'Kubla Khan' and 'Christabel', known only by recitation and private circulation in literary London. This generation included Shelley, Keats, and Byron, who did much to assist Coleridge in the period leading up to his exile in 1816.

By the beginning of 1815 Coleridge was living with the Morgans at Calne in Wiltshire, and here he began to think of bringing out a collection of his poetry. This led him to recall Wordsworth's autobiographical poem (the future *Prelude*), which was referred to during Wordsworth's life as 'The Poem to Coleridge', and to begin to develop a critical account of Wordsworth's poetic practice which soon broadened to encompass his own principles, practice and development as a poet, by way of forming a kind of critical preface to his collected verse. The project quickly grew far beyond the limits of a preface, however, particularly under the impetus achieved by Coleridge's new method of composition by dictation to John Morgan, which clearly suited him well. Given Coleridge's insistence as a thinker on reaching always for the longest perspective, and the most fundamental principles at play in an argument, discussion of his poetic practice drew him into a major exploration, not just of his personal development, but of the context of his work in English literary history, including the relationship with Wordsworth. This led in turn to philosophy, and theories of language, and in short to the *Biographia Literaria*, a kind of intellectual autobiography unparalleled in its combination of important literary criticism, brilliant local insight and chaotic disorganisation. Significant stretches of the theoretical musings in *Biographia* are more or less dishonestly plagiarised, but the whole manner of the book is so extreme in vulnerable insecurity, and so apologetic in failing to deliver the grandiose philosophical syntheses it constantly promises, that plagiarism seems beside the point. It is the wholly unique expression of a brilliant but self-consciously flawed and neurotic mind, desperate for the sympathetic ear of an audience whose judgement it dreads.

During the period of its composition Coleridge also made progress with other projects. In 1816 he wrote a new play, or rather 'dramatic entertainment', *Zapolya*, which was eventually produced in 1818. He at last published 'Kubla Khan' and 'Christabel' in a pamphlet with 'The Pains of Sleep'. *The Statesman's Manual*, first of his so-called *Lay Sermons*, appeared in December 1816. This work continued Coleridge's commitment to assist the intellectual life of his generation by teaching them to set contemporary events in the context of general issues of political and ultimately religious principle. Like all of Coleridge's mature published prose works, its ungainly stylistic obscurity failed to deter some readers, and the commitment to see the larger picture won influence and admirers. Its conservatism enraged Hazlitt, who launched a tremendous attack on Coleridge's apostasy in a review for the *Edinburgh*.

In April 1816 Coleridge presented himself at the Highgate house of the surgeon James Gillman, in search of treatment for his opium addiction. This turned out to be a decisive moment, for Coleridge moved in with the household, and found the arrangement so congenial that it was continued for the rest of his life. Coleridge's intellectual breadth and learning, and his extraordinary talk, found an enthusiastic admirer in Gillman, while the constant support and sympathetic care of the Gillmans provided Coleridge with an environment in which he could work, and be happy. He became 'the Sage of Highgate', exerting an influence on his own and younger generations mainly through the direct experience of his presence and monologous conversation. He attracted distinguished visitors such as Carlyle, Rossetti, Fenimore Cooper, and many others, and built a circle of disciples over the years which included Joseph Henry Green, Thomas Allsop, and his nephew Henry Nelson Coleridge. These latter two gradually assumed responsibility for recording Coleridge's talk, which was written up and published after his death as *Table Talk*, thus initiating a process by which Coleridge's posthumous fame came to rest on far more than the work actually completed and published in his lifetime. This process adds a further unique dimension to Coleridge's stature, for in his notebooks, marginalia and letters he left a record of speculative intellectual inquiry, and highly innovative self-analysis, which far surpasses in range, originality and sheer bulk the conventional output of any contemporary. The sense of a great genius left unfulfilled by the completed great work, which was so strong a component of his contemporary image, has been controverted for subsequent generations by the retrieving efforts of scholarship. The great late-twentieth-century scholarly editions of the *Collected Works*, and above all the *Notebooks*, under the commanding management of Kathleen Coburn, have thus created a Coleridge who could not be known in his lifetime.

Coleridge's collected poems appeared in 1817 as *Sibylline Leaves*, together with the *Biographia Literaria*, which had grown to two volumes. They confirmed his new status as a presence in literary London, a suddenly senior and much more substantial figure than the years of wandering after his departure for Germany in 1798 had seemed to anticipate. The dependency of his personality had found shelter with the Gillmans, and the twists and turns of his political allegiances and religious beliefs had settled to an orthodoxy whose justifications and history were buried in the intractable obscurity and formal irresolution of his public writings. A second *Lay Sermon* was published in 1817, addressed to 'the Higher and Middle Classes', which further developed his insistence on the need for ultimately religious principles in the negotiation of local political and social crisis. His acquaintance and celebrity widened. He returned to lecturing, with courses from 1818 on the history of philosophy, and on Shakespeare. Like his table talk, these lectures were recorded by others and came to be published. Their reliance on German and other sources is clear enough, but the extent and frankness of their derivative character is perplexingly debatable, the more so because of their unusual transmission. But their influence, and the influence of certain passages in the *Friend*, the *Lay Sermons*, and above all in *Biographia Literaria* (the discussions of Wordsworth's poetic practice and principles, and the climactic 'definition' of Fancy and Imagination in Chapter Thirteen), was undoubtedly important, and became central in the developing traditions of Anglo-American literary criticism especially after their emergence as academic disciplines in the early years of the twentieth century.

The importance that Coleridge came to have for academic literary criticism is instructive. The discipline that his own critical practice demands of poetry certainly anticipates English 'practical criticism' and the New Criticism. On the other hand his readiness to move from literary to philosophical discourse, and his general project to theorise from particulars, anticipates what might be considered a contrary strain of abstraction and theorising in English studies. Even the incompleteness and tangled rhetorical manoeuvrings of his writings have a kind of appropriateness here, foreshadowing a deep and general problem of identity in academic English, shot through with political and ethical concerns in virtue of its attention to literature, and yet neither sufficiently abstract to contribute in the disciplines of formal thinking, nor comfortable with the mere formalism of aesthetic appreciation. Coleridge has a curious quality of anticipating problems which only emerge fully in the experience and problems of later generations. There is even a kind of post-modernity in the refusal of the life, or the work, to settle into coherent narrative or any satisfying sense of consummated intention.

Coleridge's later years produced further writings. A long-cherished volume inspired by Archbishop Leighton, whose work had been a comfort in the darkest days of his addiction and illness, at last appeared as *Aids to Reflection* in 1825. This impressed many Anglicans and also found admirers in the United States. He continued to write poetry, and this later verse, almost always occasional, and mostly light and unpretentious in form, nevertheless sometimes manages an unusual bleak and wintry honesty in self-appraisal. In 1828 his *Poetical Works* were published in three volumes, followed by two further editions in his lifetime. His poetry was also published by Galignani in Paris in 1829 as part of *Poetical Works of Coleridge, Shelley, and Keats*, confirming his association with, and significance for, the major second-generation Romantics. A final important prose work, *On the Constitution of the Church and State*, appeared in 1829. This surprisingly cogent work, prompted by contemporary arguments over Catholic emancipation and the proper place and purpose of the Church, confirmed Coleridge's stature as an influential conservative Anglican thinker.

In 1822 Coleridge's wife, and his daughter Sara, had visited Highgate, and Coleridge was impressed and enchanted by Sara's beauty and formidable learning. She was to fall in love with Henry Nelson Coleridge, whom she thereafter joined in the self-imposed task of preserving her father's work and talk for posterity. Less comforting was the fate of Coleridge's eldest son Hartley. Coleridge was immensely proud of his eccentric son, and delighted when in 1819 he was elected to a Fellowship at Oriel College Oxford. But in little more than a year Hartley was removed from his Fellowship for a record of dissipation and reckless disregard of the College culture. Coleridge was completely devastated, doubtless in part because his son's behaviour appeared a cruel visitation of the father's sins. He tried everything to secure Hartley's re-instatement, but failed. Subsequently a complete separation was effected by the strange and lonely Hartley, who had no contact with his father for the remainder of his life. It was a culminating expression of Coleridge's failure as a father.

By the early 1830s Coleridge had reached something like eminence. His addiction continued, secretive and controlled. He made little money from his writing, his publisher having failed in 1819, and the sympathetic charity of the Gillmans was supplemented by small gifts and annuities, including one from the Royal Society of Literature. There were occasional meetings with the Wordsworths. In 1830 Sara and Henry Nelson Coleridge moved nearby to Hampstead, and supported him through the last few years. Coleridge died on 25 July 1834 in Highgate. A post mortem revealed evidence of serious and long-standing heart problems, suggesting a physiological basis for the laudanum dependency which had so destructively blighted Coleridge's vulnerable sensibility.

2

PAUL MAGNUSON

The 'Conversation' poems

In a copy of *Sibylline Leaves* (1817), Coleridge wrote on the page that began 'The Eolian Harp':

> Let me be excused, if it should seem to others too mere a trifle to justify my noticing it – but I have some claim to the thanks of no small number of the readers of poetry in having first introduced this species of short blank verse poems – of which Southey, Lamb, Wordsworth, and others have since produced so many exquisite specimens.[1]

In *Sibylline Leaves* 'The Eolian Harp' was placed among 'Meditative Poems in Blank Verse' with poems we now call 'Conversation Poems'. George McLean Harper coined the term 'Conversation Poems' in 1928, borrowing the subtitle of 'The Nightingale. A Conversation Poem' and following the epigram from Horace to 'Reflections on Having Left a Place of Retirement': 'Sermoni propriora', 'more fitted to conversation or prose'. Harper described them as 'poems of friendship', since they were all written to a close friend, and included in the category 'The Eolian Harp' (Aug. 1795), 'Reflections of Having Left a Place of Retirement' (Oct. 1796), 'This Lime-Tree Bower My Prison' (July 1797), 'Frost at Midnight' (Feb. 1798), 'The Nightingale' and 'Fears in Solitude' (both April 1798), 'Dejection: An Ode' (April 1802) and 'To William Wordsworth' (Jan. 1807).

Harper described the structure of 'Reflections on Having Left a Place of Retirement': 'The poem begins with a quiet description of the surrounding scene and, after a superb flight of imagination, brings the mind back to the starting-point, a pleasing device we may call the "return."'[2] Harper's use of 'return' to describe the structure is apt, since in 1807 Coleridge revised 'Frost at Midnight' by deleting the following six lines at the end of the first version in *Fears in Solitude* (1798):

> Like those, my babe! which 'ere tomorrow's warmth
> Have capp'd their sharp keen points with pendulous drops,
> Will catch thine eye, and with their novelty

Suspend thy little soul; then make thee shout,
And stretch and flutter from thy mother's arms
As thou wouldst fly for very eagerness.

Coleridge commented, 'The six last lines I omit because they destroy the rondo, and return upon itself of the Poem. Poems of this kind & length ought to be coiled with its tail round its head.'[3] As revised, 'Frost at Midnight' begins with the 'secret ministry' of the frost, makes an excursion to his childhood home at Ottery St Mary and his school, Christ's Hospital in London, and returns to the cottage and the images of frost. The other 'Conversation' poems are similarly structured.

In 1965 M. H. Abrams credited Coleridge with originating what Abrams called the 'greater Romantic lyric', a genre that began with Coleridge's 'Conversation' poems, and included Wordsworth's 'Tintern Abbey', Shelley's 'Stanzas Written in Dejection' and Keats's 'Ode to a Nightingale', and was a major influence on more modern lyrics by Matthew Arnold, Walt Whitman, Wallace Stevens and W. H. Auden. He characterised the greater Romantic lyric as spoken by the poet in an identifiable location, commonly outdoors, and constituting a conversation with a silent auditor:

> The speaker begins with a description of the landscape; an aspect or change of aspect in the landscape evokes a varied but integral process of memory, thought, anticipation, and feeling which remains closely intervolved with the outer scene. In the course of this meditation the lyric speaker achieves an insight, faces up to a tragic loss, comes to a moral decision, or resolves an emotional problem. Often the poem rounds upon itself to end where it began, at the outer scene, but with an altered mood and deepened understanding which is the result of the intervening meditation.[4]

Abrams's essay thus confirms Coleridge's claim to have introduced the short, blank verse poem into English, a form which adapted the classical ode as the model for lyric poetry. The meditative, conversational blank verse was a sharp turn from Coleridge's earlier poetry, modelled on the odes of Collins and Gray and the sentimental sonnets of William Lisle Bowles. Much of his earlier poetry (particularly his additions to Southey's *Joan of Arc* (1796), which were later incorporated into 'The Destiny of Nations'; 'Religious Musings', which concluded *Poems* (1796); and 'Ode on the Departing Year' (1796)) was allegorical and metaphysical, interpreting the events of the French Revolution in the apocalyptic terms of Revelation as a renovation of the earth. His early readers discouraged him from straining after metaphysics and the sublime. Charles Lamb urged him to 'Cultivate simplicity, Coleridge, or rather, I should say, banish elaborateness; for simplicity springs spontaneous from the heart, and carries into daylight its own modest buds and genuine, sweet, and clear flowers of expression' (Marrs 1, 60–1). The nearest model for Coleridge's blank verse is Cowper's *The Task*, which Coleridge praised in December 1796 as the 'divine Chit-chat of Cowper' (*CL* 1, 279). Cowper's *Task* is a source for 'Frost at Midnight':

> Me oft has fancy ludicrous and wild
> Sooth'd with waking dream of houses, tow'rs,
> Trees, churches, and strange visages express'd
> In the red cinders, while with poring eye
> I gazed, myself creating what I saw.
> Nor less amused have I quiescent watch'd
> The sooty films that play upon the bars
> Pendulous, and foreboding in the view
> Of superstition prophesying still,
> Though still deceiv'd, some stranger's near approach.[5]

Cowper's verse has the rhythm of ordinary speech. It avoids the mannered blank verse of Milton, which embeds clause within clause and in which the verse paragraph is the rhythmic unit, and it avoids the formal balance and antithesis of eighteenth-century heroic couplets, which influence Thomson's blank verse in *The Seasons*. Coleridge's shorter blank verse poems give a structure to Cowper's long, rambling, inconsequential amusement, as they deepen the psychological insight and the philosophical meditation on the relation of the mind to nature.

In the 'Conversation' poems, Coleridge adopts a natural symbolism in which the perceiving, remembering, imagining mind searches for images of itself and God in nature. Most of the poems begin with the poet in a state of repose, receiving sensations from nature. Receptivity changes to active speculation on the relation of the poet to nature and society, and activation of the imagination is often presented by the image of the Eolian harp. The harp is a stringed instrument with a sound box, which, when placed where the wind can blow over it, emits a natural music. In the eighteenth century it was an image of nature's music, but Coleridge transformed it into an image of inspiration in which the poet was a harp over whom the winds of inspiration blow. The harp became the first of several of his formulations of the relation of the mind to nature. In 'The Eolian Harp' the 'simplest Lute, / Placed length-ways in the clasping casement' is 'by the desultory breeze caress'd' (12–14). At first the harp is likened to a 'coy maid half yielding to her lover', and then the sound becomes the melodies of an imaginary world. In the earliest version of the poem, these speculations rose to a view of an animated universe:

> And what if all of animated nature
> Be but organic Harps diversely fram'd,
> That tremble into thought, as o'er them sweeps
> Plastic and vast, one intellectual Breeze
> At once the Soul of each, and God of all?
>
> (44–8)

In other poems, similar figures of inspiration repeat the idea of an active universe, a nature animated by God. In 'The Nightingale' the moon emerging from behind the clouds awakens

> earth and sky
> With one sensation, and those wakeful birds
> Have all burst forth in choral minstrelsy,
> As if some sudden gale had swept at once
> A hundred airy harps!　(78–82)

In 'This Lime-Tree Bower' Coleridge imagines Charles Lamb and the Wordsworths descending into a deep dell where an ash tree has grown over a roaring stream. In the depth of the dell, the ash is cut off from two sources of life and inspiration, the sun and the breeze, yet still the rush of the waterfall animates the leaves of the ash:

> that branchless ash,
> Unsunn'd and damp, whose few poor yellow leaves
> Ne'er tremble in the gale, yet tremble still,
> Fann'd by the waterfall　(13–16)

Even the cold in 'Frost at Midnight' has a 'secret ministry' that freezes the eave-drops into 'silent icicles, / Quietly shining to the quiet Moon' (73–4). At the quietest moments of the year, when water is frozen in silence, there is an active force in the world shining forth in the light of the moon reflected through the icicles.

The philosophical and theological implications of such a formulation are difficult for a twenty-first-century mind to grasp. Coleridge tried to combine antithetical materialist and idealist intellectual traditions and tried to conceptualise the means by which a transcendent God could act on the material world. First, Coleridge turned to a physician for verification of an active, immaterial force in the universe. On 31 December 1796 he wrote to John Thelwall, referring to Alexander Monro's *Observations on the Nervous System* (1783) – 'Monro believes in a plastic [i.e. shaping] immaterial Nature – all-pervading' – and then Coleridge quotes lines 44–8 of 'The Eolian Harp' (*CL* I, 294). Second, Monro's formulation of a plastic nature was in accord with Ralph Cudworth's *True Intellectual System* (1678), which Coleridge borrowed from the Bristol Library on 15 May 1795 and again on 9 November 1796.[6] A Neo-Platonist and Christian advocate, Cudworth argued against materialism and atheism and for God's direction of the world through a plastic nature 'which doth drudgingly execute that part of his providence which consists in the regular and orderly motion of matter' and which is like harmony in the arts, 'particularly those musical ones of singing, playing on instruments, and dancing'.[7] Finally, the Unitarian Joseph Priestley influenced Coleridge's figurative expression of an active force in nature. Priestley was a materialist, but his materialism, argued at length in *Matter and Spirit* (1777), conceived of matter, not as blocks of impermeable solidity, but as '*physical points* only, endued with powers of attraction and repulsion'.[8] For Priestley, matter was an energy or force. To these formulations of a plastic nature by a physician, a Neo-Platonist theologian and a Unitarian materialist, Coleridge added the characteristic of consciousness to think of an 'intellectual breeze', so the physical world trembles 'into thought'. Finally Coleridge added lines to 'The Eolian Harp' in the Errata sheet of *Sibylline Leaves* (1817):

> O ! the one Life within us and abroad,
> Which meets all motion and becomes its soul,
> A light in sound, a sound-like power in light,
> Rhythm in all thought, and joyance everywhere –
> Methinks, it should have been impossible
> Not to love all things in a world so fill'd;
> Where the breeze warbles, and the mute still air
> Is Music slumbering on its instrument.   (26–33)

In an 1802 letter to William Sotheby, Coleridge explained that

> Nature has her proper interest; & he will know what it is, who believes & feels, that every Thing has a Life of its own, & that we are all *one Life*. A Poet's *Heart* & *Intellect* should be *combined*, *intimately* combined & *unified* with the great appearances in Nature – & not merely held in solution & loose mixture with them, in the shape of formal Similes.   (*CL* II, 864)

The early 'Conversation' poems present a creative universe, sustained by God's purposes working through a plastic, shaping nature, and expressed in a symbolic mode. Yet Coleridge was wary of the figure of the harp because it implied a passivity for the poet, who at best is an idle instrument waiting for inspiration. The conclusion of 'The Eolian Harp' attributes to his wife Sara the common piety that shuns bold speculation and avoids the radical Priestleyan unity of matter and spirit, but Coleridge himself shares her reservations over his 'idle flitting phantasies' (40), bubbles that 'rise and break' (56). From his reading of the empiricist philosophers John Locke and David Hartley, Coleridge concluded that in their systems the mind is merely a lazy, passive observer of the world, not a creative soul. In the *Biographia* he ridiculed the materialist account of the mind: consciousness is 'a *result*, as a *tune*, the common product of the breeze and the harp'; and 'in Hartley's scheme the soul is present only to be pinched or *stroked*, while the very squeals or purring are produced by an agency wholly independent and alien' (*BL* I, 117).

Coleridge's reservation about the figure of the breeze and the harp led him to reformulate the relation of the mind to nature. In an early version of 'This Lime-Tree Bower My Prison' he imagines his friend Charles Lamb looking at the landscape

> till all doth seem
> Less gross than bodily, a living Thing
> That acts upon the mind, and with such hues
> As cloathe the Almighty Spirit, when he makes
> Spirits perceive His presence!

In a note to this passage, Coleridge explained to Southey 'You remember, I am a *Berkleian*' (*CL* I, 335). In his later philosophy, George Berkeley (1685–1753) developed an account of the visible world as God's language by analogy with human language. Just as one knows the existence of other minds by understanding their language, one knows of the existence of God by viewing a divine visual language in nature:

> this Visual Language proves not a Creator merely, but a provident Governor, actually and intimately present, and attentive to all our interests and motions, who watches over our conduct, and takes care of our minutest actions and designs throughout the whole course of our lives, informing, admonishing, and directing incessantly, in a most evident and sensible manner.[9]

Nature is not simply energy playing upon a human instrument, but a language to be understood. In 'Frost at Midnight' Coleridge hopes that his son Hartley will 'see and hear / The lovely shapes and sounds intelligible / Of that eternal language, which thy God / Utters' (58–61).

Coleridge's second explanation of the relationship of the mind to nature as language, like the symbol of the harp, has its difficulties for him in moments when joy is absent, in moments of dejection. At the beginning of 'Dejection: An Ode' he gazes from his window on a winter storm descending into the spring garden. In a potentially sublime storm, Coleridge laments: 'I see them all so excellently fair, / I see, not feel, how beautiful they are' (37–8). The visible forms are present, but there is no emotion, no human heart intimately connected with the appearances of nature. The visible language in nature has no communicative force, no passion and life for Coleridge. Thus when he explains his unresponsive gaze on nature, he attributes his dejection to an inner failure, and, in so doing, turns completely from the earlier figure of the harp as passive instrument of nature's active ministry:

> O Lady! we receive but what we give,
> And in our life alone does nature live:
> Ours is her wedding garment, ours her shroud!
>   And would we aught behold, of higher worth,
> Than that inanimate cold world allowed
> To the poor loveless ever-anxious crowd,
>   Ah! from the soul itself must issue forth
> A light, a glory, a fair luminous cloud
>   Enveloping the Earth –
> And from the soul itself must there be sent
>   A sweet and potent voice, of its own birth,
> Of all sweet sounds the life and element!
>
>   (47–58)

The soul must possess its proper joy or nature will be mere matter. Coleridge's turn from the figure of the passive poet as nature's instrument to one of the active, imaginative being is not merely a matter of his dejection and severe self-criticism. It reflects, rather, a shift in his thinking from a materialism he associated with David Hartley to a philosophy in which mind constructs the world.

Within the formal pattern of these poems, a reader may construe the relation of the mind to nature philosophically or theologically, but the movement of the speaker's imagination may also be read psychologically. The poems have been called crisis lyrics in which Coleridge confronts a loss, overcomes that loss through an excursion in imagination to nature and to sympathy with other minds, and often utters a blessing on the person addressed. 'This Lime-Tree Bower My Prison' begins with Coleridge's loss of 'Beauties and feelings, such as would have been / Most sweet' (3–4). What is lost to the bodily eye is gained by the spiritual eye of imagination as it follows Charles Lamb and the Wordsworths on their walk down into the dell and up to view the scene over the Bristol Channel. At the end of the poem, his bower is no longer a prison, but a natural scene in which the sunlight on the tree mirrors both the dell and the 'glorious Sun'. Coleridge's conclusion is that

> 'Tis well to be bereft of promis'd good,
> That we may lift the soul, and contemplate
> With lively joy the joys we cannot share.
>
> (65–7)

The poem is not only an imaginative apprehension of nature's joy but also an escape from loss, an act of imagination's self-recognition.

In 'Frost at Midnight' Coleridge is alone with his son in his cottage on a winter's evening in a silence punctuated only by the owl's call. He knows that the active ministry of frost and 'the numberless goings-on of life' (12) are present but cannot experience nature through his senses nor human society through conversation. A loose piece of soot on the grate reminds him of his childhood. Memory takes him back, first to his school, Christ's Hospital in London, and then to Ottery St Mary, his childhood home, where he recalls the town fair and the music of the church bells, which were a promise, a language, 'articulate sounds of things to come' (33). From his excursion into the past, he returns to the present in his cottage to bless his son, who 'thrills' (48) his heart and, while acting as an image of his own childhood and as second self, reminds Coleridge of the childhood promise. Hartley will 'see and hear' (58) God's eternal language in all seasons. Coleridge's knowledge of that same language is vicarious here and in other 'Conversation' poems. In his blessing of others, Coleridge is a benevolent guide, showing others the way to joy, but strangely distant from the immediate experience of it. There is an ambivalence in his gesture of blessing, since it is others who read nature's language. In the final version of 'Frost at Midnight' Coleridge returns to the 'deep calm' (45) on the winter midnight, but in an earlier version, he returned to the 'dead calm', a troubling indication that Hartley's role is not simply that of a second self, but of someone granted a blessing that Coleridge cannot share. His excursion in memory was merely a 'toy of Thought' (23).

The rejection of speculation in 'The Eolian Harp' and the doubts troubling 'Frost at Midnight' become more explicit in 'Dejection: An Ode'. It was originally written as a letter to Sara Hutchinson, whom Coleridge had loved since their first meeting in late 1799. Written in April 1802, the letter is almost three times as long as the final 'Ode' and confesses Coleridge's unhappy marriage and turbulent relations with the other Sara, his wife. In constructing 'Dejection: An Ode' Coleridge removed all the personal references and turned a confessional letter into a poem addressed to an anonymous 'Lady' that described his own creative failure. Although Coleridge calls it an ode, the structure and symbols resemble those of the other 'Conversation' poems. The first three stanzas describe his 'stifled, drowsy, unimpassioned grief, / Which finds no natural outlet, no relief, / In word, or sigh, or tear' (22–4), his blocked emotional expression. In the place of the usual excursion outward to nature or back in memory in the other 'Conversation' poems, Coleridge turns inward to explain the failure of his 'genial spirits' (39). The word 'genial' refers to both his creative spirit and his sexuality. He attributes his loss, which now seems to be a permanent possession, to 'afflictions' that

> bow me down to earth:
> Nor care I that they rob me of my mirth;
> But oh! each visitation
> Suspends what nature gave me at my birth,
> My shaping spirit of Imagination.
> For not to think of what I needs must feel,
> But to be still and patient, all I can;
> And haply by abstruse research to steal
> From my own nature all the natural man –
>
> (82–90)

The final two stanzas turn outward again with the hope that the winter's storm is only a 'mountain-birth' (129), a natural, not psychological, storm. Coleridge blesses the Lady with 'wings of healing' (128) and with the assurance that joy will 'lift her spirit, joy attune her voice' (134). At the beginning of the poem his expression is stifled; at the end, his voice is active only in a blessing of the other. His joy and imagination are suppressed by his 'abstruse research', his philosophical studies, which remove him from consciousness of emotional pain.

Theological, philosophical and psychological readings of the 'Conversation' poems emphasise Coleridge's individual response to nature, his imagination and his immediate circle of friends. There are few explicit references to politics in these poems. 'Reflection on Having Left a Place of Retirement' chooses the active political life over contemplative retirement, and 'Fears in Solitude', written when the government was circulating rumours of a French invasion, catalogues the nation's sins: effeminate luxury, slavery and warmongering. For the most part, however, the 'Conversation' poems appear to ignore the great national events and issues of the French Revolution and to retreat into their own interiority. Yet if the poems are read in the context of the debates of the late 1790s, they resonate with politics. In 1798 Coleridge published 'Fears in Solitude' and 'Frost at Midnight' in a slim volume with 'France: An Ode', as a defence of his public standing as a West Country radical and an opposition journalist in the *Morning Post*, who was attacked in the pages of the ministerial *Anti-Jacobin*, which had, in turn, accused him of being a Jacobin. 'Jacobin' is a slippery word, used mostly as a term of abuse covering a wide range of positions including republicanism, atheism, materialism, immorality and opposition to existing social institutions. In 'Fears in Solitude' he presents the charges against him while describing the different groups of radicals:

> Others, meanwhile,
> Dote with a mad idolatry; and all
> Who will not fall before their images,
> And yield them worship, they are enemies
> Even of their country!
> Such I have been deemed. –
> (170–5)

For Coleridge in the 1790s, idolatry is the worship of the gods of war, sexuality, thievery and drunkenness, and these, Coleridge says, are the gods of those who prosecute the war with France, enslave Africans and perjure themselves in courts. He portrays himself not only as the imaginative poet in retirement, but as the breaker of idols, one who rejects these false gods and opposes slavery and the war. At the end of 'Fears in Solitude', he returns to his family. 'Fears in Solitude' was the first poem in the volume; 'France: An Ode' the second; and 'Frost at Midnight' came last, after these two poems with explicit political themes. The affection for his family in 'Frost at Midnight' echoes that in 'Fears in Solitude'. In the public debates, domesticity was not merely a private matter, not exclusively a matter of individual psychology. Edmund Burke defined the English constitution as resting on domestic affections:

> We have given to our frame of polity the image of a relation in blood; binding up the constitution of our country with our dearest domestic ties; adopting our fundamental laws into the bosom of our family affections; keeping inseparable, and cherishing with the warmth of all their combined and mutually reflected charities, our state, our hearths, our sepulchres, and our altars.[10]

To a contemporary reader, the parallel between the constitution of the state and the constitution of the family would have been obvious. To defend himself in the court of public opinion, Coleridge added 'Frost at Midnight' to his political poems to portray himself as a loyal subject. One who loves domesticity must love one's country. Also he proves that he is not a Jacobin because he is not an atheist. While his love of domesticity and religion separates him from other radicals such as John Thelwall and William Godwin, who were materialists and atheists, they do not place him in Burke's camp. His religion led him to universal benevolence and internationalism closer to that of Dr Richard Price, whose 'Discourse on the Love of our Country' was delivered before the Society for Commemorating the Revolution in Great Britain on 4 November 1789. Price argued that we should love our country, but not exclusively, because excessive nationalism leads only to domination of other nations: 'we ought to consider ourselves as citizens of the world'.[11] Coleridge concludes 'Fears in Solitude' as a cosmopolitan, a citizen of the world, with 'the thoughts that yearn for human kind' (232), where Coleridge uses 'yearn' in an old sense of 'sympathise'. The domesticity and love of nature as God's language in 'Frost at Midnight' thus portray Coleridge as a religious advocate of universal philanthropy, not as a Burkean nationalist.

'This Lime-Tree Bower' takes a similar stand. Its form is that of a public letter addressed to Charles Lamb, who with Charles Lloyd published *Blank Verse* (1798). Lloyd's poems echoed Coleridge's radical thought, so in the public eye Lamb was associated with Coleridge and Lloyd as a radical and target of the *Anti-Jacobin*. Coleridge signed the poem 'ESTEESI', a transliteration of a Greek pun on his initials, as he explained in 1802. ESTEESI 'signifies – *He hath stood* – which in these times of apostacy[sic] from the principles of Freedom, or of Religion in this country, & from both by the same persons in France, is no unmeaning Signature, if subscribed with humility, & in the remembrance of, Let him that stands take heed lest he fall' (*CL* II, 867). Coleridge paraphrases St Paul in 1 Corinthians 10:12: 'Wherefore let him that thinketh he standest take heed lest he fall.' His signature at the end of the poem repeats the trope of standing at the centre of the poem: 'So my Friend / Struck with deep joy may stand, as I have stood' (37–8). Coleridge's standing is not merely a perspective on landscape, but rather a moral standing, since it echoes both 1 Corinthians and Milton's contrast of moral standing and falling in *Paradise Lost*. As in 'Fears in Solitude' and 'Frost at Midnight', Coleridge distinguishes himself from other materialists and radicals like Godwin, who reject contemporary standards of sexuality and marriage. 'This Lime-Tree Bower' is a poem about Coleridge's private recovery from loss but it also is a poem addressed to Lamb inviting him to share Coleridge's faith and politics, to stand with him in opposition to the government and to other radicals who embrace materialism and atheism.

Coleridge's claim of originality in creating the short blank verse meditative poem is credible considering Wordsworth's use of it, both in his shorter poems like 'Tintern Abbey' and in episodes of *The Prelude*, known before publication in the Wordsworth circle as a poem addressed to Coleridge. Coleridge's 'Dejection: An Ode' is partly Coleridge's response to having read the first four stanzas of Wordsworth's 'Immortality Ode'. These are merely two instances of an intense dialogic relationship between the two poets, which concludes with 'To William Wordsworth'. This poem was written in December 1806 after Coleridge heard Wordsworth read *The Prelude*. Wordsworth expressed imaginative strength and

> moments awful
> Now in thy inner life and now abroad,
> When power streamed from thee, and thy soul received
> The light reflected as a light bestowed.
>
> ('To William Wordsworth', 16–19)

Coleridge wakes from a depression similar to that in 'Dejection: An Ode'. *The Prelude* related Wordsworth's despondency over the failure of the French Revolution and the following restoration of his imagination in nature, yet Coleridge feels 'the pulses of [his] being beat anew' only to acknowledge that 'as Life returns upon the drowned, / Life's joy rekindling roused a throng of pains' (62–4). He reviews the genial promise of his youth and acknowledges that the promise was not fulfilled, that the gift of hope was in vain. Yet some comforting assurance returns to Coleridge from communion between himself and Wordsworth, since 'Peace is nigh / Where Wisdom's voice has found a listening heart' (86–7). The permanent brilliance of Wordsworth's genius leaves Coleridge listening passively yet also 'with momentary stars of [his] own birth, / Fair constellated foam, still darting off / Into the darkness' (98–100). Wordsworth is a friend, a 'comforter and guide', yet the voice of *The Prelude* is, in part, Coleridge's creation, since its blank verse and theme of imagination's growth through memory originated in Coleridge's earlier 'Conversation' poems. *The Prelude* is ample evidence of Coleridge's claim of originality for creating the 'blank verse poem' not in the sense that his poetry is unique and or inimitable – he reserved that claim for 'The Ancient Mariner' – but that it was generative. What Coleridge heard in December 1806 was Wordsworth's individual voice, yet that voice was an echo of his own.

NOTES

1 Mary Lynn Johnson, 'How Rare Is a "Unique Annotated Copy" of Coleridge's *Sibylline Leaves*?' *Bulletin of the New York Public Library*, 78 (1975), 472. Coleridge most likely wrote this comment in 1817–18, since the copy in which his words were inscribed appears to be a late proof copy.

2 George McLean Harper, 'Coleridge's Conversation Poems', *Spirit of Delight* (London: E. Benn, 1928), 11.

3 Coleridge's marginalia in *Fears in Solitude* were published by B. Ifor Evans, 'Coleridge's Copy of "Fears in Solitude"', *Times Literary Supplement*, 8 April 1935, 255.

4 M. H. Abrams, 'Structure and Style in the Greater Romantic Lyric', *From Sensibility to Romanticism*, ed. Frederick W. Hilles and Harold Bloom (Oxford University Press, 1965), 527–8.

5 *The Task*, IV, 286–95. *The Poems of William Cowper*, ed. John D. Baird and Charles Ryskamp, vol. II (Oxford: Clarendon Press, 1995), 194.

6 George Whalley, 'The Bristol Library Borrowings of Southey and Coleridge, 1793–8', *Library*, 4 (1949), 120, 124.

7 Ralph Cudworth, *True Intellectual System*, ed. Thomas Birch, vol. I (London: J. Walthoe, 1743), 150, 159.

8 Joseph Priestley, *Disquisitions Relating to Matter and Spirit* (London: J. Johnson, 1777), 19.

9 *Alciphron* in *The Works of George Berkeley, Bishop of Cloyne*, ed. A. A. Luce and T. E. Jessop, vol. III (London: Nelson, 1950), 160.

10 Edmund Burke, *Reflections on the Revolution in France* in *The Writings and Speeches of Edmund Burke: The French Revolution*, ed. L. G. Mitchell (Oxford: Clarendon Press, 1989), 84.

11 *Burke, Paine, Godwin, and the Revolution Controversy*, ed. Marilyn Butler (Cambridge University Press, 1984), 25–6.

3

TIM FULFORD

Slavery and superstition in the supernatural poems

At the end of 1797, Coleridge was in a quandary. He needed a new poetic language that readers would not find obscure. He wanted a new political discourse too, or at least a new analysis of politics, for events at home and in Europe left him isolated and disheartened, no longer able to believe that the millennium was at hand. In early 1798, France invaded free Switzerland. Coleridge saw this event as a final betrayal of the revolution of which he had hoped so much. It left him dispirited: the ideals of liberty, fraternity and equality had been perverted; France had become an imperialist military despotism. Already opposed to Britain's imperialist and despotic government, Coleridge was now alienated from his own nation and its revolutionary neighbour. And he was forced to ask why the population at large did not share his disgust. At home and abroad, the people were distressingly loyal to their warmongering governments. In 'France: An Ode', he recalled how Britons had been bewitched into bellicosity. 'A slavish band', they did the bidding of a cruel monarch who bound them with 'a wizard's wand' (27, 29).[1] The French had followed suit, abandoning their new-found liberty for slavish obedience to tyrants who acted in its name:

> The Sensual and the Dark rebel in vain,
> Slaves by their own compulsion! In mad game
> They burst their manacles and wear the name
> Of Freedom, graven on a heavier chain!
>
> (85–8)

'A *willing* Slave', Coleridge wrote in a letter, 'is the worst of Slaves. His *Soul* is a Slave' (*CL* I, 122). The people, he decided, were complicit with their oppressors. Brought up for generations to believe in their own inferiority, they were mental slaves who were incapable of independence because they craved a master. Those who exploited their weakness were magicians, using 'wizard spell[s]' to whip them into a mob ('Sonnets on Eminent Characters': II,

'Burke', 8). Worshipping the gods their political masters chose for them, the gods of avarice, ambition and absolutism, the people assisted at their own oppression and that of the peoples whom Britain enslaved in the West Indies.

> O Fiends of SUPERSTITION! not that oft
> Your pitiless rites have floated with man's blood
> The skull-pil'd Temple, not for this shall wrath
> Thunder against you from the Holy One!
> But o'er some plain that steameth to the Sun,
> Peopled with Death; or where more hideous Trade
> Loud-laughing packs his bales of living anguish;
> I will raise up a mourning, O ye Fiends!
> And curse your spells, that film the eye of Faith,
> Hiding the present God, whose presence lost,
> The moral world's cohesion, we become
> An Anarchy of Spirits!
>
> ('Religious Musings' (1796), 135–46)

In this passage Coleridge undermines colonialist stereotypes. The superstitious natives are not the peoples of Mexico and Africa, but the Britons who, in their lust for or complicity with wealth and power, murder and enslave across the globe.

Opposition to slavery and to the conquest of native peoples had for long been as fundamental to Coleridge as enthusiasm for the French Revolution. In 1797–8 it became more so, because it gave him the means to understand why his radicalism was unpopular. His diagnosis went like this: slavery produced superstition which in turn produced mental enslavement, perpetuating slavery. In proportion to their own powerlessness, subjugated peoples granted others powers that *seemed* supernatural. Unscrupulous tyrants took advantage of this tendency to cement their authority: they ensured those they oppressed stayed spellbound by their power. The people of Britain and France, 'slaves by their own compulsion', were mentally as manacled as the West Indian slaves whom Britain's rulers kept in iron chains.

In 1798 Coleridge began exploring mind forg'd manacles in poetry that brought 'native' and 'savage' beliefs close to home. The process is discussed in 'The Three Graves', a poem set among the farming classes of England, and written in the ballad-form of English folk poetry, but based on an understanding of superstition acquired elsewhere:

> I had been reading Bryan Edwards's account of the effects of the *Oby* witchcraft on the Negroes in the West Indies, and Hearne's deeply interesting anecdotes of similar workings on the imagination of the Copper Indians . . . and I conceived the design of showing that instances of this kind are not peculiar to savage or

barbarous tribes, and of illustrating the mode in which the mind is affected in these cases. (*CPW* I, 269)

Bryan Edwards describes a superstition born of slavery – one that existed nowhere else than Britain's West Indian colonies. The plantation slave, Edwards shows, believed in the spells and curses of obeah-men: 'Sleep, appetite, and cheerfulness, forsake him, his strength decays, his disturbed imagination is haunted without respite, his features wear the settled gloom of despondency: dirt, or any other unwholesome substance, become his only food, he contracts a morbid habit of body, and gradually sinks into the grave.'[2] Physically bound by white masters, the blacks were mentally en-slaved to the 'witchdoctors'. The Copper Mine Indians too, according to Samuel Hearne, let the curses of shamans drive them to death:

> When these jugglers take a dislike to, and threaten a secret revenge on any person, it often proves fatal to that person; as . . . he permits the very thoughts of it to prey on his spirits, till by degrees it brings on a disorder which puts an end to his existence: and sometimes a threat of this kind causes the death of a whole family.[3]

'The Three Graves' shows superstition to have a similar effect among the people of rural England – the very people who remained obedient to Church and King and amongst whom Coleridge, from 1796, was living. In rural Somerset his radical politics had been rejected by the gentry and the vil-lagers: he and Wordsworth were watched by a government spy after locals had reported them to the authorities as suspected traitors. The government, Coleridge admitted, seemed to have a 'talismanic' hold on people's minds. Belief in the rightful power of Church and State was Britain's obeah.

Coleridge was an inquisitive psychologist. He did not rest with comparing Britons' beliefs to the superstitions of 'savages'. In 'The Three Graves' he suggested that curses work when the cursed person is guilty enough to allow them to. The poem concerns love, sex and marriage. Edward, the hero, marries Mary, after seeking her widowed mother's approval. Initially, the mother gives her approval but then tells Edward to switch his affections to her. Edward rejects the mother's advances; she then curses him and his bride. It is Edward's guilt that he has provoked these advances that makes him susceptible to the curse. But he is guilty for another reason too: his dreams tell him that he desires his mother-in-law as well as his wife –

> 'A mother too!' these self-same words
> Did Edward mutter plain;
> His face was drawn back on itself,
> With horror and huge pain.

Both groaned at once, for both knew well
    What thoughts were in his mind;
When he waked up, and stared like one
    That hath been just struck blind.

He sat upright; and ere the dream
    Had had time to depart,
'O God forgive me!' (he exclaimed)
    'I have torn out her heart.'

Then Ellen shrieked, and forthwith burst,
    Into ungentle laughter;
And Mary shivered, where she sat,
    And never she smiled after.   (522–37)

It is the dream's discovery of incestuous desire, a discovery which the rational mind cannot control, that lets the curse work. Bound together in their interpretation of dreams, Edward, Mary and Ellen become guilty victims of unspeakable knowledge. They are subscribers to the curse because it articulates what they now know they had repressed.

Coleridge commented on curses in later years. 'The supposed exercise of magical power', he wrote, 'always involved some moral guilt, directly or indirectly, as in...touching humours with the hand of an executed person &c. Rites of this sort and other practices of sorcery have always been regarded with trembling abhorrence by all nations, even the most ignorant, as by the Africans, the Hudson's Bay people and others' (*Misc. C*, 202). Edwards's African obeah-men and Hearne's Hudson's Bay shamans gained their 'supernatural' power from their culture's shared guilt, from its complicity with their violation of taboos. Slaves, Edwards wrote, would almost never betray the obeah-man's identity even when dying under their curse. This complicity, Coleridge noted (in 'The Destiny of Nations'), was a covert form of resistance to enslavement. The British master's physical power over the slave was exceeded by the African obeah-man's 'magic'. Paradoxically, dying under the compulsion of an obeah-curse was a form of freedom: the superstitious soul would liberate the enslaved body in death. So too, in 'The Three Graves', death and madness under the curse would liberate Edward, Mary and Ellen from their guilty knowledge.

It was not simply guilt that produced superstition. It stemmed, Coleridge wrote, from powerlessness – a powerlessness of which the slave was the extreme case – from 'having placed our summum bonum (what we think so, I mean,) in an absolute Dependence on Powers & Events over which we have no Controll' (*CN* II, 2060). Ignorance was a form of this powerlessness: superstition sprang from 'the consciousness of the vast disproportion of our knowledge to the *terra incognita* yet to be known' (*Misc.C*, 321).

It was towards the *terra incognita australis* – the uncharted southern continent – that the Ancient Mariner was sailing. In Coleridge's most famous poem, a sea voyage into unknown areas forms an outward dramatisation of the inward conditions that, in Coleridge's diagnosis, produced superstition. The mariner journeys beyond the limits of geographic knowledge, where he finds himself helpless before powers and events over which he has no control. The further he penetrates into a physical *terra incognita*, a place of green ice and red ocean, the more he discovers his own powerlessness. On an ocean that is like 'a Slave before his Lord' (419),[4] he too is controlled by forces he cannot understand or resist. He is, in other words, a cousin of the British and French people whom Coleridge was describing at this time as a 'slavish band' in 'France: An Ode'. He resembles them in his desire to believe in the supernatural power of the forces in authority over him. He is a figure who owes his being to Coleridge's political disenchantment with both imperialist Britain and revolutionary France.

Coleridge's achievement in 'The Rime of the Ancient Mariner' was to take the popular narrative of exploration and to make it an articulation of mental as well as physical voyaging. By so doing, he found a form in which the inward self could be staged outwardly, a form all could follow. But the inward self is itself shaped by social and political conditions and crystallised in the action of the poem are Coleridge's political anxieties. In 'Fears in Solitude' (written just after 'The Rime'), he attacked the imperialism which British voyages of discovery had spread:

> From east to west
> A groan of accusation pierces Heaven!
> The wretched plead against us; multitudes
> Countless and vehement, the sons of God,
> Our brethren! Like a cloud that travels on,
> Steamed up from Cairo's swamps of pestilence,
> Even so, my countrymen! have we gone forth
> And borne to distant tribes slavery and pangs,
> And, deadlier far, our vices, whose deep taint
> With slow perdition murders the whole man,
> His body and his soul!   (43–53)

More savage than the tribes they enslaved, Britons travelled to spread their own moral diseases – the death-dealing corruption. Cairo's pestilence, here, becomes a British export. Britain is the new source of a plague usually thought to epitomise Africa's uncivilised nature.

Coleridge's conflation of a physical disease with the moral disease of colonialism was apt. In the interests of sustaining its slave colonies, Britain exposed thousands of black Africans and British sailors to yellow fever, small-pox, yaws, plague and other fatal infections. Coleridge had pitied these slaves and sailors in a public lecture on the evils of the slave-trade. In 'The Rime', he returns to the images of infection he had used in that lecture: the mariner, like a sailor on a slave-ship bound for the West Indies, enters a zone where all becomes tainted with the diseases of empire.[5] Leprosy rots the flesh of the spectre-woman who dices for the crew's lives. And the corruption spreads to the sea itself: 'the very deeps did rot' (119). In the mariner's tale, the whole world becomes infected by the events and images that show him his moral guilt.

After reading 'The Rime', Coleridge's brother-in-law Southey wrote a ballad which borrowed Coleridge's words. 'The Sailor who Served in the Slave-trade' features a repentant crew-member of a slave-ship, who believes himself cursed because he has cruelly beaten one of the captive Africans to death. It seems that Coleridge's poem prompted Southey to offer an empirical (and highly political) cause for a mariner's mental and physical anguish.[6] Coleridge himself, though, offers no such explanation. His ballad arises from his radical opposition to slavery, but it is not *about* it. It could not have been written without his experience of politics, but it is not an explicitly political poem. It is the better for not being so: distancing himself from contemporary events allowed Coleridge to find terms which would let readers share the mental state that, he argued, was produced by, and in turn reproduced, those events. In his political poems he lectured his readers on the public's fatal attraction to the powerful. In 'The Rime' he made readers feel that attraction, made them share the terror, desperation and desire of a man enslaved, in mind and body.

Coleridge later described his aim in 'The Rime' as being to imagine 'persons and characters supernatural' (*BL* II, 6). He was to make the supernatural seem so rooted in human psychology that readers would choose, for the space of their reading, to 'suspend their disbelief' in it. He was wise to choose a sea story for this purpose because his contemporaries were fascinated by the extraordinary discoveries made on recent voyages in which human psychology was put under intense pressure by isolation, danger and fear. Captain Cook had reached further south than ever before as recently as 1774. On board was William Wales, the astronomer who became Coleridge's maths teacher at school. And if Coleridge heard tales of the voyage in his classroom, he later read the massively popular printed accounts, with their details of Antarctic storms, tropical heat, strange effects of light and – shooting albatrosses. In making his mariner follow Cook and Wales, Coleridge made him topical. Cook had become a national hero because he was seen to have ventured beyond all previously known limits.

Cook had maintained discipline and subjected unknown coasts to the order of the naval chart. Coleridge's mariner, by contrast, journeys into sin,
guilt, alienation and living death. Unsailed waters leave him in uncharted
moral and social states. His mental voyage into a living death of superstition
begins, as in 'The Three Graves', with a casting-out ritual. His shipmates,
ignorantly superstitious, strive to give his shooting of the albatross supernatural significance. First they blame him, then praise him, then, on no empirical
evidence, blame him again. They try to control the weather which threatens
the ship by making him bear and purge the blame for it. And so they ostracise
and curse him. The mariner accepts the role of scapegoat because he knows
he has violated the crew's taboo. Becoming a pariah, he believes himself to
be suffering from a still worse form of alienation as he works with the living
dead, so near but yet so far from those dearest to him:

> The body of my brother's son
> Stood by me knee to knee:
> The body and I pull'd at one rope,
> But he said nought to me –
> And I quak'd to think of my own voice
> How frightful it would be!
>
> (333–8)

Here, in this ghastly scenario, Coleridge had found a dramatic language
capable of universalising the diagnosis of the age he had made in his political
poems. Alienation is brought home to the family and slavish obedience is
written on the body.[7] The mariner's zombie crewmates are embodiments of
the political plight of which Coleridge had complained, embodiments too
close to home for the public to ignore.

Close to home they are, but other-worldly too. In touching his nephew's
living corpse, the mariner violates another taboo – that which separates the
living from the dead. Later, Coleridge suggested that it is the mariner's violation of this taboo that makes him an object of terrified and superstitious
awe. Like the shaman and the obeah-man, who are treated with 'trembling
abhorrence' because they touch people with the hand of an 'executed person', the mariner becomes uncanny, a traveller haunted – or touched – by the
dead. His power, Coleridge noticed, resembled the power attributed to the
dead body by superstitious people: 'Eldridge & his Warts cured by rubbing
them with the hand of his Sister's dead Infant / knew a man who cured one
on his Eye by rubbing it with the dead Hand of his Brother's – Comments on
Ancient Mariner' (CN ii, 2048). The obeah-man, Coleridge had suggested,
worked by complicity. If a slave accepted his cure or curse, he too became
tainted by the 'moral guilt' of touching the dead. The mariner works in

this way too: as powerless as a slave, he acquires power over his fellows by making them touch his body, a living corpse that embodies his guilty violation of the boundary between life and death. He is a foreign body come home, a cursed victim who passes on guilt by the curse of his hand, eye and voice:

> I mov'd my lips: the Pilot shriek'd
> And fell down in a fit.
> The Holy Hermit rais'd his eyes
> And pray'd where he did sit.
>
> (593–6)

He spellbinds those who come into contact with him. Held in the mariner's grip, fixed by his eye, 'The wedding-guest he beat his breast, / Yet he cannot chuse but hear' (41–2). To stay and listen is to replace the loving social union of the wedding with the guilty community of the living dead. It is to become a 'savage' or a 'slave' by our own compulsion – obedient, in fear and desire, to an obeah-man. At the end the wedding guest is 'like one that hath been stunn'd / And is of sense forlorn' (655–6).

It is only at the very end of the poem that the reader hears again the narrator's voice which began it. Everything in between, in the 1798 version, is relayed to us by the mariner himself or the fascinated guest. There is no neutral 'objective' viewpoint. According to De Quincey, Coleridge had planned 'a poem on delirium, confounding its own dream imagery with external things, and connected with the imagery of high latitudes'.[8] The mariner may, for all the reader can tell, be delirious. He may be imagining everything, his guilt making him superstitiously project a supernatural drama onto the natural world. Lacking a neutral perspective, we cannot decide, with the result that if we keep reading we come to experience the world as the mariner sees and tells it. We plunge deeper and deeper into his mental journey whether or not he is as mad as his glittering eye suggests. Hallucinations, superstitions his visions may be, but they seem as real to us as they do to the mariner, as real as do the shaman's spells to the Indian.

In the 1800 edition, Coleridge subtitled 'The Rime' a 'poet's reverie'. By this he meant that the poem produced a state of mind, in writer and reader, in which internal, mental, images were projected onto the external world. A 'Night-mair', he wrote, 'is not properly a *Dream*; but a species of Reverie ... during which the Understanding and Moral Sense are awake tho' more or less confused' (*CN* III, 4046). In this half-woken state, internal blends with external: 'mere *hints* of likeness from some real external object ... will suffice to make a vivid thought consubstantiate with the real object, and derive from it an outward perceptibility' (*Friend* II, 117–18). Reveries and nightmares were responsible for ghosts and apparitions – we project our inner images onto the world without realising we are doing so. Seeing them outside us, we are frightened by their simultaneous strangeness and familiarity, exteriority and interiority.

If obeah-man and mariner were mistaking their reverie-worlds for reality, then their curses, spells and tales make their listeners share those worlds. Coleridge set out to make his poem affect the reader in the same way. Poetry of this kind becomes like obeah, like a wizard's spell or shamanistic rite, making an imaginary world seem real enough to affect readers physically – their spines tingling and hair standing on end. It places the 'civilised' reader among the 'savage' people he would like to feel superior to, making him experience the mental enslavement that is the superstitious imagination.

That it does so is a result of Coleridge's verse techniques, which draw readers inexorably into the story. Coleridge based his poem on the English ballads recently collected by Thomas Percy. This made his style, by association, oral, rural and primitive, as if it authentically emerged from a culture that believed in ghosts and spirits. But 'The Rime' is not antiquarian. Its old-fashioned diction is blended with common speech so that the combination of strangeness and familiarity is present at the verbal level. The uncanniness of the verse is also produced by parataxis – the rhetorical device in which causal links between phrases are omitted:

> It ate the food it ne'er had eat,
> And round and round it flew.
> The ice did split with a thunder-fit;
> The helmsman steered us through![9]

Does the ice split *because* the bird eats forbidden fruit? We are not sure. The reader is tantalised by the syntactic structure just as the mariner is by the structure of nature. Coleridge later said that the poem was 'incomprehensible, and without head or tail'.[10] It is his handling of prosody that makes us want to comprehend it, but prevents us from arriving at a rational order, a logic of cause and effect.

Wordsworth lamented the poem's lack of logic and regretted that the mariner 'does not act but is continually acted upon'.[11] Yet if the mariner cannot act because he believes himself without the knowledge, and therefore without the power, to do so, nevertheless Coleridge hints at how this slavery can be overthrown, at how the self can be liberated from superstitious prostration. It is by an unconscious, unknowing act that the mariner begins to throw off the living death to which his imagination has led him:

> O happy living things! no tongue
> Their beauty might declare:
> A spring of love gusht from my heart,
> And I bless'd them unaware!
> Sure my kind saint took pity on me,
> And I bless'd them unaware.
>
> (274–9)

Coleridge makes love into a saving grace, but, tantalisingly, leaves it unconscious.

Eventually, though, we arrive with the mariner back in harbour and conclude with a moral which endorses the power of love – 'he prayeth best, who loveth best / All things both great and small' (647–8). Coleridge came to feel that this moral appeared too openly in the poem and certainly it is anti-climactic, too neat to allow an effective catharsis of the fear and guilt already explored. But it is not, in fact, the end. The mariner is compelled to repeat his tale again and again. Spellbound still by the journey he relives, he continues to spellbind others. The mental world of shared superstition is not to be put by with an easy moral. When he re-published the poem in 1817, Coleridge removed some of the verbal archaisms. He also added the prose glosses, the marginal comments which seem to endorse the Christian scheme implied by 'he prayeth best, who loveth best'. They also add an impersonal authority which presents events from a perspective other than the mariner's and so, for some critics, spoil the uncanny ambivalence of the 1798 text. It is worth remembering, though, that for all their apparent Christian orthodoxy, the glosses pose further problems of interpretation. They foreground the poem's existence as a *written* text by making us conscious of the act of reading. Do we read them *after* reading each page of verse or before? Or do we read across to the margin and back? What authority do they have? We are forced to realise that we construct the world of the poem by viewing text.[12] Because we can no longer read down the page as usual, we can no longer be sure of the order of the text or of the meanings we find in it. Perhaps here too we are being tantalised like the mariner, being made desperate to discover order, so as to control the world we experience, but being disappointed.[13] If so, then we are left knowing how little we know. The poem inverts the procedure of most fiction. It is, in a sense, an anti-poem, ending not in enlightenment but endarkenment, in a feeling of how arbitrary, conventional and fallible are the means by which our little knowledge is acquired.

'Kubla Khan' is an anti-poem of a different, but related, kind. Complete yet fragmentary, it is, Coleridge warns readers, not poetry at all. Yet it portrays a poet who, like the mariner, is able to spellbind an audience into imagining a world into being. Here, however, the poet is less a shaman or obeah-man than a bard, an inspired and inspiring visionary whose words enchant his people. His power of enchantment is elevating rather than enslaving. His is a vision of harmony, beauty and music and his audience are enraptured rather than terrified. Yet they are still in superstitious awe of the poet-wizard, for he has power to exceed the limits of the world as they know it. And the bard resembles the mariner in another way – he cannot consciously control the mental act that gives him this power. The mariner blessed the water-snakes unawares; the bard cannot revive within himself the redeeming song by an act of will. Coleridge himself tells us that he conceived 'Kubla Khan' in a reverie in which mental pictures seemed real – 'the images rose up before him as *things*' (*CPW* I, 296). The reverie was broken by the interruption of the person from Porlock and the poet was unable to retrieve its thingified imagery. He offers what remains as a 'psychological curiosity' which might lead readers *into* a reverie-state of outward inwardness similar to his own, but which cannot lead them *out* again to a resolution.

Resolving reverie into conscious will was the crux of Coleridge's poetic project in 1797–8. If poetic reverie could give readers a share in imagining the world differently, then it could transform them, thus beginning the reformation of the slavish self that Coleridge considered essential if political liberty was to be achieved. But it could only do so if its origin and end could be controlled by the will. 'Christabel', the supernatural poem Coleridge began after writing 'The Rime', forces the problem to a crisis that he could not solve. It remained unfinished, with the Bard Bracy destined never to restore Christabel, Geraldine and Sir Leoline to a state of loving harmony by his healing song.

Unfinished though it is, 'Christabel' is not a failure. Coleridge explored too deep into the mental enslavement produced by his society to imagine that enslavement wholly overcome – but few writers explore so deep in the first place. None of the contemporary anti-slavery poets did; nor did the Gothic novelists from whom he borrowed the setting of the poem. Its subject is chivalry, and the gender and sexual identities people take on in the chivalric and aristocratic family. Set in medieval times, written in the style of a courtly romance, the poem seems backward-looking. Chivalry, however, was a burning political issue when Coleridge wrote, as the Gothic novelists also knew. Edmund Burke had declared in 1790 'the age of chivalry is gone'.[14] He was identifying the French Revolution as the end of a European order, an order sustained by the chivalric code in which the aristocracy, in exchange for their hereditary monopoly of power, governed with courtesy and dutiful paternalism. The governed accepted the rule of their 'betters', having learnt to admire their majesty and to fear their authority. The French Revolution, in Burke's analysis, destroyed this order.

To Coleridge and his fellow radicals, Burke's hymn to chivalry was anathema. In 1795 Coleridge termed Britain's aristocratic rulers 'leprous'. His distrust of their 'chivalry' deepened in 1796 when George, the Prince of Wales, cynically abandoned the wife he had married the year before, leaving her to return to his mistresses. Coleridge criticised the Prince in a poem, 'On A Late Connubial Rupture in High Life'. 'Christabel' returns to the subject of the aristocratic family. With the greater licence made possible by the medieval setting, Coleridge was able to explore the power-relations produced by chivalry without fear of arrest for making political attacks on Britain's rulers. At the same time, using the Gothic genre, in which superstition and the supernatural were expected, allowed him to locate in the nobility the same kinds of irrational and slavish desires that he had placed, in 'The Three Graves' and 'The Rime', amongst the lower classes. Not only peasants and savages but lords and ladies took pleasure in believing themselves dominated by powers beyond their control. Masochism, Coleridge suggested, was a national – and political – disease which monarch and minister sadistically exploited. In 'Christabel' the disease is traced to sexual roots.

Sir Leoline and Christabel have each internalised their chivalric roles. He is the stern knightly father, she the obedient daughter – her sexuality repressed so that she remains innocent in his eyes. Yet it is clear that what is repressed, on both sides, is a sexual desire that is taboo because it is incestuous: Christabel's mother is dead and she takes her place. Into this self-enclosed relationship, Coleridge sends Geraldine, a damsel-in-distress who has suffered an abuse of chivalry. She has been raped by a band of knights. Like the mariner with the wedding guest, Geraldine enthralls the innocent Christabel because she embodies the guilty knowledge that has been repressed within the castle walls. She seems quite innocent, but her violation of propriety is marked on her body:

> she unbound
> The cincture from beneath her breast:
> Her silken robe, and inner vest,
> Dropt to her feet, and full in view,
> Behold! her bosom and half her side –
> A sight to dream of, not to tell!
> (248–53)

Contact with this uncanny body spellbinds Christabel, who falls into a sexual knowledge which, as a woman who identifies herself as an innocent and dutiful daughter, she is unable to accept as anything other than guilt and sin.

As in 'The Three Graves', as in Coleridge's understanding of obeah, it is the acceptance of her guilt that makes her a mental slave. Geraldine's touch becomes 'lord of [her] utterance' (268), a stronger master of her fear and desire even than the man whom society calls her lord – her father.

Christabel's words do not betray her sexual knowledge and desire: her body does, just as Geraldine's did hers. The repressed trauma returns, disguised, in dreams and symptoms:

> Again she saw that bosom old,
> Again she felt that bosom cold,
> And drew her breath in with a hissing sound
>
> (457–9)

Leoline recognises the difference in his daughter and rejects her. His own identity as a chivalric father is dependent on protecting a daughter who must be both innocent and weak. The knowledge manifested by Christabel's body brings into the open desires that he might share, but cannot accommodate. He turns towards Geraldine instead, a woman his daughter's age who is not a blood-relation. Christabel, by contrast, he subjects to the tyrannical rage which chivalry had been invented to disguise:

> His heart was cleft with pain and rage,
> His cheeks they quivered, his eyes were wild,
> Dishonoured thus in his old age;
> Dishonoured by his only child...
> ...turning from his own sweet maid,
> The aged knight, Sir Leoline,
> Led forth the Lady Geraldine!
>
> (640–3, 653–5)

And there the poem ends, a radical critique of the chivalric code and the society which Burke wanted to stay founded on that code. Ostensibly apolitical, 'Christabel' was in fact one of the era's most profound investigations of the social and sexual relations on which the state was based. It remains profound today because, like 'The Rime', it lays bare the mechanisms by which fear and desire are produced and internalised, the processes by which, in response to the culture we live in, we shape ourselves in subservience to and/or in power over others. Coleridge, in 1797 and 1798, had arrived at a poetry in which society and the self are related with acute psychological insight. He had found a language revealing how the 'strange...self-power in the imagination' makes us what we are and how, albeit briefly and unconsciously, it might liberate us (*CN* III, 3547). Coleridge said in later years that Wordsworth was not interested enough in the superstitions of the place in which they had lived in those years. Coleridge was, and his interest is our gain. His superstitious tales and supernatural poems, flawed as they are, are his unique contribution to Romanticism and one of the greatest and most troubling achievements in all English poetry.

NOTES

1 *CPW* I, 245.
2 Bryan Edwards, *The History, Civil and Commercial of the British Colonies in the West Indies*, 2 vols. (London: J. Stockdale, 1793), II, 91–2. My discussion is indebted to two articles on obeah in Romanticism: Debbie Lee, 'Poetic Voodoo in Keats's *Lamia*', *Times Literary Supplement*, 27 October 1995, 13–14; and Alan Richardson, 'Romantic Voodoo: Obeah and British Culture, 1797–1807', *Studies in Romanticism*, 32 (1993), 3–28.
3 Samuel Hearne, *A Journey From Prince of Wales's Fort in Hudson's Bay to the Northern Ocean In The Years 1769, 1770, 1771, and 1772* (London: A. Strahan and T. Cadell, 1795), 233.
4 All quotations from 'The Rime of the Ancyent Marinere' are from the 1798 text given in *CPW* II, 1030–48, unless otherwise stated.
5 Here my reading is indebted to Debbie Lee, 'Yellow Fever and the Slave Trade: Coleridge's *The Rime of the Ancient Mariner*', *English Literary History*, 65 (1998), 675–700. See also Alan Bewell, *Romanticism and Colonial Disease* (Baltimore and London: Johns Hopkins University Press, 1999).
6 On the Ancient Mariner, Southey's poem and the slavery context, see Peter J. Kitson, 'Coleridge, The French Revolution and *The Ancient Mariner*: A Reassessment', *Coleridge Bulletin*, n.s. 7 (Spring 1996), 30–48; Malcolm Ware, 'Coleridge's "Spectre Bark": A Slave Ship?' *Philological Quarterly*, 40 (1961), 589–93; Chris Rubenstein, 'A New Identity for the Mariner', *Coleridge Bulletin*, n.s. 3 (Winter 1990), 16–29.
7 Lee, 'Yellow Fever and the Slave Trade', 682.
8 Quoted in *Samuel Taylor Coleridge. Poems*, ed. John Beer (London: Everyman, 1993), 209.
9 1817 version, ll. 67–70 (*CPW* I, 186–209).
10 'To the Author of the Ancient Mariner', ll. 3–4 in *Poems*, ed. Beer (310).
11 From the note Wordsworth appended to the poem in the second, 1800 edition of the *Lyrical Ballads*.
12 On the consequences of this realisation, see Jerome J. McGann, 'The Meaning of "The Ancient Mariner"', *Critical Inquiry*, 8 (1981), 35–66.
13 On the glosses, see Kathleen M. Wheeler, *The Creative Mind in Coleridge's Poetry* (Cambridge, MA, and London: Heinemann, 1981).
14 Edmund Burke, *Reflections on the Revolution in France*, in *The Writings and Speeches of Edmund Burke: The French Revolution*, ed. L. G. Mitchell (Oxford: Clarendon Press, 1989).

4

JAMES ENGELL

Biographia Literaria

In early March 1815, deciding what manuscripts, even older ones, might be fit for the press, Coleridge proposed to friends and publishers the project that would become *Biographia Literaria*. He had no intention of producing a two-volume work, let alone a classic of humane letters fusing literary criticism, both deeply theoretical and brilliantly practical, with autobiography, philosophy, religion and poetry. Yet, for the final result, what Arthur Symons claimed in 1906 remains true: 'The *Biographia Literaria* is the greatest book of criticism in English, and one of the most annoying books in any language' (*BL* 1906, introd., x–xi). George Saintsbury, who wrote about literary criticism more comprehensively than anyone until René Wellek, stated simply: 'So, then, there abide these three, Aristotle, Longinus, and Coleridge.' Saintsbury avowed that if all literature professors were made redundant, and the proceeds used to furnish 'every one who goes up to the University with a copy of the *Biographia Literaria*, I should decline to . . . be heard against this revolution, though I should plead for the addition of the *Poetics* and of *Longinus*' (*History of Criticism* III, 230–1).

Coleridge envisioned a short preface to a projected book of poems, *Sibylline Leaves*. Mary Lamb understood it would be five or six pages. But as early as 1811 Coleridge contemplated a 'Preface of 30 pages, relative to the principles of Poetry, which I have ever held, and in reference to myself, Mr Southey, and Mr Wordsworth'. On 30 March 1815, Coleridge wrote to Byron, awkwardly asking the younger man to read his poems and, if he judged them worthy, recommend them 'to some respectable Publisher'. Coleridge added, 'A general Preface will be pre-fixed, on the principles of philosophic and genial [having to do with genius] criticism relatively to the Fine Arts in general; but especially to Poetry' (*CL* IV, 561; see *BL* I, 264).

Then, several weeks later, Coleridge received Wordsworth's 1815 *Poems* with its new Preface distinguishing fancy from imagination. The second volume reprinted the 1800 Preface to *Lyrical Ballads*. This revived ghosts. 'It was at first intended', Coleridge had written to William Sotheby as early as

1802, 'that the Preface' to *Lyrical Ballads* 'should be written by me' (*CL* II, 811). Despite stating in 1800 that 'The Preface contains our joint opinions on Poetry' (*CL* I, 627), two years later, perhaps prompted by Wordsworth's 1802 revision of it, Coleridge protested that 'altho' Wordsworth's Preface is half a child of my own Brain...yet I am far from going all lengths with Wordsworth...I rather suspect that some where or other there is a radical Difference in our theoretical opinions respecting Poetry – / this I shall endeavor to go to the Bottom of' (*CL* II, 830). Wordsworth recalled the 'deserted Quarry in the Vale of Grasmere' where Coleridge 'pressed the thing upon me, & but for that it would never have been thought of' (*Wordsworth Prose* I, 167). Yet now, ironically, Coleridge felt too closely associated with it. (In 1810, he and Wordsworth had fallen out badly, in part precipitated by Basil Montagu's report to Coleridge that Wordsworth said his friend was rotting himself with brandy and opium. In 1812 Mary Lamb and Henry Crabb Robinson helped patch the rift.) In 1813 Coleridge complained to Southey that critics continued to find them both guilty by association with Wordsworth: 'This Slang has gone on for 14 or 15 years, against us – & really deserves to be exposed' (*CL* III, 433). Coleridge now identified *Lyrical Ballads* as 'Wordsworth's' book. While he considered Wordsworth a great poet and champions him in the *Biographia*, he recalled difficult memories. Wordsworth dropped his 'Rime' from *Lyrical Ballads* and refused to include 'Christabel', an unfinished poem that, while never completed, would remain Coleridge's longest. Not coincidentally, in 1816, shortly after he began *Biographia Literaria*, Coleridge published the poem.

So, in May 1815, having studied Wordsworth's Prefaces, Coleridge started his own long-projected Preface to stand before *his* volume of poems, one to dissociate himself from Wordsworth, one to elucidate his philosophical inquiries into language, the language of poetry, and the proper distinction between fancy and imagination. On receiving Wordsworth's new volumes, he immediately informed William of his own impending poems and his own Preface, which he would finish 'in two or at farthest three days' (*CL* IV, 576)! By 29 July 1815, Coleridge, dictating rapidly to John Morgan, extended his Preface to 'an Autobiographia literaria, or Sketches of my literary Life & opinions, as far as Poetry and *poetical* Criticism is [*sic*] concerned'. He spoke of subverting Wordsworth's 'Theory, in which my name has been so constantly included', and added that part of his own Preface had become a treatise 'on the powers of association...and on the generic difference between the faculties of Fancy and Imagination...as laying the foundation Stones of the Constructive or Dynamic Philosophy in opposition to the merely mechanic – ' (*CL* IV, 578–9). Wordsworth in his 1815 Preface defined imagination as a mode of association, but Coleridge believed that the powers of imagination to perceive, and to create, transform and unify our perceptions, could not be accounted for by explaining how we associate such perceptions once they are formed. On 10 August Coleridge directed, through John Morgan, that his own Preface and poems be 'printed in the size of Wordsworth's last edition. of Poems &c. the prefatory remarks same sized type' (VCL mss.). *Biographia Literaria* creates an extended dialogue with – and answers – Wordsworth's two Prefaces (1800 and 1815); it then criticises Wordsworth's poetry.

Yet, as early as 1803, Coleridge recorded in his notebooks, 'Seem to have made up my mind to write my metaphysical works, as *my Life, & in* my Life – intermixed with all the other events / or history of the mind & fortunes of S. T. Coleridge' (*CN* I, 1515). We cannot understand *Biographia Literaria* unless we also regard it as the record of a personal odyssey, spiritual, biographical and intellectual as well as critical. Coleridge could not separate these considerations; this alone makes the book demanding and rewarding. He offers theoretical grounding, personal history and then performs a 'practical criticism' (a phrase he coins) based on principles of psychology and philosophy. Coleridge planned and projected many works. Several he mentions in the *Biographia*, including the *Logosophia* (a work designed to set out the underlying principles of his philosophical system), and 'The Brook', a projected poem related to Wordsworth's *River Duddon* sonnets (1820). Yet *Biographia Literaria*, his most popular prose work in the twentieth century, and *Aids to Reflection*, his most popular prose volume in the nineteenth, grew in quasi-spontaneous fashion as responses, shaped by external pressures, to publications of writers he admired, engaged, but at times qualified or corrected.

At forty-two and under financial pressures, in dictating *Biographia Literaria*, Coleridge was preparing, incredibly, his first prose work published as a book. Despite lectures (he became, said Byron, a kind of 'rage' during his 1811–12 series on Shakespeare), and despite poems, reviews and essays in newspapers, the only things remotely approaching a prose volume were the *Omniana* (1812), co-authored with Southey, and the *Friend* (1809–10), later published in three volumes (1818), but originally a series of separate numbers. By early August 1815, Coleridge had dictated so much to Morgan that he began to think of the Preface as 'the main work', divided into '*Chapters*' (see *CL* IV, 584–6). Facing a deadline, in the next six weeks he completed what became the 'philosophical chapters' (5–13), in which he turned to various German sources, his own notebooks, even his own marginalia, often intermixing these from sentence to sentence, so they modify each other in interplay, all punctuated and linked by new sentences of his own. On 17 September, after twenty weeks of furious composition, he finished about three-quarters of the book as we know it today. More confident of having produced an independent work rather than a derivative commentary or short reply to Wordsworth, he dropped the plan of printing his 'preface' and its companion volume of poems in a typeface to mimic Wordsworth's: 'As to the Size and Type I care nothing, provided only the Volumes be a handsome Octavo' (CL IV, 585).

Then, in spring 1816, the printers in Bristol discovered that *Biographia Literaria*, much longer than *Sibylline Leaves*, could not accompany it as a proportionate twin. Aiming at three volumes of roughly equal length, John Gutch made the fateful suggestion that *Biographia Literaria* itself occupy two volumes (CL III, xlix–l). Coleridge agreed but, over the next months, discovered that he had to produce more, then yet more, to fill the space available. He later considered inserting his play *Zapolya*, which Covent Garden – and Drury Lane soon after – had rejected. Instead, he finally inserted 'Satyrane's Letters', an account of his trip to Germany (1798–9) already published in the *Friend* (1809). To make up the requisite space he also included his negative review of Charles Robert Maturin's *Bertram* (1816), which Drury Lane did accept. This review the *Courier* published anonymously in August and September 1816. Coleridge's reasons for inserting it seem to have been triple: (1) he had it on hand; (2) he might have felt Drury Lane took *Bertram* instead of *Zapolya* (which was not the case); (3) he was atoning for letting his review in five issues of the *Courier* appear anonymously, a practice he attacks in *Biographia Literaria*.

If the reader is now confused or, to use Symons's word, annoyed, it is because the shape of *Biographia Literaria* and its contents live up to Coleridge's description: 'an immethodical miscellany' of 'life and opinions', with shades of Tristram Shandy, Hamlet and a 'literary Quixote' tilting against the indifferent machinery of the modern critical press. The lowest common denominator of all is a kind of madness or tainted wit, though with method in it, and parts of *Biographia Literaria* are humorous. The apologia, the apologies, the excuses, the claims, the intellectual wit, complications, defensiveness and insights of the book seem by turns comic, more darkly shaded, then sheerly brilliant. Or, as Leslie Stephen remarked, the book seems 'put together with a pitchfork'. Of all important books of criticism it is the most novelistic and personal. This explains part of its appeal, for at bottom we realise that criticism is joined with life and is, as Dryden remarks, bound up with personal temperament.

Some critics, even while citing the book's failures and unevenness, posit a unity or narrative direction in the book. Others see in its delays, eddyings and self-conscious addresses to the reader a vigilant, continually intentional strategy for engagement, entertainment, digression and, ultimately, for an ingenious critical method shaping the whole. Scholars aware of its compositional history usually see an uneven text, occasionally chaotic, yet frequently unsurpassed, especially in its direct commentary on poetry and language. Structural analyses of *Biographia Literaria*, mindful of Coleridge's awareness of a potentially large, possibly sceptical, and certainly expectant public, present separate cases either for his anxiety mixed with inspired, ad hoc brilliance, or for his unorthodox rhetorical expertise aimed at provoking the reader into thought. (The book did not, in fact, enjoy a warm reception.) Coleridge regarded his literary life as something to defend but also as an admonition, a warning against wasteful and wayward habits, the nature of which he must adumbrate in the book if it is to prove to be an antidote. For this we have two indicators. First, the epigraph from Goethe's *Propyläen*, which reads in part, 'Little call as he may have to instruct others . . . he wishes to spare the young those circuitous paths, on which he himself had lost his way.' Coleridge recorded the passage in 1807 or 1808. Second, the much overlooked, short chapter 11 warns the young that literary happiness is rarely bound up with a literary profession, and that a young man might better become a minister or other professional if he wishes to retire to his library as a room of pleasure and relaxation rather than one of demand and worry. Yet, few books in English establish more firmly the concept of a learned, professionalised criticism.

As a structural whole *Biographia Literaria* contains a series of interlocking stories told almost simultaneously. These stories are autobiographical, philosophical, religious and critical. If we escape conventional experiences of continuity of subject-matter, we discover that the first volume exhibits definite chronology. The first four chapters present literary events of Coleridge's life from Christ's Hospital to 1798. Chapters 5–9 summarise his intellectual migration from various mechanistic and associative systems to rest on religious and transcendental principles. This covers roughly a decade beginning about 1795. Chapter 10, digressive and part of the material Coleridge earlier called 'the most *entertaining* to the general Reader', discusses his religious feelings. It also tries to clarify, though somewhat ambiguously and, some have claimed, disingenuously, his early political views. It closes with a defence and an apology aimed to exculpate him from the opinion that he has failed his promise, has not published much, and is a diminished man. (A century later, T. S. Eliot would still speak of Coleridge as 'a ruined man' whose ghost haunted him.) Chapters 12 and 13 re-engage a philosophical discussion leading to the short, suggestive distinctions between fancy, primary, and secondary imagination. Then, Volume II returns where chapter 4 left off, the occasion of the *Lyrical Ballads*, and first offers 'philosophic definitions of a poem and poetry with scholia'. At the start of chapter 15,

Coleridge launches into 'the application of these principles to purposes of practical criticism'. What follows, in chapters 17–20 and 22, is an outstandingly important critique of Wordsworth's poetry: a close reading of a major author in length, detail, nuanced sensitivity, and theoretical principles unprecedented (and, in many respects, unrivalled) in English letters.

Thus, the first volume explores how we form and deal with perceptions, the products of primary imagination. The second volume examines the artistic transformation of perceptions and images, especially in poetry, and thus elucidates the work of the secondary imagination, which Coleridge makes clear, several times, is what we usually call poetic imagination. At crucial junctures, he returns to the distinction between fancy and imagination, a distinction he feels Wordsworth makes improperly in the 1815 Preface. *Biographia Literaria* pivots around this distinction at the end of chapter 4 (introducing the subsequent philosophical chapters), the beginning of chapter 10, chapter 13, and chapter 14, which itself begins the second volume with its application of philosophical principles to the fine arts, particularly poetry.

Religion, too, is one of the interlocking stories. Coleridge in chapter 10 and again in chapters 12, 13 and 24 anchors his thought in religious and moral beliefs, which he feels a mechanistic view of the universe denies or denigrates. Though later afraid that he promoted pantheism in the book, and in the first volume was '*taken in*' by Schelling's polarities of mind and nature as co-equal, Coleridge is at pains in *Biographia Literaria* to warn against pantheism and promotes Christianity and the Trinity. He speaks of a 'total and undivided philosophy' in which 'philosophy would pass into religion, and religion become inclusive of philosophy' (I, 282–3). He hopes to reconcile the transcendental philosophy – not only its recent German incarnation but its older Platonic and Plotinian forms – with Christianity. The mysteries of being and knowing are to be seen together, with Jesus as a living Logos ultimately connecting, and redeeming, all. Coleridge hopes to reconcile different philosophical systems, yet believes that the first principle of philosophy or belief is best expressed by a transcendental and religious postulate ('Ich bin weil ich bin' or 'I am that I am') rather than by a materialist's creed. Coleridge's chief interest, as far as the imagination is concerned, rests with the Logos or Word, identified with both the Scriptures and Christ.

However necessary to any sympathetic grasp of the book the story of its composition is – impending debt, long-delayed plans, Wordsworth's old and new Prefaces, rapid dictation, printers demanding more material, decade-long scores to settle and set right – and however we view its final shape and narrative logic, these circumstances and characteristics fail to account for its greatness. Editors of anthologies have regularly used certain chapters and sections but ignored others. What, then, is the appeal of the whole?

With the possible exception of national or social history, this unconventional book embraces the full range of disciplines that would now be bracketed under the heading 'Arts and Humanities'. 'Interdisciplinary', as Wilfred Cantwell Smith once remarked, is a ladder-like word created by humanists to climb out of a hole they never should have fallen into in the first place. In humane letters, the ultimate tendency and highest narrative incarnation of interdisciplinary work in *form*, insofar as its object is not disembodied knowledge but the relevance of knowledge to values and the conduct of life, is biography. To approach life – and 'literary life' – in its richness, puzzle and simultaneity of experience; to give, as Coleridge says he is giving, 'Sketches' of events, activities, speculation and convictions that impinge on each other; to de-compartmentalise our specialised minds and sensibilities; to see the connections of poetry, philosophy, religion, friendship, theory and practice, and to see them grow over time, wandering and dividing, then joining and crossing – to be fully interdisciplinary is to be biographical, or autobiographical, especially when dealing with a writer as myriad-minded as Coleridge. Autobiography is a claim Coleridge essays then rejects; autobiography was a new word, a new kind of literature. Yet the book is, in many ways, what he first calls it, an 'Autobiographia literaria' (*CL* IV, 578–9), and more attention might be paid to its status as a unique classic in that genre.

Another reason for the continued appeal of *Biographia Literaria* is that it places literary engagement in the arena of the nature of the personal self, and it places the transcendent in a world where materialism and mechanism threaten alienation and loss. We may think of *Biographia Literaria* as a 'Romantic' book, yet it is a profound expression of modernity. For all his knowledge of the past and his attentiveness to intellectual and literary heritage, Coleridge's thought looks forward. He anticipates in his literary intelligence the New Criticism, yet equally the structuralists' concerns about the nature of language and the post-structuralists' indecisiveness about the logocentric. He foreshadows in his religious views the concerns, convictions and thought of Kierkegaard and Tillich.

At the end of chapter 4, distinguishing fancy from imagination, Coleridge embarks on what he hopes will be a philosophical explanation of the distinction between these two powers (chs. 5–9, 12, 13). Like much of his later prose, *Biographia Literaria* is conceived against empiricism and materialism as adequate explanations of the human psyche or soul, or of reality. The empirical psychology practised by Hartley, Priestley, Alison, Hazlitt and others extended a basis laid by Descartes, Gassendi, Hobbes, Locke and Condillac. This psychology treats how the mind reflects upon, processes, connects and associates its sense impressions and ideas derived from the senses. Coleridge does not deny the importance of this orientation. He once held associationist thought so highly that he named his first child Hartley, after David Hartley. But now he feels that associationism, explaining everything, explains nothing; that the solution of phenomena can never be derived from phenomena; and that the mind is not made out of the senses but the reverse. Wordsworth read the associationists with care, too, and his 1815 Preface defines imagination as a heightened form of associationism. But for Coleridge associationism cannot adequately explain human powers of perception, creativity, and idealisation, nor can it explain the creative, ongoing, organic processes of nature and the cosmos, which in one notebook entry he regards under the aegis of 'Logos, the Creator! and the Evolver!' (CN ii, 2546). Ideas expressed by words – most genuinely by symbols – are ultimately intellectual rather than deriving solely from sense impressions. (One larger implication of materialism for Coleridge is a society driven by things and commodities, an economic system devoid of spiritual values in which people – child labourers or slaves – are employed as utilitarian means rather than valued as ends, as souls.)

Coleridge's strategy against associationism as adequate is multiple. First, he undercuts modern empiricists by promoting, with good reason, Aristotle as first articulating the laws of association (he pointed this out to James Mackintosh in 1800, perhaps before reading J. G. E. Maass's book on associationism). Second, he explains why Hartley's 'material hypothesis' leads to self-contradiction and how Priestley, by eliminating it, eviscerates that theory. Third, he points out, correctly, that Hartley's religious beliefs do not flow from his associationist theory. Fourth, in chapters 6 and 7, Coleridge explains why the philosophical dualism of Descartes, Spinoza and Leibniz comes to an impasse. Finally, often overlooked, Coleridge emphasises that no material or associationist theory accounts for the power of the will, 'our absolute self', a faculty with which Coleridge opens the philosophical chapters, a faculty which appears at tactical places throughout them, and which also accompanies his distinction between fancy and imagination, where fancy operates by choice between already present objects and images, but the secondary imagination acts with the co-presence and control of the conscious will. Coleridge's later thought will emphasise the will. His religious and psychological explorations from this time until his death cannot be grasped without regarding the primacy of the will. In discussions of Biographia Literaria, Coleridge's stress on the will has gone relatively unnoticed, definitely undervalued.

Chapter 9 introduces the transcendental perspective. It starts not with sense impressions but with the mind's inherent faculties, their properties and categories of operation. Acts of the will – an active self-consciousness and not passive sensory receptions – determine our identity as sentient beings. The object of chapters 5–13 is overbearing for their short space: discredit materialism and the mechanical philosophy as insufficient; postulate a constructive philosophy where the mind in its dynamic, active relation to the world has primacy; reveal a power unmentioned and unaccounted for in the materialists' schemes – imagination – and explain how that power in its primary exercise is 'the living Power and prime Agent of all human Perception', permitting us to create perceptions in a manner constitutive not only with nature but with the creator of nature, God ('the infinite I AM'), and how, in its secondary agency, imagination 'dissolves, diffuses, dissipates, in order to re-create . . . it struggles to idealize and to unify'. This power produces the fine arts and poetry. Fancy is valued but confined to the reorganisation and recombination of already existing, separate sense impressions; it juxtaposes or yokes but does not transform or unify. A 'mode of memory', fancy 'must receive all its materials ready made from the law of association' (I, 304–5). Imagination metamorphoses; it creates new objects and, moreover, creates in such a way that the product potentially appears as a new whole, harmonious in its constituent parts, self-sufficient in its form. This undergirds Coleridge's definitions of poetry and a poem in chapter 14 (see below).

If disappointed at Coleridge's rather cryptic statements on fancy and imagination, we might recall that while he continued to think the distinction paramount, he became uneasy with its formulation in *Biographia Literaria*, apparently striking out part of it in a copy that has not survived. He later stated, 'All that metaphysical disquisition at the end of the first volume . . . is unformed and immature; it contains the fragments of the truth, but it is not full, nor thought out. It is wonderful to myself to think, how infinitely more profound my views now are, and yet how much clearer they are' (*TT*, 492, 28 June 1834). However, of all discussions of imagination then available, almost all familiar to Coleridge, whether by Addison, Akenside, Leibniz, Locke, Kant, Wolff, Tetens, Hartley, Burke or Wordsworth, Coleridge's ranks among the most ambitious, certainly the most seminal for criticism. Shelley's *Defence of Poetry* was not yet written, nor Keats's letters. Both would prove to be crucially significant texts in Romantic criticism; and both probably owe something to *Biographia Literaria*. For instance, Keats's 'negative capability' in all likelihood echoes the 'negative faith' of the imagination claimed by Coleridge (II, 6, 134); while Shelley's opposition between a materialistic 'reason' and a spiritual, sympathetic imagination sounds distinctly Coleridgean. Ironically, too, Coleridge's claims for imagination, although conceived against Wordsworth's 1815 Preface, fit well with Wordsworth's adumbration of that power in the very poem Wordsworth wrote to his friend, *The Prelude*, itself a poetic kind of 'Autobiographia literaria'. There, the growth of imagination begins with natal powers of human perception, where it 'Doth like an agent of the one great Mind / Create, creator and receiver both . . . – Such, verily, is the first / Poetic spirit of our human life'.

Then imagination extends itself as poetic force and intellectual love. It becomes capable of creating and unifying anew: 'all like workings of one mind, the features / Of the same face, blossoms upon one tree' (*Prelude* (1850), ii, 257–8; 260–1).

The extent of Coleridge's use of German thinkers and books, significant in the philosophical chapters, is documented completely in *Biographia Literaria* (1983). De Quincey first raised the issue of plagiarism shortly after Coleridge's death. In the next dozen years additional charges surfaced. Sara Coleridge's 1847 edition clarified the issue with some success, but it dogged the book for more than a century. The question is no longer what Coleridge employs or translates without quotation marks, but how he employs it. In recent scholarship one view contends that Coleridge does not simply string together different thoughts from various writers but that by a syncretic, even synthetic, mode of thought he integrates his sources – or attempts to integrate them – into an argument uniquely his own: one, in fact, differing from Schelling's, Kant's and others', though obviously indebted to them. Other critics withhold from Coleridge any claim to original philosophic power. Coleridge himself said, 'In the Preface of my Metaphys. Works I should say – Once & all read Tetens, Kant, Fichte, &c – & there you will trace or if you are on the hunt, track me' (*CN* ii, 2375). But this, of course, requires great time and erudition, something not all of Coleridge's accusers (or defenders) have been willing to exert and master. We should recall that Coleridge is, with Carlyle, a major intellectual figure introducing German thought to the English-speaking world. *Biographia Literaria* is a key part of that infusion. Yet, of all Coleridge's published work, as opposed to his lectures and notebooks, which he did not publish, the *Biographia* is, for good reason, the focus of his reputation as a plagiarist. No exculpation – fast dictation, intermingling and fusing of passages, the bizarre fact that in *Biographia Literaria* Coleridge either mentions by name or describes *every* book from which he takes significant material, or the surprising fact that Schelling, unperturbed at the situation, later had only kind words and praise for Coleridge (as did Ludwig Tieck) – can alter the fact that Coleridge's standard of citation falls far below not only that of modern scholarship but that of his own day as well.

Art for Coleridge is or should be a mediator between humankind and nature; as our faculties in experiencing reality should be ordered and work together according to their relative worth and dignity, so in producing and in criticising art, the same should hold true. Poetry is that verbal art capable of commanding the greatest resourcefulness of language – the greatest number of constituent parts (rhythm, meter, word choice, musicality, structure, figuration, invention) – and thus is capable of fulfilling the highest degree of integration among all our faculties by engaging us with a work so structured as to excite the pleasure of such complete activity. There is something Aristotelian about this sense of fused, constituent parts producing pleasure or eudaimonia. Beyond stressing what is conventionally regarded as 'Romantic' feeling and organic form, Coleridge's criticism partakes of Aristotelian and Platonic elements. In the *Biographia* Coleridge succeeds greatly as a 'Romantic' critic because, as do Hazlitt and Shelley, he modifies, subsumes and transforms classical criticism and thought. Here it is not much help to regard the images of a mirror (simply reflecting reality) and a lamp (illuminating and idealising it) as classical and Romantic criticism in *opposition*. *Biographia Literaria* is a crystal chandelier.

At the outset of Volume II, in chapter 14, Coleridge defines a poem and the activity of the poet in a manner consonant with his philosophical investigations in the first volume: 'A poem is that species of composition, which is opposed to works of science, by proposing for its *immediate* object pleasure, not truth; and from all other species (having *this* object in common with it) it is discriminated by proposing to itself such delight from the *whole*, as is compatible with a distinct gratification from each component *part*.' 'The poet, described in *ideal* perfection, brings the whole soul of man into activity, with the subordination of its faculties to each other, according to their relative worth and dignity.' The poet diffuses a 'spirit of unity' by the power of imagination and balances or reconciles 'opposite or discordant qualities': these include sameness and difference, the general and the concrete, the familiar and the new. This spirit 'subordinates our admiration of the poet to our sympathy with the poetry' (II, 13; 15–17).

The distinction between poetry and science (not simply modern experimental science, but all systematic knowledge) echoes Wordsworth's discussion of the Man of Science and the Poet in the 1800 Preface. This theme in criticism was as old as Philip Sidney's 'An Apology for Poetry' or 'The Defence of Poetry' (written in 1579, but not published until 1595). More recent commentators had included Alexander Gerard. From different points of view, Thomas Love Peacock and Shelley would carry the discussion further. Science and Art pervade Romantic criticism, in part because of the rise of science and applied technologies and their challenge to the importance of poetry in society and personal life. John Stuart Mill, writing in the 1850s, captures these high stakes in his remark that the two great spirits of his age are Coleridge and Bentham – the first believes in science and poetry, the second in science alone. However harshly received by some, *Biographia Literaria* helped make the intellectual climate of the English-speaking world less narrowly practical and positivist. Its impact in America – particularly on the poet and transcendentalist philosopher, Ralph Waldo Emerson (1803–82), but on many others as well – can hardly be overstated. For decades, whole educational plans were constructed around Coleridge's writing, and *Biographia Literaria* played a significant part. The American transcendentalist movement could hardly be called what it is were it not for Coleridge.

Ironically built into Coleridge's transition from philosophical principles to practical criticism is the fact that one need not understand his philosophical train of thought as transforming itself into definitions of a poem, poetry, the poet and the language of poetry. It is enough to accept those definitions as postulates of practical criticism. Not that their philosophical origin is irrelevant, but in the production and criticism of art and poetry, it is not *necessary* to be aware self-consciously of their origin: 'A great poet must be implicitè if not explicitè, a great metaphysician' (*CL* II, 810). Coleridge could have written, 'A great critic need not be a great metaphysician, but implicitly must work from principles established by one who is.' This explains why chapters 14 and 15 and the practical criticism of Wordsworth *can* stand alone. But, to formulate any theoretical definitions and postulates of criticism, one must first trek through the philosophical and psychological territory. To deny this would be to deny the route Coleridge takes, even while recognising him as one of the best practical critics of the last three centuries. At the beginning of the book, in a passage written late in its composition, Coleridge prepares readers for his volume by speaking of 'the application of the rules, deduced from philosophical principles, to poetry and criticism' (I, 5).

Although Wordsworth claims 'I never cared a straw about the theory' (*Wordsworth Prose* I, 167), and protests in the 1800 Preface that he is not being systematic, he does present what can be legitimately regarded as theoretical views. At least Coleridge thought so. He refers to Wordsworth's 'theoretical opinions respecting Poetry' and to 'Wordsworth's Poems & Theory' (*CL* II, 830; IV, 579). Coleridge's larger point is that issues of criticism are inextricably theoretical and practical. They may be separated for the purposes of analysis, but each operates as informed by the other. From Coleridge's principles and definitions flows his sustained critique of: Wordsworth's theory and practice; the language of verse considered as a larger question of all language ('poetic diction', but something more complex than mere word choice); the difference between poetry and prose; meter; and Wordsworth's consistency of style.

Coleridge believes Wordsworth's 1800 Preface emphasised too much the language of the 'rustic' (if Wordsworth had never used that word the whole dialogue might have a vastly different inflection). Despite qualifying his statement of preferring the 'language really used by men' by invoking a 'selection' of it to be 'purified', Wordsworth implied too much that the language of poetry was copying rather than creatively imitating the language of common experience and elemental passion. At least so Coleridge thinks. Reacting against strictures of neoclassical poetic diction, where individual words and phrases were ruled inappropriate for poetry, Wordsworth considers 'language' chiefly as individual words or vocabulary rather than as the larger total form of language, which for Coleridge comprises not only words and combinations of words but new uses of them, their rhythms, appropriateness together, their specific order, grammar – in short, a totality of impact achieved by the special integration of all constituent parts of language in each composition. In diction *per se* Coleridge claims that the rustic's language 'purified from all provincialism and grossness, and ... made consistent with the rules of grammar ... will not differ from the language of any other man of common-sense'. Coleridge asks: why not seek the language of those whose notions are not, like the rustics', 'fewer and more indiscriminate', but more plentiful and distinguished? 'The best part of language', he claims, 'is derived from reflection on the acts of the mind itself. It is formed by a voluntary appropriation of fixed symbols to internal acts, to processes and results of imagination, the greater part of which have no place in the consciousness of uneducated man' (II, 52, 54). Coleridge several times produces striking images of the mind: e.g., the water-skimmer floating and pushing off, both passive and active; the caterpillar metamorphosing to the air-sylph (philosophic soul); the horned fly intuiting room to be left for antennae yet to grow in its 'involucrum', or outer covering (chapters 7, 12).

In chapter 18, Coleridge pursues Wordsworth's claim that there neither is nor can be any essential difference between the language of prose and that of metrical composition. This Coleridge denies by stressing, again, that 'language' implies more than 'the mere adoption of such words' as rustics – or anyone else – 'would use, or at least understand'. Metrical composition implies an 'order', too, one that in significant poetry is directed by 'that prospectiveness of mind, that *surview*, which enables a man to foresee the whole of what he is to convey' (II, 58). As early as 1802, Coleridge held that poetry requires 'some new combination of Language, & *commands* the omission of many others allowable in other composition' (*CL* II, 812). Only in the sense that the individual words found in prose, one by one, may also be found in metrical composition (as the same quarry might provide stones for both Westminster Abbey and St Paul's, two buildings entirely different in style) can Wordsworth affirm that the language is the same in each. Fifteen years after Wordsworth's Preface, during which time neoclassical diction had been waning, Coleridge now relegates precisely what had so bothered Wordsworth to minor status: 'For whether there ought to exist a class of words in the English, in any degree resembling the poetic dialect of the Greek and Italian, is a question of very subordinate importance' (II, 62). Perhaps unfairly, Coleridge shifts the ground of Wordsworth's original argument, but in doing so he opens up a larger, more varied field of language and poetry in general. His trenchant discussion on meter argues that meter can achieve a heightened emotional effect and bring added pleasure to verbal compositions: tempering and channelling passion, meter can intensify it.

Coleridge's critique of Wordsworth's poetry is full and generally, though not universally, judged to be fair. (Wordsworth later changed a number of lines to which Coleridge had objected in *Biographia Literaria*.) It is rare for a critic to see a living, still relatively young contemporary poet as having the stature of a Milton or a Chaucer; and still more rare for later critical opinion to confirm this judgement. At the same time, Coleridge's treatment of Wordsworth is not bardolatry. Expressed in a consideration of virtues and defects, it follows a pattern of critical judgement and reviewing established in English as early as Jonson and Dryden, and practised by reviewers through the eighteenth century. Coleridge knew intimately Johnson's *Preface to Shakespeare* and *Life of Milton*. In *Biographia Literaria*, as in other places, Coleridge follows the outline of Johnson's method but lists the defects first, most of which he says are 'occasional': excessive 'matter-of-factness' in some passages; at times an incongruity between feeling expressed and the nature of the subject; choice of characters; and 'an undue predilection for the *dramatic* form in certain poems' (II, 135). Coleridge is convinced that Wordsworth, to use Wordsworth's own terms from the 1815 Preface, has a 'meditative' rather than a 'dramatic' gift. (Wordsworth thought Milton and Spenser 'meditative' and Shakespeare 'dramatic': *Wordsworth Prose* III, 34–5.) One may quarrel over this assertion and champion Wordsworth's dramatic efforts and characters, but Coleridge believes that Wordsworth is generally at his best when meditating or speaking directly. Coleridge's objection to choice of characters is not nearly as harsh as some of Wordsworth's other critics, and held for different reasons, but some have seen in it a veiled class condescension. Coleridge argues that it is the improbability of what particular characters say and how they say it – for example, the pedlar in *The Excursion* – that causes dissonance.

The virtues of Wordsworth's verse, which Coleridge says for the most part correspond to the defects (and thus in part excuse those defects) are: purity of language; perfect appropriateness of language to meaning; an earned weight and sanity of thought and sentiment combined; strength of particular lines and verse paragraphs; 'the perfect truth of nature in his images and descriptions'; 'meditative pathos' and sympathy; and 'IMAGINATION in the highest and strictest sense of the word' (II, 148, 150, 151).

Coleridge stresses the organic integration of all resources of language in poetry, something that with regard to elements of style reverberates with his definition of a poem calling the whole soul into activity, with the subordination of its faculties to each other, 'according to their relative worth and dignity' (II, 16), and reconciling opposites through a dynamic process. This marriage of the particulars of phrasing and form with the philosophical definition of a poem as a whole as it operates on us as fully responsive and experiencing creatures may be a hallmark of what has been called organic unity or Romantic organicism. But we should realise, again, that the definitions and premises Coleridge invokes are similar to Aristotle's. They stem from doctrines of harmony and form grasped imaginatively and descriptively rather than taken mechanically as prescribing certain rules. For example, chapter 16 is a 'Wish expressed for the union of the characteristic merits of both' the 'Poets of the present age and those of the 15th and 16th centuries'. Coleridge tries to avoid the excesses of either: in classicism or neoclassicism, too great a veneration for convention, stasis, strict genre, verisimilitude and poetic diction; in Romanticism, too little attention to imitation and metrical experimentation, too much attention to the personality of the poet, and a search for mere novelty of expression rather than a more grounded originality (such as Wordsworth's), which itself will last to become a classic. Coleridge nowhere states what is often attributed to him: that every poem or work of art should attain an organic unity which is absolute, or even that all good works of art must possess that quality. It helps to take his remarks in the spirit he gives them: he defines a poet 'in *ideal* perfection'; he speaks of 'delight from the *whole*, as is compatible with a distinct gratification from each component *part*'; that 'the parts . . . mutually support and explain each other' (II, 13). But to hold up an insistence on perfection, on complete, total 'unity' as a sort of litmus test (or to assume Coleridge advocates this) distorts his theory and becomes itself an abstract, imposed rule of the kind he suspected.

Appearing in July 1817, the same month as *Sibylline Leaves*, *Biographia Literaria* received rough treatment. John Wilson ('Christopher North' of *Blackwood's Magazine*), who with John Lockhart savagely reviewed Keats's *Endymion*, blistered the book in prejudiced fashion. William Hazlitt himself, with great gusto, poked fun, as did Byron and others, at Coleridge's penchant for metaphysics. Not one perceptively appreciative review appeared. Coleridge's fear of a despotic, unintellectual readership, and his anxiety over the reception of this, his own first published book in prose, seemed justified. Later, perhaps feeling guilty over his use of German writers, and possibly, too, that the philosophical chapters were inadequate, he said that he would wish to preserve only 'the second volume of my "Literary life"', 'certain parts of *The Friend*', 'and some half-dozen of my poems' (*CL* IV, 925). Yet, in many respects, the whole of *Biographia Literaria* opened gates in Coleridge's psyche. Shortly after he began actively to write and dictate it, a series of re-markable publications in prose and verse flowed from him until his death in 1834. If, as with many great works in philosophy, criticism, religion and au-tobiography, *Biographia Literaria* remains a source of unending discussion and even disagreement, this is because it generates endless fascination and insight. It brings the whole soul into activity.

5

JOSIE DIXON

The Notebooks

every generous mind . . . feels its *Halfness* – it cannot *think* without a symbol – neither can it live without something that is to be at once its Symbol and its *Other half* . . . – Hence I deduce the habit, I have most unconsciously formed, of *writing* my inmost thoughts – I have not a soul on earth to whom I can reveal them – . . . and therefore to you, my passive, yet sole < true & > kind, friends I reveal them. *Burn you I certainly shall, when I feel myself dying*; but in the Faith, that as the Contents of my mortal frame will rise again, so that your contents will rise with me, as a Phoenix from its pyre of Spice & Perfume.

(CN III, 3325)

One of the great frustrations for the student of Coleridge arises from the fleeting quality of his literary achievement, its inconsistency, patchiness and fragmentation. The voice which animates the finest of the 'Conversation' poems or the power which makes the supernatural poems so compelling are all too easily lost in the rest of his poetic output; some of his finest theoretical writing threatens to dissolve under scrutiny into a tissue of plagiarism; and much of the remaining political, religious and philosophical prose seems to waver between the doctrinaire and the arcane. As one of his most perceptive critics has put it, 'he is eccentric, even peripheral, his texts a circle whose centre is nowhere and whose circumference is everywhere'.[1] In a curious way, the Notebooks offer one answer to these frustrations, giving free play to the very qualities that are elsewhere most problematic: a naturally fragmentary form, infinite freedom to digress, a licence to borrow from other sources, and an escape from the portentousness of his public figure into the realm of the private and the occasional. Here the great talker, lecturer and theorist writes without an audience (and the bombast into which it often tempted him). He creates in this form a private space, a site of secrecy and discovery, which offers a refuge from the anxieties and failures of the public sphere. In a fascinating generic hybrid of journal, travelogue, sketchbook and commonplace book, the Notebooks show us glimpses of a more humane Coleridge, and of his work in progress, in confessional, tentative or experimental mode.

Coleridge first began keeping a notebook on a walking tour with a fellow student, Joseph Hucks, in 1794, from Gloucester through Wales to Anglesey and down the coast to Bristol. The first to have survived dates from their arrival in Bristol, and is one of sixty to have been preserved, covering the next four decades to 1834. They are mostly small pocket books (though the largest is folio size), often with leather covers and metal clasps, some more simply bound in cardboard or marbled paper. Most had pockets in the front or back for pencils or loose pages; some myrtle twigs collected on a walk have survived inside one, and folded newspaper cuttings from his German travels inside another. Some may have been home-made, to judge by the uneven stitching and collections of loose pages tied in with string and tape. Worn from carrying and often rain-streaked, the weathered condition of many of the Notebooks testifies that they were generally intended for use while travelling, though one larger volume was clearly a desk-book used for entries connected with literary work in progress.

Their physical condition tells us much about the circumstances in which the notes were written. The Notebooks' editor Kathleen Coburn comments of one of the early books, 'much of the writing is bad, done in illness, under the influence of opium or spirits, or, in the casual postures of the stagecoach or the hillside, not conducive to a clear, firm hand'.[2] Pen and pencil are punctuated by chalk scribbles contributed by Coleridge's infant son Hartley; Coleridge's biographer Richard Holmes speculates that one strangely coloured ink may be his gout medicine or even laudanum, the medicinal opiate to which he became addicted.[3] These scruffy manuscripts, not originally intended for publication, bring us in some ways closer than any of his other writings to the raw immediacy of Coleridge's insights and the conditions under which he wrote.

The Notebooks are available to modern readers in the scholarly edition prepared by Kathleen Coburn, of which the first volume was published in 1957; at the time of writing, the fifth and final volume (due in 2002) has yet to appear. These invaluable volumes provide a wealth of supplementary information about the Notebooks: physical descriptions; a table of entries with dates; indexes of people, titles and placenames; and for each volume of the Notebook texts, a corresponding volume of explanatory notes. These are not merely informative in a contextual manner, but often a vital aid to understanding the Notebook entries themselves, since Coleridge often used cryptic abbreviations, and frequently wrote entries in German, Latin or Greek, or in a private cipher, frequently retreating into these alternative private languages and codes at particularly significant, confessional moments. Coburn's scholarship is a vital resource that underlies all modern work on the Notebooks, but the extent of the edition's apparatus need not detract from the sheer pleasure and illumination of reading the entries for themselves.

How, then, do we read these private, occasional writings-without-a-genre, intended at first for no eyes but Coleridge's own? Since they represent at one level a kind of emotional and intellectual journal – Coleridge referred to his Notebooks as 'my only Confidants' (III, 3342) – one answer might be to read them autobiographically. Richard Holmes offers the caution that 'Coleridge dramatised himself in his most solitary moments (as we all, on reflection, do), and his Notebooks can never be accepted as the last word on anything (least of all as the last word from Coleridge).'[4] Personified as listeners, the Notebooks are in this sense a textual surrogate for the other, less satisfactory, audiences to whom he offered up his self-projections. Yet as one of the most attentive readers of the Notebooks, Holmes inevitably succumbs to the temptation to grant them a 'greater confessional authority' than his imaginative writings,[5] as he anatomises Coleridge's spiritual crises, along with the reading lists, shopping lists and medicinal recipes which likewise fill their pages.

Few critics have tried to read the Notebooks as literary texts in themselves, but they were frequently used by Coleridge as a testing ground for poetic ideas, and the most striking entries have a distinctive shape and rhythm of their own. There is no typical structure to the Notebook entries; eluding any formal genre, they offer free play to a whole range of styles and modes of writing, from jottings, lists and memoranda to aphorisms, extended landscape descriptions and complex philosophical arguments. There is however a recognisable idiom, grammar and punctuation which is characteristic of many of the notes; this more than anything evokes the urgency of the moment in which they were recorded and what he called 'the *streamy* Nature of Association' (I, 1770). Some of the most vivid are highly dramatic narrative renditions of dreams, such as this note from December 1803; it is a long entry of which I shall quote only the closing lines, as Coleridge emerges from a nightmare populated by surreal figures and paranoid fantasies: 'my eyes being half-opened, & still affected by Sleep / in an half upright posture struggling, as I thought, against involuntary sinking back into Sleep, & consequent suffocation / twas then I screamed, by will / & immediately after really awoke' (I, 1726). Jennifer Ford has noted how Coleridge's liberal use of the slash or solidus in this passage, breaking up the stream of consciousness into short gasps, 'conveys haste in composition, a breathlessness as well as a reluctance to elaborate...The solidus is not merely used to separate ideas, but to prevent some of them from further elucidation. As a physical mark upon the page, it blocks further potentially stressful self-exploration.'[6] One might add to this notion of interruption or suspension that it gestures energetically towards the formal lineation of poetry, giving breath to the struggling voice that emerges at the end of the dream. It has been argued (ingeniously) that the figurative power invested in Coleridge's written language of Germanic capitals, italics, slashes and dashes is literally typographical, pertaining to print and belonging to 'the secret ministry of the compositor',[7] but it is all here in the manuscript form of the Notebooks, equally – indeed perhaps especially – characteristic of his private writing.

The semantic energy of the writing, instilled in its mimetically disordered syntax, is distinctively literary, yet it offers only the formalism of formlessness, enacting the generic impossibility of channelling that associative stream into any controlled system of literary expression. Where Coleridge's published prose works fight with this tendency by keeping digression partially at bay in appendices and footnotes, the Notebooks give full sanction to the wayward and the incidental. At times, this sense of syntactic and discursive licence has a playful, even celebratory quality:

> Now how to get back, having thus belabyrinthed myself in these most parenthetical parentheses? Cut thro' at once, & now say in half a dozen a Lines what a half a dozen Lines would have enabled me to say at the very beginning / but my Thoughts, my Pocket-book Thoughts at least, moved like a pregnant Polypus in sprouting Time, clung all over with young Polypi each of which is to be a thing of itself – and every motion out springs a new Twig of Jelly-Life.
>
> (II, 2431)

The life-form characterised by these Notebook digressions is represented in this entry of February 1805 as organically self-reproducing in a way that is aptly primordial, an evolutionary precursor to higher literary forms.

It is perhaps inevitable that the Notebooks have most frequently been raided for what individual entries might offer by way of a gloss on Coleridge's theoretical writings in their more developed form. After all, in the face of such fragmentary discursive disorder, there seems less sense of violation in lifting scattered passages out of context for the light they may shed elsewhere. Certainly they reveal much about the formation of his ideas in conjunction with his reading. For example, the 1811 entries form a kind of philosophical dialogue with Jean-Paul Richter (1763–1825), the German novelist, essayist and reviewer whose analysis of associationism and imagination deeply influenced him. Coleridge is here translating and recasting for himself passages from the German original. This tells us a great deal about his working methods, and especially about the process of assimilation which has led to the charge of plagiarism. But what is most valuable about the Notebooks is rather their combination of such ideas with lived experience, and what that conjunction reveals about the fragile Coleridgean dynamics of perception, intuition and the will to theorise. This tension between outward and inward stimuli is foregrounded in one of Coleridge's few public references to the Notebooks, in the Prospectus to the *Friend*, where he alludes to the habit 'of daily noting down, in my Memorandum or Common-place Books, both Incidents and Observations; whatever had occurred to me from without, and all the Flux and Reflux of my Mind within itself'.[8] Observation and experimental record are counterpointed by the inwardly reflexive workings of the imagination, in a balance which becomes progressively harder to sustain.

The early Notebooks show Coleridge as a fine naturalist in the empirical tradition of Gilbert White (a copy of whose *Natural History and Antiquities of Selborne* has survived with Coleridge's marginalia). There is an exquisite precision and delicacy in some of his finely detailed observations, and the vividness of the moment is most urgently evoked by the sheer struggle to articulate in passages where language, without the poet's more deliberate craft, seems insufficient to catch an evanescent effect:

> the winding of a majestic River…a large Slice of calm silver – above this a bright ruffledness, or atomic sportiveness – motes in the sun? – Vortices of flies? – how shall I express the Banks waters all fused Silver, that House too its slates rainwet silver in the sun, & its shadows running down in the water like a column   (1, 549)

This entry of November 1799 is typical of many, describing in minutest terms the changing aspects of a landscape in different lights, over and over again, almost as if in the hope of imparting some fixity. Coleridge was fascinated by form, but above all the shapes which were momentarily created by movement. Later the same month he observed a flock of birds in these terms:

> Starlings in vast flights drove along like smoke, mist, or any thing misty [without] volition – now a circular area inclined [in an] arc – now a globe – [now from a complete orb into an] ellipse & oblong – [now] a balloon with the [car suspend]ed, now a concaved [sem]icircle & [still] it expands & condenses, some [moments] glimmering & shivering, dim & shadowy, now thickening, deepening, blackening!   (1, 582)[9]

This painterly tendency towards a distillation of fleeting natural phenomena into abstract, geometrical forms can be observed many times in the Notebooks, and it frequently overflows into sketchy drawings of outline shapes where words will no longer suffice. 'O Christ, it maddens me that I am not a painter…!' he exclaims in the middle of his descriptions of the landscape on a tour of Scotland in 1803 (1, 1495), and the following month, in the same vein, 'Without Drawing I feel myself but half invested with Language' (1, 1554). There is indeed a striking affinity between Coleridge's feel for transient light effects in passages such as these, and the restless cloud studies – unframed oil sketches witnessing a passionate identification with the speed of random fluctuations of light and colour – of his contemporary, the painter John Constable. Constable, like Coleridge, recorded his reaction against the eighteenth-century picturesque theorists who had sought to arrest and control the unruliness of nature in an aesthetic of fixed prospects and formal composition.[10]

Yet the Notebooks frequently show how fine the balance was for Coleridge between fidelity of observation and the search for something more enduring in – or beyond – evanescent natural phenomena. 'The stedfast rainbow in the fast-moving, hurrying hail-mist' is seized as an image 'of fantastic Permanence amidst the rapid Change of Tempest' in an entry of autumn 1802 (I, 1246), anticipating the notion articulated in *Biographia Literaria* of 'a substratum of permanence, of identity, and therefore of reality, to the shadowy flux of Time . . . Eternity revealing itself in the phaenomena of Time'.[11] The image suggests an effort to find some compromise between the vulnerable transience of natural phenomena and the inviolacy of abstractions, which had led him to reflect in an entry of November 1799, 'How perishable Things, how imperishable Ideas' (I, 576). There is a poignancy in the intuition underlying that exclamation that the impermanence may be in the vision as much as its object: Kathleen Coburn succinctly characterised the drive of many Notebook entries as 'attempts to hold onto (by observing and noting) the real world in the very moments of being drugged against it' (I, 1767n.). It is the same, fragile balance as that which animates the 'Conversation' poems, where an acute awareness of the sensuous actuality of things-in-themselves is held in creative tension with their symbolic value and a tendency to look through them, for an intuition of divinity or the 'one Life' of his early pantheist beliefs.

It is in the fragmentation of the Notebooks above all that Coleridge's desperate desire for a kind of imaginative wholeness and philosophical unity is most apparent and least capable of realisation. There is in particular a pressure in entries such as these to trace a unity, '*one* absolutely undistinguishable Form' through diverse phenomena, and to resolve the paradox of such '*oneness*, there being infinite Perceptions . . . not an intense Union but an Absolute Unity' (I, 555, 556). The image which gives rise to the first of these phrases in 1799 is, curiously, a transformation of the landscape and its reflection in Lake Ullswater into an erotic fantasy of the female body, perforated by the road 'exactly as the weiblich τετραγραμματον is painted in anatomical Books!' (Coyly, the 'feminine four-letter word' is rendered in German and Greek, and his knowledge attributed to strictly academic sources, even in a private Notebook.) Coleridge was fascinated by the effects of landscape reflected in water and frequently turned to this image in his Notebooks when straining for a cohesive vision and a unifying intuition to govern his perception. An entry of 1803 shares some of the same erotic imagery:

> O Thirlmere! – let me somehow or other celebrate the world in thy mirror. – Conceive all possible varieties of Form, Fields, & Trees, and naked or ferny Crags – ravines, behaired with Birches – Cottages, smoking chimneys, dazzling *wet places* of small rock-precipices – dazzling castle windows in the reflection – all these, within a divine outline in a mirror of 3 miles distinct vision!
>
> (1, 1607)

There is an interesting, unexpected correspondence here with the contemporary discourse of the picturesque. Eighteenth- and early nineteenth-century debates about the picturesque frequently cast nature as a woman in varying states of undress,[12] and looking at a landscape in a mirror is exactly what picturesque view-hunters of the later eighteenth century had done, with the aid of the Claude glass – a concave mirror devised as a painter's tool to reflect the view framed in miniature. The picturesque theorist William Gilpin wrote an account of using one in a travelling coach, which seems neatly paradigmatic of his frustrated efforts to reduce the dynamic unruliness of natural landscape into a fixed design: 'Forms and colours in brightest array, fleet before us; and if the transient glance of a good composition happen to unite with them, we should give any price to fix and appropriate the scene.'[13] Even as Coleridge's fidelity to the changing minute detail of natural phenomena sets him apart from the picturesque theorists, he succumbs to their visual conventions, not so much out of any real aesthetic affinity as for their ability to deliver the higher order of meaning he craves.

This tension is nicely dramatised in an entry written during the voyage to Malta in April 1804, where intense physical descriptions of the ship's sails turn into a meditation on their pure geometrical forms and finally give way to a passage of abstract reflection, showing Coleridge at his most strenuously analytical in theorising the act of perception:

> nothing more administers to the Picturesque than this phantom of complete visual wholeness in an object, which visually does not form a whole, by the influence ab intra of the sense of its perfect Intellectual Beauty or Wholeness. – To all these must be added the Lights & Shades, sometimes *sunshiny*, sometimes *snowy*: sometimes shade-coloured, sometimes dingy – whatever effect distance, air tints, reflected Light, and the feeling connected with *the* Object (for all Passion unifies as it were by natural Fusion) have in bringing out, and in melting down, differences & contrast, accordingly as the mind finds it necessary to the completion of the idea of Beauty, to prevent sameness or discrepancy.
>
> (II, 2012)

Coleridge's fine perceptual identification with the phenomena he describes threatens to give way to a search for abstractions as the symbolic imagination takes over. The paradox at the heart of even these private writings is that the very effort to capture the immediacy of lived experience is always already mediated, by the process of reflection, by the act of writing, and by the conventions he inherited.

Elsewhere in the Notebooks Coleridge's fascination with mirrors takes on a deeper significance as an emblem of the self-reflexive nature of the mind's conscious pursuit of abstractions, at one remove from the external world. Where the mind is 'every where / Echo or mirror seeking of itself' as in 'Frost at Midnight', the object of perception is distanced by its reflected surrogate in the imagination; in the final section of the poem, the child's silent presence recalls him to the seasonal vividness of the external world, but in the Notebooks, that recuperative return seems much less certain. In an entry of March 1801 he dramatises the problem for his son Hartley by reflecting a view of the mountains, which had been absorbing the child's attention, in a mirror: 'I shewed him the whole magnificent Prospect in a Looking Glass, and held it up, so that the whole was like a Canopy or Ceiling over his head, & he struggled to express himself concerning the Difference between the Thing & the Image almost with convulsive Effort.' (I, 923). Three years later in 1804, without the aid of a mirror, he returns to the idea in more explicitly philosophical terms (echoing Hartley's struggle to articulate):

> Hard to express that sense of the analogy or likeness of a Thing which enables a Symbol to represent it, so that we think of the Thing itself – & yet knowing that the Thing is not present to us ... that Proteus Essence that could assume the very form, but yet known & felt not to be the Thing by that difference of the Substance which made every atom of the Form another thing / – that likeness not identity – an exact web, every line of direction miraculously the same, but the one worsted, the other silk. (II, 2274)

The passage reads as a ruefully sceptical acknowledgement of the fine but crucial distinction which betrays the final surrogacy of symbolic apprehension, replacing direct experience with the promise of something that turns out hauntingly to be only a simulacrum.

There is an eerie instance of this on the voyage to Malta, where Coleridge describes an optical illusion seen from the ship, giving almost physical form to his homesickness for the Lake District:

> Was it the Placefell Bank of Ulswater? ... so completely did the Sea between our Ship & it become a Lake, and that black substantial Squall Cloud the Mountain that formed & rose up from its banks, that it would be a positively

[*sic*] falsehood to say, it was like. It was utterly indistinguishable... – exactly both in outline & in general surface the same as to distinctness.   (II, 2013)

He cannot circumvent the paradox that the scene is 'indistinguishable' in its 'distinctness' – a semantic betrayal of his wistful desire for something more than 'that likeness not identity'. As so often, the knowledge of delusion is built subtly into Coleridge's account, an inescapable part of his fascination with perceptual states, especially those self-induced moments of hallucinatory or otherwise surreal vision. At times these are analysed with almost scientific, experimental precision; here, for instance, is part of an entry in which he records 'on Wednesday, 24? March, 1808, I had a fact of Vision':

I again voluntarily threw myself into introversive Reflections, & again produced the same Enlargement of Shapes & Distances and the same increase of vividness – but all seemed to be seen thro' a very thin glaceous mist – thro' an interposed Mass of Jelly of the most exquisite subtlety & transparency. But my reason for noting this is – the fact, in my second & voluntary production of this Vision I retained it as long as I like ... without destroying the Delusion / – then started my eyes & something... of the Brain behind the eyes started or jirked them forward, and all was again as in common. / The power of acting on a *delusion*, according to the Delusion, without dissolving it /   (III, 3280)

Characteristically, Coleridge follows this physiological account with a philosophical train of thought, which concludes telegraphically with a reference to 'Prophets, & c–', showing him acutely aware of the correspondence between physical and imaginative illusion.

The tendency to project a symbolic and self-reflexive imaginative design on the objects of perception becomes a recurring source of anxiety in the Notebooks. In a striking entry, which begins, as many of his most consciously significant notes do, by anchoring the thought firmly in time, Coleridge reflects explicitly on this instinct as a kind of epistemological habit:

Saturday Night, April 14, 1805 – In looking at objects of Nature while I am thinking, as at yonder moon dim-glimmering thro' the dewy window-pane, I seem rather to be seeking, as it were *asking*, a symbolical language for something within me that already and forever exists, than observing any thing new. Even when that latter is the case, yet still I have always an obscure feeling as if that new phaenomenon were the dim Awaking of a forgotten or hidden Truth of my inner Nature   (II, 2546)

The fear of losing his capacity for 'observing any thing new' in this preoccupation with the inner self recognises a risk that was always inherent in maintaining 'That outward forms, the loftiest, still receive / Their finer influence from the Life within; – / Fair cyphers else'.[14] Each successive bout of dejection suffered in the early 1800s seems to turn on some version of this imaginative dilemma, when the balance of the eye and the mind is destabilised. That crisis finds its expression in a disjunction of discursive modes, whereby the solipsistic tendency for imaginative projection is fundamentally in tension both with the early Notebooks' more empirical discourse of discovery and with the religious discourse of revelation to which he increasingly gravitates.

At best, the reflexive awareness of an impoverished vision is itself productive of some of the most moving and dramatic entries in the Notebooks, like this one of November 1803:

> Wednesday Morning, 20 minutes past 2° clock. November 2nd. 1803. The Voice of the Greta, and the Cock-crowing: the Voice seems to grow, like a Flower on or about the water beyond the Bridge, while the Cock crowing is nowhere particular, it is at any place I imagine & do not distinctly see. A most remarkable Sky! The Moon, now waned to a perfect Ostrich's Eggs [*sic*], hangs over our House almost – only so much beyond it, garden-ward, that I can see it, holding my Head out of the smaller Study window. The Sky is covered with whitish, & with dingy *Cloudage*, thin dingiest Scud close under the moon & one side of it moving, all else moveless: but there are two great Breaks of Blue Sky – the one stretching over our House, & away toward Castlerigg, & this is speckled & blotched with white Cloud...Now while I have been writing this & gazing between whiles (it is 40 M. past Two) the Break over the road is swallowed up, & the Stars gone, the Break over the House is narrowed into a rude Circle, & on the edge of its circumference one very bright Star – see! already the white mass thinning at its edge *fights* with its Brilliance – see! it has bedimmed it – & now it is gone – & the Moon is gone. The Cock-crowing too has ceased. The Greta sounds on, for ever. But I hear only the Ticking of my Watch, in the Pen-place of my Writing Desk, & the far lower note of the noise of the Fire – perpetual, yet seeming uncertain / it is the low voice of quiet change, of Destruction doing its work by little & little.   (I, 1635)

Coleridge's minutely realised observation of the changing night sky gives way to a more symbolic apprehension of imaginative loss. The fading radiance enacting its struggle with the encroaching cloud, and the subsidence into a dull and more mechanical perception, marked by the ticking watch (a reminder of time almost perceptibly working an inner change), all become painfully significant in the closing lines. It is as though the phenomena he observes have become figures for the loss of perceptual immediacy constituted in the symbol-making process itself: the mind's faculty for projection turns back upon itself in an enclosed cycle that serves only to remind the perceiver of what has been lost. Poignantly, Coleridge's powers of creativity here survive only to record their own frustration, in intimations of change and inner desolation.

The 'real-time' effect of such passages, written as the phenomena they describe are actually taking place, witnesses Coleridge's fidelity to the living moment even in the act of its transcendence. The fragmentary informality of the note form enables him to embrace real-time interruption (as, famously, he could not in his account of the writing of 'Kubla Khan'), giving some entries the curious effect of oscillating between discursive modes or dimensions in time. An entry such as IV, 4547 bridges material and intellectual worlds effortlessly, as a metaphysical discussion of algebraic abstraction with Mr J. Green is punctuated by Mrs Green arriving to present them with the first cherries of the season. Jerome Christensen's fine reading of I, 1770 hinges on the interruption of a difficult philosophical entry, straddling two days in December 1803, by a single interpolated sentence in which Coleridge reflects on the act of writing by candlelight, the 'Beautiful luminous Shadow' of his pencil 'going before it & illuminating the word, I am writing'.[15] In the midst of Coleridge's strained intellectual pyrotechnics, the momentary return to the material, personal act and observation is strangely moving, running counter to the tendency, increasing in the later Notebooks, to move out of the living moment, from the site of observation to the site of record, and from literal description to figurative abstraction. Where the 'Conversation' poems' restorative movement offers a circular path back to the living scene, guaranteed by the presence – and sometimes the interruption – of his silent companion, the Notebooks' more solitary and labyrinthine discourse holds fewer reassurances.

The (im)balance between his identification with the external life of things in themselves and the philosophical superstructure to which they are increasingly subordinated has a rhetorical dimension, as Coleridge was ruefully aware:

Now this is my case – & a grievous fault it is / my illustrations swallow up my thesis – I feel too intensely the omnipresence of all in each, platonically speaking – or psychologically my brain-fibres, or the spiritual Light which abides in the brain marrow as visible Light appears to do in sundry rotten mackerel & other *smashy* matters, is of too general affinity with all things / and tho' it perceives the *difference* of things, yet is eternally pursuing the likenesses, or rather that which is common / bring me two things that seem the very same, & then I am quick enough to shew the difference, even to hair-splitting – but to go on from circle to circle till I break against the shore of my Hearer's patience, or have my Concentricals dashed to nothing by a Snore – that is my ordinary mishap.   (II, 2372)

The self-reflexivity of this 'concentrical' labyrinthine discourse is linked not least to a social failure – eliciting incomprehension or boredom – a possibility kept wordlessly at bay by the silence of his interlocutors in the 'Conversation' poems. In the later Notebooks, as the abstraction of the 'thesis' increasingly overtakes the materiality of the 'illustrations', driven by the desire for more figurative meaning, fine descriptions tend to shade off into allegorical or moralising codas. A storm scene with a ruined castle illuminated by lightning flashes[16] ends with the reflection 'how hieroglyphic of human Life – of a man cast on shore, and raising himself up by both arms from his prostration' (III, 3258). The notion articulated in an entry of 1819, of 'that slavery to the Eye from which the Philosopher should take every means to emancipate his mind' (IV, 4518), was implicit in much earlier dialogues with Wordsworth, but emerges with increasing explicitness here, as descriptions of natural phenomena seem to surface chiefly as similes for abstract ideas. It is thus a philosophical proposition, rather than the object itself, which now excites his wonder: *'How luminous! As plain to be seen, as an Eel in an old Fish-pond, from which the water has been just let off, or the Sun glittering on the mud and sparkling on the Duck-weed!'* (IV, 4521). These descriptive flashes are now set in long philosophical and – increasingly – scientific disquisitions, punctuated with Latin and Greek, which take his remorseless appetite for speculation into new territory: geometry, chemistry, galvanism, animal magnetism, mesmerism and pathology.

Where these new and more literally experimental sources of stimulus and fascination coincide with the visionary mode of his earlier writing, the effect is at once comic and poignant, an irresistible source of imaginative bathos:

> that in birds of prey...the gastric juice is of the nature of an Alcali may be conjectured from the indistinguishable Likeness of the Mice which had fallen into a bason of caustic Alkali at the Royal Institution with the Nostoc or tremulous transparent Jelly vomited by Hawks, Kites and Owls...one Mass of which that fell swop on my Hat at the foot of Bowscale, behind Skiddaw – & which seen falling by the Light of a crescent moon, immediately after a shooting Star had been noticed, might naturally be referred to the latter.
>
> (IV, 4646)

This wonderfully playful subversion of the empirical by the revelatory and vice versa is as disarming to the reader as the insistent sense that Coleridge himself, even in his private note-taking, is conscious of the inadequacy of his every rhetorical move ('N.b. – I am not at all satisfied with the preceding, It does not solve the difficulty if the assumption were true': IV, 4604). In the absence of the recuperative manoeuvres which he found available in poetic forms, the Notebooks' tangled rhetorical involution is somehow remorselessly honest, displaying Coleridge's extraordinary – humane, yet ultimately self-defeating – talent for anticipating the weaknesses of his own 'belabyrinthed' position.

Such infinitely self-subverting possibilities are particularly characteristic of the Notebooks' range of discursive modes. Reading them successively, the effect is like that of a kaleidoscope offering brilliant flashes of meaning, each of which is always shifting, in search of a pattern that is new and yet somehow fundamentally the same. While the search is variously imaginative, erotic, religious, philosophical or scientific, each of these modes of apprehension promises in turn to deliver a version of the symbolic wholeness which Coleridge so craved. The notion returns us to the central preoccupations of the passage quoted as the epigraph to this chapter, where the Notebooks themselves become his stand-in friend and confidant, a surrogate for the social and spiritual fulfilment – that supplement to the 'halfness' of the self – sought in the lifetime companion he never quite found. In its vision of the Notebooks as a phoenix rising from the flames to which he had mentally consigned them, the passage captures something of their ambiguous textual status. Addressing one of these private manuscripts as 'sole confidant of a breaking Heart', Coleridge yet projects a sublimated vision of their afterlife (delivering a frisson to the modern reader of Coburn's edition), in an intimation of this public literary posterity for which they scarcely seem designed.

NOTES

1 Jerome Christensen, *Coleridge's Blessed Machine of Language* (Ithaca, NY: Cornell University Press, 1981), 16.
2 Kathleen Coburn, ed., *The Notebooks of Samuel Taylor Coleridge* (London: Routledge and Kegan Paul, 1957–), 1 (Notes), xxxii.
3 Richard Holmes, *Coleridge: Darker Reflections* (London: Harper Collins, 1998), 94. Holmes follows Coburn, *Notebooks*, ed. Coburn, ii, 3041n.
4 Richard Holmes, *Coleridge: Early Visions* (London: Hodder and Stoughton, 1989), 91n.
5 *Ibid.*, 308.
6 Jennifer Ford, *Coleridge on Dreaming: Romanticism, Dreams and the Medical Imagination* (Cambridge University Press, 1998), 73.
7 Christensen, *Blessed Machine*, 264.
8 *Friend*, ii, 16–17.
9 Square brackets indicate Coburn's conjectural readings where the original is faint or stained, supplied with the help of a later transcription of the passage in 1803 (1, 1589).
10 Constable condemned the tendency for 'running after pictures and seeking the truth at second hand' in a letter to John Dunthorne of 29 May 1802; in the second of his lectures at the Royal Institution in 1836 he derided Boucher's painting as a 'bewildered dream of the picturesque', relating that he 'never painted from the

life, for that nature put him out': C. R. Leslie, ed., *Memoirs of the Life of John Constable* (1843; revised 1845, ed. Jonathan Mayne; London: Phaidon Press, 1951), 15, 312.

11 *BL*, II, 234.

12 Nature was variously imagined in the 'starchd Apron, & Ruffles' of landscape gardening (as William Mason wrote to William Gilpin in 1782) or in what John Clare later termed in a letter to the painter Peter de Wint 'her every day dess-abille'. Gilpin writes almost priggishly of nature 'in her best attire in which it is our business to see her', a wanton female 'chastened by the rules of art'. Coleridge was clearly more of de Wint's persuasion! J. W. and Anne Tibble, eds., *The Letters of John Clare* (London: Routledge and Kegan Paul, 1970), 239; Gilpin is quoted in Carl Paul Barbier, *William Gilpin: His Drawings, Teaching and Theory of the Picturesque* (Oxford University Press, 1963), p. 141; William Gilpin, *Three Essays: On Picturesque Beauty; On Picturesque Travel; and On Sketching Landscape* (London: R. Blamire, 1792), 75, 52.

13 Quoted in Elizabeth Wheeler Manwaring, *Italian Landscape in Eighteenth-Century England* (New York: Oxford University Press, 1925), 186.

14 'Lines Written in the Album at Elbingerode in the Harz Forest', 1799.

15 Christensen, *Blessed Machine*, 268–9.

16 Coburn suggests it may be a description of the painting of Peele Castle by George Beaumont, which inspired Wordsworth's 'Elegiac Stanzas'.

6

J. C. C. MAYS

The later poetry

How might 'later poetry' be defined? Some of the expectations raised by this category were determined by W. B. Yeats in *New Poems* (1938), by T. S. Eliot in *Four Quartets* (1944) and by Ezra Pound after the *Pisan Cantos* (1949). Previous determining instances are Tennyson's 'Flower in the Crannied Wall' and 'Crossing the Bar' and Hopkins's 'terrible sonnets'. Later ones include William Carlos Williams's *Pictures from Brueghel* (1962) and George Oppen's *Primitive* (1978). In all these instances, we see the poet summarising a career in writing as it reaches a (possibly) final stage, and setting truth down plainly. Style is radically simple – simple because of the pressure to be testamentary, radical because the stripped-down formulation rests on a lifetime dedicated to art. Beethoven's late quartets are frequently cited as antecedents, Rembrandt's late paintings and Cezanne's cut-outs as analogues, Flaubert's *Bouvard et Pécuchet* and Beckett's *Stirrings Still* provide examples in prose fiction. Composition under such conditions does not prevaricate because it has nothing to gain and everything to lose:

> Who,
> swinging his axe
> to fell kings, guesses
> where we go?
> (Basil Bunting,
> *Briggflatts*, 1965)

Against such a background, Coleridge's later poems constitute an odd case. They are customarily taken to begin after the time he met Sara Hutchinson (November 1799) and settled in the north of England (early 1800). The titles begin with 'Love' (1799) and 'Dejection: An Ode' (1802) and continue with notebook poems written in Malta and, in particular, a number written in a resurgence of verse-writing activity during the 1820s. The first oddity is that, at the beginning of this process, Coleridge was less than thirty years old and less than half-way through his life. Also, while his writing career began at school and university, he had only thought of himself as a poet incidentally and for a short time before he shifted into a 'later' phase. Secondly, his poetry after 1800 is different from that of the later Tennyson, Eliot and others in that the relation it bears to what precedes it is more accurately described as dialogic than retrospective. It looks back in order to negotiate a way forward, not to cement a long-sought position. It is less a final winnowing of truth than a restatement so as to begin a different argument concerning previous themes.

As far as Coleridge wrote a distinctive later poetry on these terms, it can only be understood in relation to the poems he wrote at Stowey, when the Wordsworths lived at Alfoxden, but there is a third feature also: the dialectic of the earlier–later relationship rests on a selective base. Coleridge wrote different kinds of poems besides 'The Ancient Mariner' and 'Christabel' before 1800 and he continued to do so afterwards. For instance, his parodic Higgenbottom sonnets which so upset his friends Lamb and Southey represent a strain of satire which continued until the month in which he died:

> Mine eye perus'd
> With tearful vacancy the *dampy* grass
> Which wept and glitter'd in the *paly* ray
> ('Sonnets attempted in the Manner of
> Contemporary Writers', 1, 4–6)

His later poetry extends beyond 'The Solitary Date-tree' and 'The Pang More Sharp Than All' in several directions. He continued to write translations and *jeux d'esprit*, satirical poems and verse-dramas, album verses and adaptations, all of which are beside and beyond the conventional Romantic view of poetry. The concept of a break in Coleridge's poetry around 1800 ignores the kinds of writing to which he was continuously devoted through his career. As far as his later poetry constitutes another kind, it needs to be understood in relation to a surrounding context which did not develop antithetically.

Coleridge's later poetry is often misunderstood as a poetry of and about personal failure – failure to write a kind of poem he had written for a brief period earlier. But the subject it contains is a developing one and larger than simply personal expression. He did not write another 'Ancient Mariner' because the poem said everything that could be said at the time, and more. 'The Ancient Mariner' prompted him to begin 'Christabel', which he did not finish, but he wrote other poems which articulate the necessity of that incompleteness and thereby articulate his mature relation to the earlier kind of poetry. Meanwhile, he continued to write different kinds of poetry in a similar way to before. Coleridge's later poetry is not a falling-off, as Wordsworth's or Robert Frost's or Marianne Moore's later poems might be deemed to be. It does not characteristically parody his earlier style or reiterate earlier arguments in different words. Instead, it attempts a rapprochement with similar themes on separate grounds.

Coleridge's later poems include occasional and other kinds of verse which have too often been dismissed as unserious, for they show a degree of energy and wide-ranging interest which kept the core of his poetry alive. Coleridge's claim to be a great poet lies in the continued pursuit of the consequences of 'The Ancient Mariner', 'Christabel' and 'Kubla Khan' on several levels. If his verse after the Nether Stowey experiment had attempted retrospection merely, like later Eliot or Oppen, it would be less than wise and certainly less adventurous. It has been said that Coleridge ceased to write poems like 'The Ancient Mariner' because he was overtaken by German metaphysics, illness, opium and an unhappy love affair. He in fact stopped writing poems of such a kind in early summer 1798, after he completed the first part of 'Christabel' and the fragmentary 'Ballad of the Dark Ladiè'. During the following twelve months, at a time when Wordsworth wrote the majority of the poems he contributed to *Lyrical Ballads*, as well as 'Peter Bell', and then in Germany developed the method of 'The Pedlar' into the beginnings of *The Prelude*, Coleridge wrote only a handful of occasional poems besides the translations he accumulated for sale to newspapers. The Alfoxden–Stowey collaboration brought Wordsworth into his own and at the same time gave Coleridge pause. His ambitions in this sort of poetry were suspended in about May 1798 without anxiety, regret or comment. They did not revive until he wrote 'Love' in November–December 1799 and not in a sustained way until 1801–2.

Though 'Love' and poems thereafter are connected with Coleridge's feelings for Sara Hutchinson, it should be borne in mind that his relationship with her is as much an effect as a cause of his mental condition. Martin Greenberg states the matter justly when he describes how Coleridge's concentration of longing onto a person with whom he could not consummate his love was a way of condemning the natural man. It is anticipated, even at the moment of his betrothal, in the 'mild reproof' which his wife-to-be administers to the 'shapings of his unregenerate mind' ('The Eolian Harp', 49, 55). 'Sara Hutchinson was an "Ideal Object" to him rather than a real one, a "yearning Thought that liv[ed] but in the brain" rather than a "living Love" – so he describes her in "Constancy to an Ideal Object". She was the idea of love, not a woman whom he would or could love in marriage; addressing that "Ideal Object", that "yearning Thought", he writes, "She is not thou, and only thou art she" .'[1]

When Coleridge returned to revisit the themes of his Stowey poems after an interval of several years, he picked up with the impasse which they registered rather than a new situation which had developed in the interim.

'Love' was first published under the title, 'Introduction to the Tale of the Dark Ladiè', as if to underscore the point. Subsequent poems which describe his blocked feelings for Sara Hutchinson are as much concerned with what blocked his feelings in May 1798 as about her as a person in her own right. As Wordsworth wrote in the Preface to *Lyrical Ballads* (1800), 'the feeling therein developed gives importance to the action and situation and not the action and situation to the feeling'.[2] Coleridge's themes are moral and metaphysical no less than psychological.

A letter Coleridge wrote to the young Thomas Allsop in March 1820 (*CL* v, 22–3) describes the conditions of the later poetry. Coleridge quotes a passage from the October eclogue of 'The Shepheardes Calender' and explicates Spenser's turn from a sense of power stirring and capacity reviving, how this is interrupted by a reminder of loss, which produces 'a natural sigh', and how the passage evolves into a meditation on the inability to realise hope. The explication articulates a sequence of affirmation, interruption, reflection: 'yes – but (sigh) – well'. The sigh falls between the motion and the act like the shadow in Eliot's 'The Hollow Men' and reverberates through Coleridge's later poems. The part of 'Youth and Age' separately entitled 'An Old Man's Sigh' in some manuscripts underscores the paradigm. The later poetry exists in a condition of 'if only'. It is suspended over interruption, 'oft and tedious *taking-leave*'. It supposes a hiatus – 'Hope leaves not us but we leave Hope.' The interruption is indeed a loss but it liberates a further statement of a distinctive sort.

> O! might Life *cease*, and selfless *Mind*,
> Whose Being is *Act*, alone remain behind!

A question therefore arises in retrospect: did the realisation embodied in the later poetry suggest to Coleridge that he had previously been on the wrong track – that the promise of *Lyrical Ballads* was delusory? Had he ventriloquised himself into writing, across the table from Wordsworth, poetry which amounted to an accidental diversion, nonsense in the way Charles Lamb suggested 'Kubla Khan' lacked moral coherence? The answer is that he never thought so, even while he continued to need the supposition of a false start. He needed the magical moment to pass in order to grasp its significance, to decide that his career as a poet was finished in order to begin to articulate what blocked (what should indeed block) its development. This explains why his later poetry begins so early; and another way of saying this is to acknowledge that Coleridge's career rests on necessary failure. Wordsworth helped him discover it in a way Coleridge might almost have designed, as he designed to fall in love with a woman he could not marry, to borrow what he omitted to acknowledge, to renege on commitments while hating himself for it. The contradictions provide insight into emotional and intellectual truths hidden by ordinary success.

The Stowey poems discovered that truth does not lie in the knowledge of good and evil simply but in the working-through of a moment of choice. It is as if the debate between the two daemons who accompany the Ancient Mariner homeward, one with a voice like honey-dew, the other sterner, remained unresolved; as if the moral stain which comes to disfigure Christabel cannot be cleansed. Coleridge maintained his faith in Schiller's ideal of the *schöne Seele*: 'The poet, described in *ideal* perfection, brings the whole soul of man into activity' (*BL* ch. 14). But in a fallen world, where perfection waits to be realised, the notion of intention involves the notion of inadequacy, which in turn involves the notion of exterior assistance or divine grace. Coleridge's later poetry, as I said, complements and enlarges his lifelong argument, does not simply repeat or compromise it.

The core argument centres on the poems addressed to and associated with Sara Hutchinson. Several of the more public ones are collected in the (unpublished) anthology she made, entitled *Sara Hutchinson's Poets* (1802), the more anguished ones until recently remained unpublished in his notebooks. 'The Picture' and 'The Keepsake' are examples of the first kind; fragmentary lines which Coleridge's son-in-law published under the titles 'Phantom' and 'An Angel Visitant' provide examples of the second (*CN* II, 2441, 2224 f 81). Others, like 'Farewell to Love', are adaptations – in this instance from the Elizabethan poet Fulke Greville (1554–1628). Poems addressed to Mary Morgan and Charlotte Brent and, later, to Anne Gillman and Highgate acquaintances contribute to the same argument concerning unrequited, unrequitable love, its difference from friendship, its flowering in successful marriage, and so on.

The connections and overlap with the poems Coleridge wrote at Stowey are inevitable, the subject of the later poems being Coleridge's dialogue with himself. 'Alice du Clós', for example, picks up the theme of jealousy, describing how stifled love festers and becomes destructive. It goes back to 'The Three Graves' which Coleridge took over from Wordsworth in the summer of 1797, and, revealingly, at one point (line 91) Coleridge mistakenly wrote the name of the earlier heroine (Ellen) for the later one (Alice). Glycine's song in *Zapolya* II. i. 65–80 celebrates a bird suspended in a shaft of sunlight which is emblematic of delight like a Wordsworthian rainbow. Yet the bird is imagined as constructed – 'His eyes of fire, his beak of gold, / All else of amethyst' – like Kubla's palace of art. The suspended rhythms resemble those in the closing lines of 'Kubla Khan' ('I would build that dome in air . . . And all who heard should see them there'); and the idea is the same, that the construction is transitory. The later statement, however, adds a moral dimension, 'Love's dreams prove seldom true'. The subsequent imperative, 'We must away', thereafter links author and reader in a joint action which is different from contemplative stasis ('Weave a circle round him thrice').

Further examples of later poems which revisit and rewrite earlier themes are plentiful, though it is important to appreciate the significance of such revisitation.[3] 'The Pang More Sharp Than All' appears to have been begun as early as 1807 though it probably did not develop into its present form until 1822–5. It is sustained by a mood which was strong following Coleridge's return from Malta and it was later focused by Coleridge's developing relation with his son, Hartley. The phrase 'believing mind' (5) carries forward from 'Frost at Midnight' (24), as 'that crystal orb' ('The Pang More Sharp Than All', 39) rewrites the 'mirror seeking of itself' in the earlier poem (22). Again, 'the magic Child' and 'the faery Boy' ('The Pang More Sharp Than All', 37, 56) follow continuously from the 'little Child, a limber Elf' of 'Christabel' (656). Coleridge in other words rewrites his understanding of Hartley in relation to previous poems in which Hartley has appeared, in a process in which earlier values are renegotiated. In a similar way, 'The Garden of Boccaccio', which was composed in June–August 1828, draws on feelings associated with Sara Hutchinson and memories of the Tuscan landscape in 1806, but also alludes to and summarises themes from Stowey poems like 'This Lime-Tree Bower my Prison' and from even before (compare, e.g., 67–8 with 'The Eolian Harp', 12–25). The point of such reworking is restatement and enlargement in relation to a surrounding later interpretation.

Not all restatements succeeded to Coleridge's satisfaction and 'The Garden of Boccaccio' is a case in point. He allowed successive printings to accumulate errors without correction and one can speculate that circumstances tempted him too far into an earlier conversational manner which he afterwards realised was slack. It is important that the later style differs in its register and organisation from the earlier conversational or meditative mode: 'The Keepsake', even parts of the original 'Letter to Sara', sound like nothing written before. Coleridge's developed version produced a style more adjusted to contemplation as distinct from exploration. The Stowey experiment explored incantation and rhythm (what Coleridge called 'chaunting') to manipulate forces of nature which are supernatural in that they lie beyond the conscious mind. It supposed that poems can act like charms to call forth the powers residing in names and thereby adjust or control them. The later poems, differently, work like riddles, naming not summoning, working through pictures not sound.

The later poems characteristically work with emblems and allegory – images in relation to an idea. The subtitle to 'Love's Apparition and

Evanishment' – 'An Allegoric Romance' – describes the genre. The fit is partly obscured by what Coleridge has to say about allegory in *The Statesman's Manual*, where he suggests it is an inferior mode – 'a translation of abstract notions into a picture-language which is itself nothing but an abstraction from objects of the senses' (*SM* 30). We should not be fooled when Coleridge afterwards accelerates into a contrasting description of symbol and his wheels take fire from their motion. Allegory is a form associated with a divided or alienated consciousness, to be sure, and it matches Coleridge's mature conviction concerning our adulterated presence in the world. So many late poems are like ballet performed at a distance from the person who describes and who reads: both are in the position of observers, the reader with no more control than the writer/describer. Emblematic figures of Love and Hope, Time Real and Imaginary, appear without explanation, and the larger story which is suggested by their recurrence is not glossed. We have a poem entitled 'Reason for Love's Blindness' but the reason remains mysterious.

Coleridge's later poems, as I have said, embrace the larger part of his career as a poet and they evolved across a span of thirty-five years. In Germany and on his return, he picked up a technical interest in writing hexameters; but, when he travelled to Malta, his interest in Italian verse forms was from the outset more sophisticated. His interest in consciously re-modelling his technique represents an attempt to approach his subject-matter differently. His notebooks are filled with adaptations and experiments which take over the lighter, dispersed stress patterns of Italian models. His rhyme-schemes, at the same time, became more simple, falling either into groups of lines rhyming ABAB or into couplets handled so loosely that they are frequently misremembered as blank verse (e.g. 'The Garden of Boccaccio'). In this respect, Coleridge is at odds with the prosodical tendency of his time. The second generation of Romantic poets, Keats, Byron and Shelley, were turning to varied and elaborate stanza forms (ottava rima, terza rima, Spenserian stanzas) while Coleridge's rhymes became simpler. The pattern of sound is more evenly distributed within a more predictable framework than in the supernatural poems. It is no less complicated in itself though it might appear to be so, functioning as it does less like a corkscrew and more like a peg.

Jerome McGann believes that Coleridge's later poems are 'disturbing' because they are 'self-absorbed and introspective'. He charges: 'In these poems Coleridge is not exploring politics, society, or the apparatuses and ideologies of the state, he is applying an allegorical deconstruction to what he himself saw as the most fundamental objects of the mind, the heart, and the soul itself.'[4] Part of the answer is that Coleridge interprets private themes at a representative level, even in writing which he left unpublished because of its private reference. Dialogue with his earlier self engages issues raised by philosophers (Spinoza, Kant, Schelling) and by traditional theology (free will, original sin, redemption). He writes about adult relationships in a societal context in 'The Improvisatore' and about 'Love, Hope, and Patience in Education'. The list could be extended and the range of subject-matter which also covers marriage, baptism and death is broad. In the context of poems about the relation between men and women, which McGann writes about in another book,[5] Coleridge's contribution is unique: he occupies a position between eighteenth-century sensibility and nineteenth-century censoriousness which is simultaneously difficult and subtle.

However, McGann's charge raises the point that political matters as they are ordinarily understood are ignored. He suggests that Coleridge focuses on psychological and moral themes to the exclusion of the world of action and power. This is true only in that Coleridge did not write about sexual politics overtly. But he wrote political poems throughout his life, and perhaps more of them after 1800 than in the 1790s, certainly no less in the 1820s. His later, largely private poems are surrounded by – sustained by – a context of public writing of many different kinds. I say sustained because the intentness of privacy presupposes an envelope of public concern.[6] Retired into respectable surroundings at Highgate Coleridge might have been, but this did not prevent him from writing 'The Bridge Street Committee' and on the Catholic Question ('Sancti Dominici Pallium'), on the new University of London ('Association of Ideas') and the Reform Bill ('The Three Patriots'). It is true that later poems on public issues are written in a different style from the private ones but the differences are less clear-cut than between, say, 'The Devil's Walk' and 'Christabel'.

What perhaps misled McGann is the unfortunate division in the old standard edition of Coleridge's poems which classified many of his political poems along with *jeux d'esprit*, epigrams and metrical experiments and relegated them, out of sequence, to an appendix in a separate volume. The assumption which guided an editor in 1912 was that true poetry dealt with the sublime and permanent and that writing to the moment should be removed like chaff. The selective canon of pure poetry none the less misrepresents Coleridge because the winnowings contain successful poems of other kinds and these together make up an enabling context. Coleridge always slid between kinds of poetry – from the sublime to the humorous, from magical to doggerel and back again – in a way which suggests he would have been inhibited by being restricted to a single kind. The 'other poems' which accompany not only his late poems but his entire poetic output function like oxygen and produce their own rarities. There is a connection between

Coleridge's continuing availability to socially and politically aware themes and his 'failure' to continue as a Wordsworthian poet. ('Refusal' is too strong a word; 'disinclination' suggests the decision was easy; 'failure' at least incorporates the matter of principle and communicates the regret.)

I have written about the abundant variety of Coleridge's verse in another context.[7] Here one needs to remember that, alongside poems as solipsistic and dark as 'Limbo', Coleridge wrote 'A Droll Formulary to Raise Devils'. As a companion piece to the 'Letter to Sara', he wrote 'A Soliloquy of the Full Moon, She being in a Mad Passion', and, at the time he converted the first into 'Dejection: An Ode', he was translating scores of satirical epigrams. 'The Pains of Sleep' was accompanied by a humorously deprecating self-description, 'Epitaph on Poor Col, by Himself'. After lacerating verses on his failed marriage he wrote a comically affectionate verse-letter to his estranged wife and a fragmentary satire on the wedding of a friend, Mr Baker. 'The Suicide's Argument' is overtaken by 'Lavatorial Lines'. So the story continues to the end. While he pondered 'Love and Friendship Opposite' and 'A Guilty Sceptic's Death Bed', he wrote 'An Autograph on an Autopergamene' and lampoons on social-climbing medical men. The verses he wrote in the months before his death were of the same sort: album verses, satire, a parody motto, a scabrous Latin address. The more intense, private poems which criticism has concentrated on were ventilated and nurtured by generous breezes. The last poem he wrote was not the solemn injunction 'Stop, Christian passerby!' which closes the old editions and is now engraved on his memorial: it was a doggerel letter for an autograph. Coleridge wrote the way he did because not all the verse he wrote, in his terms, was poetry.

He is himself responsible for the idea of a selective canon. Even as his confidence in his abilities as a poet revived, in the writing of *Biographia Literaria*, he organised the selection of his poems in *Sibylline Leaves* to privilege the Wordsworthian kind, and *Sibylline Leaves* became the basis of subsequent collections in his lifetime which in turn influenced those which came after. Coleridge, too, for his own creative reasons, is responsible for the muddled sequencing which obscures the relation between his poems. He excluded several he wrote after his return from Malta from *Sibylline Leaves* – for instance, 'The Suicide's Argument, with Nature's Answer' – with the result that when they were collected (this last in *Poetical Works* 1828) they appeared to represent a late revival in an allegorical mode which in truth dates from earlier. 'Time Real and Imaginary', also dating from after the return from Malta, was included in *Sibylline Leaves* but only at the very last moment. Other poems remained uncollected – 'Farewell to Love' was published only in newspapers – and those which would have embarrassed family and friends were naturally withheld altogether.

An understanding of Coleridge's poems as a whole – poetic alongside political, philosophical interrupted by personal, finished alternating with trial versions – is important if one is trying to understand the emergence of the allegoric, emblematising method. Coleridge in Malta and afterwards contemplated his situation as static, stuck, fixed. Travelling light as a traveller does and brooding on problems, they appeared a thing apart, though thereby no less easy to resolve. Some statements of his position are literally emblems, such as those written for Mathilda Betham. Others articulate his relation with Wordsworth by means of images of roots or birds met in his reading or they take passages directly from a book to develop into verse. There is an instructive contrast to be drawn from the immediate, semi-public statement of his response to hearing Wordsworth reading *The Prelude* and the private meditation on his feelings written in Latin, 'Ad Vilnum Axiologum', which develops out of his reading in Goethe and Schiller. Coleridge's adaptations of Greville, Daniel, Donne, as well as his translations from the German and Italian, which form an increasing part of his output in the early 1800s, reflect the modification contained in his later poetry. One might compare his adoption of personae like the 'poor Bird'/ 'poor Bard' in 'A Character'. Allegory, emblems, borrowed passages, personae all enabled him to articulate his sense of a disunited condition.

Coleridge's writing holds together in a way contrary to first appearance and ordinary logic. His later poems continually hint at, draw upon, even summon into existence an unwritten narrative concerning failure in love and a blocked emotional situation. Even though the writing can be supplemented with biographical narrative, its method leaves it allusive and fragmentary. It sets before us a discourse employing moral counters which are intensely perceived but they do not engage us with flesh and blood. The separate poems participate in a larger unwritten text, unwritten because they continually frustrate attempts to translate it into wide-awake experience; as Lee Rust Brown puts it, 'the whole text which constitutes the fragment's meaning is absent'.[8] However, Brown points out that when Coleridge collects the earlier poetry to which the later poetry refers, he relabels it so that 'The Three Graves', 'The Wanderings of Cain', 'Christabel', 'Kubla Khan', 'The Ballad of the Dark Ladiè' (and more) are all described as fragments. Their fragmentary nature is typically attributed to an external cause (a man from Porlock, etc.), in distinction from the later poems where the supposition is that the complete meaning is too private or painful to be fully articulated. But in both instances, the fragments by their fragmentariness summon into existence a fiction of textual wholeness which does not materially exist.

The feature of this creative fragmentation which is invariably overlooked is Coleridge's occasional writing. It is overlooked because it appears intrinsically of lesser worth, especially to literary readers intent on poetical poetry. At the same time it forms a large part of the whole and it was evidently important to Coleridge. What is the relation between his irrepressible burbling about shaving pots and medical matters, on the one hand, and 'Love's Apparition and Evanishment', on the other? The answer is that Coleridge's life as a poet depends on evasive mobility: obstacles cleared while his attention appeared to stray. The central enabling condition was thinking in verse, unrestricted as to kind; the apparent interruptions form the cement. To this extent, the category of his later poetry is a misnomer: it is a kind of verse he began writing in relative youth; it exists in a symbiotic relationship with some of the poetry he had been writing for only a few years before, the categories of his earlier magical and conversational poems and his later poems exist alongside political and occasional poems which do not divide into earlier and later in the same way and whose method, in an important sense, sustains the more private themes and manner. When Coleridge the poet comes properly into his own it will be as a whole, on more than one level, and partial categories will dissolve.

NOTES

1 Martin Greenberg, *The Hamlet Vocation of Coleridge and Wordsworth* (University of Iowa Press, 1986), 62.
2 George Whalley's sensitive reading of the poems in terms of the biographical situation is misleading to the extent that ideas and beliefs contributed to them equally. See *Coleridge and Sara Hutchinson and the Asra Poems* (London: Routledge and Kegan Paul, 1955).
3 In this respect, Marshall Suther, *Visions of Xanadu* (New York: Columbia University Press, 1965), and Morton D. Paley, *Coleridge's Later Poetry* (Oxford: Clarendon Press, 1996), are recommended.
4 Jerome McGann, *The Romantic Ideology: A Critical Investigation* (University of Chicago Press, 1983), 97.
5 Jerome McGann, *The Poetics of Sensibility: A Revolution in Literary Style* (Oxford: Clarendon Press, 1996).
6 'The Devil's Walk' and 'Cholera Cured Beforehand', in a polemical way, and 'Israel's Lament' and 'The Tears of a Grateful People', more subtly, supply examples. On the political dimension of the last two poems, see Tim Fulford, *Romanticism and Masculinity: Gender, Politics and Poetics in the Writings of Burke, Coleridge, Cobbett, Wordsworth, De Quincey and Hazlitt* (London: Macmillan, 1999), 155–76.
7 J. C. C. Mays, 'Coleridge's New Poetry', *Proceedings of the British Academy* 94 (1997), 127–56.
8 Lee Rust Brown, 'Coleridge and the Prospect of the Whole', *Studies in Romanticism* 30, 2 (1991), 235–53 (238). See also 244.

2

DISCURSIVE MODES

7

The talker

S.T. Coleridge Ætat. Suae 63.
Not / handsome / was / but was / eloquent
COLERIDGE.[1]

Dorothy Wordsworth would have concurred: 'At first I thought him very plain, that is, for about three minutes: he is pale, thin, has a wide mouth, thick lips, and not very good teeth, longish, loose-growing, half-curling, rough, black hair...But, if you hear him speak for five minutes you think no more of them' (*IR*, 45). Dorothy's account is exceptional in its humane amusement; but the extraordinary effect she attributes to Coleridge's speech is quite usual. Leigh Hunt recalled Byron leaving Coleridge's company, 'saying how wonderfully he talked', and added: 'This is the impression of every body who hears him' (*IR*, 219). In what Hazlitt acerbically characterised as 'an age of talkers' (*CT*, 255), Coleridge became famous as the greatest of them all. Tourists on the culture-trail, in Highgate years especially, would approach him, a great curiosity, expecting an extraordinary exhibition (which they normally received). He seems to have quietly delighted in the facility, and the celebrity it won him; and, perhaps, to have relied too much upon his power to charm: 'I have heard him say', recollected a fellow traveller in Germany, 'fixing his prominent eyes upon himself (as he was wont to do, whenever there was a mirror in the room), with a singularly coxcomical expression of countenance, that his dress was sure to be lost sight of the moment he began to talk; an assertion which, whatever may be thought of its modesty, was not without truth' (*IR*, 74). Occasionally, he wearied of the duty to perform, which he could find exhausting: 'He deemed Himself obliged to Play first Violin', wrote a bemused and bored Lady Jerningham after a visit, 'and was much fatigued with the violent exertion He made' (*IR*, 134). Visitors in his last years were sometimes warned not to draw him into too exciting a conversation, as the sheer physical demands of discoursing struck Dr and Mrs Gillman, his protective hosts, as seriously life-threatening.

After Coleridge's death, his fame as a talker only increased, thanks largely to the compilation of *Table Talk* made by his devoted son-in-law and nephew, Henry Nelson Coleridge, published in 1835, the year after his death. The book gathered fragments from the great man's conversation, some quite lengthy, arranged (allegedly) by date (see *TT* I, xc–xci). Many of the most quotable dicta appear here: 'I have a smack of Hamlet myself, if I may say so', 'Shakspeare [*sic*] is the Spinosistic deity, an omnipresent creativeness', 'The pith of my system is to make the senses out of the mind – not the mind out of the senses, as Locke did' (*TT* II, 61, 86, 179). Coleridge emerges from these pages as hugely wide-ranging; gifted with an immense memory and the command of extraordinarily various fields of knowledge; religiously respectable; broadly Tory (the publication of pejorative remarks about the 1832 Reform Bill caused some consternation in the circle: see *TT* I, cix–cxii). The first edition sold very well: most unusually – as Carl Woodring says, it was 'a work of commercial success such as Coleridge's prose had never enjoyed' (*TT* I, xcviii); and a revised edition was published the following year. In 1851, a lightly emended version of the 1836 text was published by Sara Coleridge (Coleridge's daughter, and Henry Nelson Coleridge's widow); and there were many subsequent new editions and reprints throughout the latter half of the nineteenth century, making it (said Lucy Watson) 'perhaps the most popular of all books either relating to or written by S. T. Coleridge' (*TT* I, c). Alongside the poems, *Table Talk* is the key work for any attempt to understand what Coleridge meant to the nineteenth century, just as *Biographia* is to the twentieth.

There were other accounts of his talk, notably Thomas Allsop's *Letters, Conversations and Recollections of S. T. Coleridge*, first published in 1836, and issued in new editions in 1858 and 1864. Allsop's Coleridge is subtly but importantly different from Henry Nelson Coleridge's: a little more scurrilous, outspoken on religious matters (and, according to the 'Preface' finally published in the third edition, far from orthodox). There seems to have been a subdued battle of the rival books of table talk, the family certainly not approving of Allsop. What Coleridge said in his largely improvised lectures ('the words of the moment!': *CL* III, 471) was also often recorded, and the records gathered throughout the succeeding years, until they constituted the impressively large body of texts to be found in Volume V of the *Collected Coleridge*. Henry Nelson Coleridge was first here too, moving on from *Table Talk* to the *Literary Remains* (1836–9), in Volume I of which he gathered various fragments to represent Coleridge's lecture series of 1818. Sara Coleridge produced a larger volume of *Notes and Lectures on Shakespeare* in 1849, drawing on extensive newspaper reports of what he had said; in 1856, John Payne Collier published his notes on several of Coleridge's 1811–12 lectures on Shakespeare and Milton; and another, still larger gathering of *Lectures and Notes on Shakespeare*, made by Thomas Ashe, appeared in 1883.

Alongside *Table Talk* and the other records of him speaking, a large nineteenth-century literature of memoir and reminiscence portrayed the wonderfully talkative man – and it proved, no doubt, quite as important to Coleridge's lasting garrulous celebrity. Wordsworth, De Quincey, Hazlitt, Lamb, Peacock, Carlyle: most of his great contemporaries wrote their versions of Coleridge, in tempers ranging from the rapt and indulgent to the jokey and satirical, even to the scandalised; and so too did a host of minor writers, contributing to the collective portrait of a recognisable type. The incidents and encounters their various memoirs are based upon do not need to be fictional for them to establish, not Coleridge exactly, but a myth of him – a kind of exemplary genius, who spoke (as Hazlitt said) 'as if the wings of his imagination lifted him from off his feet' (*IR*, 68). Myth-Coleridge overlaps a good deal with S. T. Coleridge, who indeed is largely responsible for creating him; but nevertheless we should try and discriminate the one from the other (without denying the importance of either).

Part of the point of the myth is that you cannot really represent him at all. After *Table Talk* was published, several commentators politely observed that the task was futile: how could you put Coleridge the talker into cold print? Julius Charles Hare, for instance, a devoted Coleridgean, doubted whether H. N. C. had really caught very much of the master's conversations, remembering 'their depth, their ever varying hues, their sparkling lights, their oceanic ebb and flow; of which his published Table-talk hardly gives the slightest conception' (*TT* I, cix). But this doubt was only picking up H. N. C.'s own anxieties. He wrote, after recounting the events of one afternoon:

> When I look upon the scanty memorial, which I have alone preserved of this afternoon's converse, I am tempted to burn these pages in despair. Mr. Coleridge talked a volume of criticism that day, which, printed verbatim as he spoke it, would have made the reputation of any other person but himself. He was, indeed, particularly brilliant and enchanting, and I left him at night so thoroughly *magnetized*, that I could not for two or three days afterwards reflect enough to put any thing on paper. (*IR*, 252)

He recalled, no doubt with fellow feeling, the similar difficulties faced by a short-hand writer attending one of Coleridge's lectures (Gurney was a famous short-handist):

> A very experienced short-hand writer was employed to take down Mr. Coleridge's lectures on Shakspeare, but the manuscript was almost entirely unintelligible. Yet the lecturer was, as he always is, slow and measured. The

writer – we have some notion it was no worse an artist than Mr. Gurney himself – gave this account of the difficulty: that with regard to every other speaker whom he had ever heard, however rapid or involved, he could almost always, by long experience in his art, guess the form of the latter part, or apo-dosis, of the sentence by the form of the beginning; but that the conclusion of every one of Coleridge's sentences was a *surprise* upon him. He was obliged to listen to the last word.   (*IR*, 149)

A sort of tacit admission of failure accompanies every page of *Table Talk*; and expressions of regret at the impossibility of transcription, at the in-adequacy of one's own language to capture such extraordinary discourse, recur again and again in the accounts of Coleridge speaking. 'It is impossible to carry off or commit to paper his long trains of argument', said another nephew (*IR*, 197); and one way of expressing this sense of a discourse be-yond words was to describe it, not as language, but as a kind of music: what Julius Mayne Young called 'The melody of Coleridge's voice' (*IR*, 268) is re-peatedly invoked by the memoirists. 'His elevated tone, as he rolled forth his gorgeous sentences, his lofty look, his sustained flow of language, his sublime utterance, gave the effect of some magnificent organ-peal to our entranced ears', wrote Cowden Clarke (*IR*, 271); 'With his fine, flowing voice', said Thomas Hood, 'it was glorious music, of the "never-ending, still-beginning" kind; and you did not wish it to end' (*IR*, 217); 'a strange rich, mellow, rhythmical, yet somewhat monotonous music, peculiarly suited to his ever-varying yet continuous flow of transcendent eloquence' (*IR*, 279). Even less poetical accounts still invoke the idea of music with telling frequency: 'All he says is without effort, but not unfrequently with a sort of musical hum, and a catching of his breath at the end, and sometimes in the middle, of a sentence, enough to make a slight pause, but not so much as to interrupt the flow of his language' (*IR*, 141); and his friend, the painter Leslie: 'His voice was deep and musical, and his words followed each other in an unbroken flow, yet free from monotony' (*IR*, 179). Even the amused Mary Russell Mitford, who thought Coleridge's accent bleating and provincial, freely conceded that he had 'so much of the electric power of genius – that power which fixes the attention by rousing at once the fancy and the heart – that the ear has scarcely the wish to condemn that which so strongly delights the intellect' (*IR*, 155). In a less qualified spirit, the young Anne Chalmers wrote, 'I can give no idea of the beauty and sublimity of his conversation. It resembles the loveliness of a song' (*IR*, 272).

The failure of her words before Coleridge's voice makes it a bit like an inexpressible and sublime object, like an Alp or God. 'I seemed rather to listen to an Oracular voice, to be circumfused in a Divine ὀμθή, wrote a rapt William Rowan Hamilton, 'than, as I did in the presence of Wordsworth, to

hold commune with an exalted man' (IR, 286). Thomas Hood reported his
return to earth after immersion in the Coleridgean music:

> To attempt to describe my own feeling afterward, I had been carried, spiralling,
> up to heaven by a whirlwind intertwisted with sunbeams, giddy and dazzled,
> but not displeased, and had then been rained down again with a shower of
> mundane stocks and stones that battered out of me all recollection of what I
> had heard, and what I had seen! (IR, 217)

And, like the sublime, the power could prove oppressive as well as awe-
inspiring: John Payne Collier had sat listening for less than an hour, anxiously
keen to remember what was said, before feeling 'obliged to leave the room
for some time, that I might lighten the weight' (IR, 141). This new source
of sublimity is not mountainous grandeur or divinity, but the speaking consciousness: the auditor stumbles into inarticulacy before the overwhelming
plenitude of the voice; and this idea, that consciousness (revealed in spontaneous speech) has a kind of sublimity, picks up on a range of Coleridge's own
thoughts about the God-like mind and its organising powers. He was repeatedly drawn to imagine the totality of creation as a vast harmonic sounding
(as in 'The Eolian Harp'), and the creativity of the genius is often granted a
kind of musical authority too: Wordsworth, for instance, whom Coleridge
heard reciting 'An Orphic song indeed, / A song divine of high and passionate thoughts / To their own music chaunted!' ('To William Wordsworth',
45–7).

So, the figure of myth-Coleridge draws on a genuinely Coleridgean repertoire (just not on the entire repertoire); and one of the most important,
besides the metaphor of music, is Coleridge's habitual characterisation of
consciousness as river-like:[2] 'Samuel Taylor Coleridge was like the Rhine',
declared Barry Cornwall, '"That exulting and abounding river"' (IR, 223);
'The stream flowed on and began to widen', reported a listener, as Coleridge
began his 'multiform mellifluous monologue' (IR, 270). (Cowden Clarke re-
sourcefully combined images and found his metaphor in a river at its most
sublime – 'He was like a cataract filling and rushing over my penny-phial
capacity. I could only gasp and bow my head in acknowledgment' IR, 208.)
Talfourd recollected:

> At first his tones were conversational; he seemed to dally with the shallows
> of the subject and with fantastic images which bordered it; but gradually the
> thought grew deeper, and the voice deepened with the thought; the stream
> gathering strength, seemed to bear along with it all things which opposed
> its progress, and blended them with its current; and stretching away among
> regions tinted with etherial colours, was lost at airy distance in the horizon of
> fancy. (IR, 211)

De Quincey also pictures Coleridge shifting gear from the mundane to the sublime as his entrance into a great rivery sweep: 'these little points of business being settled, – Coleridge, like some great river, the Orellana, or the St. Lawrence, that had been checked and fretted by rocks or thwarting islands, and suddenly recovers its volume of waters, and its mighty music, – swept at once, as if returning to his natural business, into a continuous strain of eloquent dissertation' (*IR*, 113).

The sublime and mythical Coleridge easily slips into the merely obscure and monstrous. For instance, a story told by Samuel Rogers:

> He talked uninterruptedly for about two hours, during which Wordsworth listened to him with profound attention, every now and then nodding his head as if in assent. On quitting the lodging, I said to Wordsworth, 'Well, for my own part, I could not make head or tail of Coleridge's oration: pray, did you understand it?' 'Not one syllable of it', was Wordsworth's reply.   (*IR*, 225)

Myth-Coleridge here becomes an outstanding example of a favourite English comic type: the intellectual. Coleridge the intellectual (as opposed to Coleridge the poet, who led a largely discrete afterlife) still retained a strong enough iconic life at the beginning of the next century for Max Beerbohm to base on it a cartoon version. 'Samuel Taylor Coleridge Table-Talking', in *The Poet's Corner* (1904), shows a pudgy Coleridge sounding forth obliviously, doubtless on some abstruse philosophical issue, to a company of helplessly snoozing diners;[3] and the joke draws on a strong line stemming from Peacock (in *Melincourt* and *Nightmare Abbey*) and Lamb:

> 'I was', he said, 'going from my house at Enfield to the India-house one morning, and was hurrying, for I was rather late, when I met Coleridge, on his way to pay me a visit; he was brimful of some new idea, and in spite of my assuring him that time was precious, he drew me within the door of an unoccupied garden by the road-side, and there, sheltered from observation by a hedge of evergreens, he took me by the button of my coat, and closing his eyes commenced an eloquent discourse, waving his right hand gently, as the musical words flowed in an unbroken stream from his lips. I listened entranced; but the striking of a church-clock recalled me to a sense of duty. I saw it was of no use to attempt to break away, so taking advantage of his absorption in his subject, I, with my penknife, quietly severed the button from my coat and decamped. Five hours afterwards, in passing the same garden, on my way home, I heard Coleridge's voice, and on looking in there he was, with closed eyes, – the button in his fingers, – and his right hand gracefully waving, just as when I left him. He had never missed me!'   (*IR*, 230–1)

(A likely story.)

Lamb (as always) is kindly about his friend as well as funny; but myth-Coleridge's monologuing is often given severer treatment. Madame de Staël naturally provides the epigraph to any discussion of this point: 'when I saw Madame de Staël in London, I asked her what she thought of him: she replied, "He is very great in monologue, but he has no idea of dialogue"' (IR, 148) – a remark that gets repeated throughout the long tradition of Coleridge memoir. De Quincey is quite as eloquent on Coleridge's 'conversation, if that can be called conversation which I so seldom sought to interrupt, and which did not often leave openings for contribution' (IR, 114); and, in a long late essay on 'Coleridge and Conversation', he analysed, with typical comic pedantry, the principal reasons for the unsatisfactoriness of Coleridge's 'habit of monologue': it is antisocial, impertinent to women, and predisposed to *longueurs*.[4] This dubious reputation was abroad in his own lifetime: the illustrator David Scott observed, 'The moment he is seated, as has been said, he begins to talk, and on it goes, flowing and full, almost without even what might be called paragraphic division, and leaving colloquy out of the question entirely' (IR, 257). Rivers reappear here, since they are happily oblivious of the objects that stand in their overwhelming way: 'His was a mild enthusiastic flow of language; a broad, deep stream, carrying gently along all that it met with on its course, not a whirlpool that drags into its vortex, and engulfs what it seizes on' (IR, 257). 'The fact was', judged a well-disposed Thomas Methuen,

> that his words, as well as his ideas, had so much of that majestic flow which characterizes certain rivers in the western world, that (to say nothing of the difficulty of restraining a mind so productive as his) he was generally heard with that degree of silent admiration, that 'the art of stopping' must have been to him singularly difficult, and his volubility of speech, to a considerable extent, pardonable.

Still, even Methuen conceded that, 'On the whole, perhaps, his vast conversational powers were too little exercised in *dialogue*' (IR, 163, 165). The star-turn is Carlyle's unforgiving portrait from the *Life of Sterling* (1851) which brilliantly joins the several metaphors I have been identifying in the tradition of myth-Coleridge, and gives them all their most pejorative twist:

> it was talk not flowing anywhither like a river, but spreading everywhither in inextricable currents and regurgitations like a lake or sea; terribly deficient in definite goal or aim, nay often in logical intelligibility; *what* you were to believe or do, on any earthly or heavenly thing, obstinately refusing to appear from it. So that, most times, you felt logically lost; swamped near to drowning in this tide of ingenious vocables, spreading out boundless as if to submerge the world.

To sit as a passive bucket and be pumped into, whether you consent or not, can in the long-run be exhilarating to no creature; how eloquent soever the flood of utterance that is descending. But if it be withal a confused unintelligible flood of utterance, threatening to submerge all known landmarks of thought, and drown the world and you! – I have heard Coleridge talk, with eager musical energy, two stricken hours, his face radiant and moist, and communicate no meaning whatsoever to any individual of his hearers, – certain of whom, I for one, still kept eagerly listening in hope; the most had long before given up, and formed (if the room were large enough) secondary humming groups of their own.   (*IR*, 237–8)

The river of the mind has become a pointless flood; sublime immersion in the musical cataract has become the comic indignity of being treated like a bucket. It is a powerful charge all right; and Coleridge's abuses of conversational nicety have retained their notoriety. For instance, the uncomprehending encounter with Wordsworth and Rogers (quoted above) appears in Theodore Zeldin's little handbook on conversation, as an example of how rhetoric destroys the proper sort of mutual exchange:[5] Zeldin is following in the footsteps of De Quincey, who complained that Coleridgean talk 'defeats the very end of social meetings'.[6]

Coleridge was certainly guilty of breaking the written rules: 'It is an impertinent and unreasonable Fault in Conversation, for one Man to take up all the Discourse', counselled Steele;[7] and Chesterfield specifically ruled out what Lamb had imagined Coleridge doing to him – 'Never hold anybody by the button...if people are not willing to hear you, you had much better hold your tongue than them.'[8] Anne Chalmers offers one response to the habitual Coleridgean manner, not a daft one: 'I have heard people say that it showed a disagreeable admiration of himself, Coleridge's flow of talk; but I should think that person very conceited who, after having been admitted to an interview with him, should feel inclined to talk rather than listen' (*IR*, 273).[9] Besides that, it might in fairness be said that not everyone found him so oppressive a speaker anyway: it seems to have been a habit that grew as he aged (it is hard to think that the conversations with Wordsworth in the 1790s were so simply one-way); but even in his late years, William Rowan Hamilton found 'that he took very graciously, and in good part, any few words I ventured to throw in; and allowed them to influence, and in some degree to guide his own great, and sweet, and wondrous stream of speech' (*IR*, 286–7) – which generously grants as much as the irresistible river metaphor will allow. (John Frere records a dialogue too, though Coleridge does have most of the lines: *IR*, 274–7.) He was not always going at full stretch anyway, and would swap puns and rhymes with intimates: 'He never disdains to talk on the most familiar topics, if they seem pleasing to others', reported Collier (*IR*, 141); and his Highgate neighbour Anne Mathews found him a very pleasing conversationalist on small matters ('I do not know whether he was not a more charming companion when he stooped his magnificent mind to the understanding of the less informed and little gifted, than when he conversed with higher intellects': *IR*, 193). There is some evidence, indeed, though it is hard to piece together very compellingly, that his off-duty conversation with women, especially, was quite different to the kind of talk that the records normally preserve. Still, all this feels something like pleading; and whatever allowance might be made, it seems certain enough that Coleridge's talk usually lacked the democratic and collaborative impulse that linguists tend to attribute to the conversational idioms they prefer: as, say, 'All participants share in the construction of talk in the strong sense that *they don't function as individual speakers.*'[10] 'The speaker, however, it must be fairly admitted, did not "give and take". His generosity was illimitable, for he would receive nothing in return', said Dibdin, tongue not wholly in cheek: 'It was true, there were very few who could *give* as they had *received*; but still, as an irritated hearer once observed by the side of me, "fair play was a jewel"' (*IR*, 118).

Knowingly (I assume), Dibdin alludes there to a Coleridgean source:

> O Lady! we receive but what we give,
> And in our life alone does Nature live[.]
> ('Dejection: An Ode', 47–8)

And the echo is important because it alerts us to a much more general feature of the critical memoirs of Coleridge talking: the most vigorous and thoughtful accounts often gather strength by being an oblique kind of literary criticism, using his regrettably monologuing conversational style to symbolise a distinctive brand of Romantic doctrine. The case against might run: Coleridge's (supposed) idealism re-locates reality within the individual spirit, removing him from the rooting stabilities of the world without; and the way this preference is registered in conversational style is in monologue, enchanting, self-delighting, intransitive. 'Thinking and speaking were his delight; and he would sometimes seem, during the more fervid moments of discourse, to be abstracted from all and every thing around and about him, and to be basking in the sunny warmth of his own radiant imagination' (*IR*, 119): that would be the kind way of putting such shining selfness; but Coleridge's abuse of the proper give-and-take might well carry a darker implication, confirming a suspicion that the Romantic mind is lost in abstraction and blind to external fact, a mind whose solipsistic speech is an incomprehensible noise issued in total disregard of the needs or interests of any audience in the world without. Talfourd wrote: 'Whether he had won for his greedy listener only some raw lad, or charmed a circle of beauty, rank, and wit, who hung breathless on his words, he talked with equal eloquence; for his subject, not his audience, inspired him' (*IR*, 210–11). Hazlitt, typically, is sharper and funnier:

> C—— is the only person who can talk to all sorts of people, on all sorts of subjects, without caring a farthing for their understanding one word he says...I firmly believe he would make just the same impression on half his audiences, if he purposely repeated absolute nonsense with the same voice and manner, and inexhaustible flow of undulating speech! (*CT*, 254)

– a complaint that runs happily in parallel with the negative remarks he makes about Coleridge's philosophical temperament ('He is without a strong feeling of the existence of any thing out of himself'[11]). Coleridge the monologuist, like Coleridge's Hamlet (another soliloquiser), dwells on what he takes to be the superior reality of the world within: put to the test of normal human exchange, he can only speak his self-dwelling thoughts, not so much escaping his solipsistic imprisonment as seeking to absorb his would-be interlocutors into it.

One of Coleridge's most characteristic distinctions, however, is to anticipate his most telling critics; and the morbid psychology of Coleridgean monologuing already has its most desolate (though not unsympathetic) account in 'The Ancient Mariner', whose central character is less gifted with his 'strange power of speech' than burdened by it. Memoirists repeatedly draw a comparison between the poet and his single most famous creation, obviously enough in many cases ('Like his own bright-eyed marinere; he had a spell in his voice that would not let you go': *IR*, 217); but the parallel could have a bleaker significance. John Sterling's comment is haunting: 'It is painful to observe in Coleridge, that, with all the kindness and glorious far-seeing intelligence of his eye, there is a glare in it, a light half unearthly, half morbid. It is the glittering eye of the *Ancient Mariner*' (*IR*, 254–5). Talking, said Procter, was for Coleridge 'like laying down part of his burden' (*IR*, 223); and you sense a similar sort of awful compulsion even in Carlyle's unsympathetic picture. This is the act of uttering as a desperate '*out*ering, getting rid of' (*CN* IV, 4954), an attempt to evade the prison of the unhappy self and make contact with a redeeming world without: 'Have Mercy on me, O something *out* of me!' (*CN* II, 2453).

An alternative to the monologuist, exercising a correctly democratic style of conversation, might be called, in the tacitly adversarial title of one of Hazlitt's books of essays, the 'Plain Speaker' – one whose mode of talking goes hand in hand with a full-blooded realism, just as Coleridge's self-spawning stream necessarily accompanies the self-involutions of the idealist imagination. The case is no-nonsense and feels sturdy and firm-hearted, and it is not only Hazlitt's; there is a nice example of it in Robert Owen's *Autobiography*:

> Mr. Coleridge had a great fluency of words, and he could well put them together in high-sounding sentences; but my words, directly to the point, generally told well; and although the eloquence and learning were with him, the strength of the argument was generally admitted to be on my side. Many years afterwards, when he was better known and more celebrated, I presented him with a copy of my '*Essays on the Formation of Character*', and the next time I met him after he had read them, he said – 'Mr. Owen, I am really ashamed of myself. I have been making use of many words in writing and speaking what is called eloquence, while I find you have said much more to the purpose in plain simple language, easily to be understood, and in a short compass. I will endeavour to profit by it.'
> (IR, 14)

(Less plausible even than Lamb's button-holing, unless Coleridge was having a joke.) Owen's vanity nicely shows the way that being a Plain Man can be but another brand of egotism. Even if not that, Plainness is itself a kind of style, which (in Hazlitt, for instance) works very adroitly to achieve an entirely literary effect. (It must be a moot point, by the way, how much more genuinely 'dialogic' Hazlitt was in his conversations than Coleridge in his; he seems, if anything, to have tended to taciturnity, and – latterly – ill-temper, which merely abuses conversational propriety in a different way.[12]) Anyhow, it is enough to say here that Plain Speaking's merits are not simple or self-evident, and that a defence might yet be mustered for the Coleridgean idiom in its own right. But such a defence needs to leave behind the tenacious figure of myth-Coleridge that the Victorian mind found so compelling, and turn instead to the virtues of S. T. Coleridge's voice, a more intricate and ambiguous noise; so I shall begin a new section.

As I hope I've said enough to imply, Coleridge's lasting notoriety as a talker alone would justify a treatment of the subject in a *Companion*; but the theme turns out to be rather more than a diverting aspect of his biography (though it certainly is that); and more, too, than an important part of his ambiguous posthumous reputation (though it is that as well). Talk might look set to keep a merely anecdotal or biographical place in so substantial and writerly an achievement; but in fact it plays a secretly formative role across the immense Coleridge range.[13] The voluminous notebook entries, for example, and the thousands of scribbled commentaries in the margins of books, are occasional, nonce-writings, which emulate the passing, one-off language uttered at the table or improvised at the lecture-podium; and the letters are often dazzling recreations of the speaking voice. Henry Nelson

Coleridge felt no compunction about filling out quiet days in the *Table Talk* with short passages from letters (see *TT* I, lxxxix), and silently incorporated notebook entries into the second edition of *Table Talk* as though they were recollections of the great man speaking (see *CN* III, 3497n.); when he compiled the section, 'A Course of Lectures', in the *Literary Remains* (1836–9), he produced (says R. A. Foakes) a 'medley of notes, reports, and marginalia' (*C. Lects* I, lxxx); and Allsop too, in his *Recollections*, freely mingled remembered snippets of conversation and fragments of Coleridge's letters and notes. You can certainly disapprove on textual principle; but both editors were recognising, legitimately enough, a basic kinship between his manner in notebook or correspondence and the conversational style they knew so well from the life.

The boundaries between Coleridge the talker and Coleridge the writer are always breaking down like this – just as do attempts to discriminate between the formal, essential or central Coleridge works and the informal, peripheral ones. Notebooks and marginalia, lectures and letters, might seem at first sight incidental contributions to the canon; but really there is no difference in kind (though, of course, there is in degree: a favourite Coleridgean distinction) between their type of rhetorical existence and the spoken life of the *Friend* or *Biographia Literaria* – both of which were composed by dictation, and which retain at least something of the tell-tale characteristics of Coleridge talking. 'Many who read the abstruser parts of his "Friend" would complain that his works did not answer to his spoken wisdom', wrote Lamb: 'They were identical' (*TT* I, xli) – which is a little exaggerated no doubt, but exaggerates a genuine truth. (Emerson found 'the largest part of his discourse . . . often like so many printed paragraphs in his book': *IR*, 289.) The self-evidently oral origins of *Table Talk* and the *Lectures on Literature* make especially obvious the prominent place which the talking Coleridge should properly occupy in our sense of those works; but Coleridge the talker is firmly behind the other prose writings too: he used the notebooks while dictating *Biographia* in much the same way he did while lecturing on Shakespeare and Milton. And not only behind the prose writings: it was a conversational paradigm that underwrote the poetic experiment he made with Wordsworth, to bring poetry closer to the spoken tongue ('to ascertain how far the language of conversation in the middle and lower classes of society is adapted to the purposes of poetic pleasure'); and in his own invention, the 'Conversation' poem, he worked independently to much the same end ('Well, they are gone, and here must I remain').

But what was it about Coleridgean talk that made it so enabling a mode of expression for him? Our best guide here is Coleridge himself. He was the most conspicuous of talkers, and he was conspicuously fascinated by talking:[14] especially by the way that (as Michael Ignatieff puts it nicely, in a description of Isaiah Berlin, another great talker) 'a style of speaking is a style of thinking'.[15] In the *Friend* he discriminates at length between good and bad styles of discourse. The 'ignorant man' produces speech with no internal organisation other than the order of recollection; his sentences are articulated by the most vestigial or thoughtless of connections ('the "*and then*", the "*and there*", and the still less significant, "*and so*"'). The 'man of education', on the other hand, cannot but display in his speech an 'unpremeditated and evidently habitual *arrangement* of his words, grounded on the habit of foreseeing, in each integral part, or (more plainly) in every sentence, the whole that he then intends to communicate. However irregular and desultory his talk, there is *method* in the fragments' (*Friend* I, 449). 'Method' recognises not only things, but the relation between things; a Shakespeare character like Mistress Quickly or the Nurse from *Romeo and Juliet* quite lacks such a skill (*Friend* I, 452). As a criterion of excellence it sounds decisive: a reconciliation of things with the relationship between things, of 'each integral part' with the 'whole'; and, in that holistic marriage of manyness and oneness it is unmistakably Coleridgean. Indeed, Coleridge is describing, within the spontaneous art of speech, much the same synthesis of opposites that he sought in great poetry: which should offer you, for example, 'such delight from the *whole*, as is compatible with a distinct gratification from each component *part*' (*BL* II, 13). Much the same methodical orderliness should underwrite the highest prose works too, of course – as Coleridge was ruefully aware when he apologised in *Biographia* for producing 'so immethodical a miscellany' (*BL* I, 88). But, as that last example shows, the serene balances and reconciliations of Coleridgean theory can sometimes contrast unforgivingly with the much more fruitfully contested life of Coleridgean practice.

When, by chance, Keats met Coleridge on Hampstead Heath in 1819, it was the astonishing, wandering diversity of the speech that he found comic and captivating:

Last Sunday I took a Walk towards Highgate and in the lane that winds by the side of Lord Mansfield's park I met Mr. Green our Demonstrator at Guy's in conversation with Coleridge – I joined them, after enquiring by a look whether it would be agreeable – I walked with him a[t] his alderman-after dinner pace for near two miles I suppose. In those two Miles he broached a thousand things – let me see if I can give you a list – Nightingales, Poetry – on Poetical Sensation – Metaphysics – Different genera and species of Dreams – Nightmare – a dream accompanied by a sense of touch – single and double touch – A dream related – First and second consciousness – the difference explained between will and Volition – so say metaphysicians from a want of smoking the second consciousness – Monsters – the Kraken – Mermaids – southey believes in them – southeys belief too much diluted – A Ghost story – Good morning – I heard his voice as he came towards me – I heard it as he moved away – I had heard it all the interval – if it may be called so.

(*KL* II, 88–9)

In a letter sent some time before that encounter, Keats had criticised Coleridge's over-theorised abstraction, remarking that he 'would let go by a fine isolated verisimilitude caught from the Penetralium of mystery, from being incapable of remaining content with half knowledge' (*KL* I, 194); but *that* Coleridge, blinded by idealism and theory to the particular specifics of the world without, is suspiciously close to myth-Coleridge. Coleridge on the Heath, by contrast, seems almost parodically alert to a diversity of truths and possible truths, almost helplessly unable to let *anything* 'go by': indeed, he might even seem to emulate rather well the quality of mind with which Keats had, originally, unfavourably contrasted him ('*Negative Capability*, that is when a man is capable of being in uncertainties, Mysteries, doubts, without any irritable reaching after fact & reason': *KL* I, 193–4). The most obvious characteristic of Coleridge's speech on the Heath is also the most important: its abundant plurality ('a thousand things'); the immense range of diverse subjects covered. Keats's listing letter reads like one of the more expansive headings in *Table Talk*: 'Mr Coleridge's Philosophy – Sublimity – Solomon – Madness – C. Lamb – Sforza's Decision', or 'Humour and Genius – Great Poets Good Men – Diction of the Old and New Testament version – Hebrew – Vowels and Consonants' (*TT* II, 179, 254). And this kind of apparently bewildering transition from subject to subject is recorded elsewhere too: 'We then got, I know not how, to German topics', as a puzzled nephew wrote, not an untypical response (*IR*, 136). Attributing precise and undeviating 'Method' to such displays often takes a generous leap. Sitting through one of Coleridge's more rambling lectures, Charles Lamb withheld the benefit of the doubt, but showed a kind of generosity all the same: 'when Coleridge was running from topic to topic, Lamb said, "This is not much amiss. He promised a lecture on the Nurse in 'Romeo and Juliet,' and in its place he has given us one in the *manner* of the Nurse"' (*IR*, 151).

Keats's hostility to myth-Coleridge (and, perhaps, his warm indulgence of Coleridge on the Heath) springs from his own Hazlittian resistance to theory and system; and that antipathy towards all totalising or unifying philosophies has often been seen as the gist of 'Romanticism'.[16] This kind of disposition naturally ennobles talk as an expressive medium (as in Hazlitt's books, *Table Talk*, *The Plain Speaker*, *The Round Table*). Talk is the natural expression of open-ended, anti-systematic thought, for, as Robert Grant remarks (in the course of a discussion of Oakeshott's characterisation of conversation), it is not only 'an end in itself', but also 'endless... in being permanently inconclusive'.[17] Several commentators have used the paradigm of conversation to try and catch the essence of such anti-systematic thinking: Richard Rorty, for instance, distinguishes between 'therapeutic', 'edifying' philosophies and 'constructive', 'systematic' ones, the former aiming at 'continuing a conversation rather than at discovering truth'.[18] The idea of a 'conversation' philosophy has a happy coincidence with a poet known for 'Conversation' poems;[19] and Coleridge has accordingly been cast in that philosophical rôle, following an edifying route of 'anti-rationalism' and purposefully proceeding 'in a disorderly, miscellaneous fashion'.[20] For such a world-view, the everlasting, wandering processes of talk, not the finalised product of systematic account, is the only fitting medium.

But, of course, Coleridge was hardly so committed an irrationalist, nor so single-minded a pluralist: on the contrary, he espouses vehemently the opposing virtues of unity, wholeness, and system – everything, indeed, that a properly 'Romantic' diversitarian would most deplore; and he exhibits, at times, an almost disturbing antipathy to the simply plural, 'the universe itself... an immense heap of *little* things' (*CL* I, 349). An occasionally overwhelming sense that such multitudinousness must be controlled or tamed – whether it be by the Imagination of poets ('Gods of Love who tame the Chaos': *CN* II, 2355) or by the metaphysical Will ('whose function it is to controul, determine, and modify the phantasmal chaos of association': *BL* I, 116) – recurs again and again in Coleridge's thought. The imagery of rivers, which I mentioned before, is natural enough if you are describing 'an unfailing flow' (*IR*, 223) in someone's speech ('For nearly two hours he spoke with unhesitating and uninterrupted fluency': *IR*, 118): it lends itself naturally to describing the associative stream of a consciousness properly belonging to the endlessly plural universe. But Coleridge deplored and distrusted the 'streamy Nature of Association, which Thinking = Reason, curbs & rudders' (*CN* I, 1770); and his river imagery often has other, rather different implications, implications wholly opposed to the continuous streamy plurality of the associating mind, suggesting a quite different impulse prompting his talk.

Coleridge shared his refined watery idiom with Wordsworth, who used it gallantly in *The Prelude* to praise his friend's eminence; and there it described, not Coleridge's fluidly associative openness to the multiplicity of things, but, on the contrary, his instinctive grasp that, beneath its apparent plurality, the world is deeply one:

> But who shall parcel out
> His intellect, by geometric rules,
> Split like a province into round and square?
> Who knows the individual hour in which
> His habits were first sown, even as a seed?
> Who that shall point as with a wand, and say,
> 'This portion of the river of my mind
> Came from yon fountain?' Thou, my friend, art one
> More deeply read in thy own thoughts, no slave
> Of that false secondary power by which
> In weakness, we create distinctions, then
> Believe our puny boundaries are things
> Which we perceive, and not which we have made.
> To thee, unblinded by these outward shews,
> The unity of all has been revealed[.]
>
> (*Prelude* (1799), II, 243–65)

Here, the river subsumes the isolated elements perceived by a falsely discriminative consciousness into the unity of a single purposeful flow: the unity of the mind reflects the greater unity of reality at large. Washington Allston, whose own aesthetic writings show how much he absorbed from Coleridge, remembered:

> He used to call Rome 'the silent city', but I could never think of it as such while with him, for meet him when and where I would, the fountain of his mind was never dry, but, like the far-reaching aqueducts that once supplied this mistress of the world, its living stream seemed specially to flow for every classic ruin over which we wandered; and when I recall some of our walks under the pines of the Villa Borghese, I am almost tempted to dream that I have once listened to Plato in the groves of the Academy. (*IR*, 102)

– partly polite eulogy, no doubt, but the Platonic reference may well be more than casual, implying a broad kind of philosophical allegiance, somehow enacted in his conversational technique.

For Plato is Coleridge's great spokesman for unity; and Coleridge's most characteristic river metaphors for his talk express a Platonic opposition to the disparate disconnections of atomistic, separative thought which, he felt, had blighted the eighteenth century: the pseudo-philosophy of discrete 'ideas' and 'images' which had given rise to associationism. Just as Pope expressed this mind-set in verse, with his poetry a sterile '*conjunction disjunctive*, of epigrams' (*BL* I, 19), so Dr Johnson was its exemplary exponent in the art of conversation. '[H]ere I am returned quite Coleridgified', wrote Mitford, after a trip to London to hear Coleridge lecture, 'much in the same way, I suppose, as Boswell was after a visit to Johnson' (*IR*, 155); but Coleridge would have been only half-pleased with the comparison, since he judged the very transcribability of Johnson's talk to mark the limits of his genius. (Of the 'bettermost sort of Remark of Dr Johnson's recorded by Boswell', he was only prepared to concede: 'a notable Flea-skip for so grave a Bug': *CN* III, 4104.) Disciples loyally followed the line: 'Boswell would have found his occupation gone at Highgate', wrote a young admirer, 'The genius of Coleridge very rarely broke out in those flashes of poignant satire and eloquence, that taught men to tremble before the Lion of Bolt Court' (*CT*, 363). The contrast that Coleridge drew between the 'short sharp things' of Johnson's 'bow-wow manner' and the sublimity of Burke, who 'like all men of Genius who love to talk at all, was very discursive and continuous' (*TT* I, 405), is transparently intended to be self-vindicatory. There is a certain pathos (even if it is tinged with sour grapes) in basing your superiority on your non-memorability, no doubt, which Coleridge was ready to spot: 'As Conversationalists is not S.T.C. [compared with] Dr Johnson as Eol[ian] Harp is to Single Drum[?] Hence the stores of remembered Sayings of the latter – while S.T.C. sparks / Sparks that fall upon a River, / A moment bright, then lost for ever'.[21] 'A true Boswell would have found ample matter for record', said Thomas Colley Grattan (*IR*, 258); but a true *Boswell*, ears open for short sharp things, would have been at sea.

Coleridge's anti-Johnsonian awareness of the connectedness and inter-relatedness of the whole could only get expressed in the most comprehensively inclusive and totalising of systems: a system which would 'reduce all knowledges into harmony' (*TT* I, 248). Throughout his life he seriously entertained the most enormous ambitions for a *'last & great work'* (*CN* I, 1646), an authoritative philosophical system expressing his colossal and all-encompassing world-view. More precise conceptions of the work changed somewhat as his philosophical positions shifted about, but the looming presence of the unrealised master-work remained constant, pretty much throughout his thinking life, finally gathering around the much-laboured, never-finished *magnum opus*. Now, such a work is obviously quite at odds, as much at odds as can be, with the necessarily fragmentary, ad hoc, 'Improvisatore'-genre of *talk*; and yet, in practice, it was in talk, and in works emulating the virtues of his talk, and not in the great work, that Coleridge thrived. Stalled by the prospect of writing, he was liberated by the opportunity of talking (as H. N. C. reported: *IR*, 98). The gathering, centripetal activity of a system-builder, seeking for the unity beneath secondary divisions, dissipates into the endlessly multiple life of momentary, irresolved speech. This need not mean that Coleridge's ambitions for system failed through plain indolence, of course; less still that those ambitions were bogus: on the contrary, his talk would not have been the immense creative opportunity that it evidently was, had it not existed within a context of unfulfilled, but quite genuine, systematic ambitions. Thomas McFarland, in a remarkable essay, says the 'reflexive pressure of the *magnum opus* made the whole of Coleridge's prose achievement provisional in its nature'[22] – and what McFarland astutely implies there is the way the spirit of speech, rather than that of system, animates Coleridge's prose. Coleridge writes in (and of) the Notebook: 'I trust, that these Hints & first Thoughts, often too cogitabilia rather than actual cogitata a *me*, may not be understood as my fixed opinions – but merely as the suggestions of the disquisition; & acts of obedience to the apostolic command of Trying all things' (*CN* III, 3881). Such talk-like provisionality freed him from the obligation to be 'fixed', allowing him to write 'things thinkable' rather than 'things thought by *me*': the same saving evasion of the authorial 'I' that he enjoyed in *Table Talk*, a book he wrote without being its author.

Coleridge's fluent talk is his perfect medium, because in it the rival impulses of detail and whole (whose happy reconciliation is intimidatingly expected by his theory) are left free to exist in fruitful irresolution, their final methodical reconciliation endlessly deferred: the failure of system is re-experienced as an enabling virtue. Like his work at large (of which, indeed, it is the paradigm), the encompassingly erratic progress of his talk embraces in its moment-to-moment life quite opposing inclinations: the would-be systematic philosopher discovers in the open-ended contingency of speech an off-duty idiom, one which may express the untidied manyness of the world; but, as Coleridge used it, his talk could also intimate an abiding Platonic conviction of the connectedness of everything to everything. As usual, however, he is his own best analyst:[23]

There are two sorts of talkative fellows whom it would be injurious to confound / & I, S.T. Coleridge, am the latter. The first sort is those who use five hundred words more than needs to express an idea – that is not my case – few men, I will be bold to say, put more meaning into their words than I or choose them more deliberately & discriminatingly. The second sort is of those who use five hundred more ideas, images, reasons &c than there is any need of to arrive at their object / till the only object arrived at is that the reader's mind's eye of the bye-stander is dazzled with colours succeeding so rapidly as to leave one vague impression that there has been a great Blaze of colours all about something. Now this is my case – & a grievous fault it is / my illustrations swallow up my thesis – I feel too intensely the omnipresence of all in each, platonically speaking – or psychologically my brain fibres, or the spiritual Light which abides in thate brain marrow as visible Light appears to do in sundry rotten mackerel & other *smashy* matters, is of too general an affinity with all things / and tho' it perceives the *difference* of things, yet is eternally pursuing the likenessnesses, or rather that which is common / bring me two things that seem the very same, & then I am quick enough to shew the difference, even to hair-splitting – but to go on from circle to circle till I break against the shore of my Hearer's patience, or have my Concentricals dashed to nothing by a Snore – that is my ordinary mishap. (*CN* II, 2372)

If you understand the Platonic 'unity of all', digressiveness is redeemed, for genuine irrelevance becomes inconceivable (everything is related to everything else); and yet the desire to express a unified 'thesis' still persists. Just as his poetics (as they appear in 'On Poesy or Art') play off 'unity' against 'multeity', and the 'centripetal' against the 'centrifugal force',[24] so here, in his talk, a would-be singularity of argument finds itself sidetracked into vivid particulars. Intended to be subordinated to their illustrative function, they exceed their purpose and acquire for themselves an independent (delightful) existence. The interdependent tangle of the one and the many is entirely Coleridgean: an abundance of imagining keeps over-flowing the rectitude of a rigorous exposition; but such abundance cannot show itself without that thwarted ambition, for it only comes to mind thanks to the unity which it repeatedly bewilders.

It is a conversational 'failing', but also a kind of success. If you re-read the memoirs with this kind of formative dilemma in mind, it is very striking how often witnesses single out the power of his 'images', as well as the extraordinary range of his information – both forces to divert him from the expository straight and narrow. William Mudford found 'Coleridge, full of his subject, and his mind teeming with images, and facts, and illustrations' (*IR*, 180); Cowden Clarke remarked how 'the gorgeousness of his imagery would increase and dilate and flash forth such coruscations of similies [*sic*] and startling theories that one was in a perpetual aurora borealis of fancy' (*IR*, 208); 'I was less struck by the logic than by the beauty of the language, and the poetry of the images', James Fenimore Cooper admitted (*IR*, 220). Wordsworth, a brilliantly perceptive interpreter of Coleridge, picked up on the way this digressive, imagistic superfluity habitually submerged any unity of discursive purpose in an embarrassment of riches:

a majestic river, the sound of or sight of whose course you caught at intervals, which was sometimes concealed by forests, sometimes lost in sand, then came flashing out loud and distinct, then again took a turn which your eye could not follow, yet you knew and felt that it was the same river...there was always a connection between its parts in his own mind, though not one always perceptible to the minds of others. (*CT*, 379–80)

Much the same sense of productive conflict – between the great unified arc of argument and the distracting local delights along its course – animates De Quincey's justly famous account:

Coleridge, to many people, and often I have heard the complaint, seemed to wander; and he seemed then to wander the most, when in fact his resistance to the wandering instinct was the greatest, – viz. when the compass, and huge circuit, by which his illustrations moved, travelled farthest into remote regions, before they began to revolve. Long before this coming-round commenced, most people had lost him, and naturally enough supposed that he had lost himself. They continued to admire the separate beauty of the thoughts, but did not see their relations to the dominant theme. Had the conversation been thrown upon paper, it might have been easy to trace the continuity of the links; just as in Bishop Berkeley's Siris, from a pedestal so low and abject, so culinary, as Tar Water, the method of preparing it, and its medicinal effects, the dissertation ascends, like Jacob's ladder, by just gradations, into the Heaven of Heavens, and the thrones of the Trinity. But Heaven is there connected with earth by the Homeric chain of gold; and being subject to steady examination, it is easy to trace the links. Whereas, in conversation, the loss of a single word may cause the whole cohesion to disappear from view. However, I can assert, upon my long and intimate knowledge of Coleridge's mind, that logic, the most severe, was as inalienable from his modes of thinking, as grammar from his language.

(IR, 113–14)

De Quincey is being kind, attributing to Coleridge an undeniable success; but he suggests as he does so the way that Coleridge's pluralistic attention to detail might well find itself in a more conflictual relationship with any overall sense of purpose.

Transient as the medium was, his conversation clearly lingered enough to influence many of the best young minds of the next generation. Wordsworth thought so (CT, 378–9); and Coleridge defended himself on similar grounds, maintaining (reasonably) that he had 'atchieved [sic] ten fold more' by conversation 'than by all my public Efforts, from the Press or the Lecture-Desk' (CL v, 310). But the most lasting performances of his conversational inconsequence, of course, were those approximations that made it into print. His prose works, especially, strive to maintain the digressive capacity of a spoken language, a fact which made them especially liable to criticism from practitioners of a straighter-lined prose. Southey lamented the way that Coleridge wrote 'in so rambling and inconclusive a manner; while I, who am utterly incapable of that toil of thought in which he delights, never fail to express myself perspicuously, and to the point' (IR, 126); and contributed (at Coleridge's request) a letter to the Friend, detailing the complaint: 'do you not yourself sometimes nose out your way, hound-like, in pursuit of truth, turning and winding, and doubling and running when the same object might be reached in a tenth part of the time by darting straightforward like a greyhound to the mark?' (Friend ii, 498–9). 'I do not care twopence for the Hare', Coleridge later said, in private, 'but I value most highly the excellencies of the scent, patience, discrimination, free Activity; and find a Hare in every Nettle, I make myself acquainted with' (*CL* v, 98): 'free Activity' there is something like the informal life of speech, with its inclusive qualifications and sidetracks. '[A] book of reasoning without parentheses' implied 'a *friable* intellect' (*CL* iv, 685), a discontinuous intellect like Dr Johnson's: Coleridgean parentheses, contrariwise, are designed to enact 'the *drama* of Reason – & present the thought growing' (*CL* iii, 282).

If Coleridge was prone to monologue, then, it was (so to say) monologue of a peculiarly dialogical kind: 'he seemed to be addressing, not the auditors, but replying to his own thoughts' (*CT*, 129). S. C. Hall indulgently observed: 'probably there has never been an author who was less of an egotist: it was never of himself he talked' (*IR*, 184); and Coleridge sought, not dissimilarly, to excuse his apparently self-assertive boisterousness to Thelwall by explaining how he became 'ever so swallowed up in the *thing*, that I perfectly forget my *opponent*' (*CL* i, 260) – and not only in the thing, you might add, but in the relations of the thing too. Hazlitt's mockery of the Shandyesque incapacity at show in *Biographia* is the unkind description of a real quality. *Tristram Shandy* is famous for digression, a play between the would-be purposefulness of the narrative line that Tristram seeks to pursue, and the proliferation of absorbing details, incidents, and qualifications that obstruct that path. *Biographia*, similarly, sidetracks its own progress into digressions, parentheses, lengthy footnotes, incidental chapters, self-interrupting changes of idiom, assumed voices, anticipated objections – all seeking to replicate the capaciously self-checking, self-distracting rhythms of Coleridge's talk. Freed from the duty to be the great system by its self-declared provisionality, *Biographia* surreptitiously becomes the masterpiece of the Coleridgean voice which the *magnum opus* could never be. In *Biographia*, as in his talk, the rival perceptions of reality which his reconciliatory theory sought to unite could find the properly wavering expression of their running irresolution.

And with such matters in mind, the term ' "Conversation" poem' might seem to signify a little more than merely the attempt to capture for verse a speaking tone: for in those poems, the rival tugs that Coleridge identifies in the wandering life of his own talk are formalised and cast as poetry. The poems articulate quite diverse visions of nature: the naturalist's perception of concrete realities, on the one hand, an over-arching sense of sublimely inclusive unity, on the other; and, for the spoken length of the poem, the visions converse. The fluent, knowing play between imagistic manyness and hopeful oneness enacts in metre the rhythms of Coleridgean consciousness that found spontaneous expression in his speech: 'a recognition and a re-sistance', in Geoffrey Hill's words, 'it is parenthetical, antiphonal, it turns upon itself'.[25]

NOTES

1 *CL* vi, 969.
2 Cf. John Beer, 'Coleridge and Wordsworth: Influence and Confluence', *New Approaches to Coleridge: Biographical and Critical Essays*, ed. Donald Sultana (London: Vision, 1981), 192–211.
3 Cf. Morton D. Paley, *Portraits of Coleridge* (Oxford: Clarendon Press, 1999), 124–5.
4 *The Posthumous Works of Thomas De Quincey*, ed. Alexander H. Japp, 2 vols. (London: Heinemann, 1891–3), ii, 17, 17–18.
5 Theodore Zeldin, *Conversation: How Talk can Change your Life* (London: Harvill, 1998; repr., 1999), 5–6.
6 *Posthumous Works of Thomas De Quincey*, ii, 18.
7 *The Spectator*, ed. Donald F. Bond, 5 vols. (Oxford: Clarendon Press, 1965), iv, 4.
8 To his son, 19 October OS 1748: *The Letters of Philip Dormer Stanhope Fourth Earl of Chesterfield*, ed. Bonamy Dobrée, 6 vols. (London: Eyre and Spottiswode, 1932), iv, 1245. See Peter Burke, *The Art of Conversation* (Cambridge: Polity Press, 1993), 111, where Steele and Chesterfield are also quoted.
9 Armour and Howes offer a defence, and dispute Coleridge's reputation as an unbroken monologuist: *CT*, 81–3.
10 Jennifer Coates, 'The Construction of a Collaborative Floor in Women's Friendly Talk', *Conversation: Cognitive, Communicative and Social Perspectives*, ed. T. Givón (Amsterdam/Philadelphia: Benjamins, 1997), 55–89, p. 55.
11 *Coleridge: The Critical Heritage*, ed. J. R. de J. Jackson (London: Routledge and Kegan Paul, 1970), 251.
12 This is a paradox that Raymond Williams worries over at amusing length in his book on Orwell, one of the great practitioners of conversational idiom. Hazlitt was taciturn as a young man by his own admission ('On My First Acquaintance with Poets'); his later manner was rebarbative enough even to alienate at times the saintly and fiercely loyal Lamb. E. V. Lucas judges Hazlitt to have been 'positively anti-social': *The Life of Charles Lamb*, 2 vols. (London: Methuen, 1905), i, 250.
13 I am gratefully following Armour and Howes: 'That Coleridge was basically a talker is an interpretation suggested by numerous critics but never fully explored. Thoroughly understood, it projects a unifying concept into the seeming chaos of his intellectual life. It also offers the key to many difficulties presented by his printed works' (*CT*, 22).
14 He inspired talk in others too, if there is anything to the comical story repeated by Maginn (*IR*, 242–3).
15 Michael Ignatieff, *Isaiah Berlin. A Life* (London: Chatto and Windus, 1998), 3–4. Cf. A. C. Goodson's remark, 'For Coleridge, conversation reflected habits of mind; it was only as interesting as the informing intelligence': A. C. Goodson, ed., *Coleridge's Writings. Vol. III: On Language* (Basingstoke: Macmillan, 1998), 3–4.
16 A. O. Lovejoy influentially suggested that Romanticism holds that 'not only are there diverse excellences, but that diversity itself is of the essence of excellence': 'Optimism and Romanticism', *Publication of the Modern Language Association of America*, 42 (1927), 921–45, p. 943. Cf. F. W. Bateson, *A Guide to*

English Literature, 2nd edn (London: Longman, 1967; rev. repr., 1970), 146–7. The argument is furthered in several works by Isaiah Berlin – e.g. 'The Apotheosis of the Romantic Will' in his *The Crooked Timber of Humanity: Chapters in the History of Ideas*, ed. Henry Hardy (London: Murray, 1990), 207–37.

17 Robert Grant, *Oakeshott* (London: Claridge Press, 1990), 65.

18 Richard Rorty, *Philosophy and the Mirror of Nature* (Oxford: Basil Blackwell, 1980), 5, 373.

19 As Stephen Bygrave says: *Coleridge and the Self. Romantic Egotism* (Basingstoke: Macmillan, 1986), 81.

20 Kathleen M. Wheeler, *Romanticism, Pragmatism and Deconstruction* (Oxford: Basil Blackwell, 1993), xi, 16.

21 Quoted in Kathleen Coburn, ed., *Inquiring Spirit: A New Presentation of Coleridge from his Published and Unpublished Prose Writings* (London: Routledge and Kegan Paul, 1951), 185.

22 Thomas McFarland, *Romanticism and the Forms of Ruin: Wordsworth, Coleridge, and Modalities of Fragmentation* (Princeton University Press, 1981), 343.

23 I discuss part of this entry along much the same lines in Seamus Perry, *Coleridge and the Uses of Division* (Oxford: Clarendon Press, 1999), 93–4.

24 'On Poesy or Art', in S. T. Coleridge, *Biographia Literaria . . . with his Aesthetical Essays*, ed. J. Shawcross, 2 vols. (Oxford: Clarendon Press, 1907) II, 262.

25 Geoffrey Hill, *The Lords of Limit: Essays on Literature and Ideas* (London: Deutsch, 1984), 94.

8

DEIRDRE COLEMAN

The journalist

When I hear of the French casting *cannon*, I think nothing of that at all,
provided you can only prevent them from casting *types*.
(Charles Stuart to Henry Dundas, 1793)[1]

When it came to the power and influence of the daily press, and the crucial
role of newspaper offices in supplying politicians with the latest intelligence,
especially in war-time, Charles Stuart knew what he was talking about. One
of a trio of entrepreneurial Scottish brothers who descended on London
in the 1780s to make their fortunes in printing and publishing, Charles was
firmly and lucratively ensconced in the pay of the Treasury, as was his brother
Peter, proprietor of a ministerial paper and eager servant of whatever party
was in power.[2] The third brother was Daniel Stuart, editor–proprietor of the
Morning Post, the daily London newspaper whose founding in 1772 has been
described as one of the most significant events in the history of journalism.[3]
When Stuart purchased the *Morning Post* in 1795 its circulation had declined
to 350 copies per day. Within three years, he had increased this to 2,000 copies
per day, reaching an unprecedented sale of 4,500 copies per day in 1803, the
year he sold it and bought the evening paper, the *Courier*. Coleridge wrote
prose and verse for both of Daniel Stuart's newspapers, but his best efforts
were for the *Morning Post* during its period of spectacular recovery,[4] starting
with poetry contributions in 1797 and rising to essays and leading columns in
1800. So successful were Coleridge's essays at this time, particularly his astute
psychological anatomy of William Pitt (March 1800), that he appears to have
been offered a proprietary interest in the paper (*EOT* 1, lx). David Erdman
has collected together Coleridge's prose contributions to both the *Morning
Post* and the *Courier* in three substantial volumes, and written a lengthy and
fascinating introduction, tracking the mazy and sometimes tortuous twists
and turns of Coleridge's early political engagement, as he struggled to remain
an admirer of the French Revolution whilst deploring France's invasion of
Switzerland in 1798. A simple way of measuring the oscillating temperature

of Coleridge's politics at this time, from violently red-hot to temperate, is to read the two poems he contributed to the *Morning Post* within three months of each other: 'Fire, Famine, and Slaughter' (January 1798) and 'Recantation: An Ode' (April 1798) (see *CPW* I, 237–40, 243–7).

The political fray, the speed of print circulation, the power and influence of newpaper writing: all these were as powerfully attractive to Coleridge as to the Stuart brothers. This is particularly clear in the mid-1790s, when Coleridge stepped forward as a radical young lecturer, preacher, and journalist. In a lecture of 1795, attacking the two recent Government Bills designed to restrict the right of assembly and the free discussion (and publication) of political issues, he declared himself stoutly for the unfettered liberty of the press and freedom of speech. The evil of the Gagging Acts (as they were popularly called) lay in their destruction of the nation's entire nervous system: 'By the almost winged communication of the Press, the whole nation becomes one grand Senate, fervent yet untumultuous . . . By the operation of Lord Grenville's Bill, the Press is made useless. Every town is insulated: the vast conductors are destroyed by which the electric fluid of truth was conveyed from man to man, and nation to nation' (*Lects. 1795*, 313).[5] For certain ruling-class observers, however, Coleridge's 'fluid of truth' was a toxic substance inciting the lower classes to sedition and insurrection. Nor did the influence of the press seem confined (as Coleridge suggests) to the international, European scene; some believed it even operated at the imperial margins. In the 1788 debate in the House of Lords on a Bill to regulate the trade in and transport of African slaves, the Duke of Chandos complained that in Jamaica the 'negroes read the English newspapers as constantly as the ships from England came in'. From the debates in both Houses they would (he regretted) be tempted to conclude that their emancipation was at hand.[6]

Coleridge's excitement about the speed and reach of newspaper influence peaked at the very moment Wordsworth was decrying the reading public's 'craving for extraordinary incident which the rapid communication of intelligence hourly gratifies'.[7] But what particularly captivated Coleridge in 1800 was the flattering reflection that what the individual journalist 'writes at 12 at night will before 12 hours is over have perhaps 5 or 6000 Readers! . . . Few Wine merchants can boast of creating more sensation.' The intoxification was at its most intense when words approximated political deeds, when (as Coleridge boasted to one correspondent in 1800) he could hear bandied about his own 'particular phrases in the House of Commons' as if he were 'grand Monopolist of all good Reasons!' (*CL* I, 569).[8] Coleridge's self-aggrandisement as journalist could sometimes assume grotesque proportions, such as the suggestion that his *Morning Post* essays had been single-handedly responsible for re-starting the war between England and France in 1802, or his claim that, when he was in Italy in 1806, Napoleon was determined to hunt him down and punish him personally.[9] But the odd moment of high drama could not make up for the many flat times, when journalism seemed nothing more than pure drudgery: 'We Newspaper scribes are true Galley-Slaves – when the high winds of Events blow loud & frequent, then the Sails are hoisted, or the Ship drives on of itself – when all is calm & Sunshine, then to our oars' (CL 1, 569). At such times journalism was no more than a 'bread and beef' occupation, 'the absolute necessity of scribbling prose' in conflict with the higher and more enduring achievements of, say, poetry or philosophy (CL 1, 635, 545). Even the 'immediate, & wide impression' guaranteed by speedy circulation was often, Coleridge had to concede, only 'transitory' (CL 1, 582). Frequently troubled by the ephemeral nature of journalism, he considered a pamphlet re-issue of his *Morning Post* essays (CL 1, 627), and even book publication of his most admired pieces, to be entitled 'The Men and the Times' (CN 1, 1577, 1646).

Neither plan materialised, principally because of Coleridge's ambivalence about the 'trade' of journalism, and the accompanying suspicion that his newspaper essays for the *Post* and the *Courier* were not worth collecting (CL 1, 623), a view seconded by E. P. Thompson in our own time.[10] By referring to the '*Press as a Trade*' Coleridge meant 'reviewing, newspaper-writing, and all those things in which I proposed no fame to myself or permanent good to Society' (CL 1, 372). Despite his denigration of paid writing as inferior to the pursuit of fame and the greater good of society, Coleridge was not greatly troubled by the close link between writing and commerce. Of course, like all professional writers, he jibbed at the dependency upon 'Vampire Booksellers' and 'Scorpion Critics' (CL 1, 185), but he knew he possessed marketable skills, and in the early years he insisted on the proper fee for his hire. When James Perry of the *Morning Chronicle* invited him to London to write for him in 1796, Coleridge declined, suspecting that the editor wanted to employ him 'as a mere Hireling without any *proportionate* Share of the Profits' (CL 1, 226). With so many editors in the pay of political factions, hired writing was an on-going and very real pressure, exposing one to great anxieties and uncertainties, and 'many temptations to do evil', Coleridge confessed; it also made it difficult to preserve 'a delicacy of moral feeling and moral perception' (CL 1, 376). This vexed issue of independence became especially acute later in his life, during periods of illness or low confidence, leading Thompson to conclude that 'Coleridge never used his opportunities in the national press; he was always *used*.'[11] One such low point was 1811, the year he wrote for T. G. Street's *Courier*, a newspaper generally regarded at this time as 'a vane fixed on the pivot of ministerial policy'.[12]

Finally, writing for a newspaper, whether his own or someone else's, involved Coleridge in the pressure of deadlines, the hasty business of having 'to publish as well as to compose extempore', without time for second thoughts and revision. Although he conceded the necessity of deadlines in order to complete a task, Coleridge projected himself as temperamentally unsuited to task work: 'O way-ward and desultory Spirit of Genius! ill canst thou brook a task-master! The tenderest touch from the hand of *Obligation* wounds thee, like a scourge of Scorpions!' (*CL* I, 186).

In addition to writing for the two big London dailies, the *Morning Post* and the *Courier*, Coleridge ran two newspapers of his own, the *Watchman* (1796) and the *Friend* (1809–10). Both were weeklies, although the *Watchman* was published every eighth day in order to avoid the stamp-tax (*BL* I, 179), an improvisation which was to become characteristic of the versatile and expanding radical weekly press in the early nineteenth century.[13] Although written in very different circumstances, with different aims and audiences in mind, there are some striking links between these two newspapers, particularly in terms of the very personal way in which they pitch themselves to targeted audiences. The two papers are also linked through Coleridge's concern to argue for the continuities and consistency of his political position over the years. Notably, he paid tribute in the *Friend* to the impossible idealism of Pantisocracy, the utopian scheme devised by himself and Robert Southey to settle an egalitarian community on the banks of the Susquehanna. Visionary and strange this idea may have been 'yet to the intense interest and impassioned zeal, which called forth and strained every faculty of my intellect for the organization and defence of this Scheme, I owe much of whatever I at present possess, my clearest insight into the nature of individual Man, and my most comprehensive views of his social relations' (*Friend* II, 146–7). Coleridge's journalistic activities during 1794 and 1795 were crucial to the 'organization and defence' of Pantisocracy. There was, of course, the question of financing the scheme, and the Bristol lectures of 1795 on politics, religion and history were explicitly designed with that purpose in mind. But, more importantly, Coleridge's profound commitment to the pantisocratic ideal entailed intensive philosophical and moral thinking about the nature of the self and contemporary society, speculations which fuelled and shaped his activities at this time. Nor, when Southey's departure for Portugal definitively scuppered the Susquehanna Pantisocratic scheme in mid 1795, did Coleridge cease to hope that he might re-establish Pantisocracy, albeit in a new guise. The geographical location of Pantisocracy had already migrated, from America to a farm in Wales, so there was nothing to stop Coleridge wishing for 'a Pantisocracy in England' too, as he confided to a friend in March 1795 (*CL* I, 155). But in the end, Pantisocracy was about not so much an ideal location as an ideal of male friendship. For Coleridge, friendship, intimate and domestic, was the necessary starting-point of social life, 'the *center* of the Ball' which would then grow bigger in time, fostered by warm feelings of benevolence and philanthropy: 'I love my *Friend* – such as *he* is, all mankind are or *might be*!' (*CL* I, 86).

This highly personal and idealistic view of friendship coloured much of Coleridge's thinking, including his reflections on the dynamics of the writer–reader relationship. Much has been written of the transition in the eighteenth century from a system of patronage to that of the impersonal commercial marketplace, but both of Coleridge's newspapers involved the informal and often generous patronage of friends, together with subscription schemes which were designed to deliver a fraternity of like-minded supporters, bonded together in brotherly love. At the heart of each subscription scheme were known friends, sympathetic to Coleridge's aims, who would either personally sign up their friends or at least pave the way for Coleridge to do so. After the demise of Pantisocracy in the mid 1790s, Coleridge attempted to reconstitute its communitarianism, intimacy and friendship through what Jon Klancher has called 'an alternative society of the text'.[14] No scheme was fool-proof against reader rejection, but in the rapidly expanding world of print Coleridge needed to feel that he knew his readers, that they had in some way been hand-picked for him, and that he had their unwavering confidence and support. This is particularly true of the period after Coleridge's return from Malta in 1806. The experimental design for his weekly newspaper the *Friend*, printed on stamped paper so as to go free to all parts of the Kingdom, reflects a dogged determination to 'find dispersedly what [he] could not hope to meet with collectively' (*Friend* II, 273), a community of élite readers who preferred instruction to amusement, and who did not shrink from hard brainwork.[15] Incongruous as the newspaper format was for Coleridge's weighty and difficult essays, instant circulation offered him the chance of interacting with his readers in a 'friendly' way, monitoring and even taking into account their responses as the weeks passed. Daniel Stuart, irritated by his friend's newspaper ambitions, accused Coleridge of an unworthy 'desire of producing on the public and receiving on yourself an instant impression' (*Friend* II, 493), but it was not so much vanity as imperative psychological need which propelled Coleridge to undertake his strange experiment. For unlike Wordsworth who had the confidence and equanimity to look to posterity, believing that every great and original writer needed to create the audience by which he was to be appreciated, Coleridge craved the approval of his contemporaries. On his own admission, his was 'no self-subsisting Mind' but prone to 'faint away inwardly, self-deserted & bereft of the confidence in my own powers...the approbation & Sympathy of good & intelligent men is my Sea-breeze, without which I would languish from Morn to evening' (*CN* II, 1054).

Throughout 1794 Coleridge and Southey spawned numerous plans for either selling their poetry to magazines and journals, or working as news-paper reporters. They also planned to start their own periodicals, one of which was to be called the *Citizen*, the other the *Provincial Magazine*. None of these plans came to very much, except the series of lectures delivered by the two young men in Bristol between January and June 1795. Coleridge's anti-war, anti-ministerial lectures appear to have caused a sensation. One news-paper trumpeted that 'he spoke in public what none had the courage in this city to do before, – he told Men that they have Rights' (*Lects. 1795*, xxxi); for this he incurred the 'furious and determined' antagonism of the Tories, but at the same time he became the darling of the oppositionists, so much so that when it came to setting up the *Watchman* Coleridge benefited enormously from the patronage of some of Bristol's leading Unitarian friends and fellow liberals. The alternative society which they offered Coleridge at this time was not just humanitarian, liberal and progressive; it was also a close-knit society with important links to the world of publishing and the book trade.[16] An initial subscription fund enabled him to travel across the Midlands early in 1796, carrying with him letters of introduction which opened many doors throughout the well-off manufacturing towns of Worcester, Birmingham, Derby, Nottingham and Sheffield. Wherever he went he found himself feted, even 'marvellously caressed' (*CL* I, 179). The cynosure of all eyes, he was 'the figurante of the circle', a ballet-dancer performing on demand. And whereas in Bristol he had been criticised for his slovenly person – lecturing in dirty stockings and sporting uncombed hair (*Lects. 1795*, xxx) – on the subscription tour he boasted that he 'christianized' himself, i.e. 'washed and changed' before meeting potential supporters (*CL* I, 175).

The year 1795, the year in which Coleridge lectured and planned for the *Watchman*, formed a precious interlude between euphoria and repression. At the end of 1794, the dissenting radicals Thomas Hardy, Horne Tooke and John Thelwall had been tried by the State for treason and acquitted. A year later there would be renewed persecution in the shape of the Gagging Acts (November 1795), designed ('for the safety of his majesty's person') to stamp out seditious meetings. In the lull between, there is an ebullience and seamlessness to Coleridge's political and religious activities. Lecturing was a form of sermonising (and vice versa), and popular oratory merged into journalism. Already famous for his eloquence, Coleridge's 'talk' spilled over into print, creating many points of connection between the 1795 lectures and the *Watchman*. He even recycled some of his more successful and flamboyant lectures, such as the one against the slave trade, originally delivered in a

Bristol coffee-house on the Quay, within sight and sound of that prosperous city's slaving ships.[17] Boycotting the consumption of sugar was one of the popular means of undermining the trade, a strategy Coleridge buttressed with unforgettably Gothic images of the guilty sipping tea 'sweetened with Brother's Blood', an act accompanied, not with music, but with shrieks and groanings, 'and the loud peals of the lash!' (*Watchman*, 139). There were also good legal reasons for translating talk into print. His first public lecture he was '*obliged* to publish, it having been confidently asserted that there was Treason in it' (*CL* I, 152). Although he claimed that the lecture was 'printed as it was delivered', he probably tempered some of its sentiments, for while publication was a safeguard against misrepresentation, it was also more risky than talk because more permanent. Later in the year, he revised it again under the new, lofty title of *Conciones Ad Populum, or Addresses to the People*. The blurring here of sermon and political address can be seen in the title of his pamphlet (a 'concio ad clerum' was a Latin sermon), but there was no blurring of its political message, the Preface declaring: 'Truth should be spoken at all times, but more especially at those times, when to speak Truth is dangerous' (*Lects. 1795*, 27).

In the *Watchman*'s Prospectus, Coleridge advertised himself as the radical author of *Conciones* and 'The Plot Discovered', his incisive tract against the 'ministerial treason' of the Gagging Acts. He also selected a motto which continued the earlier emphasis on truth: 'That All may know the Truth; and that the Truth may make us free!' Determined to be the voice of opposition in the provinces, which were not well served except with ministerial rags, Coleridge unapologetically declared that the entire orientation of the *Watchman* was to be political; even its original essays and poetry, designed to complement the Parliamentary reports and the international and domestic news, were to be 'chiefly or altogether political' (*Watchman*, 5). Paradoxically, the emphasis on the daily-ness and immediacy of his newspaper's concerns co-existed with a concern for permanence, evident in the octavo format of the *Watchman*; the newspaper's Prospectus informs us that, whilst individual numbers would look and appear 'as regularly as a Newspaper' they could be 'bound up at the end of the year' so as to become 'an Annual Register', a less perishable and therefore more attractive 'vehicle' for 'Men of Letters' whose contributions he hoped to publish (*Watchman*, 5).

The years 1794–6 were famine years, with wheat more than doubling in price between May and July 1795,[18] hence the emotive topos of hunger running through every number of the *Watchman*. Brilliantly, and dangerously, Coleridge links the scarcity, not to the failure of crops, but to an unjust war begun and supported 'by the rich and powerful' against the interests of the poor (*Watchman*, 54). For instance, the fashion for hair-powder, made of flour, is linked to the shortage of bread, a seemingly preposterous connection until it is pointed out that the tax on the powder funds the war, a war which has caused the dearth in the first place. Similarly, in the high-spirited 'Essay on Fasts' (March 1796) which lost Coleridge so many subscribers, he introduced a topical joke into his discussion of fasting as one of the impurities introduced into Christianity by prelacy. Linking hunger to the Gagging Acts with a pun, he protested that 'by two recent Acts of Parliament the mouths of the poor have been *made fast* already' (*Watchman*, 54).[19] Finally, hunger is linked both to insurrection and to the annihilation of the family as society's fundamental unit; this seemed especially true of Ireland's 'starving, oppressed, and degraded' peasants: 'If a man who labours from morning till night cannot *earn* bread to eat for himself and family, the bond of protection and obedience, the very end of society is broken' (*Watchman*, 118).

Despite the democratic egalitarianism and universalism of the *Watchman*'s motto, 'That All may know the Truth; and that the Truth may make us free!', there were some for whom truth needed careful exposition, and others who were not qualified at all to receive it. The shilling fee at the door of his public lectures, designed 'to keep out blackguards', had already demonstrated some exclusivity (*Lects. 1795*, xxxi), and the *Watchman* was to continue the lecturer's cautious policy of pleading '*for* the Oppressed, not *to* them' (*Lects. 1795*, 43). Coleridge's desire to address a polite rather than popular audience reflects the uncomfortably close connection for him at this time between intellectual radicalism and the popular societies, an anxiety exacerbated by his disbelief that truth could be smoothly communicated downwards from the educated to the labouring classes. Unlike Godwin, for whom society resembled a continuously linked chain along which truth moved without rupture, Coleridge firmly believed that connection and conversation only took place amongst the upper ranks, ' "the Nobility, Gentry, and People of Dress" '. Playfully mocking this fashionable group by attributing their description to a Perfumer's advertisement,[20] Coleridge nevertheless proceeds to make a serious point: 'But alas! between the Parlour and the Kitchen, the Tap and the Coffee-Room – there is a gulph that may not be passed' (*Lects. 1795*, 43). Writers in this period had a habit of characterising the class status of reading audiences according to where the act of reading took place, so Coleridge's paired oppositions of private and public space are revealing. For members of the ruling class, the taproom – that part of an alehouse where labouring-class men did their serious drinking and socialising – was one of the most feared and stigmatised sites of plebeian culture, with alehouses typically associated in the 1790s with conspiratorial and seditious Jacobinism.[21] The coffee-house functions as the opposite in Coleridge's rhetoric, a site for the dissemination of news, certainly, but also for polite conversation and genteel sociability. When writing for the *Morning Post* in 1800, for instance, Coleridge confessed to Stuart that he tailored his style to an imagined co-hort of '[Lond]on Coffee house men & breakfast-table People of Quality'. While feeling a certain condescension towards the fashionable world of coffee-house philosophers and politicians, none of whom would welcome the rigours of 'austerest metaphysical [re]asoning' (*CL* I, 627), Coleridge was obliged to concede their respectability and ply his trade of authorship amongst them. How accurately he imagined his newspaper audience in 1800 is questionable, however, for when his friend Thomas Poole offered Stuart an essay critical of male servants for their 'encroachments . . . on the employ-ments of women',[22] Stuart rejected it for the following reasons: 'The Livery Servants are a numerous body and very powerful among the Purchasers of the Morning Post. Very few families purchase a Newspaper which is not first read by the Servants, and their influence is great with respect to the circulation of Papers; at least their hostility might be very dangerous' (*EOT* III, 165).

The public house appears in the first number of the *Watchman* as the undesirable alternative to the private, domestic fire-side. Too poor to buy his own newspaper, the labourer flies to the alehouse for the news of the day, only to find biassed, ministerial prints; his opinions are then corrupted, he falls into bad company, and 'contracts habits of drunkenness and sloth' (*Watchman*, 11). Thus the taxes which make newspapers a luxury, and the alehouse which opens the world of print to the poor man, constitute serious 'impediments to the diffusion of Knowledge'. Coleridge then proceeds to out-line the various means by which Providence counteracts these impediments, such as the 'large manufactories' where 'it is the custom for a newspaper to be regularly read'. At this point in his argument, faced with the vision of a large gathering of working men, 'whose passions are frequently inflamed by drunkenness', the 'coil of resistance' lurking in any Coleridgean commitment issues in an abrupt reverse,[23] with the hated Gagging Acts invoked positively for their potential to 'render the language of political publications more cool and guarded, or even confine us for a while to the teaching of first princi-ples, or the diffusion of that general knowledge which should be the basis or substratum of politics' (*Watchman*, 13–14). Ultimately, Coleridge's fear of an unruly, uneducated, potentially violent mob moved him from youthful visions of the whole nation as one 'grand Senate', united by a free press, to middle-aged rumblings in 1814 against 'malcontents and pot-wise senators of alehouses' (*EOT* II, 377).

From the start the *Watchman* advertised itself as a miscellany, inviting its readers to become writers in a democratic and communal fashion, as though it were indeed a 'spacious coffee-house': 'The Miscellany is open to all *ingenious* men whatever their opinions may be', Coleridge informed his readers (*Watchman*, 197).[24] This openness is paraded in Number v where Coleridge reprints an abusive letter by 'Caius Gracchus' which had been published in the *Bristol Gazette*. In refutation of Caius Gracchus's charges of prejudice and illiberality, Coleridge protests: 'I ought to be considered in two characters – as the Editor of the Miscellany, and as a frequent Contributor', a double role which enabled him to welcome criticism on the principle that 'where the poison is, there the antidote may be' (*Watchman*, 197). But despite Coleridge's protestations that the *Watchman* was an open forum for a free and frank exchange of views, he ran out of patience with his readers, and the alternative society of the text failed to materialise. Complaining about the conflicting demands upon him, with some readers wanting only political news and debates, and others calling for more poetry and less 'democratic scurrility' (*CL* I, 202, 195), Coleridge suddenly realised he was no longer the 'figurante of the circle'; indeed, he had been upstaged by his audience, with the average 'Subscriber instead of regarding himself as a point in the circumference entitled to some one diverging ray, considers me as the circumference & himself as the Centre to which *all* the rays ought to converge' (*CL* I, 202).

Coleridge's oscillation at this time between egalitarian and hierarchical concepts of the writer–reader compact was paralleled stylistically in the contrast between the *Watchman*'s meek and neutral persona, outlined in Number I, and Coleridge's highly personal, impassioned and figurative essay style. At a time when choice of style and register were read as indicators of political allegiance – take, for example, the contrast between Tom Paine's plainness and Edmund Burke's ornateness – Coleridge gave off a mixed message. Initially, his sales pitch is for a cool and neutral presentation of facts, relating the political events of the day 'simply and nakedly, without epithets or comments', accompanied by a neutral summary of the different accounts to be found in the opposition and ministerial prints (*Watchman*, 14). Mindful, perhaps, of the recent slur against him as one of a group of 'factious Aliens' scattering 'the seeds of discord and sedition' in Bristol (*Lects. 1795*, 329, 389), Coleridge defiantly announces: 'though I may be classed with a party, I scorn to be of a faction' (*Watchman*, 14). But the cautious and mild tone of this 'Introductory Essay' is followed by an extraordinarily pungent essay on Edmund Burke, full of complexity and profound paradox, and alive with the 'throb and tempest of political fanaticism', the very rhetorical violence which (ironically) Coleridge charges to Burke. To instance just one marvellous sentence: 'At the flames which rise from the altar of Freedom, [Burke] kindled that torch with which he since endeavoured to set fire to her temple' (*Watchman*, 39). Irritated by Coleridge's professed 'spirit of meekness', Caius Gracchus concluded of the essay on Burke: 'Inconsistency in the character of this Philosopher, seems a prominent feature' (*Watchman*, 194–5).

The radical political lecturer John Thelwall was also at this time remonstrating with Coleridge about his inconsistency – the puzzling contradiction between the 'outrageous violence' of phrases like 'th'imbrothell'd Atheist's heart' and Coleridge's supposed Christian meekness (*CL* I, 212).

In his essay 'Modern Patriotism' in Number III of the *Watchman* Coleridge further alienated radical friends like Thelwall by pitting his own brand of Christian patriotism against a demonised version of radicalism-as-sexual-immorality. Without naming William Godwin, he denounced his philosophical principles, such as the argument against marriage, as 'vicious', and his book as a 'pimp' and 'Pandar to Sensuality' (*Watchman*, 196, 100). As Coleridge increasingly detached himself from the radical movement, Christian quietism and consensus-seeking came to prevail over party and controversy, leading Alan Liu to argue that the 'origin of the journalism of impartiality lies in apostasy', with Coleridge as 'the master amphibian of test-the-water politics' in the post-*Watchman* years.[25] Another way of viewing Coleridge's political journalism would be to see its various contortions as expressive of a deep-seated psychological and creative attachment to moving forward through resistance, a dialectic he first hints at in a letter of 1800 to Godwin, advising him to give up his theory of 'Collision of Ideas, & take up that of mutual Propulsions' (*CL* I, 636). The experiment of the *Friend*, as we shall see, involved precisely this, a strategy of moving forward stealthily through a symbiotic dialectic between writer and reader involving active and passive motions, attacking and yielding.

In the tenth and last number of the *Watchman*, Coleridge announced that he would 'cease to cry the State of the political Atmosphere', his explanation being simply that 'the Work does not pay its expences'. The failure to retain subscribers was, however, only a partial explanation. Coleridge had stuck his neck out, and the times were dangerous: James Montgomery, radical editor of the Sheffield *Iris*, was clapped into prison for criminal libel just as Coleridge began his tour for subscribers in January 1796, the orator John Gale Jones was arrested in Birmingham in March, and few radical journals were to survive the year.[26] In addition to state-organised terror, the news from France was growing more and more discouraging. Gradually, Coleridge's highly personalised authorial presence begins to disappear from the paper, and by May he confessed himself 'depressed . . . beneath the *writing-point* in the thermometer of mind' (*CL* I, 212). The letters trace a steady disengagement from radical commitments: 'local and temporary Politics are my aversion', he wrote in July, and by October he has 'snapped' his 'squeaking baby-trumpet of sedition', piously denouncing 'politicians and politics – a sort of men and a kind of study . . . highly unfavourable to all Christian graces' (*CL* I, 222, 240).

Renunciation was never Coleridge's strong point. Even the rural retreat of a pantisocratic farm in Wales had to be located 'near some Town, where there is a speedy Communication with London' (*CL* I, 155). During 1809–10, Coleridge succumbed one more time to the lure of running his own newspaper, subjecting himself again to the dreaded scourge of a weekly deadline. In his sights were two new radical weeklies, William Cobbett's *Political Register* (1802) and Leigh Hunt's *Examiner* (1808). In terms of format, Coleridge insisted that the *Friend* be modelled precisely upon Cobbett's newspaper (*CL* III, 196–7); at one point he even confessed that the 'paramount *Object*' of the *Friend* lay in strangling the bad passions awakened by Cobbett's prose (*CL* III, 141, 143). Few friends believed that Coleridge was capable of carrying on this newspaper, especially one written in Grasmere and published from so remote a place as Penrith, but Coleridge persisted in his plan nevertheless, carrying the Prospectus 'wet from the pen to the printer, without consulting anybody, or giving himself time for consideration',[27] and sustaining the periodical for nine months, three times the duration of the *Watchman*. And whereas the *Watchman* was devoted to addressing the politics of the day, the *Friend* (ostensibly) turned its back on politics, 'except as far as they may happen to be involved in some point of private morality' (*Friend* II, 27). Any writing which did not pass the test of holding itself aloof from current affairs went elsewhere, into the venal *Courier*, for instance, which was helping out in other ways too, through advertisements for the *Friend* and credit for stamped paper (*EOT* I, cxxxii).

The private and personal are hall-marks of the *Friend*, a tactic which was not just temperamentally congenial, as we have seen, but part of a concerted tilt at another new phenomenon in the literary marketplace, the 'synodical individuum' of the *Edinburgh Review* (founded 1802), in which the anonymous writer hid behind the 'disguise of a pretended Board or Association of Critics' (*Friend* II, 108). Not that Coleridge lacked disguises of his own. In order to cover over the 'indelicacy' of speaking of himself 'to Strangers and to the Public' (*CL* III, 151), he presented the *Friend*'s Prospectus as an extract from a private letter, a ruse which enabled him to speak frankly of the experiment he was intending to perpetrate on his readers. For instance, he decared that the format of the weekly essay offered him 'the most likely Means of winning, instead of forcing my Way':

> Supposing Truth on my Side, the Shock of the first Day might be so far lessened by Reflections of the succeeding Days, as to procure for my next Week's Essay a less hostile Reception, than it would have met with, had it been only the next Chapter of a present volume. I hoped to disarm the Mind of those Feelings, which preclude Conviction by Contempt, and, as it were, fling the Door in the Face of Reasoning by a *Presumption* of its Absurdity.   (*Friend* II, 17)

Progress is to be made through the alternate motions of readerly resistance and yielding, a pattern mirrored in Coleridge's own alternation between authorial attack and accommodation. Such an experimental methodology could only be carried out over time and through the close monitoring of his readers' reactions. So novel was Coleridge's project of weekly attrition against his readers that none of his close friends appeared to understand exactly what he was trying to do. As far as Southey was concerned, Coleridge's desire for intimate friendship with his readers was humbug, involving an 'unmanly *humblefication*' which the ambitiously high pedagogical aim of his paper gave the lie to (Warter II, 120). The other great weakness was his 'rambling and inconclusive' prose style, a function of Coleridge's 'inordinate love of talking' (Warter II, 188), and the oral dictation of whole numbers of the *Friend* which were then printed without re-transcription.[28]

Unfortunately for Coleridge, his subscribers failed to appreciate his experiment upon them. As far as they were concerned, the solicitude for their comfort came too late, so that what remained uppermost was the assault, succinctly summed up in Coleridge's modelling of the writer–reader relationship on that of the physician and patient. As for the many (and understandable) complaints of 'unintelligibility', these were deflected by the charge that unintelligibility was just as likely to be the fault of the reader as of the writer, especially if the reader had an 'ideotic understanding'. In illustration of this point Coleridge cited the case of one of his subscribers who wrote to abuse him for ' "learned non*sence* and unintelligible Jar*gin*" ' (*Friend* II, 275). Having fallen into the hands of the dangerously illiterate, Coleridge had come to resemble the physician who absurdly recommended 'exercise with the dumb bells, as the only mode of cure, to a patient paralytic in both arms' (*Friend* II, 152). His ambition to write, not for the 'multitude', but for those who 'by Rank, or Fortune, or official Situation, or Talents and Habits of Reflection, are to *influence* the Multitude' (*CL* III, 143), had not quite come to pass.

There is a general truth in the claim that the *Friend* marketed itself for a more establishment and professional coterie than the middle-class dissenters and friends of freedom targeted by the *Watchman*.[29] But it is important to note that many of the *Friend*'s subscribers were friends and associates from earlier days, and that when the eminently practical Thomas Clarkson offered him a ready-made readership in the shape of dozens of well-off and well-read Quakers, the needy Coleridge was happy to accept their vote of confidence in him. But whilst willing to accept Quaker support, he would not then take direction about how to accommodate their special interests and views, with the result that they dropped their subscriptions, leaving Coleridge incensed by their desertion.[30] In a telling phrase about the failure of his idiosyncratic and intensely personal aspirations to establish a devoted readership, he described the *Friend* as 'a secret entrusted to the Public'.[31]

In *Biographia Literaria* (1817) Coleridge dismissed newspapers as entirely unsuitable reading matter for Christians, full of 'merely political and temporary interest'. He also lampooned his own efforts as a journalist, saying the work was not fit for a learned gentleman like himself, a point reinforced by his distorting reduction of the *Watchman* subscription tour to an encounter with two philistine types – a lower-class, evangelical tallow chandler and an opulent cotton merchant, both of whom refused to subscribe (*BL* I, 182–4). Any ambition he might have had to be a 'popular writer' foundered on his political independence (he claimed), on opinions 'equi-distant from all the three prominent parties, the Pittites, the Foxites, and the Democrats', with the result that most of his first newspaper ended up in the grate (*BL* I, 187). Later, Coleridge referred to the *Watchman* as 'an obscure and short-lived periodical publication, which has long since been *used off* as "winding sheets for herrings and pilchards"' (*Watchman*, 139, n. 2).

The *Friend* received better treatment from its author, rising like a phoenix out of its newpaper covers in 1812 as a 'Series of Essays', then again in 1818, when it appeared in thoroughly revised book form. By this time Coleridge's excitement at the speed of newspaper circulation had evaporated into alarm at the size and rapidly changing composition of the reading public, with the consequence that 'circulation' now became an internalised metaphor of bodily integrity. Warning his young readers in *Biographia Literaria* to avoid the trade of authorship, Coleridge argues that thoughts, like other bodily secretions, 'must be taken up again into the circulation, and be again and again re-secreted in order to ensure a healthful vigor, both to the mind and to its intellectual offspring' (*BL* I, 231). Similarly, the experimental methodology of 'mutual Propulsions', initially devised by Coleridge as an alternative to radicalism and public controversy, became an increasingly internalised metaphor. The small water insect on the surface of a rivulet which '*wins* its way up against the stream, by alternate pulses of active and passive motion, now resisting the current, and now yielding to it in order to gather strength and a momentary *fulcrum* for a further propulsion' is the very 'emblem of the mind's self-experience in the act of thinking' (*BL* I, 124).

NOTES

1 Wilfrid Hindle, *The Morning Post, 1772–1937* (London: Routledge, 1937), 85.
2 See A. Aspinall, *Politics and the Press, c. 1780–1850* (London: Home and Van Thal, 1949).
3 See Lucy Werkmeister, *The London Daily Press, 1772–1792* (Lincoln: University of Nebraska Press, 1963), vi.

4 Hindle gives a lively account of the newpaper's rise to eminence in chapter 5 of *The Morning Post*.

5 See Young's *Travels in France* (1792), a text quoted by Coleridge in the Prospectus to the *Watchman*. For 'electric sensibility' as the vehicle of a 'universal circulation of intelligence' in Britain, see Young's *Travels*, ed. J. Kaplow (New York: Anchor Books, 1969), 160. The contrast between well-informed British labourers and ignorant French provincials is a major focus of Young's text; see also pp. 140–1, 162–3, 171–2, 180.

6 Duke of Chandos, 'Debate in the Lords on the African Slave Bill' (1788) in *Parliamentary History of England* (London: T. C. Hansard, 1806–20), xxvii, 648.

7 Preface to *Lyrical Ballads* (1800), *The Prose Works of William Wordsworth*, ed. W. J. B. Owen and J. Smyser, 3 vols. (Oxford: Clarendon Press, 1974), I, 128.

8 Coleridge reiterated the claim in 1814; see *CL* III, 510, 531, and Erdman's commentary in *EOT* I, clx.

9 *EOT* I, 401–2, n. 12.

10 See Thompson's 1979 review of Erdman's edition: 'A Compendium of Cliché: The Poet as Essayist', repr. in E. P. Thompson, *The Romantics: England in a Revolutionary Age* (New York: The New Press, 1997), 143–55.

11 E. P. Thompson, *The Romantics*, 153. See William Christie, 'Going Public: Print Lords Byron and Brougham', *Studies in Romanticism*, 38, 3 (Fall 1999), 443–75.

12 Quoted by Erdman who thinks that the metaphor might be Hazlitt's (*EOT* I, clxxiv).

13 See Kevin Gilmartin, 'Radical Print Culture in Periodical Form', *Romanticism, History, and the Possibilities of Genre: Re-forming Literature, 1789–1837*, ed. T. Rajan and J. Wright (Cambridge University Press, 1998), 43.

14 See Jon Klancher, *The Making of English Reading Audiences, 1790–1832* (Madison and London: The University of Wisconsin Press, 1987), 23.

15 See Deirdre Coleman, *Coleridge and 'The Friend' (1809–1810)* (Oxford: Clarendon Press, 1988).

16 Peter Kitson aligns Pantisocracy with Unitarianism. See 'The Whore of Babylon and the Woman in White: Coleridge's Radical Unitarian Language', *Coleridge's Visionary Languages: Essays in Honour of John Beer*, ed. T. Fulford and M. D. Paley (Cambridge: D. S. Brewer, 1993), 6.

17 Coleridge's essay against the slave trade was published between the debates on Wilberforce's second (unsuccessful) Bill against the trade in the House of Commons; for the boycott campaign and associated Gothicism, see Deirdre Coleman, 'Conspicuous Consumption: White Abolitionism and English Women's Protest Writing in the 1790s', *English Literary History*, 61 (Summer 1994), 341–62, and Charlotte Sussman, 'Women and the Politics of Sugar, 1792', *Representations*, 48 (Fall 1994), 48–69.

18 Roger Wells, *Wretched Faces: Famine in Wartime England, 1763–1803* (Gloucester: Alan Sutton Publishing, 1988), 46–50.

19 Compare Anna Laetitia Barbauld, *Sins of Government, Sins of the Nation* (London: J. Johnson, 1793), repr. Lucy Aikin, *The Works of Anna Laetitia Barbauld*, 2 vols. (London: Longman, 1825), II, 381–412.

20 For the importance of advertisements to the success of newspapers, see Hindle, *The Morning Post*, 83–4.

21 See the entry for 'taverns and alehouses' in Iain McCalman, ed., *An Oxford Companion to the Romantic Age: British Culture 1776–1832* (Oxford University Press, 1999), 724–5; and chapter 6 of McCalman's *Radical Underworld: Prophets, Revolutionaries, and Pornographers in London, 1795–1840* (Cambridge University Press, 1988).

22 Mrs Margaret Sandford, *Thomas Poole and His Friends*, 2 vols. (London: Macmillan, 1888), I, 282.

23 See *EOT* I, cxxvi.

24 A 'spacious coffee-house' is how James Anderson described his new periodical, the Edinburgh *Bee* in 1790; for discussion of the *Bee*, see Klancher, *English Reading Audiences*, 22–6.

25 Alan Liu, *Wordsworth: The Sense of History* (California: Stanford University Press, 1989), 416.

26 The *Watchman* followed the case of Jones and his associate John Binns in some detail, since attempts to prosecute them involved the new Gagging Acts. See Thompson, *The Romantics*, 118.

27 *Selections from the Letters of Robert Southey*, ed. J. W. Warter, 4 vols. (London: Longmans, 1856) II, 120. Further references will appear in the text as 'Warter'.

28 For Coleridge's method of composition, see Dorothy Wordsworth's letter (*MY* I, 391).

29 See Klancher, *English Reading Audiences*, 152.

30 See *BL* I, 175–6; and chapter 5, 'Coleridge's Quaker Subscribers', in Deirdre Coleman, *Coleridge and* The Friend.

31 'The "Friend" is a secret which I have entrusted to the public; and, unlike most secrets, it hath been well kept', from Thomas Allsop, ed., *Letters, Conversations and Recollections of Samuel Taylor Coleridge*, 2 vols. (New York: Harper and Brothers, 1836), I, 233.

9

ANGELA ESTERHAMMER

The critic

Coleridge thought, talked and wrote about poetics and criticism throughout his life. Until 1820, these were often primary concerns; at other times,
and later in his life, his ideas about literature were ancillary to his work
on philosophy, religion, psychology, history or language. Yet the task of
summarising Coleridge's philosophy and practice of literary criticism is a
challenging one, because he prepared almost none of his criticism for publication and his notes were left in a chaotic form. Most of what we know
about his critical opinions derives from the 'Shakespearean criticism' – not
a coherent text, but surviving notes and reports concerning public lectures
that Coleridge presented between 1808 and 1819. There is also a multitude
of passages on literary criticism in Coleridge's Notebooks and in his copious
marginal annotations to editions of Shakespeare and other books. Both the
Notebooks and the marginalia overlap extensively with the public lectures,
for Coleridge tended to lecture *extempore* based on scraps of paper and annotated volumes that he brought with him into the lecture hall. Some of his
major ideas about criticism did take published form in *Biographia Literaria*
(1817), but examining the notes and fragments that testify to his practice as
a critic before and after the publication of *Biographia* allows us to see how
those principles developed, and how Coleridge applied them to the study of
Shakespeare, Milton and major European writers.

Coleridge offered eight courses of public lectures on literary topics, mainly
in London and occasionally in Bristol. These were conceived as money-
making ventures, to be attended by admission-paying, literary-minded gentlemen and ladies, although some were more successful than others in
realising their financial objectives, and some had to be cut short because
of Coleridge's illnesses, depressions and opium addiction. Audience appreciation of the lectures and the lecturer was extremely variable. One listener
reported that Coleridge was 'sometimes very eloquent, sometimes paradox-
ical, sometimes absurd' (*C. Lects* I, 143). Henry Crabb Robinson probably
spoke for others who knew Coleridge personally when he observed in his

diary that Coleridge's private conversations on Shakespeare, which often touched on the same points as his lectures, were far superior to them, for in the latter he digressed, apologised at great length for the digressions, repeated himself and so on. Many listeners were in awe of Coleridge's breadth of knowledge, especially about Shakespeare, yet others complained about his ignorance. 'In his lectures [Coleridge] appears grossly ignorant', William Godwin apparently commented (*Sh C* II, 172), but a journalist reporting on the Shakespeare lectures gushed with praise: 'no man living, no man perhaps, among all those who have at any time undertaken to analyze and expound the writings of Shakespeare, ever studied him so profoundly' (*C. Lects* II, 248). There was equally diverse reaction to Coleridge's frequent habit of speaking without notes, or without referring to his notes if he had brought them. A reviewer in the *Sun* newspaper in 1811 warmly recommended to Coleridge 'to *speak* as much, and to *read* as little as possible' (*C. Lects* I, 196), but other listeners complained that the lectures consisted of nothing but digressions, that they were unorganised and therefore incomprehensible, or that he never got to the topic on which he had promised to speak. Coleridge's enthusiasm and his ability to mesmerise an audience seldom went unnoticed, however. According to his friend James Gillman, 'In his lectures he was brilliant, fluent, and rapid; his words seemed to flow as from a person repeating with grace and energy some delightful poem';[1] and a young shorthand recorder was practically rendered speechless by performances that, as he put it, were 'not only beyond my praise but beyond the praise of any man, but himself' (*C. Lects* I, 203).

It is likely the lectures themselves were as mixed as the reviews – periods of brilliance interspersed with ramblings aggravated by illness and drug abuse. The topics of the courses varied, although all of them covered some of the same material. The topic mentioned by Coleridge in one of his earliest references to the plan of public lecturing is significant, however: 'the Principles of Poetry conveyed and illustrated' (*CL* III, 29–30). From the beginning, he is committed to a criticism founded on fixed philosophical principles, although this was far from the norm in his day. Eighteenth-century critics and contemporary reviewers were much more likely to practise a type of criticism that focussed on isolated passages of particular works, pointing out their 'beauties' or (more frequently, in the case of reviewers) their 'defects'. The pieces that commonly appeared in partisan periodicals like the *Edinburgh Review*, the *Quarterly Review* and the *Examiner* are, Coleridge complains, 'filled with personalities' and superficial judgements (*C. Lects* I, 189). Reviewers are successful at encouraging the spread of shallow ideas, but discourage thoughtful reading practices; they neglect the profound resonances of poetic language and its ability to convey 'not . . . merely what a certain thing is, but

the very passion & all the circumstances which were conceived as constituting the perception of the thing by the person who used the word' (*C. Lects*
I, 273). Coleridge attempts to correct this tendency with a criticism founded
in expansive theories of language, representation and aesthetics.

Although Coleridge developed his philosophical approach to criticism over
many years, its foundations are already evident in the first literary lecture he
presented in January 1808, where he sets out to define the 'fixed Principle'
behind the common eighteenth-century critical term 'taste' (*C. Lects* I, 27).
Elucidating fixed principles involves defining terms and distinguishing them
from closely related or alternative terms, or practising what Coleridge frequently referred to as 'desynonymization'. Thus, he distinguishes taste from
other modes of perception (sight, hearing, touch) that might have been
adopted for this metaphorical usage by demonstrating that taste has both
an active/perceptive and a passive/reactive component: 'Taste then may be
defined – a distinct Perception of any arrangement conceived as external to
us co-existent with some degree of Dislike or Complacency conceived as resulting from that arrangement' (*C. Lects* I, 30). The definition of taste, as
a starting point for aesthetic theory, indicates Coleridge's belief that there
is both a subjective and an objective component to aesthetic response: taste
may be different for everyone, but there are universal principles that enable
us to understand and often acquiesce in others' tastes. Here at the outset of
his lectures, and frequently thereafter, Coleridge adopts vocabulary familiar from eighteenth-century criticism (taste, beauty, imagination, fancy), but
strives to give it more exact definition and more philosophical grounding.
He also stresses the moral import of literature and criticism, claiming that
'the main Object, for which I have undertaken these Lectures, is to enforce at
various times & by various arguments & instances the close and reciprocal
connections of Just Taste with pure Morality' (*C. Lects* I, 78).

In keeping with his desire to found criticism on fixed principles, Coleridge
deduces a definition of poetry that recurs often in his lecture courses, as
well as in *Biographia Literaria*. This crucial definition is worth citing in two
different formulations. Poetry, says Coleridge, is

> the art . . . of representing external nature and human Thoughts & Affections,
> both relatively to human Affections; to the production of as great immediate
> pleasure in each part, as is compatible with the largest possible Sum of Pleasure
> in the whole.   (*C. Lects* I, 75–6; cf. *CN* III, 3286, 3615)

> Poetry is a species of composition, opposed to Science as having intellectual
> pleasure for its Object and attaining its end by the Language natural to us
> in states of excitement; but distinguished from other species, not excluded
> by this criterion, by permitting a pleasure from the Whole consistent with

a consciousness of pleasurable excitement from the component parts, & the perfection of which is to communicate from each part the greatest immediate pleasure compatible with the largest Sum of Pleasure on the whole.

(C. Lects I, 218; cf. CN III, 4111).

Coleridge's definition resonates strikingly with Wordsworth's Preface to *Lyrical Ballads* (1800), showing that the early poetic theory of both men derives from their collaboration and conversation in the late 1790s. Both subscribe to an expressive theory of poetry; both believe that poetry recalls, and produces, states of excitement; and both distinguish poetry (whose object is pleasure) from science (whose object is truth). In notebook entries of 1800, Coleridge refers to the 'recalling of passion in tranquillity', and includes an evocative image: 'a child scolding a flower in the words in which he had himself been scolded & whipt, is *poetry*' (*CN* I, 787, 786). But besides these collaborative ideas about poetry's expressive nature, Coleridge's definition encompasses some philosophical principles about the status and form of poetry that constitute the basis of his critical practice. Two of these, to be discussed in what follows, are the status of representation and the relationship of part to whole.

Poetry, writes Coleridge, is 'the art...of representing external nature and human Thoughts & Affections'. His notion of what it means for art to 'represent' is closely tied to the most often repeated claim in his critical prose: that art is not a *copy* but an *imitation* of nature. It does not aim to *be* reality, but to *represent* reality. Artistic representation therefore always includes an element of resemblance to the real world, but also an element of difference from it. The pleasure we derive from art is that of perceiving likeness *and* difference, identity *and* contrariety; indeed, this is what Coleridge calls 'the universal Principle of the Fine Arts', which is also 'the condition of all consciousness' (*C. Lects* I, 83–4).

The principle of likeness-in-difference leads directly to Coleridge's theory of dramatic illusion. Coleridge believes that much misunderstanding of drama and dramatists has come about because people expect a verisimilitude to everyday life that drama was never meant to provide. The purpose of drama is not to *delude* the audience into taking it for reality; rather, its purpose is to produce *illusion* by placing the spectator in a state that is comparable to dreaming, but involves more conscious control. The theatrical experience depends on 'a sort of temporary Half-Faith, which the Spectator encourages in himself & supports by a voluntary contribution on his own part, because he knows that it is at all times in his power to see the thing as it really is' (*C. Lects* I, 134). Coleridge insists on the spectator's or reader's active involvement in this state through an exercise of will – more specifically, through a willing suspension of judgement, the mental faculty that normally determines whether or not a thing really exists. Thus, if we see a forest scene represented on stage, 'the true stage Illusion both in this and in all other Things consists not in the mind's judging it to be a Forest but in its remission of the judgement, that it is not a Forest' (*C. Lects* I, 130). In *Biographia Literaria* this condition, expanded beyond drama to poetry in general, comes to be known by a memorable formula: 'that willing suspension of disbelief for the moment, which constitutes poetic faith' (*BL* II, 6).

The central distinction between copy and imitation has wide-ranging implications for Coleridge's criticism. It leads him to place a rather modern emphasis on language and fictionality. 'The very Essence of a Play', Coleridge notes in the margin of an edition of Ben Jonson, 'the very language in which it is written, is a Fiction to which all the parts must conform' (*CM* III, 172–3). As a verbal creation, a play is both similar to and distinct from reality, and its fictional status permeates the dramatic structure. One of Coleridge's most noteworthy achievements is his shift of attention from the local characteristics of Shakespeare's and other writers' language, to the realisation that language as a whole, as a system of representation, distances art from nature, and necessitates a set of principles for interpreting and appreciating art that are separate from the faculties of perception and understanding that we use to 'interpret' nature. 'Poetry', Coleridge concludes, 'is purely *human* – all its materials are *from* the mind, and all the products are *for* the mind' (*C. Lects* II, 218; cf. *CN* III, 4397).

Because art is a human imitation of nature, the creation and appreciation of poetry involve the active exercise of judgement on the part of both poet and reader. This principle deeply influences Coleridge's practical criticism, colouring his opinions about the success or failure of individual dramas and dramatists and the faults of readers or reviewers. Throughout his career as a critic, Coleridge campaigned for the recognition that a great work of literature is one in which all the parts are under the control of its creator; and, in a move that he believed was one of his most revolutionary contributions to criticism, he chose Shakespeare as the great exemplar of conscious artistry. Coleridge frequently criticised eighteenth-century Shakespeare critics for describing Shakespeare as a 'delightful Monster', a 'wild, irregular, pure child of nature', or an 'Automaton of Genius' (*C. Lects* I, 79; *CN* III, 4115) – that is, as a writer who needs to be *excused* for breaking the rules of dramatic structure and appreciated *despite* his irregularity. Coleridge insists – in an assertion he expects will appear sensational to his contemporaries – that, far from being an unruly monster, Shakespeare possesses a superior faculty of judgement. In his notes for the beginning of a lecture series on Shakespeare in 1818, he writes:

However inferior in ability to some who have followed me, I am proud that I was the first in time who publicly demonstrated to the full extent of the position, that the supposed Irregularity and Extravagances of Shakespear were the mere Dreams of a Pedantry that arraigned the Eagle because it had not the Dimensions of the Swan. In all the successive Courses, delivered by me, since my first attempt at the Royal Institution, it has been and it still remains my Object to prove that in all points from the most important to the most minute, the Judgement of Shakespear is commensurate with his Genius – nay, that his Genius reveals itself in his Judgement, as in its most exalted Form.

(C. *Lects* III, 263–4)

Coleridge believes that the popular opinion of Shakespeare as an unruly genius proceeds from the unwillingness of critics to expend the mental energy needed to comprehend the unity and integrity of his plays, and from a failure to realise that every work of literature should be judged according to the character and characteristics of its own kind (*CM* III, 886). Some eighteenth-century English critics followed the French neoclassicists in maintaining that plays should adhere to the traditional 'three unities': they should observe a unity of time, a unity of place and a unity of action. Coleridge contends, however, that the three unities, derived from the example of ancient Greek drama, are historically specific to the Greek stage, and that it is ludicrous to apply them indiscriminately to all drama whatsoever. Only drama that relies on a Chorus being present throughout the action has a need to avoid lapses of time or changes of location.

Nevertheless, a differently conceived unity is crucial to Coleridge's interpretation of literary works: he argues that the third unity, the unity of action, is the essential condition of successful drama, although he thinks that a more helpful term for it would be 'unity of interest'. The harmony of a play is caused by 'a single energy, modified *ab intra* in each component part' (*Sh C* III, 4–5). Coleridge dates his own recognition of this characteristic to around 1800, writing in a marginal note of 1811:

As late as 10 years ago, I used to seek and find out grand lines and fine stanzas; but my delight has been far greater, since it has consisted more in tracing the leading Thought thro'out the whole. The former is too much like coveting your neighbour's Goods; in the latter you merge yourself in the Author – you *become He*.

(*CM* II, 220)

Inevitably, Coleridge's analyses of particular Shakespearean plays seek to demonstrate the harmony that connects each of the parts with the whole, thus demonstrating Shakespeare's ingenious sense of form and his mastery of poetic representation. The parts that contribute to the overall unity of interest in a play can include major and minor characters (such as Mercutio, Tybalt or Rosaline in *Romeo and Juliet*), specific scenes, images, word-play, even instances of rhythm or syntax. One characteristic of Coleridge's Shakespearean criticism is the detailed attention he pays to opening scenes, in order to show how the drama develops organically out of the situation presented there, just as character grows out of an original 'germ'. Coleridge's readings of Shakespearean drama become increasingly close and detailed in the later lectures of 1818–19, for which the lecture notes are essentially marginalia on specific passages in *The Tempest*, *Richard II*, *Hamlet*, *Macbeth*, *Othello* and other favourite dramas. Coleridge presumably drew on these individual notes when lecturing in order to build an argument about the unity of each play. He extends the same critical approach to other literary works as well, and his final lecture series of 1819 contains a lecture on *Paradise Lost* as the epic poem that 'alone really possesses the Beginning, Middle, and End – the totality of a Poem or circle as distinguished from the ab ovo birth, parentage, &c or strait line of History' (*C. Lects* II, 389; cf. *CN* III, 4494). Coleridge's central definition of the poem, then, 'the perfection of which is to communicate from each part the greatest immediate pleasure compatible with the largest Sum of Pleasure on the whole' (*C. Lects* I, 218), develops in tandem with a practice of criticism that consists largely of demonstrating the integral relationship between parts and wholes.

Much of Coleridge's criticism involves the psychological analysis of Shakespearean characters. But, far from falling into the trap of treating fictional characters as if they were real people (as he has sometimes been accused of doing), Coleridge applies the distinction between copy and imitation in this case as well. He strives to show that Shakespeare's characters are not directly copied from life, but are the product of meditation. More precisely, they are products of 'observation which was the child of meditation' – of Shakespeare's ability to observe people and interpret what he observed as confirmation of a philosophical theory of life (*C. Lects* I, 306). Coleridge frequently characterises the poet as Proteus, the god who can take on the shape of anything in nature, and again Shakespeare is his outstanding example. The philosophical cast of Shakespeare's mind provides a kind of medium in which the most multifarious characters can be seen distinctly. 'Shakespear always *Master* of himself and his Subject – a genuine Proteus', read Coleridge's notes; 'we see all things in *him*, as Images in a calm Lake – most distinct most accurate – only more splendid more glorified – this is correctness in the only philosophical sense' (*C. Lects* I, 528).

Shakespeare's ability to combine observation with imagination means that his work contains universally relevant imitations of real life; it is 'nature idealized into poetry' (*Friend* I, 471). When he takes on the shape of a character such as Lear and speaks the 'language of nature' that Lear would have uttered, we recognise the likeness to *and* the difference from real life; thus Lear's words, like the language of all great tragedy, 'might give pain, but not such pain as was inconsistent with pleasure' (*C. Lects* I, 227). By contrast, inferior writers of sentimental drama attempt to arouse pathos by copying nature. 'In its highest excellence', Coleridge remarks archly, this art 'only aspired to the genius of an onion, the power of drawing tears and...the Author acting like a Ventriloquist distributed his own insipidity' (*C. Lects* I, 351). Shakespeare's characters represent classes, not individuals, and this aspiration towards essential or ideal qualities rather than contingent ones distinguishes him from other Renaissance dramatists like Ben Jonson, as well as from writers contemporary with Coleridge, like the popular German dramatist August von Kotzebue.

However, Shakespeare also provides the inspiration for modern drama, and Coleridge repeatedly refers to his plays as 'romantic dramas' or 'dramatic romances'. In doing so, he is not using the term 'Romantic' the same way we do today, but referring to the ideal, dream-like character of plays like *The Tempest*, and their appeal to the imagination rather than to historical or everyday verisimilitude. In general, Coleridge treats Shakespearean plays more as texts to be read than as productions to be seen on stage. He theorises that the less elaborate stages and the more learned audiences of Shakespeare's day prompted him to write a type of drama that appeals strongly to the imagination, and that is in fact the forerunner of the 'closet drama' that Coleridge's own contemporaries were writing: '[Shakespeare] found the stage as near as possible a closet, & in the closet only could it be fully & completely enjoyed' (*C. Lects* I, 254). But the comparison of Shakespearean to modern drama also has to do with Coleridge's severe judgement on the quality of Shakespearean acting in the early nineteenth century, causing him to prefer reading Shakespeare in his 'closet' rather than watching him performed. Modern theatres 'drove Shakespear from the stage, to find his proper place, in the heart and in the closet; where he sits with Milton, enthroned on a double-headed Parnassus' (*C. Lects* I, 563).

In his criticism of Shakespeare, Coleridge attempts to put into practice his fundamental beliefs about great poetry: that it is an imitation and not a copy of nature; that it is the expression of an authorial mind and bears everywhere the traces of that author's philosophy and imagination; that it gives pleasure through the integral relation of parts to the whole. He also attempts (with varying success) to achieve a historical perspective on Shakespeare's drama, or Milton's poetry, or the three unities of classical drama, by relating each of these forms of art, via the mind of the author, to the characteristics of the era in which they originated. All of this forms part of Coleridge's general belief about the relation of art to rules. No aesthetic or formal rule may be applied indiscriminately, he argues; rather, we must first know and appreciate 'the end, the nature, the Idea of a work' before we can understand what kind of rules should apply (*C. Lects* II, 70). Although the spirit of poetry requires rules of organisation, these rules must derive from within the work of art itself, rather than the form being a product of pre-existing strictures. After 1811, Coleridge frequently adopted the terms introduced by his German contemporary A. W. Schlegel for this distinction, referring to the need for a principle of 'organic form' rather than 'mechanical form' when discussing works of art. Organic form is a form determined by the essential principle within a thing, such as a growing plant, which manifests itself in external features because all its parts develop in conformity with an internal law.

To Coleridge, recognising the integral, organic form of a poem, and developing the permanent philosophical principles upon which practical criticism must be based, involves more intellectual labour than most critics and reviewers have been willing to bestow. He urges readers to exercise their judgement, rather than passively seeking sensation or verisimilitude. In his lectures and Notebooks, Coleridge semi-seriously divides readers into four categories according to the mental effort they expend when reading literature:

> 4 Sorts of Readers. 1. Spunges that suck up every thing and, when pressed give it out in the same state, only perhaps somewhat dirtier – . 2. Sand Glasses – or rather the upper Half of the Sand Glass, which in a brief hour assuredly lets out what it has received – & whose reading is only a profitless measurement & dozeing away of Time – . 3. Straining Bags, who get rid of whatever is good & pure, and retain the Dregs. – and this Straining-bag Class is again subdivided into Species of the Sensual, who retain evil for the gratification of their own base Imaginations, & the calumnious, who judge only by defects...4 and lastly, the Great-Moguls Diamond Sieves – which is perhaps going farther for a Simile than its superior Dignity can repay, inasmuch as a common Cullender would have been equally symbolic/ but imperial or culinary, these are the only good, & I fear the least numerous, who assuredly retain the good, while the superfluous or impure passes away & leaves no trace.
>
> (*C. Lects* I, 65–6; cf. *CN* III, 3242)

Coleridge's allegory of the types of readers reflects his beliefs about the moral purpose of literature, which should provide its readers with examples of the 'good & pure', but can only do so if they are willing to read with an active mind and a waking judgement. But it also relates to his critique of readers and reviewers in his own day, the object of frequent diatribes in Coleridge's work. There are certain traits in human personality that, according to Coleridge, lead readers to make false judgements; some of these are our prevalent desire to claim knowledge without really thinking, our consequent readiness to accept the opinions of others, and our habit of using vague terminology.

But Coleridge also identifies specific historical and sociological factors he believes are causing the proliferation of false criticism in his age. These include the shallow, sensation-seeking readers of popular novels (sponges and sandglasses, presumably), a readership formed by the unsettling political events of the time; the vogue of public speaking, which encourages showmanship and ill-thought-out remarks; and the popularity of journalism, reviewing and gossip about public characters. Most reviewers writing in contemporary periodicals, Coleridge would claim, are 'Straining Bags' who 'get rid of whatever is good & pure' and 'judge only by defects'. He attributes the 'pernicious' nature of modern reviews to the fact that reviewers 'decided without any reference to fixed principles' (*C. Lects* i, 189), revealing again his conviction that literary criticism must have a philosophical structure of its own in order to be able to understand literature as a particular mode of representation, an imitation and not a copy of life.

How original or revolutionary were Coleridge's ideas about literature and literary criticism? The question often arises, both for the sake of placing Coleridge's work in historical context, and for the more specific purpose of evaluating his relationship to the German critics and philosophers whom he was famously accused of plagiarising, in his own time and since. There is no simple answer to the question, however. Other critics in both Britain and Germany were saying similar things about Shakespeare and the principles of poetry – for instance, emphasising Shakespeare's conscious control over his medium or going beyond the dogmatic application of the 'three unities' – even if Coleridge sometimes writes as if he were the first to assault the dominance of wrong-headed eighteenth-century Shakespeare criticism. Yet Coleridge remains justified in this claim inasmuch as he took issue with many interpretations that his lecture audiences would still have considered standard and orthodox, and in his elucidation of new critical ideas he often developed them more subtly than anyone else or gave them their most influential formulation.

The German writer most often mentioned in connection with Coleridge's lectures on literary criticism is August Wilhelm Schlegel, whose own lectures on dramatic art and literature (*Ueber dramatische Kunst und Literatur*) Coleridge claims to have read for the first time in December 1811, just before presenting lecture 9 of his 1811–12 series. From then on Coleridge frequently drew on Schlegel's lectures for specific observations about Shakespearean drama, as well as for a key distinction between classical and Romantic art. Following and expanding on Schlegel, Coleridge contrasts the Latin language with the Romance languages that developed from it, and classical Greek drama with Shakespearean or modern drama. Romance languages, and Shakespearean drama, lack the simple and perfect symmetries of classical language and art; however, they are 'more rich, more expressive, & various'. By analogy with the term 'Romance' (as applied to 'mixed' languages), Coleridge applies the term 'romantic' to 'the true genuine modern Poetry', and baptises the new hybrid genres of Shakespeare 'romantic Dramas, or dramatic Romances' (C. Lects I, 466). Classical art, associated with the clear lines of statuary or with rhythm and melody in music, is repeatedly contrasted with modern art, whose characteristics are the richer, more complex tones of painting or of musical harmony.

Whether, as Coleridge argued vehemently, he had arrived at most of his opinions about Shakespeare and modern drama before encountering Schlegel's work, or whether his most important critical principles were derived from German contemporaries, by propagating these ideas about classical and Romantic art Coleridge participated in shaping modern literary history and the discipline of comparative literature. The first three lectures of his 1818 series at the London Philosophical Society are devoted to a history of European literature from the Dark Ages onward, a type of literary history that was being practised contemporaneously by A. W. Schlegel and his brother Friedrich Schlegel in German and by Germaine de Staël in French. In this series Coleridge also pursues a sociological type of criticism that is typical of de Staël, in which the characteristics of a nation's literature are explained with reference to its geography and climate, its political and familial organisation, its system of morals and beliefs, its treatment of women and so on. Perhaps because of a renewed openness between Britain and Europe after the end of the Napoleonic Wars in 1815, Coleridge pays increased attention to European literature in his lecture series of 1818 and 1819. In what was reported to be one of his most popular lectures, he expounds on Cervantes's *Don Quixote* by performing a philosophical-psychological analysis on the protagonist, describing Don Quixote as a man with perfect reasoning faculties but no faculty of judgement, and remarking on Cervantes's genius in creating Don Quixote and Sancho Panza as complementary characters – two halves of a complete personality.

In defending himself against the charge of plagiarising Schlegel, Coleridge points out that they might well have reached the same conclusions simultaneously, given the many similarities in their education and reading; they had, for instance, studied under the same professors at the University of Göttingen. He particularly stresses that the key influence on both their critical ideas was the philosophy of Kant, 'the distinguishing feature of which [is] to treat every subject in reference to the operation of the mental Faculties, to which it specially appertains' (CL III, 360). From Kant's *Critique of Pure Reason* (1781) and *Critique of Judgement* (1790), Coleridge learned that the human mind is not a passive receptor of sensations from the material world, but that the mental faculties act autonomously to synthesise sensory impressions into phenomena, or manifestations of reality shaped by the forms and categories of human understanding. The fundamental principles of Coleridge's criticism bear a clear resemblance to the Kantian account of epistemology and mental process. For Coleridge, the mind of the poet, the reader and the critic is in each case active and synthesising. Just as the great poet or dramatist does not slavishly reproduce external reality, but rather produces an imitation of reality adapted to the conditions of language and artistic representation, so the critic, reader or spectator should not receive the work passively, as pure sensation. Instead, the interpreter must judge a work of art according to fixed principles of criticism, principles that are comparable to Kant's forms of understanding. This application of an act of the mind in order to discover the relations among things, or in order to proceed from random phenomena to organised principles, is what Coleridge refers to as *method*, a term he applies to both literary criticism and scientific investigation in the 'Essays on the Principles of Method' that he published in the *Friend*.

Coleridge's achievement as a literary critic is fundamental to modern criticism – and that situation has been both celebrated and deplored. 'It is impossible to understand Shakespeare criticism to this day, without a familiar acquaintance with Coleridge's lectures and notes', wrote T. S. Eliot, but he added, 'Coleridge is an authority of the kind whose influence extends equally towards good and bad.'[2] Similarly, but more bitingly, F. R. Leavis claimed that 'Coleridge's prestige is very understandable, but his currency as an academic classic is something of a scandal.'[3] When scholars analyse the extent of Coleridge's influence on major schools of twentieth-century criticism in both Britain and America, four achievements are generally noted.

(1) *Psychological criticism.* Although psychological analysis of fictional or dramatic characters was common in eighteenth-century criticism, Coleridge refines this approach by bringing to it a new awareness of the status of aesthetic representation and the importance of unity within a literary work. He also grounds his conception of the psychology of characters, poets and readers in a new, Kantian vocabulary of mental faculties.

(2) *Philosophical criticism.* 'The distinction of Coleridge, which puts him head and shoulders above every other English critic', wrote Herbert Read in the mid twentieth century, 'is due to his introduction of a philosophical method of criticism'.[4] Coleridge would have felt that this judgement corresponded exactly to his aims: to ground the reading and appreciation of literature and art on a set of fixed principles derived in part from the British philosophical tradition, in part from Kant and German idealism.

(3) *Practical criticism.* Utilised and demonstrated in his public lectures as well as in *Biographia Literaria*, the term 'practical criticism' is original with Coleridge and was made more famous by the twentieth-century critic I. A. Richards when he used it as the title of an influential book on 'literary judgement' in 1929. The term encapsulates Coleridge's belief that criticism must begin with fixed principles, but must always apply these to particular works with the goal of understanding and appreciating the way parts of a work contribute to the pleasure generated by the whole. In his lectures, Coleridge applied the principles of criticism primarily to Shakespeare, Milton and other canonical writers, but a complete understanding of his critical practice would also take into account his engagement with Wordsworth's poetry in *Biographia Literaria* and his numerous reviews and interpretations of other contemporary writers. In all cases, Coleridge pays precise attention to details of literary language, noting in the course of an analysis of Walter Scott's *Lady of the Lake* 'how little instructive any criticism can be which does not enter into minutiae' (*CN* III, 3970).

(4) *Sympathetic or genial criticism.* Coleridge's frequent tirades against contemporary reviewers, and against eighteenth-century Shakespeare critics, form part of a campaign to reform criticism. He tries to show that it is more productive for reviewers to point out and account for the excellences of a work rather than its defects. In his essays 'On the Principles of Genial Criticism' (1814), he maintains that critical principles should be based on an awareness of the particular character of each poem as determined by the poet's controlling imagination, which can make even apparent irregularities in a poem work towards the effect of the whole.

These characteristic features of Coleridge's criticism have been recognised, to varying degrees, since his critical notes and fragments began to be published in the late nineteenth century. In light of what has been called the 'linguistic turn' in late twentieth-century criticism, however, a much more recent trend is to credit Coleridge with being one of the first to base his literary criticism on a theory of language. Paul Hamilton's *Coleridge's Poetics* and A. C. Goodson's *Verbal Imagination*, both published in the 1980s, demonstrate in different ways how thoroughly Coleridge's criticism is informed by ideas about language drawn from both eighteenth-century British traditions and the idealist philosophy developing in Germany during Coleridge's lifetime. Thus Coleridge's frequent insistence that art is not a copy but an imitation of nature, that the greatness of great poets lies in the way they *represent* character and life, and that poetry derives from the mind, also needs to be understood as part of a wide-ranging philosophical system centring on the word or Logos as the medium through which we all – artists or not – apprehend the world. As a young man of twenty-eight, Coleridge longed to write a major work devoted to 'Poetry & the nature of the Pleasures derived from it' (*CL* II, 671). But by his late forties his literary criticism became totally subsumed into philosophy and theology – that is, into a theory of what he called the Logos. Coleridge's only substantial study of a literary work after 1819, a lecture of 1825 on Aeschylus' *Prometheus Bound*, concerns itself with 'the mythic import of the work' (*SWF* II, 1264), assimilating dramatic characters entirely to theological principles. As his late work shows, Coleridge ultimately regarded the language of poetry and drama as a subcategory of a more general theory of language, Logos, and discursive reason.

NOTES

1 James Gillman, *The Life of Samuel Taylor Coleridge* (London: Pickering, 1838), 335–6.
2 T. S. Eliot, 'Shakespearian Criticism: 1. From Dryden to Coleridge', *A Companion to Shakespeare Studies*, ed. Harley Granville-Barker and G. B. Harrison (Cambridge University Press, 1966), 298.
3 F. R. Leavis, 'Revaluations (XIII): Coleridge in Criticism', *Scrutiny*, 9 (1940–1), 69.
4 Herbert Read, *Coleridge as Critic* (London: Faber and Faber, 1949), 18.

10

PETER J. KITSON

Political thinker

Throughout his life, S. T. Coleridge was a politically engaged thinker. From his student days as an undergraduate at Jesus College, Cambridge, when he participated in agitation in support of his hero, William Frend, to his later years as the 'Sage of Highgate' criticising the pervasion of materialist thinking and commercial ethics through all aspects of life, Coleridge was a deeply political man. His writings reveal him as someone who closely followed the contemporary political scene as it unfolded during one of the most turbulent and exciting periods in the nation's history, a man steeped in the leading ideas of European political philosophy. Coleridge gave political lectures, wrote leaders, essays and editorials for the press, in which he commented on the major issues of the time, published journals full of political comment, and produced three substantial political treatises. As a young man he published sonnets on key political figures of the time, such as Burke, Pitt, Priestley and William Godwin; poems of political and religious dissent; and a number of poems about his response to the French Revolution, most notably 'Fears in Solitude' and 'France: An Ode'. All this is remarkable in a writer known chiefly as the composer of several of the greatest poems in the English language.

If the range and scope of Coleridge's political *oeuvre* is daunting, equally difficult are the arguments which surround it. In his own time Coleridge was known as one of the English 'Jacobins', a vague and imprecise term which was used, often pejoratively, to indicate a supporter of the French Revolution and Parliamentary reform and opponent of the repressive measures of the government of William Pitt. He was the disciple of the dissenter Joseph Priestley and the close friend of the radical political lecturer John Thelwall. In later life it was claimed he reneged on his support for radical politics and religion, becoming, in the years of post-war reaction, a supporter of the established Church and State. Most typical of this view of Coleridge was that of his erstwhile admirer, William Hazlitt, who represented the former radical as an apostate who 'at last turned on the pivot of a subtle casuistry to the *unclean side*' (Howe XI, 34). Coleridge with his fellow poets William Wordsworth and Robert Southey thus constituted what Francis Jeffrey labelled the 'Lake School' of poets, men who had turned their backs on radical and reformist youth, retreating to the Lake District and replacing ideas of political renewal with escapist visions of natural sublimity. This picture was echoed by Byron's attack on the three 'epic renegades' in the Dedication to the first Canto of *Don Juan* (1818).

The position, however, is much more complicated than Hazlitt's trajectory of democrat to reactionary would suggest. Certainly Coleridge did move from being a radical dissenter to being a proponent of the established Church and State, from being a democrat and republican to being a monarchist and a defender of a restricted franchise, from being a severe critic of the rights of property to being one of its stoutest defenders. Nevertheless there were aspects of Coleridge's thought that remained constant. Additionally neither his early radicalism, nor his later conservatism, were straightforward adoptions of currently held opinions. Even Hazlitt, while contemptuously criticising Wordsworth and Southey for entering the citadel of reaction, emphasised the marginality of Coleridge's situation: '[B]ut Mr. Coleridge did not enter with them; pitching his tent upon the barren waste without, and having no abiding place nor city of refuge!' (Howe XI, 38). Criticism of Coleridge has tended to fall into two camps, those stressing the lack of continuity between dissenter and conservative and those who emphasise the continuity of his work.[1] Nicholas Roe, in particular, showed Wordsworth and Coleridge to be at 'the epicentre of British radical life'.[2] Coleridge's dissent has been further related to earlier traditions of political ideas, especially his debt to an older tradition of political dissent deriving from the Commonwealth thought of seventeenth-century republicans, such as John Milton, James Harrington and their eighteenth-century mediators John Toland and Moses Lowman. Certainly Coleridge's early political thought should not be regarded as he himself was prone to in later life, as a youthful aberration; instead it was a deeply thought and felt response to an established tradition of English radicalism, dating back to the great political controversies and experiments of the English Revolution.[3]

Undoubtedly there were ideas and themes which ran consistently through Coleridge's political career from the Bristol lectures to his *On the Constitution of the Church and State*: he always advocated the positive role of government in promoting the welfare of its people; he stressed the necessity to ground political conduct and speculation on 'fixed and determinate principles of action' (*EOT* I, 24); he believed that improvement would occur, in the first instance, through the efficacy of a small group of enlightened thinkers; he upheld the freedom of the press; and, most importantly, his political opinions were always informed by his religious beliefs, however his faith altered. Such a consistency of belief would grant support to Coleridge's own claim that there was 'not a single political Opinion' which he held in youth that he did not continue to hold in later life (*Friend*, 719). This is, of course, not the whole truth. Coleridge clearly disavowed much of his earlier radicalism and changed his opinions relating to the issue of property and how it should be represented in political structures. In his *Biographia Literaria* of 1817, he played down his part in the radical agitation of the time, affirming his enthusiasm for the dissenting opinions he held but describing these opinions as 'in many and most important points erroneous' and proclaiming the opposition of 'his principles...to those of jacobinism or even of democracy' (*BL* I, 180, 184). Yet in 1794, Coleridge could write to Robert Southey in extreme republican terms: 'The Cockatrice is emblematic of Monarchy – a *monster* generated by *ingratitude* on *Absurdity*. When Serpents *sting*, the only remedy is – to *kill* the *Serpent*, and *besmear* the *Wound* with the *Fat*' (*CL* I, 84). These were strong words for 1794, a year after Louis XVI of France had been executed for crimes against the new French Republic.

Coleridge had been radicalised at Cambridge though his association with William Frend. It was probably Frend who converted Coleridge to Unitarianism, a dissenting sect of Christians who wished to return to the doctrinal purity of the early Church. They believed that many, if not most, of the beliefs of the established Church were, in fact, corruptions. These corruptions involved such key beliefs as the divinity of Christ and the atonement. Affirming the humanity of Christ excluded the Unitarians from participating in the civic life of the state, according to the Test and Corporation Acts, which they tirelessly campaigned against. The leading exponent of Unitarian Christianity in the late eighteenth century was the scientist and theologian Joseph Priestley, whose works Coleridge devoured. When Frend was tried by the vice-chancellor's court for 'sedition and defamation of the Church of England' Coleridge was notable in his support. Coleridge himself applauded one of Frend's remarks during the trial.[4] After Cambridge, Coleridge with his fellow radical, the poet Robert Southey, devised a scheme for emigration to America to found a Utopian colony on the banks of the Susquehanna river. The system of 'Pantisocracy' was organised on the principle of the equal rule of all and involved the communal ownership of property. It would have involved the families of twelve men (the number of the disciples). Clearly the two poets had not fully thought out the implications of what they were doing, and the scheme ended in ignominious failure when Southey inherited money, placing him in the position of contributing much more to the venture than others. Southey had also scandalised Coleridge by his proposal that a servant should accompany them. Nevertheless Pantisocracy was not simply the whim of two young men but a scheme related to a long tradition of communal settlement in America. Its origins were less in Southey's acknowledged Godwinian beliefs, than in Coleridge's Christianity. Coleridge believed, at this time, that property was 'beyond doubt the Origin of all Evil' (*CL* I, 214). The 'leading Idea of Pantisocracy' was 'to make men *necessarily* virtuous by removing all Motives to evil' (*CL* I, 114). In his 'Lectures on Revealed Religion' delivered in Bristol, in 1795, he referred to the example of the early Church which followed Christ's teaching: 'In Acts II. 44. 45. we read "And all that believed were together, & had all things in common – and sold their possessions & goods and parted them to all men, as every man had need"'(*Lects. 1795*, 219). Coleridge also noted that the Hebrew constitution of Moses enforced the equalisation of property. The land was divided equally and debt was curtailed by the prohibition on charging interest on money and the requirement that all debts were remitted every seventh year (*Lects. 1795*, 124–30). In the Mosaic dispensation Coleridge understood one of the key ideas of his political philosophy, 'Property is Power and equal Property equal Power':

['']The Land shall not be sold, for the Land is mine, saith the Lord, and ye are strangers and sojourners with me.['] There is nothing more pernicious than the notion that anyone possesses an absolute right to the Soil, which he appropriates – to the system of accumulation that flows from this supposed right we are indebted for nine-tenths of our Vices and Miseries. The Land is no one's – the produce belongs equally to all, who contribute their due proportion of Labour.   (*Lects. 1795*, 125–6)

Coleridge himself would go further in proposing an 'abolition of all individual Property' as the only security against accumulation (*Lects. 1795*, 128). This was a belief that he versified in the poetic summary of his theological, political and philosophical opinions, 'Religious Musings' (composed 1794–6), where, at the poem's millenarian climax, 'the vast family of Love / Raised from the common earth by common toil / Enjoy the equal produce' (341–3).

Coleridge's ideas about property went much further than most radicals and dissenters would countenance. The radical philosopher William Godwin argued for equalisation of property in his *Enquiry Concerning Political Justice* (1793), but not its communal ownership. John Thelwall desired only an equality of rights not of property, 'a system so wild and extravagant' which would only serve to give 'rascals and cut-throats an opportunity . . . of transferring all property into their own hands'.[5] Priestley himself was a keen proponent of commerce. Coleridge's true antecedents were the protestant sectaries of the seventeenth-century Commonwealth, most notably the communistic Diggers led by Gerrard Winstanley who, with thirty or forty associates, gathered for the purpose of digging up and cultivating the common land of St George's Hill near Cobham in Surrey in 1649.[6] Thelwall perceived this difference between the views of Coleridge and other 'Friends of Liberty' when he fulminated against what he saw as his former friend's exculpation from the charge that he had been a Jacobin. In the margins of his own copy of *Biographia* Thelwall complained that Coleridge was 'far from Democracy, because he was far beyond it…he was a down right zealous leveller & indeed in one of the worst senses of the word he was a Jacobin, a man of blood'.[7] It was precisely Coleridge's philosophical extremism and his concern with what Thelwall described as 'the republic of God's own making' that separated him from the mainstream of the English radical and reformist movements in the 1790s.[8] Thelwall, a materialist, was exasperated by Coleridge's attachment to religion and Coleridge, a zealous dissenter, determined to influence Thelwall to his own beliefs. This tension between the two men provided one of the chief reasons for their friendship. The sincere and close friendship between Coleridge and Thelwall which followed with Coleridge's desperate attempts to settle the reviled and persecuted radical in the Nether Stowey neighbourhood, should not disguise this fundamental difference in political opinions that existed between them, no matter how united they were in their opposition to the war against revolutionary France and their contempt for the repressive measures of Pitt's government at home.[9]

In the *Biographia* Coleridge drew attention to his isolation from the reformist movements of the time, highlighting not his attacks on the government but, instead, his critique of '*modern patriotism*' (*BL* I, 185). This is true but selective. Coleridge attempted to ground his own political beliefs on a religious basis and his opinions were certainly idiosyncratic, yet these things would not, in themselves, isolate him within the various and fractured groupings of reformers and radicals of the 1790s, not all of whom derived their political opinions from the work of the secular thinkers, Thomas Paine or William Godwin. The debate about the significance and value of the French Revolution was properly begun by Edmund Burke's *Reflections on the Revolution in France* (1790). For Burke the Revolution was the product of Enlightenment philosophers, lawyers and other professional groupings, intent on tearing up the fabric of French society, government and religion. Burke stressed, instead, the notion of society as a partnership between the past, present and the future and he emphasised the value of precedent, tradition and prejudice. His attack on the revolutionaries in France occasioned many replies, most notably by William Godwin and Thomas Paine. Paine's *The Rights of Man* (1791–2) argued that mankind had certain natural rights that were suspended when we enter a state of civil society, but that if the government failed to promote and protect these rights then the people were allowed to remove the government, whatever its form, and begin again. Paine was also a Deist, dismissive of the established Church. William Godwin, in his *Enquiry Concerning Political Justice* (1793), also opposed Burke but steered a different track from Paine. His philosophy stressed the importance of three cardinal virtues, Reason, Truth and Justice, arguing that all institutions should be subject to the test of Reason without recourse to emotions of gratitude or deference. These institutions included government, religion, the family and marriage.

Coleridge took his political bearings from a different radical tradition and found the examples of Godwin and Paine to be highly troubling. The early influences on his political thought were those of David Hartley and Joseph Priestley. Hartley, in his *Observations on Man* (1749), provided a mechanistic account of how the mind arrives at knowledge of the world. Hartley argued that our knowledge of the world is built up through sensation by a process Locke called the 'association of ideas'. This denied that there were any innate ideas in the mind which was thus an empty vessel or blank sheet of paper, a *tabula rasa*, awaiting the experience of the world to write upon it. Hartley argued that we progress from simple to complex ideas, eventually building up moral ideas and moving to a love of God. The moral nature of the human being was thus determined by environment. Mankind was in theory perfectible, and progress was determined by necessity. Hartley's epistemology had been absorbed by Joseph Priestley who made the doctrines of necessitarianism and optimism a part of his political philosophy. Coleridge subscribed to Priestley's Unitarian synthesis. In a letter to Southey of December 1794 he admitted 'I am a compleat Necessitarian – and understand the subject as well almost as Hartley himself – but I go farther than Hartley and believe the corporeality of thought—namely, that it is motion – ' (*CL* 1, 137). Priestley did not discriminate between matter and spirit, regarding them as manifestations of the same substance, and Coleridge seems to have concurred with this conflation of matter and spirit.[10]

The attraction of Hartley's and Priestley's ideas for Coleridge was that they removed the element of chance and the random from the world. These ideas demonstrated how the necessary workings of associationist psychology transformed self-interest into disinterested benevolence: 'Jesus knew our nature – and that expands like the circles of a Lake – the Love of our Friends, parents and neighbours lead[s] us to love of our Country to the love of all Mankind' (*Lects. 1795*, 163). Here Coleridge attacks Godwin for his rejection of the values of family and community as irrational, recuperating them for a radical politics which supplies the major deficiency of Godwin's system, a motivation to act. At the same time Coleridge argues against Burke that familial values are not necessarily the foundation of paternalism and monarchy. Coleridge was also ill disposed to Godwin because he believed that his rejection of Christian values led to atheism, libertinism and depravity. In the *Watchman* (1796) Coleridge accused the followers of Godwin of considering 'filial affection folly, gratitude a crime, marriage injustice, and the promiscuous intercourse of the sexes right and wise' (*Watchman*, 99–100).

In a sense Coleridge was right about his earlier dissent. In publications, such as *Conciones ad Populum* (1795), *The Plot Discovered* (1795) and *The Watchman* (1796), he was concerned not only to attack the war with France and to argue for political reform, but also to place his dissent within a tradition of religious radical thought. In the *Conciones*, a published version of political lectures delivered in Bristol as a means of funding the Pantisocracy project, he stressed the 'necessity of *bottoming* on fixed principles', a recurrent theme in his political writing (*Lects. 1795*, 33). He sees the French Nation teaching the lessons that 'the Knowledge of the Few cannot counteract the Ignorance of the Many' and 'that general Illumination should precede Revolution', stressing the importance of a moral reformation of the people as a prelude to political reformation, also a lifelong concern of his work (*Lects. 1795*, 34, 43). Coleridge categorises the 'Friends of Liberty' into four classes. The first are fair-weather supporters, alternatively Republicans or Aristocrats; the second class are thoughtless extremists motivated by hate, susceptible to the 'inflammatory harangues' of political demagogues; and the third are the propertied middle-class dissenters and reformers, selfishly dragging down what is above them but jealous of any attempt to alleviate the sufferings of those below them (*Lects. 1795*, 37–9). The final group is the 'small but glorious band' of 'thinking and disinterested patriots', men who regard 'the affairs of man as a process', understanding that 'vice originates not in the man, but in the surrounding circumstances' (*Lects. 1795*, 40). The notion of an intellectual vanguard that will safeguard political change would transmute into Coleridge's concept of the clerisy. Central to his thought is Coleridge's criticism of Godwinian claims that Reason will provide a motivation for action for all classes, gradually trickling down the social chain to the lowest links. Instead he argues that only the Christian dispensation will do this and that we 'should plead *for* the Oppressed, not *to* them'. A reformer should be among the poor teaching them 'their *Duties* in order that he may render them susceptible of their *Rights*' and preaching the gospel as a way of effecting change (*Lects. 1795*, 43–4). Such sentiments are widely divergent from those of Paine and Thelwall who would rather enable the labouring poor to obtain their political rights. Coleridge, however, combines this preliminary discourse with a swingeing attack on the government for its conduct of the war with France and its repressive measures at home. His *The Plot Discovered* (1795) similarly attacks the restricted franchise and ministerial corruption of the constitution, drawing upon the English republican tradition of 'Milton, Locke, Sidney and Harrington'.[11] For Coleridge the best form of government is that in which all the people are *'morally* present' through representation (*Lects. 1795*, 306). Given the state of the present restricted franchise in Great Britain the only thing saving the country from an effective despotism is 'the Liberty of the Press' by which 'the whole nation becomes one grand Senate' (*Lects. 1795*, 312–13), and this the present government was attempting to curtail.

The *Conciones ad Populum, The Plot Discovered* and the *Watchman* constitute the high-points of Coleridge's radical dissent. Subsequent works involve a re-thinking of his political commitments. In 1798, the French invaded the peaceful cantons of Switzerland and Coleridge took this as an opportunity to recant from his former support of the Revolution which he now considered, with much justice, to have betrayed its own ideals. In 'France: An Ode', first published in the opposition newspaper, the *Morning Post*, in April 1798 under the title 'The Recantation', Coleridge furthered his criticism of the Godwinian radicals at home, 'the "Sensual and the Dark"' who burst their manacles only to wear the 'name of freedom, graven on a heavier chain' (85). But then he went further, distinguishing the tarnished concept of revolutionary political 'Freedom' from that of true 'Liberty', a power found not in the works of man, but in the forms of nature, 'earth, sea, and air' (102–5). Similar concerns are expressed in Coleridge's 'Fears in Solitude' written during a period of alarm at a possible French invasion. Infused with a sense of guilt for the many national crimes his country has occasioned, the poet now moves towards the recovery of a sense of a national community, redefining patriotism in terms which gender the conflict of English masculinity and piety against a feminine French sensuality:

> Stand forth! be men! repel an impious foe,
> Impious and false, a light yet cruel race,
> Who laugh away all virtue, mingling mirth
> With deeds of murder; and still promising
> Freedom, themselves too sensual to be free
>
> (139–43)

People get the governments they deserve. Simply to change the forms of 'constituted power' will make no difference if 'our own rank folly and wickedness' remain unchecked (162). The redemptive values of the English countryside are now placed against corrupt and war-mongering politicians, atheistic radicals and hypocritical French sensualists.

It is not easy to date the beginning of Coleridge's passage from idiosyn-cratic dissenter to idiosyncratic conservative.[12] In a series of essays 'On the French Constitution', for the *Morning Post*, Coleridge re-defined his polit-ical creed. Although in *The Plot Discovered* he had argued for the 'moral' representation of all, now he defined good government thus: 'For the present race of men Governments must be founded on property' (7 December 1799; *EOT* I, 32). Now Coleridge affirms the value of the British constitution in al-most Burkeian terms as a proper balance of 'the influence of a Court, the pop-ular spirit, and the predominance of property' (26 December 1799; *EOT* III, 47–8). It was only a short step from this position to becoming a keen sup-porter of the war with Bonapartist France – which he now saw as an am-bitious military dictatorship – when it was resumed in 1802 after the brief peace of the Treaty of Amiens in 1801.

Although many of his concerns remained constant Coleridge had altered his view on a number of issues by 1805. Most importantly he had aban-doned his Unitarian dissent for an acceptance of the Trinity, and the estab-lished Church was to play a more and more important role in his thinking from then on. In his essay 'Once a Jacobin Always a Jacobin' he defined a Jacobin as someone who 'builds a Government on personal and natu-ral rights' and denied he had ever departed from the axiom in politics that 'property must be the grand basis of government' (*Lects. 1795*, 370, 373). This political philosophy was developed and refined in a series of essays for the *Friend* (1809–10, revised 1812 and 1818). Here Coleridge applied the distinction between the Reason and the Understanding that he had learnt from the German philosopher Immanuel Kant. This distinction maintained that the Understanding was the faculty 'of thinking and forming *judgments* on the notices furnished by the sense' (similar to Hartley's and Priestley's notion of how the mind worked) and the Reason was 'the power by which we become possessed of principle . . . and of ideas' such as 'Justice, Holiness, Free-Will etc' (*Friend* I, 177). Coleridge distinguished between three types of government, that founded on fear (as in the theories of Thomas Hobbes), that founded on expediency (as advocated by Burke), and that founded on pure Reason (as described by Rousseau and his Jacobin followers). Dismissing government by fear as applicable to beasts not men, and government by expediency as oblivious to the 'sublime Truths of our human nature' (*Friend* I, 173, 185), Coleridge proceeds to develop a critique of those systems founded on an appeal to Reason.

In Coleridge's view, governments founded on pure Reason, such as that advocated in Rousseau's concept of the 'General Will', mistake the nature of the Reason itself which should have no place in the practical arrangements of governing. Reason provides the primary principle for all of Coleridge's later political philosophy:

> Every man is born with the faculty of Reason: and whatever is without it, be the shape what it may, is not a man or PERSON, but a THING. Hence the sacred principle, recognized by all Laws, human and divine, the principle indeed, which is the *ground-work* of all law and justice, that a person can never become a thing, nor be treated as such without wrong.   (*Friend* I, 189–90)

In terms of Reason all men are equal as all equally possess the faculty, but all are not equal in terms of their Understanding which depends on environment and education. Reason belongs to the sphere of morality, politics to the Understanding. Those who determined that government should be founded on personal right were then led to make endless qualifications. Rousseau had to fall back on the General Will in the belief that Reason was best shown in the aggregate. Women and children, all possessed equally of Reason, had to be excluded from the franchise and women are 'a full half … of the whole human race' (*Friend* I, 195). For Coleridge government begins not in the protection of personal rights but in the protection of property. Man is not a creature of 'pure Intellect' and thus his 'Reason never acts by itself, but must clothe itself in the substance of individual Understanding and specific Inclination, in order to become a reality and an object of consciousness and experience' (*Friend* I, 201). Jacobinism thus becomes, in Coleridge's *The Statesman's Manual*, a '*monstrum hybridum*, made up in part of despotism, and in part of abstract reason misapplied to objects that belong entirely to experience and the understanding' (*SM*, 63–4).

The *Friend* laid the groundwork of Coleridge's later political philosophy, commonly referred to as conservative, but always oddly so and still carrying on some of the concerns of his early radical thinking. Suffused with a belief in the importance of the positive role of government which he had outlined back in the pages of the *Watchman* of 1796, this philosophy stressed the values of tolerance and always showed a concern for the social (if not the political) welfare of the labouring classes. The years following the end of the Napoleonic War in 1815 were troubled. Britain experienced the painful transition from a war-time to peace-time economy, new industrial and technological working practices made redundant many traditional craftsmen, such as the hand-loom weavers who responded with 'Ludd-ite' frame breaking. Farmers, fearing competition from cheap foreign grain, demanded protection; financiers, merchants, businessmen were worried by inflation. The government of Lord Liverpool responded to the crisis with the protectionist Corn Law of 1815 and a series of repressive measures. Fears of revolution were re-kindled by the revival of the reform movement, led by a new breed of radical demagogues demanding the reform of Parliament and the repeal of the Corn Laws. Social protests and disturbances, such as The Spa Fields Riot, the Peterloo Massacre, and the notorious Cato Street Conspiracy, led the government to introduce the repressive Six Acts of 1820. To cap it all, at the death of George III in 1820, the Prince Regent attempted to divorce his estranged wife Caroline of Brunswick to prevent her becoming his Queen. The resulting trial was exploited by radicals and reformers who depicted the leaders of the nation as unscrupulous hypocrites.[13]

One of the major themes of Coleridge's later writing is that the landed interest and the traditional leaders of society had abdicated their duties and responsibilities. The Corn Laws, which he saw as a selfish measure on the part of one class to protect itself at the expense of the nation, were evidence of this. Similarly he was scandalised by the spectacle of a libidinous monarch attempting to divorce his wife on grounds of adultery, instead of behaving as his rank demanded. To address this crisis Coleridge published two of three 'Lay Sermons' designed to appeal to the various classes of society (the third, for the working classes, was never written). The first of the sermons, *The Statesman's Manual* (1816), was addressed to the 'higher classes of society' and attempted to combine Kantian ideas of the Reason and the Understanding and German Higher criticism of the Bible with the realities of political economy. Coleridge argued that the difficulties that the country was experiencing resulted, in part, from the general and unquestioned acceptance of the empiricist philosophy and Utilitarian economics by all classes of society. Against this trend he upheld a synthesis of Christianity and Idealist philosophy which stressed the importance of principles. To the charge that the notion of the Bible furnishing the best political strategy for a contemporary politician was somewhat quixotic, Coleridge answered that in the Scriptures we have 'a history of Men' not 'a shadow-fight of Things and Quantities' (*SM*, 28). The political economies of the time are 'the *product* of an unenlivened generalizing Understanding' whereas the Scriptures give us 'the living *educts* of the Imagination . . . a system of symbols, harmonious in themselves, and consubstantial with the truths, of which they are the *conductors*' (*SM*, 29). In the Scriptures the ideas of pure Reason are clothed with the images of sense, providing principles for action beyond the motivations of the self-interest of the empirical Understanding. Coleridge's *A Lay Sermon* (1817), addressed to the middle classes, is more focussed on the current discontent. It shows his uneasiness, first glimpsed in the *Conciones ad Populum* of 1795, with the demagogues, 'false prophets', who plead '*to* the Poor and Ignorant' but are never found 'actually pleading *for* them' (*SM*, 142–5, 148). Coleridge diagnoses society's main problem to be dependence on the 'Overbalance of the Commercial Spirit' and the 'Absence or Weakness of the Counter-Weight' (*SM*, 169). The true counter-weights should be the landed interest and religion but one is enfeebled by an acceptance of commercial ethics and the other by the growing importance of dissent, in particular Unitarian dissent, the sect that Coleridge himself had adhered to as a young man. Against those who regard the evils of economic depression 'as so much superfluous steam ejected by the Escape Pipes and safety valves of a self-regulating Machine' maintaining that in a 'free and trading country *all things find their level*', Coleridge opposes the humanist point that 'Persons are not *Things* – but Man does not find his own level!' (*SM*, 205).

Coleridge finally pitched his tent outside the citadel of orthodoxy with his last major, political treatise, the extraordinary *On the Constitution of the Church and State* (1829), ostensibly a part of the debate about the repeal of the civil disabilities of Catholics, but a work that goes much further into the realms of political philosophy. Coleridge argues in quasi-Platonic mode that there exists an 'Idea' of the State prior to experience and not abstracted from any particular state, but that this 'Idea' could only be manifest in the works of individual nations and societies. The 'Idea' could not exist in its pure rational state in the forms of men but it could be regulative of existing arrangements which may or may not conform to it. The social state in ideal form reflects two forces, the interests of 'Permanence' and the interest of 'Progression' (*Church and State*, 24). The interests of permanence are served by the landed classes, and the interests of progression by the commercial classes, the mercantile, the manufacturing, the distributive and the professional. The idea of the State approximates to that of the British Parliament where the landed interest is represented in the House of Lords and the other in the Commons, while the king 'in whom the executive power is vested' functions as 'the beam of the constitutional scales' or balance of interests (*Church and State*, 29–30). There were things that the State was not able to do, however, no matter how ideally constituted. The idea of the Nation, thus, includes both that of the State and that of the 'National Church', 'two poles of the same magnet; the magnet itself, which is constituted by them, is the CONSTITUTION of the Nation' (*Church and State*, 31). Coleridge, as in his radical days, took his lead from the biblical Hebrew Commonwealth. Here the 'NATIONALITY', an endowment of property, was settled on one of the twelve tribes, a body entrusted with the moral and intellectual improvement of the people. The National Church is, therefore, the '*third* great venerable estate of the realm', charged with securing and improving 'that civilization, without which the nation could be neither permanent nor progressive' (*Church and State*, 42, 43–4). This is done through the endeavours of a national 'Clerisy' – a class or order of learned educators, guardians of the nation's culture. Coleridge is keen to distinguish the National Church from the Church of Christ which belongs to another world, though it is a glorious historical accident that in Britain the National Church is Christian.

In *Church and State* we can see many of the concerns of the younger Coleridge: the concern with education and the positive functions of government; the stress on the acts and examples of an enlightened elite in achieving general illumination; the strong scriptural underpinning of politics with religion; the related interest in the Hebrew Commonwealth as a model for government; and the various concerns with the relation between property and power. Throughout, the strong humanitarian and social concern is there, where the 'machinery of the wealth of the nation' is made up of 'the wretchedness, disease and depravity of those who should constitute the strength of the nation!' (*Church and State*, 63). Finally defending the Church establishment he had vilified as Antichrist in the 1790s and chastising the members of the dissenting sects to which he had formerly belonged, Coleridge remained throughout a Christian, patriot and Commonwealthsman, no matter how much those words themselves changed for him over his long political life.

NOTES

1 Both John Colmer, *Coleridge, Critic of Society* (Oxford: Clarendon Press, 1959), and John Morrow, *Coleridge's Political Thought: Property, Morality and the Limits of Traditional Discourse* (Basingstoke: Macmillan, 1990), stress the continuity of the poet's thought. For those more critical of Coleridge's break with his radical past see E. P. Thompson, 'Disenchantment or Default: A Lay Sermon', *Power and Consciousness*, ed. C. C. O'Brien and D. Vanech (London and New York: University of London Press, 1969), 149–81; and Nicholas Roe, *Wordsworth and Coleridge: The Radical Years* (Oxford: Clarendon Press, 1988).

2 Roe, *Wordsworth and Coleridge*, 14, 4.

3 Nigel Leask, *The Politics of Imagination in Coleridge's Critical Thought* (Basingstoke: Macmillan, 1988); Morrow, *Coleridge's Political Thought*; Peter J. Kitson, ' "The Electric fluid of truth" ', *Coleridge and the Armoury of the Human Mind*, ed. Peter J. Kitson and Thomas N. Corns (London: Frank Cass, 1991), 36–62; ' "Sages and patriots that being dead do yet speak to us": Readings of the English Revolution in the Late Eighteenth century' *Pamphlet Wars: Prose in the English Revolution*, ed. James Holstun (London: Frank Cass, 1992), 205–30.

4 Richard Holmes, *Coleridge: Early Visions* (London: Hodder and Stoughton, 1989), 47–9.

5 John Thelwall, *Peaceful Discussion, and not tumultary violence, the means of redressing national grievance* (London: printed for J. Thelwall, 1795), 14.

6 See Peter J. Kitson, ' "Our Prophetic Harrington" ', *Wordsworth Circle*, 24 (1993), 97–102.

7 B. R. Pollin, 'John Thelwall's Marginalia in a Copy of Coleridge's *Biographia Literaria*', *Bulletin of the New York Public Library*, 74 (1970), 73–94.

8 Quoted in Thompson, 'Disenchantment or Default?', 162.
9 See Nicholas Roe, 'Coleridge and John Thelwall: The Road to Nether Stowey', *The Coleridge Connection: Essays for Thomas McFarland*, ed. Richard Gravil and Molly Lefebure (Basingstoke: Macmillan, 1990), 60–82.
10 See H. W. Piper, *The Active Universe. Pantheism and the Concept of the Imagination in the English Romantic Poets* (London: Athlone Press, 1962); Leask, *Politics of Imagination*, 19–30; Ian Wylie, *Young Coleridge and the Philosophers of Nature* (Oxford: Clarendon Press, 1989), 27–46.
11 See Kitson, '"Electric fluid of truth"'.
12 David Erdman 'Introduction', *EOT*, ix–ixvii; Morrow, *Coleridge's Political Thought*, 43–72.
13 Tim Fulford, *Romanticism and Masculinity* (Basingstoke: Macmillan, 1999), 155–76.

II

PAUL HAMILTON

The philosopher

Is Coleridge philosophically interesting? His philosophical output was prodigious and remarkably untidy. His letters abound in comments and judgements on his philosophical reading; they document his current theoretical allegiances and his plans to publish them. His Notebooks, kept throughout his life, extend this activity into private areas safe from public accountability, showing a corresponding increase in adventurousness and ambition but fewer signs of decisions being taken and consistent positions being occupied. The fascinating Notebook entries are 'acts of obedience to the apostolic command of Trying all things' (CN III, 3881). Early publications like the 1795 *Lectures on Politics and Religion* reveal a young intellectual engrossed by the possible philosophical justifications for radical sentiments in politics that he considers congruent with his religious beliefs. At that time those beliefs were Unitarian, mapped out in his poetry of the time (especially 'The Destiny of Nations') as a convergence of different knowledges appropriate to a God who shared his aspects amongst different religions. Unitarianism fitted with Coleridge's championing of intellectual enfranchisement, however sceptical he was growing of Jacobin enlargements of the political franchise in France. In the Prospectus to the *Watchman* in 1796, he equated communicative and political action, arguing that 'the *forms* of Government ... are but the Shadows, the virtue and rationality of the people at large are the substance, of freedom ... We actually transfer the Sovereignty to the People, when we make them susceptible of it' (*Watchman*, 4–5). This repeats ideas central to William Godwin's topical *Enquiry Concerning Political Justice* (1793) whose idealistic rationalism must also have nurtured the transcendental tendency in Coleridge, as much as did his growing dissatisfaction with the Hobbesian psychology of empiricism popularised by John Locke and developed most exhaustively by David Hartley.

The psychology was based on theories of the association of ideas, and it is his extrication from this intellectual matrix which Coleridge pronounces to be his birth at last into authentic philosophical activity, an incarnation he dramatised again in the first volume of *Biographia Literaria*. In February 1801 he wrote to Thomas Poole: 'If I do not greatly delude myself, I have not only completely extricated the notions of Time and Space; but have overthrown the doctrine of Association, as taught by Hartley, and with it all the irreligious metaphysics of modern Infidels – especially, the doctrine of Necessity' (*CL* II, 706). Coleridge had been grateful to Tom Wedgwood, brother of his patron Josiah, for having stated to him 'some very valuable truths' which he guessed had 'been noticed before, & set forth by Kant in part & in part by Lambert' (*CL* II, 675). Lambert need not detain us, but Coleridge's phrasing suggests that he probably knew of Kant's starting place, the transcendental aesthetic with which the *Critique of Pure Reason* begins, in which we find the transcendental exposition of the forms of space and time. Kant then demonstrates that categories such as causality or natural necessity are logical prerequisites internal to our experience of the world rather than externally imposed by it on us. Kant's reversal of empiricist priorities released in Coleridge the sense of an ultimate human freedom which Kant should have exploited further.[1]

The dynamic view of life, testifying to our unavoidable implication of its nature in our own processes of understanding it, could be derived by Coleridge from Kant, but only as a regulatory precept, not as an idea constitutive of the actual state of things in themselves. However, Coleridge, like other post-Kantians, immediately traced the dynamic view in earlier, more unabashedly animistic thinkers, such as Giordano Bruno, Jakob Boehme and the Cambridge Platonists. Coleridge's subsequent philosophical writings adopt the post-Kantian idiom in which the primary issue becomes that of how to describe an Absolute activity common to mind and nature although reducible to neither. Coleridge's claim to Poole quickly moves on to his ambitions, rather than his achievements, which are no less than 'to solve the process of Life & Consciousness' (*CL* II, 706). This formulation anticipates his reading of (especially) Schelling's *Naturphilosophie* which his *Theory of Life* utilised in 1815 (unpublished until 1849) to intervene in a dispute about the nature of animation raging in contemporary reviews. Coleridge is typically post-Kantian in his point of departure, but his ubiquitous religious commitment to Christian doctrine inhibits his full participation in scientific and philosophical debate. At some point, he always retreats to question the conclusiveness of any answer framed in terms which are not finally religious, and, within religion, doctrinal. The marvellous description of imagination, primary and secondary, at the end of the first volume of *Biographia* is thus reworded at the end of the second volume in case the reader has missed the crucially devout orientation of the former – 'its pure Act of inward adoration to the great I AM, and to the filial WORD that reaffirmeth it from Eternity to Eternity, whose choral echo is the Universe' (*BL* II, 240). The need for an Absolute identity to explain the relationship between mind and nature which makes possible perception of the one by the other is answered less by an epistemology than by a paean of praise to God from both sides. Mind and nature are connected because they worship in a common Church.

Biographia Literaria dramatises a philosophical emancipation from a main-stream British empirical tradition in order to establish credentials within a new German tradition. Coleridge does not let himself be swallowed entire by post-Kantianism but takes with him a host of religious animists with whom to build a critical emplacement within the idealist promised land. The failure to prosecute the full transcendental deduction promised in the first volume is displaced by the second volume's display of critical empowerment in the literary criticism of Shakespeare, Milton and, above all, Wordsworth. But many readers have also pointed out that the Schellingian cast of the first volume's development had pantheistic implications inimical to the Christian ones Coleridge would have desired, and which he emphatically affirmed, as we have seen, in Trinitarian terms at the book's end – Father ('the great I AM'), son ('the filial WORD') and a Comforter of sorts (the universe's 'choral echo'). Many critics have tried to retrieve the book's failure to be systematic, redescribing it as a successful expression of a religious commitment escaping philosophical reduction. This would match Coleridge's philosophical tactics with those of Lessing, Schleiermacher and Kierkegaard – formidable company.[2]

On the way to the dramatic philosophical irresolution of *Biographia*, Coleridge produces another journal, the *Friend* of 1809–10, whose title, as Elinor Shaffer claims, signals the move from the paradigm of an eighteenth-century periodical to 'a romantic and hermeneutic model'.[3] Coleridge's jour-nalistic friendship conjures up an audience capable of recognising their crit-ical self-reflection in his writing. Arguably he will use the same hermeneutic tactic in *Biographia*, and his re-hash of the 1809 *Friend* is issued a year later.[4] 'But what are my metaphysics?', asks Coleridge at one point and answers, 'to expose the folly and legerdemain of those who have thus abused the blessed machine of language' (*Friend* II, 108). The *Friend*, then, divides between a coterie interest in fostering a sympathetic audience which will eventually become that idea central to Coleridge's later political theory, a 'clerisy', or educated class, planted throughout the land like a National Church to estab-lish respect for moral and intellectual authority. It also continues his abiding interest in and investigation of the phenomenon of language, particularly of its encompassing of the polarities of epistemology, thought and thing. This concern dates from Coleridge's much earlier rebuke of September 1800 to the grammarian Horne Tooke, and his advice to Godwin that language was the subject he should be writing about:

> I wish you to write a book on the power of words, and the processes by which human feelings form affinities with them – in short, I wish you to *philosophise* Horne Tooke's system . . . Are not words &c parts & germinations of the Plant? And what is the Law of their Growth? – In something of this order I would endeavour to destroy the old antithesis of *Words & Things*, elevating, as it were, words into Things, & living Things too. (*CL* I, 625–6)

Coleridge's own idea of language comes to figure the Absolute identity that post-Kantian epistemology needs. Both these concerns of the *Friend* help rationalise Coleridge's projected 'Logic', or the 'Elements of Discourse', which he worked on with his disciple J. H. Green in the 1820s. Yet, to adapt Jerome Christensen's brilliant commentary on the *Friend*'s method, to reduce a text to the reading of a text – to reduce its meaning to its reading – only 'figures' a philosophy: it does not yet state it.[5] Hence the need for the 'Logic' and Coleridge's persistent and harmful promise of a systematic philosophy, always hovering off-stage, for which he otherwise devises a series of substitutes. Is the problem entirely an individual one, though? Is it not partly owing to Coleridge's immersion in a tradition which has always proved uncongenial to the mainline intellectual and academic traditions of British culture? Dr Johnson famously dismissed Berkeley's idealist proposition (that everything exists only in so far as it is perceived) by the simple action of kicking a stone. Does Coleridge in fact use this native prejudice against anything disputing commonsensical explanation to indemnify his frequent departures from the idealist idiom, to which he seems philosophically committed, for a religious discourse in which mystery and doctrine can be conventionally and unexceptionably evoked?

When Coleridge gave his philosophical lectures between December 1818 and March 1819, he borrowed copiously from the German historian of philosophy, W. G. Tennemann, to whose *Geschichte der Philosophie* (1798–1817) he had already had recourse in the *Friend* and in *Biographia*. Coleridge's most influential twentieth-century editor, Kathleen Coburn, thought that Coleridge disagreed with Tennemann and livened him up enough for his borrowings from the German not to count as plagiarism. She does concede, though, that it was Tennemann who gave him 'a systematic presentation' of his subject.[6] Yet Tennemann, or Coleridge's dependence on him in the *Philosophical Lectures*, forces Coleridge into one of his rare philosophical overviews *not* impregnated with a theological interest liable to give birth to an unphilosophical discourse. In Lecture III, Coleridge disagrees with Tennemann's Kantianism (carried 'into all his views') in order to praise Greek philosophers such as Pythagoras, Thales and his followers for having been, in effect, post-Kantians before their time. They are praised because they

> detected two great truths neither of which has yet been used to the full extent and which ... are to produce their effects thousands of years after them: first, that the final solution of phaenomena cannot itself be a phaenomenon; and next, the law that action and reaction can only take place between things similar in essence.
>
> (*Phil Lects*, 145–6)

Both these 'truths' raise the question of the Absolute identity assumed by difference without being itself differentiated, but here Coleridge does not use the divine to ease the difficulties in abstaining from naming this common principle. Much of the rest of the *Philosophical Lectures* which is original concerns language and anticipates the more sustained work on the 'Logic'.

'"Aye, hear now! (exclaimed the Critic) here come Coleridge's *Metaphysics*"' (*BL* II, 240). And we all know what to think of his metaphysics, is the implication. Ruefully, Coleridge here anticipates the fate of his philosophical reputation. Metaphysics has done badly enough in the British analytic tradition in philosophy. Add to the metaphysical content dismissed from Hume to A. J. Ayer the teasing obliqueness of Coleridge's writings and their highly questionable originality, and the anxiety of Coleridge's philosophical reader becomes predictable. Coleridge apparently presents an inability to publish an authoritative, systematic account of his thought as if this failure signified the philosophical possession of that which passeth outward show. Recently, more sympathetic and textually minded readers have plausibly matched this reticence to near-contemporary ironic strategies formulated by the German Romantics. In any case, goes the sympathetic argument, the vast corpus of Coleridge's unpublished writings contains more than enough for the reconstructor of his missing system. That magnificent editorial enterprise, the *Collected Coleridge*, sets new standards for just such an archaeological reconstruction. We have Coleridge's *Logic*, his *Marginalia* which frequently annotate philosophical texts in detail, periodical ventures, lecture transcriptions and numerous shorter works, and we confidently await the published text of his *Opus Maximum*. As for the rest, their miscellaneous character only confirms the desire expressed at one point in his Notebooks to match philosophical speculation to the messiness of life: 'to write my metaphysical works, as *my Life, & in* my Life – intermixed with all the other events/ or history of the mind & fortunes of S. T. Coleridge' (*CN* I, 1515).

Sometimes it is tempting to put the problem as follows: Coleridge says a lot of philosophically interesting things. But his academic readers have vested interests in making his opinions belong to him in definitive ways. It seems impossible not to present Coleridge these days without overtly constructing him as the kind of object vindicating a particular kind of scholarly enterprise. The hermeneutical circle appears at its most vicious where Coleridge is concerned. He always gives us answers to our questions, whatever we ask. And his professional interpreters seem bound by academic discipline not to take his answers as anecdotal; they are professionally compelled instead to take them as an incomplete redaction, to be edited and published as fragments of a system – one he invites them to complete or which he marvellously invokes by ironic attenuation. But an equally Romantic model of reading Coleridge's scattered philosophical insights would be as part of that kind of infinite conversation, inspired by every occasion, which Carl Schmitt deplored and Maurice Blanchot celebrated.[7] Or if these imaginative afterlives sound historically unsafe, we can always recall Leslie Stephen's judgement in the *DNB*: 'Coleridge suffers when any attempt is made to extract a philosophical system from his works. His admirers must limit themselves to claims for what he undoubtedly deserves, the honour of having done much to stimulate thought, and abandon any claim to the construction of a definite system.' Schmitt's important critique of this Romantic validation of the anecdotal or the occasional over the principled commitment to system renews early Victorian prejudice against German Romanticism which Carlyle's writings forcefully disputed. The prejudice is amusingly and typically documented when an irritated Gabriel Betteredge in Wilkie Collins's novel, *The Moonstone*, describes the approach to the novel's mystery initially offered by Mr Franklin Blake. 'Have you ever been in Germany?', Blake asks him, and then proposes an explanation which, 'taking its rise in a Subjective–Objective point of view', claims that 'one interpretation is just as likely to be right as the other'.

The suspicion persists for many that Coleridge's case is symptomatic of something more complicated than that of a brilliant pedagogue who never published enough and so is remembered for his occasional insights – a latter-day Socrates whose questions lack a systematic framework or overview. Because continental philosophy is the subject on which Coleridge's respectability founders, he was on a hiding to nothing anyway. Arguably Coleridge knew this at the time, hiding his sources because of his fear that recognition of the German origins of his ideas would deny them a fair hearing. Even Rene Wellek, in the midst of his magisterial exposure in *Immanuel Kant in England 1793–1838* of Coleridge's fast and loose way with his German borrowings, left the door open to rehabilitation by allowing that what was most characteristic of British readings of Kant was their assimilation of his thought to native philosophical traditions. Ostensible distortion and misunderstanding of another writer can be redescribed as effective assimilation and redeployment of him in the different idiom appropriate to a different context. There is no Coleridgean initiate who has not felt the challenge to explain their philosophical interest in Coleridge in this way. Owen Barfield's is perhaps the most exhausting and trusting attempt to champion Coleridge's thought as the original exposition of his *own* tradition, a religious vitalism for which he found support rather than original material in the Germans. The continental tradition is made to *stand for* rather than *be* the rebarbative quality of Coleridge's thinking. The inspiring teacher is linked to a systematic effort which in philosophical circles is usually thought eccentric or animistic, glossing at length that intriguingly unconditional claim of Coleridge's that 'the rules of imagination are the very powers of growth and production'. One finds the same praise for intellectual stimulation combined with advocacy of a new kind of systematicity in the most ambitious recent claims for Coleridge's philosophical significance: 'potentially as generative of critical thought in the areas of psychology, philosophy and religion as, for example, the systems of F. W. J. Schelling and G. W. F. Hegel'.[8]

This kind of claim sounds inflated, and 'potential' is once more a virtue which excuses Coleridge for not having been a major philosopher and returns us to the realm of unpublished possibility. But within the British reception of German idealism he certainly was always regarded as having played a crucial part. His critical fortunes do trace the distinctive character of an important aspect of the history of philosophy in this country, specifically its queasy relations with continental philosophy. This includes both an intermittent receptivity to German ideas and a lasting scepticism about French ones. The accusations of plagiarism levelled against Coleridge evidence not only uncertainty about the man but also the insecure hold of British intellectuals on the German thought he was supposed to have plundered. There was no orthodox assimilation of Kant, Fichte and Schelling to which Coleridge's evocative imitations might be contrasted. A philosophical radicalism based on Lockean empiricism held sway: that movement which grew in sophistication from David Hartley to Bentham and James Mill, mellowing into the liberal utilitarianism of John Stuart Mill which set the dominant tone of gradual reform in the Victorian age. The younger Mill's *Examination of Sir William Hamilton's Philosophy* then scotched the next attempt to appropriate German idealism. Despite the efforts of Hegelians such as Bradley, Bosanquet, Greene, McTaggart and their followers later in the century, Coleridge remained a minatory figure of the failure to let German thought make a permanent contribution to British philosophy, someone therefore misunderstood or suspect depending on your intellectual sympathies. In his book, *Coleridge as Philosopher*, Coleridge's early twentieth-century philosophical defender, J. H. Muirhead, saw him 'as a stage in the development of a national form of idealistic philosophy... the voluntaristic form of idealist philosophy, of which Coleridge was the founder, and remains today the most distinguished representative'. Coleridge, he maintains, substituted a 'personalistic metaphysics ... for the pantheistic impersonalism of Schelling'. However when Muirhead fills out the 'personalistic' quality which allows Coleridge's work comparison with the rigour of Schelling he encounters 'a reconstruction of orthodox Christian dogma'. His defence is therefore thrown back once more on the familiar suggestiveness, a richness escaping philosophical decisiveness. Again, as the advocacy of Coleridge's seriousness and originality as a philosopher approaches the systematic, an alien system threatens to supervene, casting Coleridge in the role of Christian apologist rather than that of philosopher proper. As regards the distinction between dogmatics and philosophy I am following a well-worn view of Coleridge's tendency to personalise the Absolute, and so turn a logical function into a character from Divinity.[9]

As a Christian apologist, Coleridge had a distinguished influence on John Keble, F. D. Maurice, Augustus Hare, Newman and others, who, if not exactly young Hegelians, were movers and shakers in the more parochial sphere of middle England's religious life. They were less aware than he of connected philosophical issues definitively brought to philosophical consciousness by the higher criticism from Herder onwards, with which Coleridge wrestled, most publicly in his *Lay Sermons*, and which drew later responses from more secular thinkers such as George Eliot and Browning.[10] More important for his followers was Coleridge's pre-empting of philosophical closure through what John Coulson has called 'fiduciary' statements: in other words, statements grounded in and reaffirming his Christian beliefs.[11] This initiative led him to a close study of theological language and to computations of the logical room available for its characteristic propositions, that tantalising space between the literal and the metaphorical. 'It is one of the miseries of the present age', wrote Coleridge in one of his lay sermons, *The Statesman's Manual* (1816), 'that it recognises no medium between *Literal* and *Metaphorical*' (*SM*, 30). The act of believing before you can understand, basic to Coleridge's main published treatise on fiduciary language, *Aids to Reflection* (1825), can of course cut two ways. It can rely on aesthetics or on dogmatics. As the former, it moderates the poetic use of symbol to fit religious purposes; as the latter it dwells on the axiomatics of traditional Christian doctrine, predominantly the Trinitarianism of which Coleridge's early, enthusiastically poetic Unitarianism had no need. David Pym's excellent *The Religious Thought of Samuel Taylor Coleridge* provides a mirror image of Muirhead's worries. Coleridge, he complains, was 'obsessed with the notion that the only really valid theology sets forth God, man and nature in a logically flawless edifice ... [H]is attempt to be systematic was praiseworthy, but if only he could have been systematic as a Romantic, content to leave much unsaid to speak to the heart of man for itself'. Here philosophy is the villain, becoming Coleridge's master, and dragging 'some sublime thinking into the mire of nonsense as a result'.[12]

A little earlier than Pym, Roy Park argued persuasively that Coleridge's intellectual development might best be grasped through his shift from construing imagination on analogy with practical reason to construing it on analogy with constitutive reason. Park clarifies the distortion of Kant's philosophy implied by Muirhead's influential perception that Coleridge's idealism was voluntarist.[13] For Coleridge, the exercise of a good will evinces a harmony with the divine will, a sympathetic correlation through which we can actually know God. Summarising in his Preface to the second edition of *The Critique of Pure Reason*, Kant had written of that space 'beyond the limits of all possible experience' for which speculative reason has 'at least made room' and which we can occupy 'by practical data of reason'.[14] If practical reason becomes cognitive, then Kant's point of preserving this space for practical reason is lost. Coleridge's theological desire to overcome the distinction between literal and metaphorical uses of language is part of a plan to occupy the religious hinterland under cover of practical reason in order to annexe it for speculative reason. Analogously, imagination (which formerly coped with the unknowable) now collapses into a kind of knowledge, and so loses its discursive distinctiveness. In the terminology of Coleridge's famous definition of imagination at the end of the first volume of *Biographia Literaria*, the secondary imagination becomes primary. In other words, as his orientation grows more theological, Coleridge relocates our idealising grasp of perfection at the level of perception. But for a Christian like Coleridge, such irradiation of individual experience by the divine revealed in moral truth cannot remain an indeterminate, aesthetic judgement. It must be dogmatic or doctrinally substantive. The space contrived between the literal and the metaphorical diminishes rather than enhances imaginative effort.

Philosophy is as much a casualty as imagination in this scenario. Acting with a good will becomes a kind of knowledge of the divine, a grasp of ourselves *sub specie aeternitatis*. Kant would have felt vindicated by the Christian tale which Coleridge's thinking was now impelled to tell. Philosophy had become something else. Coleridge had said in *Biographia Literaria* that he had always thought that Kant had meant 'more' by his noumenon or thing in itself 'than his mere words express' (*BL* I, 100). But now more is less, unlike in Schelling, whom Sara Coleridge thought her father echoed here. For Schelling, the idea of an Absolute Will offered not an invitation to Christian dogmatics but a solution to the problem of explaining identity in difference. Schelling's philosophy of identity is preoccupied with the difficulty of describing that stability necessary for differentiation which could nevertheless itself never be named without thus becoming differentiated. Relativised rather than absolute, its meaning would thus depend on the differences whose common order it was supposed to guarantee. The affinity of mind and nature, for example, which Kant's *Critiques* could only evoke dialectically, becomes in Schelling the common principle by which they can be differentiated, something whose own necessarily undifferentiated quality led Kant needlessly to talk of noumenal otherworldliness.[15]

In *Biographia* Coleridge's grasp of Fichte and Schelling always appears monitored by a Christian commitment whose specifics threaten both imaginative and philosophical speculation alike. As Walter Pater appreciated, he sometimes 'uses a purely speculative gift for direct moral edification', because, Pater might have added, the life lived according to Christian precept releases, in Coleridge's view, the highest speculative truth.[16] 'Christianity', he wrote in *Aids to Reflection*, 'is not a Theory, or a Speculation; but a *Life*; – not a *Philosophy* of Life, but a life and a living Process'(*AR*, 136). While this may well be true, it does not make for philosophical expansiveness, and yet Coleridge asserted straightforwardly in *Aids* that 'The Practical Reason alone *is* Reason in the full and substantial sense' (*AR*, 277n.). Once its living process was referred to Christian doctrine for explanation, this '*is*', this moral being or experience, frequently foreshortened Coleridge's philosophical surmises. By making the Absolute Will into something with which we can be personally acquainted, practical reason converges on exposition of and prescriptions for the Christian life lived in relation to God. The alternative, as Pym argued, is a Romantic openness to the unsaid, colluding with imaginative suggestiveness and arbitrariness.

Can we make Coleridge's intermittent openness to theory and idea sound like a plausible philosophical alternative to systematic reasoning? Many have tried. John Stuart Mill and Leslie Stephen were both willing to acknowledge Coleridge's cultural importance. They saw his contribution as opposite in kind that of the systematic Utilitarian, Jeremy Bentham; and they provide early examples of this liberalism of interpretation. They are happy to displace his philosophical importance and settle for his innovativeness in what we can now perceive as the emergent human sciences: for him, 'the very fact that any doctrine had been believed by thoughtful men, and received by whole nations or generations of mankind, was part of the problem to be solved, was one of the phenomena to be accounted for'.[17] More recently, some influential critics of Coleridge have tried to reconcile a strictly epistemological reading with Coleridgean indecisiveness without redescribing him as a cultural theorist rather than a philosopher. Coleridge's method was 'reticulative', Thomas McFarland has urged, a principled vacillation in the service of preserving a theological alternative to pantheism, but philosophically rigorous for all that.

McFarland reads Coleridge's writings as a web-like artefact whose 'concern for as many interconnections as possible' exemplifies a viable philosophical position.[18] Only 'the academically inert' fail to see that his 'mosaic' method of composition mounts a finely judged attack on monism.[19] McFarland calls systematic totalities in philosophy 'Spinozism'. Coleridge's philosophy replaces the Spinozistic drive for systematic explanation on a consistent plane (idealist or materialist) with an eclectic openness to the irreconcilable. When Schelling's Absolute solves the mind/body opposition for him, he has to create another division to avoid a single systematic exegesis. Eventually, though, this differs from mere incoherence by possessing 'A Trinitarian Resolution', and so Coleridge's philosophy has to be underwritten by Anglican theology after all.[20] Again, this may be a plausible description of what happened, but it does not rescue Coleridge's interest as a philosopher. More germane are attempts to read him as a Romantic ironist. Kathleen Wheeler's pioneering reading of *Biographia Literaria* sees it as the product of a sophisticated philosophical intelligence well versed in the techniques of Friedrich Schlegel, Ludwig Tieck and Karl Solger. Incoherence, on this account, remains properly unresolved, but is contextualised by a knowingness about the provisionality of definition and by a playful invocation of our inveterate tendency to complete any fragment. Coleridge becomes a philosophically interesting example of the advantages and limitations of philosophical irony and no longer has to suffer in comparison with the great systematic philosophers of his time.

Wheeler's explanation works best where Coleridge employs a genre habitually overdetermined by ironic tactics, such as autobiography. Even *Biographia Literaria*'s pretensions to totality, though, often seem straightforward rather than disingenuous. If Coleridge's philosophy is inescapably committed to a transcendental deduction that does not work, then, one might rather feel inclined to say, so much the worse for his philosophy: that is not the way to read his writings at all; a writer as captivating and expressive in philosophical failure as Coleridge has no need of philosophical success. Seamus Perry has written an excellent account of Coleridge's 'uses of division', one which shows how the neo-Empsonian reader can find in Coleridge's failure 'the very texture of his work'.[21] One can still, perhaps, complement this disabused appreciation with an account of Coleridge's ubiquitous self-consciousness about his own medium, and the extent to which he tabled his own uses of language as amendments to the charges of failure. The compensations of 'his compulsive metaphor-making' which, as Perry points out, is 'something which makes the experience of reading him so different from reading, say, Schelling', can still be philosophical.[22] This is because, for

Coleridge, language embodies that prior identity of differences, the unity of subject and object itself never stateable as a proposition, which his transcendental philosophy needs. To make such claims for his philosophical interest stick, we have to summarise, somewhat drastically but in technical detail, the post-Kantian options available at the time.

Schelling's philosophy of identity breaks with Fichte and goes on to attack Hegel. Both Fichte and Hegel tried to ground knowledge Absolutely. Every time Kant reflected on how knowledge was possible, he appeared to create a subject-position whose relation with *this* knowledge remained unexplained. Fichte's originality lay in describing knowledge as production instead of correspondence, an unconscious action to which reflection is always subsequent. But his explanation could not stop reflection from generating yet another knowledge to be explained. Knowledge of the world becomes the reflection back to us of our own productive limits, leaving unanswered the question of how the self recognises its own product, represents it, and so relates to it in a knowledgeable way. Coleridge commended the dynamism of Fichte's productive orientation but feared Fichte's egotism.[23]

Hegel, on the other hand, historicises the Kantian account of self-consciousness. When, as philosophers, we reflect on knowledge we realise that certain objects are historically tailored to certain kinds of knowledge. Again, this reflection must be made from outside the current epistemological paradigm it identifies, and so itself must still lie in need of explanation. But, in time, such reflection will itself be reflected upon; it will itself be shown to belong to its era, and to pose falsely as an Absolute certainty, or to account for *all* knowledge. The process continues until conceptual possibilities are gradually exhausted and we are provided with the Idea of all possible knowledge. For those in Schelling's camp, this position could never be reached because it itself could always be added to the sum of knowledge up till now. There is no reason to think that it could lift itself out of the temporal process and achieve a transcendental viewpoint. History will not end just because it has been explained so far. Schelling's later philosophy goes on to become more mystical, but it also stresses contingency and temporality.[24] The only knowledge inviolable by such changes is an Absolute identity already presupposed by any differentiation, amounting to the continuity in which comparison between differences becomes possible.[25]

Derrideans would no doubt see things the other way round and argue that our notion of sameness depends on our notion of difference. Deleuze, in a move Foucault thought defined twentieth-century thought, also looks in this direction in his famous revision of Nietzsche: what eternally recurs is not the same but difference.[26] But now we have a philosophical debate on our hands, one whose contemporary positions the Romantics have foreshadowed.

Coleridge, then, is part of a genealogy of philosophical arguments very much alive today. He enters the dispute on Schelling's side, and he has something original to say where his scattered remarks on the subject concern language. The Notebooks record his desire to construct 'the great anti-Babel of metaphysical Science'. This was to be achieved through desynonymy, an activity which both detected further differences in meaning and simultaneously reaffirmed their linguistic homogeneity. In a typical entry we hear:

> How the human soul *is* affected / this is by Language: an almost infinite sphere of variety: for whatever accompanies any perception, act, or sensation, may be the language of that p., a. or s. – but this p. a. and s. *are* again the logoi of and to the spirit – directly to the spirit with whom they are conjoined, and immediately to any other whom it communes with. (*CN* III, 3910)

In his opposition of language and Babel, Coleridge demonstrates that a commitment to absolute unity (the Logos) rather than to absolute difference is hard to abandon. On those occasions in the *Philosophical Lectures* when he talks about language, you know he is not just translating the thought of others. And his linguistic remarks most often bear upon the question of showing the identity on which the progressive differentiations of our expanding knowledge depend. His logic anticipates Schelling's pupil, J. J. Goerres, in its sexualising of metaphysics, although again with Coleridge's characteristically linguistic steer. The two basic linguistic forms, verb and substantive, may, Coleridge speculates, be a 'Grammatical Allegory' of 'the two Sexes, their derivation from the Homo Androgynous, and the retiring of the latter from the world of the senses into the invisible world of Self-consciousness, in the fable of Plato and of the Rabbinical writers'.[27] In a treatise otherwise derivative mostly from Kant, the drive to explain, without conceptualising or differentiating, an ulterior unity leads Coleridge to construe generation not, for once, as St John's doctrinal Logos, but as a kind of generative grammar.[28]

In his biological speculations, Coleridge argues that from Plato onwards the most persuasive philosophical tradition explains progress in knowledge and proliferation in nature as an access of communication or information:

> Plato, with Pythagoras before him, had conceived that the phenomenon or outward appearance, all that we call thing or matter, is but as it were a language by which the invisible (that which is not the object of our senses) communicates its existence to our finite beings ... Plato argued that, as there was that power in the mind which thinks and images its thoughts, analogous to this was the power in nature which thought and imaged and embodied its thoughts, in consequence of which he resolved the ground of all things into the dynamic. (*Phil Lects*, 187)

This is no mysticism but something more like our own current use of a communication paradigm to explain life-processes. Coleridge's recourse to language can seem almost obsessive, but no more so, perhaps, than the information models used to explain genetics now. In his linguistic self-consciousness, Coleridge appeared able to approach positions in Schelling's philosophy whose pantheistic implications would otherwise have warned him off. The identity of Reason and Being that explains to Schelling why there is something rather than nothing is imaged by Coleridge's 'SYNONYMYSTIC', or a biological self-division whose growth through individuation is best grasped as the proliferation of words within a homogeneous language.[29] And vice versa: 'I am persuaded that the chemical technology, as far as it was borrowed from Life and Intelligence, half-metaphorically, half-mystically, may be brought back again ... above all, in the philosophy of Language – which ought to be experimental and analytic of the elements of meaning' (CN III, 3312). I. A. Richards's famous statement in *Coleridge on Imagination* that Coleridge's 'general theoretical study of language' releases psychological insights 'comparable to those which systematic physical enquiries are giving us over our environment' is deceptively belated and forgetful of an original *unity* of scientific and linguistic study, implied by Schelling's identity philosophy, and now beginning to recover intellectual respectability.[30]

Coleridge's philosophy of life as a process of 'progressive individuation' whose identity through change is modelled on the 'physiognomy of words' reflects upon the rest of his thinking.[31] Generally, his enthusiasm for emancipation from the 'despotism of the eye' marries the break with empiricism to ideas of education and moral improvement or, as he puts it at the end of the *Treatise on Logic*, 'emancipation from the influences and intrusions of the senses, sensations and passions generally'.[32] The *Treatise on Logic* grew out of one of his pedagogical schemes after he had settled in Highgate with the Gillmans to make some money by educating a select group of young gentlemen from the professional classes. Coleridge's projected philosophical class was thus intended to recruit for a properly equipped ruling class, teaching 'that sort of *Knowledge* which is best calculated to re-appear as Power – all that a Gentleman ought to possess'. In *On the Constitution of the Church and State According to the Idea of Each*, Coleridge set out his plan for, this time, a social model replicating the ideal unity in which he believed all social difference had an interest. Coleridge's political emphasis is part and parcel of his logical interest in the permanence behind any progression. His other extended political critique – of Rousseau in the *Friend* – attacked false claims to represent this rational ideal which, just as it ought to remain undifferentiated in philosophy, ought to be taken out of society's natural class competitiveness and live off a common endowment like a 'National Church'.[33]

'He [Wordsworth] is a great, a true Poet', Coleridge once wrote disparagingly of himself in a letter, 'but I am only a kind of a Metaphysician' (*CL* I, 658). There are good reasons for concluding, though, that in the end the philosophical patterning of Coleridge's thinking appears as significant as his frequent religious, moralising and political displacements of it.

NOTES

1 Immanuel Kant, *Immanuel Kant's Critique of Pure Reason*, trans. Norman Kemp Smith (London: Macmillan, 1970). The 'Transcendental Aesthetic' follows Prefaces and Introduction.
2 Coleridge never completed his proposed 'Life of Lessing', an ambition dating from 1798. For Lessing on the 'leap' required of religious faith, see especially *Uber den Beweiss des Geistes und des Kraft*, translated by H. Chadwick in his *Lessing's Theological Writings* (Stanford University Press, 1967).
3 Elinor Shaffer, 'Coleridge and Schleiermacher', *The Coleridge Connection: Essays for Thomas McFarland*, ed. Richard Gravil and Molly Lefebure (London: Macmillan, 1990), 213.
4 See Kathleen Wheeler's original and clear exposition of the hermeneutic case of *Biographia* in *Sources, Processes and Methods in Coleridge's* Biographia Literaria (Cambridge University Press, 1980): 'Coleridge's preoccupation with his readership justifies us in applying these theses [of chapter 12 of *Biographia*] to the reading situation for clarification', 86.
5 Jerome Christensen, *Coleridge's Blessed Machine of Language* (Ithaca, NY, and London: Cornell University Press, 1981), 264.
6 *The Philosophical Lectures*, ed. K. Coburn (New York: Philosophical Library, 1949), 19.
7 Carl Schmitt, *Political Romanticism*, trans. Gary Oakes (Cambridge, MA: MIT Press, 1986); Maurice Blanchot, *L'entretien infini* (Paris: Gallimard, 1969).
8 Mary Anne Perkins, *Coleridge's Philosophy: The Logos as Unifying Principle* (Oxford: Clarendon Press, 1994), xiii.
9 See J. H. Muirhead, *Coleridge as Philosopher* (London: George Allen and Unwin, 1930); Frederick Burwick repeats this praise for Coleridge's personalising of an impersonal Schellingian Absolute in 'Coleridge and Schelling on Mimesis', *The Coleridge Connection*, ed. Gravil and Lefebure, 178–200.
10 Elinor Shaffer, *'Kubla Khan' and 'The Fall of Jerusalem'* (Cambridge University Press, 1975).
11 J. Coulson, *Newman and the Common Tradition* (Oxford: Clarendon Press, 1970).
12 David Pym, *The Religious Thought of Samuel Taylor Coleridge* (New York: Barnes and Noble, 1978), 26–7.
13 See James Boulger, *Coleridge as Religious Thinker* (New Haven: Yale University Press, 1961): 'Kant's notion of a categorical imperative giving support for regulative principles becomes in Coleridge's deductions a mode of cognition dealing with areas anathematized by Kant', 124. And Boulger repeats Muirhead's belief in Coleridge's theological distaste for an impersonalism endemic in philosophical discussion – 'Coleridge realised that approaching the idea of God in this way, from a conception of the will as source of all being, involved the danger of

entirely separating the objective Absolute Will from the subjective, personal God as Father', p. 131. This is hardly a philosophical danger, though.

14 Immanuel Kant, *Immanuel Kant's Critique of Pure Reason*, 24–5.

15 This is a lasting philosophical conundrum which, as Andrew Bowie has argued, is at the heart of Schelling's quarrel with Hegel and links him to Derrida. See *Schelling and Modern European Philosophy – An Introduction* (London: Routledge, 1993), especially chapter 4. See the succinct summary on p. 71: 'Any determinate answer to the question of what the Absolute is would of course introduce relativity. A thing is, as a thing, that which is not other things and can be identified in a predicative utterance: the Absolute is therefore not a thing.' See also Peter Dews, 'Deconstruction and German Idealism', *The Limits of Disenchantment* (London: Verso, 1995), 115–48, especially 138.

16 Walter Pater, *Appreciations, With an Essay on Style* (London: Macmillan, 1910), p. 72.

17 John Stuart Mill, *Essays on Bentham and Coleridge*, ed. F. R. Leavis (London: Chatto and Windus, 1950), 100.

18 Thomas McFarland, *Coleridge and the Pantheist Tradition* (Oxford University Press, 1969), xl.

19 *Ibid.*, 110.

20 *Ibid.*, ch. 4.

21 Seamus Perry, *Coleridge and the Uses of Division* (Oxford: Clarendon Press, 1999), 87.

22 *Ibid.*, 56.

23 'Fichte's Wissenschaftslehre, or *Love* of Ultimate Science, was to add the keystone to the arch: and by commencing with an *act*, instead of a *thing* or *substance* ... supplied the idea of a system truly metaphysical ... But this fundamental idea he overbuilt with a heavy mass of mere *notions*, and psychological acts of arbitrary reflection. This his theory degenerated into a crude egoismus' (*BL* I, 101).

24 See, amongst others, Manfred Frank, *Der unendliche Mangel an Sein* (Frankfurt: Suhrkamp, 1973); Slavoj Zizek, *The Indivisible Remainder: An Essay on Schelling and Related Matters* (London: Verso, 1996).

25 In Andrew Bowie's terse formula, 'seeing something as different entails access to the same'. See *Aesthetics and Subjectivity: From Kant to Nietzsche* (Manchester University Press, 1990), 111. Thomas Pfau spells out the implications here in his excellent introduction to *Idealism and the Endgame of Theory: Three Essays by F. W. J. Schelling*, trans. and ed. with critical introduction by Thomas Pfau (Albany, NY: SUNY Press, 1994), when he discusses 'Schelling's theoretical probing of identity as the *one* paradigm that enables us to *think* difference while, at the same time and for the same reason, its sole purpose lies once again strictly in thinking *difference* (and not in establishing itself as an autonomous form of closure to the practice of philosophy/theory ...). Here identity proves central to the multiple critical discourses and post-Freudian debates on gender theory and "sexual identity", as well as on questions of racial and ethnic identity' (4).

26 Gilles Deleuze, *Difference and Repetition*, trans. Paul Patton (London: Athlone Press, 1997), especially ch. 1; M. Foucault, *Language, Counter-Memory, Practice: Selected Essays and Interviews*, ed. with intro. by D. Bouchard (Oxford: Basil Blackwell, 1977), 194.

27 *Treatise on Logic*, British Library MS Egerton 2825, I, 32.

28 Contrast, for example, the discussion of Logos in Notebook no. 39, British Library Add. MS 47, 534.

29 Schelling, *System of Philosophy in General*, in Pfau, ed., *Idealism and the Endgame of Theory*: 'that ultimate question posed by the vertiginous intellect hovering at the abyss of infinity: "Why [is] something rather than nothing?"' (p. 152). The link with Heidegger's *Seinsfrage*, and so with Derrida's critique of Heidegger, is obvious. For Schelling, the Absolute escapes any differentiation at all and so is an absolute 'indifference'. See the formulation in F. W. J. Schelling, *Ideas for a Philosophy of Nature*, trans. Errol E. Harris and Peter Heath, intro. Robert Stern (Cambridge University Press, 1988): 'If, therefore, philosophy, in order to know in an absolute way, can only know of the absolute, and if the absolute stands open to her only through knowing itself, then it is clear that the first idea of philosophy already rests on the tacit presupposition of a possible indifference between absolute knowing and the absolute itself, and consequently on the fact that the absolute ideal is the absolute real' (p. 44).

30 I. A. Richards, *Coleridge on Imagination* (London: Kegan Paul, 1935), 232.

31 *Hints towards the Formation of a More Comprehensive Theory of Life*, ed. Seth B. Watson (London: Churchill, 1848), 50, 41–2.

32 *Treatise on Logic*, II, 403.

33 *Friend* II, 193–200; *On the Constitution of the Church and State*, Part I.

12

MARY ANNE PERKINS

Religious thinker

The categories according to which Coleridge's various admirers and critics have represented him often appear irreconcilable: he has been portrayed, for example, as a radical Unitarian, a mystic, a theosophist and an orthodox Anglican with conservative leanings. Such descriptions sometimes reflect the nature of a critic's interest in a particular period of his life, or in one aspect of his thought and often as much evidence can be found to challenge as to support them. This is not only because of the complexity of Coleridge's evolving ideas but also because he was convinced that truth is revealed only by means of apparent oppositions, because of 'the *polarizing* property of all finite mind' (*Friend* I, 515n). Even his early lectures, given at Bristol, contained a mixture of radical and conservative views. However, the development of his thinking, when traced across the spectrum of letters, notes and marginalia, is coherent and cogent. It shows the close relationship between his current reading and the religious ideas and questions which preoccupied him, and also his vast erudition and rigorous power of analysis and argument. He was always unwilling to subordinate his critical faculties to dogma of any kind, whether that of revolutionary radicalism, evangelical 'bibliolatry' (see below) or established Anglican convention. For this reason it is likely that his work and moral character would have attracted criticism from one quarter or another even if his private life had been respectably regular and conventional, which it was not. Yet it was precisely this wide-ranging critical spirit, blended with an intense desire for truth, which gave his writing on religion such penetrative power and which influenced and inspired many of both his own and succeeding generations.

Those who recognise the complexity of his religious thought and its evolution have sometimes suggested that it reflects the vacillations of his emotional life. Despite widespread admiration for his poetry and literary criticism, critics, particularly among his compatriots, have often dismissed his religious and philosophical arguments as muddled metaphysics. It has been argued that he 'straddled too many fences' and 'lacked the . . . power of integration necessary to launch a true theological movement'.[1] Such views have been sustainable partly because, until recent years, many of his most interesting arguments and accounts of his own beliefs and religious experience were inaccessible in published form. Many of the intellectual, moral and spiritual difficulties with which he passionately engaged were themselves consequences of his unrelenting pursuit of a systematic unity which would 'reduce all knowledges into harmony' (*TT* I, 248). As early as 1805, he insisted on the necessary interdependence of, on the one hand, the inner witness of conscience, faith and feeling and, on the other, the evidence of history, fact and external testimony (*CN* II, 2405, 2453). For him, philosophy, history, poetry, religion and science all bore witness to the truth of Christianity, to the unique value of the human person, and to history as a redemptive scheme through which the whole created order would be fulfilled and perfected. However, his was no blind faith; what makes his work far more stimulating than that of many of his pious contemporaries is the relentlessness with which he subjected his own beliefs to the challenge of historical, scientific and philosophical criticism.

Although there was always a reciprocity between Coleridge's religious views and his political and social ideals, this was perhaps most radically expressed in his youth. Between 1795 and 1800 he combined political commentary (in, for example, the editions of his own short-lived periodical, the *Watchman*, and in the *Morning Post*) with his Bristol lectures on the social and political implications and imperatives of Christianity, and wrote two of his greatest poems: 'The Rime of the Ancient Mariner' and 'Christabel'. The curiosity and keen insights which were characteristic of all his work on religious and spiritual issues are already evident in both poems. Central to the former is the theme of the self-imposed separation of the human individual from the rest of creation which is itself then plunged into chaos and fragmentation as a result of this act of alienation. Through spiritual redemption, the whole creation is then restored to a unified, harmonious community in which the individual (the Mariner) finds his own spiritual home. This idea of a created order which reaches the apex of its beauty and unity only through the Fall and Redemption of humanity became a constant motif of Coleridge's own spiritual and intellectual journey. His political and social commitments at this time, such as the plans to found a Pantisocracy – a classless Utopian society – in America, were born out of his search for the principles upon which human community, fragmented by the degeneration of morality and intellect, might be restored. His deep desire to find unity and coherence as the ground of reality was sometimes expressed in pantheistic terms; for example, in references to a universal Spirit: 'Life', he wrote to Thomas Wedgwood in 1803, 'seems to me then a universal spirit, that neither has, nor can have an opposite. God is everywhere . . . and works everywhere; & where is there *room* for Death?' (*CL* II, 916). Soon after this, however, his notebook entries and letters demonstrate an intellectual conviction, at least, that God was both immanent (incarnate in mind, nature and history) and transcendent. In 1806 he set out his idea of God as essentially Unity and Distinction, a tri-unity in which, just as 'that Unity or Indivisibility is the intensest, and the Archetype, yea, the very substance and element of all other Unity and Union', so too is 'that Distinction the most manifest, and indestructible of all distinctions'(*CL* II, 1196). Here he identifies the principles of 'Being, Intellect, and Action' with 'the Father, the Word, and the Spirit'. This tri-une relationship, he argues, 'will and must for ever be and remain the "genera generalissima" of all knowledge'. The passage is followed by an explicit rejection of the 'intelligential' position of Unitarianism. From this point his letters and notes adopt the Christian Trinity as the only adequate (more accurately, the least inadequate) symbol of ultimate reality. In a late notebook, he described its 'sublime perfection & prominent Object' as 'to effect what in no other way can be effected, the union of Personality with Infinity in the Godhead' (*CN* IV, 5262). It was both a revealed truth which required the response of faith *and* an intellectual principle: 'The Trinity', he declared, 'is indeed the primary Idea, out of which all other Ideas are evolved – or as the Apostle says, it is the Mystery (which is but another word for Idea) in which are hidden all the Treasures of knowledge' (*CN* IV, 5294). It was 'the only form in which an idea of God is possible, unless indeed it be a Spinozistic or World-God' (*CM* II, 1145). In his mature and later years he vehemently opposed those sects which refused to accept God as tri-une in accordance with the doctrines and creeds established by the great Councils of the Church. The 'Socinians', who denied that Christ was the Logos, eternally with God 'from the beginning' (*CM* III, 305), and the 'Arians' who believed the Son of God was a created being (though far surpassing all others) were his main targets. Their positions were, he believed, intellectually and morally flawed.

By his middle years, Coleridge's reading, psychological speculations and examination of his own dream states, moods and motives, had convinced him that the primal reality – the primary term of the Trinity – must be Will rather than Being, and that this was reflected in human nature. The relation of will to reason became, thereafter, an intensely important issue to him. But if 'Coleridge's own stake in Christianity was existential' it was not only, as Thomas McFarland suggests, in the sense that it gave his 'miserable and shattered' life final meaning.[2] For Coleridge, as later for Søren Kierkegaard (1813–55), the *will* was the crucial factor through which finite and infinite reality could be reconciled and through which the individual achieved personhood and redemption. This pre-eminence of the will subverted the materialistic, mechanistic philosophies which he had admired in his youth.[3] He never abandoned a critical scientific approach which accepted the determining power of natural law, yet he believed, with the German thinkers who influenced him – for example, Jacobi, Kant, Fichte and Schelling – that the opposite pole, that of human free agency, was an essential characteristic of human history beyond the scope of physical science.

In the *Biographia Literaria* (1817), Coleridge wrote tolerantly of pantheism which, at this point, he declared 'not necessarily irreligious or heretical; though it may be taught atheistically' (*BL* I, 247), but as he became focussed on the principle of 'distinction-in-unity' he increasingly distanced himself from any notion of an '*anima mundi*' (world spirit). Later, he argued emphatically that pantheism and atheism were synonymous: to say that 'all is God' was to deny God. It was, except in the barest logical terms, an insignificant proposition; if there is nothing which is *not* God, the term 'God' is meaningless and superfluous. His criticism of a tendency to pantheism in the work of his German contemporary, Schelling, and, to a lesser degree, in that of Jakob Böhme (1575–1624) and Spinoza (1632–77), is in marked contrast to his admiration for what might now be termed the 'pan*en*theism' ('all *in* God') of the early Christian writer, Origen (c. 185–c. 284), and of John Scotus Erigena (810–77).[4] Even in the early poems, lines such as ' 'tis God/Diffused through all, that doth make all one whole' ('Religious Musings') are more representative of this latter tradition than of pantheism in which Nature and God are identified. Although Coleridge writes, in *The Eolian Harp* (1796–1828), of the 'one intellectual breeze' which sets vibrating the 'organic harps' of 'animated nature' and is 'At once the Soul of each, and God of All', in the poem as a whole – as in 'Religious Musings', with its 'Monads of the infinite mind' – his imagery has more in common with the Christian metaphysics of the German philosopher, Leibniz (1646–1716), than with the monism of Spinoza. Like the former, he struggled to get beyond the dichotomy of monism and dualism.

With his increasing commitment to the search for a unified system, his focus on political and social criticism began to shift. Religion was now no longer simply the basis for personal and social improvement. There could be no contradiction, he maintained, between its doctrines and principles and the whole range of human reason and experience. For example, the discoveries of the physical sciences, properly understood, must be compatible with Christian belief and teaching. His Notebooks reveal that his interest in, for example, evolutionary theory, magnetism, electricity, hypnosis ('animal magnetism') and astronomy was inspired, at least in part, by a drive to understand how they could be seen in the context of fundamental Christian principles about God, nature and man. The philosophies of the Enlightenment had produced a 'science of man' which was inadequate in that its dominant mechanistic model of cause and effect could not explain some of the most fundamental human experiences: those, for example, of the poetic imagination, of free agency, of the sublime, of revelation. Coleridge found in the work of his contemporaries, particularly in the new German philosophies of nature,[5] ways of thinking which acknowledged these aspects of reality. These ideas, furthermore, were consistent with some of the most enduring and recurrent ideas about reality; ideas which he had already encountered in his avid reading of intellectual history. The philosophies of German Romanticism and Idealism emphasised the need to reconcile finite with infinite reality. Philosophies of nature, theories of history, aesthetic principles were perceived as essentially intertwined with spiritual truths. Coleridge's own attempt to develop a 'dynamic system' was aimed at a similar integration of ideas, feelings, experience, conscience and actions. For example, the famous statement concerning the primary and secondary imagination in the *Biographia Literaria* (I, 304) is only one of many which propounds a relationship between the human imagination and the divine act of creation. Imagination is that power which perceives and realises unity in multiplicity; which recognises symbols as not just representing, but participating in, universal, infinite and eternal realities. It reflects both God's *fiat* ('Let there be...and there was', Genesis 1) and the divine energy which infuses all the forms and the life of nature. Imagination, in the poet, the prophet, the historian ('a poet facing backwards'), the mystic, is the power which reconciles the multiplicity of life and thought in a higher unity.

From the time of his acceptance of ultimate reality as tri-une, the concept of *Logos* became a seminal principle in Coleridge's system. He explored all its many interrelated meanings and associations in both Greek philosophy and Christian thought. The *Logos*, for example, is the 'Idea' of God: 'God is the sole self-comprehending Being, i.e. he has an Idea of himself, and that Idea is consummately adequate, & superlatively real.' This Idea 'is the same, as the Father in all things, but the impossible one of self-origination. He is the substantial Image of God, in whom the Father beholds well-pleased his whole Being' (*CL* II, 1195). Coleridge also drew on the ancient theology of the Word of God 'which was from the beginning' (John 1:2), the Word which, 'spoken' by God, becomes the 'seed' of all creation and the life which sustains it. He explored the idea of *Logos* as the principle of distinction, the God who is 'Other and the same' – *Deus alter et idem* – expressed within Christian doctrine as the Son who is consubstantial with God the Father and through whom the multiplicity of life and being is generated. He found a correspondence between these ideas and ancient Greek concepts of

Logos as the principle of reason, and of difference, distinction and opposition (all essential to intelligibility), propounded by Heraclitus, Pythagoras, Plato and the neo-Platonists. In these early roots of western thought, *Logos* had been identified with the hidden power of the act of naming, with the root of language itself, with the energy produced by opposition, and with a divine–human principle.[6] On this basis, and further inspired by the work of the German Romantics, Coleridge developed his own philosophy of language: words, as 'living powers' (*AR*, 10) participate in, and reflect, the power of the divine Word as the life and light of thought. When laziness, ignorance or malice leads to the distortion or abuse of language, this in turn, he argued, led to intellectual and moral degeneration, not only of the individual, but of society. His 'logosophic system' attempted to reconcile the principles of Idealist philosophy, particularly that of self-knowledge, with his own theological speculations. In the *Biographia Literaria*, for example, he drew parallels between the Idealist concept of the Absolute as 'the SUM or I AM' in which 'object and subject, being and knowing, are identical' and the biblical account of God's self-revelation, 'I AM THAT I AM', confirmed in his direction to Moses 'Thus shalt thou say unto the children of Israel, I AM hath sent me unto you' (Exodus 3:14). The *Logos*, incarnate in Christ, became, for Coleridge, the quintessential Self, both the archetype and the constitutive principle of an ideal humanity.

He was inspired by the recurrence in western thought of the idea of Logos as intellectual principle, as the incarnation of God in Person, as Creator (source of the dynamic of polarity through which life evolved), and Reconciler (medium of reconciliation between opposites). Foreshadowed in ancient philosophy, this idea reappeared in the Renaissance synthesis of Greek and Christian thought. Coleridge admired Giordano Bruno's physics and metaphysics which were based on the idea that 'the greatest secrets of nature' were to be found in 'the minima and maxima of contraries and opposites'.[7] He also traced the development of this idea of a relational reality symbolised by Logos in the writings of great Christian thinkers such as John Scotus Erigena and the fifteenth-century cardinal, Nicholas of Cusa. For the latter, the union of the two natures of Christ was the paradigm of diversity-in-unity. Coleridge judged the philosophical insights of his own time partly according to their consonance with this ancient and enduring metaphysical theme. For example, his admiration for Immanuel Kant's new system of 'trichotomous' logic was based on its contrast to the old Aristotelian model, and its acceptance of the principle that all reality, whether ideal or actual, exists and can be understood only through the dynamic relationship of opposite poles. Opposites were not contraries – they did not cancel each other out; this truth, he argued, was known to the ancients and expressed in the philosophies of Pythagoras and the Jewish Kabbalah. On this basis he adopted the 'noetic' or 'dynamic' pentad as a geometrical model of relational reality, claiming that 'the Forms of Logic are all borrowed from Geometry' (*AR*, 179–83). The figure was sometimes used as a paradigm for the expression of spiritual realities or religious concepts (*SWF* II, 837–8; *CM* II, 562–3), and as a kind of transferable template it could be profitably applied, through a suitable modification of its terms, to any particular branch of knowledge (Newsome, *Two Classes of Men*, 100–10). It could symbolise, for example, the science of colour, or physical and chemical processes, or the Constitution of the nation. The Logos, as the principle of polarity and distinction-in-unity, was the key to this *schema*, as it was of the heptad and tetrad which Coleridge sometimes used instead. He represented the historical process itself, in both nature and society, as progressing by means of a dynamic of opposition. The 'general law' of polarity (*SWF* I, 517–20) was expressed, for example, as individuation and attachment, or permanence and progression (*Church and State*, 24). The energy produced from each opposition was the life process itself. From it emerged in each case a further, 'higher' form of being or thought. Again, the Logos was the source and process of this life.

Coleridge's margin notes during his reading of the sixteenth-century mystic, Jakob Böhme, reflect his interest in the latter's references to the Gospel of John and the Logos idea. Coleridge himself seems always to have felt drawn to this Gospel which, with the Epistles of St Paul, was at the heart of his own faith (*CL* VI, 552, 556). Critical of some of Böhme's more fantastic alchemical speculations, he nevertheless deeply admired his visionary representations of the divine Word which was also, mysteriously, the ideal Humanity. He was similarly inspired by the prolific and exotic prophecies of Swedenborg, particularly by references to a 'divine Humanity' which would be fully manifested when the great redemptive scheme of nature and history was complete. Swedenborg, like other mystics before him, suggested that the human principle was in fact mysteriously with and in God and, following the supreme revelation of Christ, was progressively realised in human history until its final manifestation. For Coleridge, the possibility of self-knowledge and self-making,[8] both essential to the realisation of personhood, as opposed to mere individuality, is hidden in the Logos which (or who) is the inner principle of intellect, of creation and reconciliation, as well as the external ultimate principle of Reason and source of Life. Christ, as the incarnate Logos, had to be understood as source, symbol and revelation of this ideal Humanity. The last line of Coleridge's poem 'Know Thyself' (1834) reflects this belief and nicely counters Alexander Pope's famous lines, written a century earlier,[9] with the contrary admonition: 'Ignore thyself, and strive to know thy God!'

In middle life Coleridge began to test both philosophical and scientific theories – particularly those within German philosophy which seemed to confirm his own – against Christian doctrine and claims for biblical revelation. In the 'Confessions' of the mid-1820s he derided the futility of a literal interpretation of the Bible which sought to depict God as directly manipulating the minds and hands of ordinary human individuals, overriding their humanity in some infallible dictation. Rather, the Scriptures spoke to the *inner* being – the heart, conscience, spirit, will of the reader – using symbols, analogies and other figures to convey truths which were eternal, infinite and universal: 'it is the Spirit of the Bible, and not the detached words and sentences, that is infallible and absolute' (*SWF* II, 1156). To him the idea of inspiration was completely at odds with that of divine dictation. One of the greatest threats to Christianity, he believed, was the attempt to reduce it to something which could be proved – in the way that facts about the phenomenal world could be proved according to scientific method and laws; this led to a concept of God as one truth amongst many, merely a part of the created order instead of its source, life and goal. He argued that religion itself had been corrupted since the end of the seventeenth century, by this mechanical way of thinking. The witness of the heart was the crucial test: 'in the Bible' he avowed, 'there is more that *finds* me than I have experienced in all other books put together...the words of the Bible find me at greater depths of my being;...whatever finds me brings with it an irresistible evidence of its having proceeded from the Holy Spirit' (*SWF* II, 1123).

Although some of the great figures of Romanticism, such as Friedrich Schlegel, studied and admired the language, religion and culture of Asia and the East, Coleridge's attitude to non-Christian religions was sometimes merely dismissive. Writing on 'Indian religion', for example, he concluded that Buddhism was simply a form of 'religious Atheism' and denounced the 'incongruities and gross contradictions' (*AR*, 283) of the Brahmin mythology. He admired Judaism, however, as the root of Christianity, and was deeply appreciative of aspects of Jewish mysticism (*Phil Lects*, 299–305). He wrote of his reluctance to attempt any kind of conversion of his friend Hyman Hurwitz, whose Hebrew and Rabbinical scholarship he respected and valued, and, in 1830, expressed disgust that a Jew should have to give up the Covenant of Abraham before he could receive the Covenant of Christ (unpublished notebook (N)44, f77–8). His views of the practices and beliefs of Christian or pseudo-Christian sects or parties changed little in his middle and later life; in 1830 he set out five uncompromising articles of faith as necessary to Christians. According to these, Roman Catholics 'and Socinians, especially the modern Unitarians' were self-excluded, the former for their worship of the Virgin Mary and the saints. On the other hand, the scope of his acceptance

of 'the Ministers of all other Churches, Lutheran or Calvinistic, Arminian ...
Presbyterian or Independent ... as members of the *Christian* Church in England' (*SWF* II, 1484–6) was unusual in this period, and he often distinguished
between the members of a particular group and the institution to which they
belonged.[10] He admired the work of the Quakers George Fox and William
Penn, but in 1823 criticised what he saw as the 'extremely vague and misty'
aspects of their creed (*CN* IV, 5068n). A few years later he described Quak-
erism as the 'Rind & Bark in wondrous preservation counterfeiting *a tree* to
the very life' when what he sought was 'the Heart of Oak' (N35, f34–v). At
this point, increasingly lionised both in Britain and in America, engaged in a
huge correspondence but with deteriorating health,[11] he wrote of his longing
for 'Church Fellowship'. His notes express an empathy with the Moravians,
who lived a simple, dedicated life of faith, but he believed they would not tolerate the spirit of free enquiry, and he feared 'a wilful Stupor with the sacrifice
of Reason under the name of Faith' and the 'Tyranny of *Dogmas*'. His faith
co-existed with doubt; although he clung to it through all difficulties, it was
never a means of escape from them. The theologian and educational reformer,
F. D. Maurice, maintained that Coleridge's own conflicts, doubts and failings
gave his religious thought an authority which it would otherwise lack.[12]

One of the aims of *Aids to Reflection* (1825) was to demonstrate that
prudence, morality and spirituality were quite distinct, and to show that the
tenets of the first two led inexorably, unless language or reason were abused,
to the recognition that the core, the essence, of humanity is 'spirit'. The truths
of Christianity, for example, were not a matter of rational evidence. Although
supported and confirmed by reason, the knowledge of spiritual truth was
'of necessity immediate and *intuitive*'. However, it required a response of the
will; to Coleridge, Calvinism's portrayal of a passive will appeared deeply
flawed. In the arguments of *Aids to Reflection* he drew on the works of
Archbishop Leighton and other seventeenth-century divines. Their insights
into the human condition and spiritual truth had been lost, he believed,
through a relentless distortion of language and thought in the mechanistic and materialistic philosophies of the eighteenth century. Although the
style of the *Aids* now seems at times to obscure rather than to enlighten,
he addressed moral and religious doubts and difficulties with great precision, honesty and thoroughness, acknowledging a shared humanity with the
reader. 'Christianity', he wrote, 'is not a Theory, or a speculation, but a
Life. Not a *Philosophy* of Life, but a Life and a Living Process ... TRY IT'
(*AR*, 202). At the same time, he remained true to his own aphorism that 'He,
who begins by loving Christianity better than Truth, will proceed by loving
his own Sect or Church better than Christianity, and end in loving himself
better than all' (*AR*, 107).

Coleridge's Notebooks, particularly those of the last five years of his life, demonstrate his painstaking study of the Bible according to critical principles which were then less acceptable, on the whole, to British theologians, than to German. He addressed fundamental questions concerning the authenticity of miracles, the person of Jesus Christ and the idea of evil. This last issue, in particular, was one which he thought had been dangerously neglected by some of the greatest thinkers, such as Spinoza. Evil, in his own experience, was a dread reality which at times overwhelmed both individuals and societies (Perkins, *Coleridge's Philosophy*, 286). His sense of sin and despair at times made him contemplate suicide, but he believed, as the poem 'The Suicide's Argument' (1811) shows, that this would be an offence against the life-giving power which infused all nature. Again, two years before his death, his notebook entries record an anguished inner conflict over whether or not suicide must be judged a mortal sin. The concept of evil was inextricably linked to questions concerning the nature and direction of the human will which, together with his Logos theme, was the issue through which he sought to reconcile intellectual, spiritual and psychological experience. Following the teachings of St Augustine of Hippo and of Martin Luther, he emphasised the will as the spiritual crux of, and for, human nature. He supported that strand of Christian tradition (for example in the writings of Origen in the third century) which depicted an original spiritual 'Fall'. From an aweful and mysterious alienation in the primacy of Will had emerged a deathly spirit of self-contradiction and fragmentation (*CN* IV, 5076–8). God had seeded this dark chaos with life and form through his Spirit and Word in order to bring about the redemptive scheme of creation. Humanity had been, and was, continuously seduced by the evil principle of a corrupted Will – a concept which Coleridge explored in his poem 'Ne Plus Ultra' (1811) – but 'original sin' need not be seen as an arbitrary condemnation of innocent individuals through a supposed tainted line of corruption; the phrase, he suggested, simply asserts that sin had an origin, was *originated* by the will, and is therefore not an eternal principle (*AR*, 270–1). Just as it had a beginning, it will have an end – with the final realisation of God's kingdom in which all things would be made new.

Like many of the Romantics who, in their youth, were inspired by what appeared to be a new dawn of political and social reform following the French Revolution, Coleridge, in early manhood, had interpreted the teaching of Christ as primarily a call to renewal and the establishment of a new order of justice and freedom. Gradually his early radicalism was modified, not by loss of passion for those ideals, but by his acceptance of an intellectual paradigm which presented reality as constituted by oppositions and polarities. 'Right', he now believed, 'is a word without meaning except as the correlative of Duty' (*SM*, 64) and 'Reason as the science of All as the Whole, must be interpenetrated by a Power, that represents the concentration of All in Each'; this power was religion (*ibid.*). *The Statesman's Manual* (1816) and the *Lay Sermon* of 1817, intended to be the first two of three sermons (the third was never written), were addressed to the 'Higher' and 'Middle' social classes and sought to establish certain religious and philosophical principles as the foundations of a civilised and moral society. *On the Constitution of the Church and State* (1829) continued to emphasise these principles; here Coleridge argued that the idea of the nation should be understood in terms of a polarity of state and 'National Church' (*Church and State*, 31). The National Church was based upon his premise that civilisation must be grounded 'in the harmonious development of those qualities and faculties that characterise our *humanity*' (42–3). Its object was 'to secure and improve that civilization, without which the nation could be neither permanent nor progressive' (44). It should be led by a 'Clerisy' of learned men 'of all denominations' (46) and would develop the latent humanity and citizenship in all 'natives of the soil' (48). He took pains to distinguish the 'National' from the Christian Church which 'is no state, kingdom, or realm of this world' but rather 'the appointed Opposite to them all *collectively*' (114), truly universal, or 'catholic': 'neither Anglican, Gallican, nor Roman, neither Latin nor Greek' (124). In *Church and State*, Coleridge explained his stand against the Catholic Emancipation Act of 1829. In earlier years he had felt torn between his acknowledgement of the just demands of Irish Catholics and his own fear of a state within a state. Roman Catholics, he argued in 1811, were under the control of a 'numerous and most powerful magistracy' which 'will not suffer itself to be placed under either the control or the superintendence of the Sovereign'. Indeed, they swore allegiance to a foreign sovereign: the Pope (*EOT* I, 243).

Church and State, together with his *Logic*, the *Philosophical Lectures*, *Aids to Reflection* and the work published as 'Hints Towards a More Comprehensive Theory of Life', was to be part of Coleridge's great *Opus Maximum* which would demonstrate that 'CHRISTIAN FAITH IS THE PERFECTION OF HUMAN REASON' (*AR*, 541). The final prospectus for this work was set out in 1828.[13] Conceived in some form as early as 1799 (*CL* I, 519), by 1814 it had at its core the idea of Logos (*CL* III, 480), but Coleridge finally recognised that he would never complete it. The relationship of the various parts of the work, which he sometimes called the *Logosophia*, has often remained obscure to those without access to his manuscript notes or time to explore them.[14] However, his attempt to reconcile metaphysical and theological principles with sound philosophical argument, scientific progress, social and political axioms and human experience, had a significant influence upon nineteenth-century religious thought. *Aids to Reflection*, for example, was published in twelve editions in fifty years.[15] His work was valued not only by devoted disciples such as F. D. Maurice and Archdeacon Hare – who took up his ideas concerning the relationship of Reason and Will within religious faith – and the American, James Marsh, who established the University of Vermont on Coleridgean principles, but also by those who were more critical. John Henry Newman believed Coleridge 'indulged a liberty of speculation which no Christian can tolerate' yet credited him with inspiring an interest in the cause of Catholic truth. John Tulloch, in the *Fortnightly Review* of January 1885, argued that Coleridge had transformed Christianity 'from a mere creed, or collection of articles, into a living mode of thought, embracing all human activity' and showed how all theological problems were related to the 'really vital question... whether there is a divine root in man at all – a spiritual centre answering to a higher spiritual centre in the universe'.[16] More recent criticism has remained polarised between those who argue that Coleridge foreshadowed aspects of twentieth-century theology (Barth, *Coleridge and Christian Doctrine*, 196) and those who see him as 'an Ancient, whose thought, for that reason, remains effectively unavailable for any appropriately modern enterprise of theological reformulation'.[17] Coleridge's last letter to his godson (*CL* VI, 989) certainly affirms his unambiguous acceptance of the ancient and orthodox principles of Christian faith, but he also challenged the accepted 'radical discontinuity' between the natural and the supernatural, emphasised the role of the Will in faith, and acknowledged the 'human solidarity' of sin (Barth, 197). 'We cannot', Coleridge asserted, 'believe anything of God but what we find in ourselves' (N41, f79). It is this kind of penetrating insight which, at the end of the twentieth century, appears startlingly modern.

NOTES

1 J. D. Boulger, *Coleridge as Religious Thinker* (New Haven: Yale University Press, 1961), 219.

2 T. McFarland, *Romanticism and the Forms of Ruin: Wordsworth, Coleridge, and Modalities of Fragmentation* (Princeton University Press, 1981), 365.

3 See Trevor Levere, *Poetry Realized in Nature: Samuel Taylor Coleridge and Early Nineteenth-Century Science* (Cambridge University Press, 1981), 9–10.

4 M. A. Perkins, *Coleridge's Philosophy. The Logos as Unifying Principle* (Oxford: Clarendon Press, 1994), 111, 121n, 151n.

5 R. Modiano, *Coleridge and the Concept of Nature* (London: Macmillan, 1975), 138–206.

6 These ideas are explored more fully in Perkins, *Coleridge's Philosophy*.

7 Giordano Bruno, *De la causa, principio e uno* in *Dialoghi italiani*, 3rd edn, ed. G. Aquilecchia (Florence: Sansoni, 1958), 573; quoted McFarland, *Romanticism and the Forms of Ruin*, 292.

8 S. Happel, *Coleridge's Religious Imagination*, 3 vols. (University of Salzburg Press, 1983), II, 523–4.

9 See the opening lines of Pope's second Epistle in the *Essay on Man* (1734): 'Know then thyself, presume not God to scan; / The Proper study of Mankind is Man.'

10 See J. R. Barth, SJ, *Coleridge and Christian Doctrine* (New York: Fordham University Press, revised reprint, 1987), 197.

11 Cf. Richard Holmes, *Coleridge: Darker Reflections* (London: Harper Collins, 1998), 530–55.

12 F. D. Maurice, *The Kingdom of Christ* (London: J. G. F. and J. Rivington and Darton and Clarke, 1842), 'Dedication'.

13 See the Folio Notebook in the Huntington Library, HM MS. 17299 fols. 132–69.

14 The critical edition of the *Opus Maximum* is being prepared for publication as part of the *Collected Works* at present.

15 John Beer, 'Coleridge's Religious Thought: The Search for a Medium', *The Interpretation of Belief. Coleridge, Schleiermacher and Romanticism*, ed. D. Jasper (London: Macmillan, 1986), 48–9.

16 John Tulloch, 'Coleridge as a Spiritual Thinker', *Fortnightly Review*, n.s. 37 (Jan. 1885), 11–25; in *The Critical Heritage. Samuel Taylor Coleridge*, ed. J. R. de J. Jackson, 2 vols. (London: Routledge, reprint 1995), vol. II: *1834–1900*, 161.

17 Kevin Lewis, 'The Impasse of Coleridge and the Way of Blake', *The Interpretation of Belief*, ed. Jasper, 225–34, 225.

3
THEMES AND TOPICS

13

JULIE CARLSON

Gender

Coleridge was not a feminist, although he included women amongst his best friends. Nor was his work directed systematically at issues of gender, definitions of masculinity and femininity, or the relations between the sexes, except as these matters intersected with other topics that fundamentally informed his work such as the French Revolution, social reform, faculties of mind, the professionalisation of poetry and the poet. Still, Coleridge is useful for thinking about gender and its articulation in the early nineteenth century, occasionally in what he wrote and more frequently in what he 'was' as writer and man. To proclaim in the early 1800s that 'there is a sex in our *souls*' when the revolution in female manners was being conducted on the opposite principle and was barely off the ground was to disassociate oneself from feminist causes and to align oneself with gender essentialists *(Friend* II, 209).[1] Most of Coleridge's comments on gender supported the social conservatism that usually follows from essentialist claims. They positioned women in the private sphere, viewed love as women's primary preoccupation, and characterised femininity as maternal, nurturing, dependent, and domestic. Even Coleridge's advocacy of androgyny, regarded ever since Virginia Woolf as his major positive contribution to gender analysis, supported a masculinist agenda, for it was attributed only to the genius of male minds.[2]

That being said, any case for essentialism is difficult to maintain when its spokesperson is Coleridge, a man whose character and relations with others were construed by everyone, including himself, as weak, subordinate, dependent, and whose essential condition was lack. The case is further challenged by the power of his fictions and the attention that his work devoted to potentiality, receptivity, performativity and the determining role of form on content. What should we make of a man whose writings on women were often manifestly unsympathetic but who on occasion rose to their occasion and, more than any other male Romantic writer, made 'femininity' his subject position? How do we categorise the poet who composed 'Christabel' and made a philosophical commitment to 'potential man'?

Adding to the curiosity of Coleridge's positions on gender is the way that his treatment of this topic diverges from the usual difficulties of interpreting his ideas. There were no radical shifts in his thinking about gender, nothing analogous to the complexities and retractions that make generalisations about his other political positions so hazardous to venture.[3] This is all the more striking when we recall how women and revolutionary enthusiasm intersected in Coleridge's personal experience. As is well known, the most radical expression of his support for revolutionary principles – his plan to establish a communitarian agrarian society on the banks of the Susquehanna in 1795 along with eleven other men and twelve women – was conservative on the score of gender and sex. No haven of free love, Pantisocracy stipulated that adult members be married. True to his enthusiasms, Coleridge married Sarah Fricker after a very brief courtship, her most attractive feature being that she was the sister of Edith Fricker, to whom fellow Pantisocrat, Robert Southey, was engaged. Coleridge's perceptions of this woman certainly changed shortly after their marriage, but these changes did not affect fundamentally his opinions regarding women's proper place.[4] From start to finish, Coleridge affirmed the sanctity of marriage, the equation of women with domesticity, and some notion of equality *within* the private sphere between husband and wife. Maintaining a balance between the sexes even extended to his opinions on housework, which showed him committed to fulfilling his fair share and woefully ignorant about what a share entailed.[5]

Beyond the tantalising announcement of a series of lectures on female education and occasional comments regarding female suffrage, prominent women writers and intellectuals, or factory labour, Coleridge provided no extensive commentary on, or reliable support for, women's emancipation. On the contrary, his comments on women and gender usually arose in the context of traditionally 'feminine' topics – love, marriage, childrearing and, to a lesser extent, spirituality and beauty – and are to be found primarily in his letters and notebooks, his early poems, and his writings on and for the theatre. We might say that these writings provide the raw materials for gender analysis by detailing Coleridge's thoughts on love between the sexes and introducing what Heather Jackson calls 'Coleridge's women', under which phrase I include both living and fictional women.[6] When considered separately, his treatment of both love and women can feel undernuanced, overly schematic, at times (sub)standard for the period. More interesting conceptual possibilities emerge if we view the two together as a never-coming-together of his women and love.

Coleridge conveniently schematised his views on heterosexual love in an essay fragment entitled 'True Love, Illustrated . . . Geometrically'. Presenting a triangle (love) composed of two 90-degree triangles (husband and wife) that had two ascending horizontal lines parallel with the bottom, Coleridge characterised each line in terms of what brought the two sides together. The bottom line represented 'the common basis of their human nature', the middle line 'what they have common to each other, but different from the rest of Mankind', and the upper line, itself intersected into two, the qualities of each partner that were 'opposite yet correspondent' to the other (*SWF* I, 285). This highest line grounded 'perfect' love between the sexes and was based on a fundamental philosophical conviction of his: extremes meet, with its related distinction between 'Contraries that preclude or destroy, and Opposites that require and support each other' (*SWF* II, 960). Ideally, then, heterosexual love required difference in order to achieve the unity and humanity it sanctified; in Coleridge's view, difference perpetuated not simply the species but the harmony of daily life (cf. *CL* III, 305).

This conviction entailed two corollary claims that informed Coleridge's depictions of gender. The 'human Being rises above the brute in exact proportion as those sexual *opposites in correspondency* . . . extend thro' the whole Being', encompassing each partner's features, expressions, understanding, moral affections, even 'the very texture of the Body', all these 'having a common basis of Identity' in the couple but 'in each so modified, that in the man they shall be masculine, in the woman feminine – i.e., Opposites & yet correspondencies' (*SWF* I, 286). For example, 'the meekness, and tenderness, and patient Fortitude of the woman' is reflected in her lover's 'perfect Sympathy with Men' and his corresponding traits of 'Gallantry of Spirit, Courage, Patriotism, Sense of the Profound in Truth, the Sublime in Nature or Imagination' (*SWF* I, 287). (Apparently, Coleridge was better at geometry than arithmetic.) More generally, this meant not only that individuals needed love but that man needed woman (and woman man) for self-perfection. This balance, in turn, required the priority of love over sexual desire, a relation that Coleridge curiously figured as that between parent and child in the fragmentary essay, 'Well-Being, Friendship, Love, and Desire': 'Love then is the Parent of all {such} sexual Desire, as a pure and dignified Nature will permit itself to feel! Love alone begets it; shelters, and shelt'ring at once warms and hides it . . . and itself {in return} receives support & renewal of vivacity from its offspring!' (*SWF* I, 291).

Coleridge's attempts to realise these views foundered on another philosophical preoccupation of his, coordinating real with ideal. His actual experiences of love manifested a structural – even geometrical – contradiction between idealising the couple and enacting it as a triangular and serial configuration. (Further complicating twoness was his definition of love as 'unity in duplicity'.) Determinant here was the series of living Saras – Sara(h) Fricker, Sara Hutchinson, Sara Coleridge – and the triangles they composed with

Dorothy and Mary Wordsworth and by means of them. Crucial too were the polarities that the series of living Saras and their fictional counterparts (pensive Sara, disabling Sara, dearest Sara, Asra) signified, polarities that structured Coleridge's notion of 'the feminine': lover v. wife, muse v. drone, ideal v. real, then v. now or never. These women bring into focus two constituents of Coleridge's amatory–literary desires. Complexity was on the side of the fictional, only in part because of the overdetermination of Sara. While love was fundamental to his views on humanity, divinity and the human, living women were intertextual, substitutable, at times even expendable, and fictional women were often subtexts for beloved men.

With the exception of female figures in 'Christabel' – on all counts an exceptional text – Coleridge's depictions of women in his poems were not very adventurous. Nor did women figure prominently in most of his poems. Generally, they functioned as backdrop, delineating the home-space as the place from and to which men came and went. 'Fears in Solitude' is the best-known example of a group that includes 'Reflections on Having Left a Place of Retirement', 'To the Rev. George Coleridge' and 'The Nightingale', all three of which evacuated the 'pretty Cot' or 'home' of whatever 'sweet girl' originally was there. With the exception of 'Frost at Midnight', no man in Coleridge's 'Conversation' poems or lyrical ballads is found indoors. Even in 'Frost at Midnight', he did not wish to stay there, straying in thought not only to earlier times but to times that would place him henceforth out of doors via a son who would melt the ice perceptible through the pane of the house. In this regard, all of the poems in *Lyrical Ballads* could be said to follow the anti-domestic strain of its opening poem with its seaman whose primary aim was to sever 'wiser' men from maidens. Not one of the poems depicted a working relation between husband and wife, except (Wordsworth's) 'Simon Lee', which equated it with infirmity. Apparently when revolutionary poetry entailed 'a man speaking to other men', conversation between the sexes of the same generation was precluded. Exchanges were already fairly one-sided in the conversations that came before. 'My pensive Sara' was basically invoked to 'dart' a 'mild reproof' to '[t]hese shapings of the unregenerate mind' which she 'holily dispraised'. Two years later, she was reduced to a headnote to 'This Lime-Tree Bower My Prison' that equated housewifery with warden-like tactics to keep husbands from walking. Nor did women in less compromised roles have much to say for themselves. '[O]ur Sister', the 'Lady' and the 'most gentle Maid' fused with a Nature whose nature was mute ('Nightingale'). Even the song of the Abyssinian Maid was a vision.

'Dejection: An Ode', especially the genesis of it, is particularly revelatory of Coleridge's attitudes towards women and women's effects on Coleridge's attitude. Its initial version as 'A Letter to – –' of 4 April 1802, usually referred to as 'Coleridge's Verse Letter to Sara Hutchinson', went the farthest of any of his poems in poeticising his series of Saras in regards to the polarities that structured his concept of femininity. '[D]earest Sara', the 'Heart within my Heart' whose 'lov'd haunt' was 'the weather-fended Wood' is opposed to the unnamed Sara responsible for the 'coarse domestic life' that itself sapped life because it yoked together 'two unequal Minds' and 'two discordant Wills'. Dearest Sara, that is, linked nature to innocence and love through her capacity for joy, whereas drone Sara impeded all four. The latter's life-draining powers even extended to embryonic daughter Sara, one of the 'little Angel Children' whose needs literally depressed their father's spirits by 'bind[ing] and pluck[ing] out the wing-feathers of my Mind'.[7] But whereas both inmates of domesticity represented an immediate drain on the speaker's creativity, only the wife depleted the source – not only of the joy necessary for inspiration but of the fund of 'fair forms' through which to express the poet/husband's 'Sorrow'. 'Verse Letter' also introduced Coleridge's unusual rendition of the classic polarity of femininity, madonna/whore. Since wife and mother proved deflating to every aspect of this speaker's pro-creativity, 'maid', 'friend' and 'sister' assumed the eroticism caused by the poem's occasion and form – published on the day of Wordsworth's wedding to Mary Hutchinson, the date of Coleridge's wedding to Sarah Fricker seven years earlier, and in a form associated with erotic pastoral.[8] This conflation triggered the repression that accompanied the speaker's depression, whereby he at once downplayed the 'eye-lash play' of 'innocent Sara' and heightened it in her surprising depiction as 'conjugal & mother Dove'. Such a move raises a complexity that we will develop shortly concerning anxieties triggered by the mother. In this context, it highlights how much more got repressed in the 'Dejection' to follow. Not only did 'Dejection' repress the covert expression in 'A Letter to – –' of sexual feelings for the wrong woman but it effaced all the particular women who influenced the former speaker's depression – and thus his potential poetic genius. More tellingly, 'O Lady' not only stood in for those women but for an intervening man, the Edmund/William who, as legend still has it, really inspired this author's dejection and shaping powers of imagination.

It would be oversimplifying things only slightly to construe the gender substitutions in and between these versions of 'Dejection' as characteristic of Coleridge's literary/love life. His poetic masterpieces depended on women to get and keep them going but associated their depths of interiority, certainly their ups and downs, with men. Nor did this situation alter significantly in Coleridge's drama, despite the greater visibility of women in theatre and in his plays. For reasons that involve conventions of theatre as well as characteristics of Coleridge, his writings on theatre comprised his most extensive commentary on women and their roles in society.[9] Theatre, from the Restoration on, accentuated women, even when it stereotyped and marginalised female roles, by making a spectacle of their bodies. Coleridge's plays increasingly followed this tradition. From the collaborative *Fall of Robespierre* (1794, with Southey), to *Osorio* (1797), to its staged revision as *Remorse* (1813), to *Zapolya* (1815), all delineated the state of their respective states in terms of domestic relations and, as the progression of titles suggests, granted increasing prominence to women – *Zapolya* being truly distinguished in this period (and only for this reason) in featuring three female roles, Queen Zapolya, Lady Sarolta and Glycine, 'all prominent, though not equally so, and each altogether distinct from the other two', and consequently dependent 'for it's [*sic*] fate, certainly for it's success, on the talents of the Actresses – in an equal, perhaps, in a greater degree than on those of the Actors' (*CL* IV, 617, 620).[10] But as was true of his poems, the plays' depictions of domestic relations were usually highly conventional, as exemplified by *Zapolya*'s resounding conclusion, 'None love their country but who love their home.' Of more interest is how this maxim expatriated its author and how these plays' status as theatre placed women outside the confines of home.

Two characteristics of Romantic theatre generally help to particularise Coleridge's treatment of gender in his plays. The first underscores the importance of theatre as aesthetic venue and metaphor to assessments of the French Revolution and thus adds a political component to longstanding objections regarding the immorality and traffic in bodies associated with acting. After the Terror, the mere status of action, particularly of taking matters into one's own hands, was subject to misgivings regarding the violence that allegedly accompanied the autonomy and greater democracy of Reason. Related to these misgivings is a standard complaint made against Romantic plays both then and now, that they were all talk and no action. Both characterisations sharpen the peculiarity of Coleridge's treatment of women and introduce yet another polarity into his conception of femininity. Pitted against the exemplary women who embodied the wise passiveness of ideal domesticity and, in their relative silence, were the dramatic counterparts to the women of the 'Conversation' poems (Adelaide in *The Fall of Robespierre*, Maria in *Osorio*, Teresa in *Remorse* and Lady Sarolta in *Zapolya*) were the female characters who acted and whose acting compromised them morally, but not sexually (especially Alhadra in *Osorio* and *Remorse*). But whether Coleridge's female characters acted or reacted, they were given little to say that was either rational or poetic about the self-divisive consequences of acting. This silencing made quite a statement in a drama known for the liberality of its speeches.

Extremes met, however, in this polarity between acting and being around the doubly negative connotations of acting in the case of women. The initial moralised opposition between troublesome women who acted and virtuous women who existed increasingly gave way to an opposition that linked hyperactive men like Ordonio and Emerick to all women and distinguished them from exemplary men who waited. This alliance reconfigured traditional features of masculinity and femininity, as the later plays increasingly stressed. When male exemplarity needed to become visible as wise passiveness or even self-division on the score of taking action, uncomplicated women were left to run the show. Sword-wielding Alhadra, who ultimately wreaked her revenge on the man who had murdered her husband, both set the standard of commanding action and articulated its double standard. Her acting compensated for male inadequacy. Both versions of the play made clear that whereas she, while a nursing mother, withstood lengthy confinement in a prison of the Inquisition, even a 'month's imprisonment would kill' her husband (*CPW* II, 527). Nor did her marginal status as a Moor isolate her in this regard from Christian women, almost all of whom repeated Alhadra's avenging acts and her indifference to words. Maria, Teresa and Glycine all rescued their men at considerable risk to themselves by making their way into secret dungeons, falling on their beloved's assailant (Maria/Teresa), even spearing their fiancé (Glycine). Entailed in such acts was also a risk to essential femininity, for each 'put aside the customs and terrors of a woman' to act like a man – or like men used to act before they needed to reflect their powers of self-reflection. This hint that gender is constructed occasioned a further splitting between female acting and being. Women's 'natural' ability to dissemble kept the most virtuous woman under suspicion.

For reasons primarily of form, Coleridge's plays were more explicit than his poems about the sexual suspicion that suffused women's status as actors, though poems too expressed male antipathy towards marriage and anxieties regarding the sexual activities of mothers. In the plays, however, women voiced reservations about marriage, equating it with funerals and construing it as slavery.[11] Glycine makes irreverent assessments of the institution of marriage and the desirability of men. To Lady Sarolta's womanly counsel regarding 'the duties of a wife', Glycine asserted,

> It is a wife's chief duty, madam
> To stand in awe of her husband, and obey him,
> And, I am sure, I never shall see Laska
> But I shall tremble. (*CPW* II, 903)

But rather than using this critique, as did Joanna Baillie, to construct a more egalitarian, because rational, basis for heterosexual relations, Coleridge's plays exposed what kept the sexes apart when united in marriage.[12] The category of woman was ontologically unstable, because of the undecidability of whether she was what she seemed. Critics have construed as artistic weakness the virtuous Albert/Alvar's blindness to Maria/Teresa's constancy. Read in connection with *Zapolya*, this appears to be not creative oversight but insight into women's nature as sexual suspects. The usurper Emerick believed that he could win, not force, his best friend's wife's 'love' on the grounds of female 'vanity / And [Lady Sarolta's] resentment for a forced seclusion' in the domestic sphere (*CPW* II, 917). Moreover, once she assented, he was confident that she could 'decoy' her husband (Casimir), for '[i]f the dame prove half as wise as she is fair, / Casimir may still pass his hand and find all smooth' (*CPW* II, 927). Such potential for deception made the foundations of the happiest homes radically insecure and elicited some serious, but ineffectual, attempts to quarantine female sexual energy (for example, son and heir-apparent Bethlen discovered his mother in a 'werewolves' cave' (*CPW* II, 925)). The nation's welfare, too, suffered under the prospect of female overactivity. Part I of *Zapolya* closed with the confident prediction that the son of 'Royal Andreas' will restore the State by reclaiming the 'palace of his fathers' (*CPW* II, 900). Part II declared that usurpation ended when 'She comes again' (901).

More useful for gender and feminist analysis than Coleridge's characterisations of women or men in his poems and plays was his life-long investigation of the problematics of identity. Coleridge understood the capacity of language to speak against the subject and the body's power to overrule determinations of will or reason better than most writers of the period. In delineating these topics, his writings anticipated performative accounts of identity and psychoanalytic discussions of the phallus or the misrecognition in love. Still, his writings rarely explored these problems systematically, accepted self-division as an ontological condition, or applied sympathy for the experience of self-disruption to both genders. He associated complex interiority – for better and worse – with men. '19 to 25 [is] the time when Females are most likely to manifest the depth of their nature if they have any' (*SWF* II, 915).[13] Readers sympathetic to the depths of Coleridge's suffering may be inclined to interpret more positively his ascription of lack of interiority to women as evidence that Coleridge envied 'femininity' its relative security because of its reduced spheres of responsibility and mandated activity. If so, he could have expressed more compassion for the ways that woman's existence for the other threatened her integrity, rather than belittling her for manifesting undue concern with appearances or construing her duplicity as moral rather than ontological. Instead, disappointment over Sara Coleridge taught him to instruct prospective husbands in some fundamental queries.

'Has she an inward Being, a reality more valuable & precious to her than all without? Or is she a mere Dependent on Shew, and *lives* only in the eyes and ears of others?' (*SWF* II, 915). Granted, Mary Wollstonecraft voiced similar concerns in *A Vindication of the Rights of Woman* (1792) over the damage that women's cultivation of surfaces does to marriage, childrearing and equality between the sexes, but she portrayed this superficiality as enjoined by cultural notions of beauty and love, as condoned by both sexes, and as alterable if both sexes would comport themselves in line with the assumption that women were reasonable and autonomous beings. Besides, Coleridge never conceived of women's receptivity as exposing them to anything like the 'femininity' that his dependencies occasioned.

One positive dimension of Coleridge's experiences of femininity was that they rendered masculinity an achievement, not an unmarked category, in his writing. Coleridge was not alone in drawing attention to the problematic status of masculinity in this period. As Godwin's *Caleb Williams* made clear, one question that (post-)Revolutionary English culture needed to direct to 'things as they are' was where is the honour in being a man?[14] Certainly, Coleridge's profession as poet posed a categorical threat to standards of masculinity that prized rationality, physical strength, taciturnity, heroism or utility. His profession was also threatened as never before by both the growing number of women writers turning authorship into a trade and those 'devotees of circulating libraries' who do not know how to distinguish between genius and 'novels, or books of quite ready and easy digestion' (*BL* I, 30).[15] But Coleridge was singular in the degree to which this lived reality informed his conceptual and professional categories and, from his perspective, isolated him from his fellows. 'Have I one friend?' was an existential, literary-critical *and* gendered lament that further alienated him from everybody. Not only market but dark forces threatened this lady, repeatedly mishandled by more worldly men, 'whom hundreds abuse and no one thinks it worth his while to defend' (*CL* IV, 701).

Forced by categories as well as circumstances to rise to his own occasion, Coleridge attempted to defend his manhood and livelihood by devising several conceptual oppositions that made feminine traits the dominant features of statesmen. Pairings such as absolute versus commanding genius, potential man versus actual citizen promoted traits of interiority, passivity, potentiality as the qualities requisite for worthy leaders of the nation. Despite important differences, the chief point of both sets was to define civic activity as virtually synonymous with imaginative activity. Political leaders not only needed vision but the capacity to envision which contingent particulars best accorded with the idea of England as it had been manifested through history. Actual citizens expressed the true voice of the people to the extent that each reflected the idea by reflecting on it in private rather than in public assemblies where men leave their better faculties at home. Such priorities influenced Coleridge's depictions of government, the constitution of Church and State, national education, the statesman's best manual – all of which, though committed to fostering potentiality, were not concerned with advancing women's liberation. Instead, they composed a 'new' man who, by being less manly, hoped to find his right to rule less under attack.

Gender warfare between men over what comprised the leading man was more conflicted when the arena was poetry, which conceded so much to femininity (but so little to women) in the Romantic age. As played out between Coleridge and Wordsworth, this battle entailed some surprising reversals that ultimately prove fruitful for reconfiguring the relation between poetry and gender in this period.[16] On the one hand, poetic pride of place went to Wordsworth, as descriptions in 1799 of the 'growth of the poet's mind' and changes to the second edition of *Lyrical Ballads* (1800) made clear. Even between 1795 and 1797, when assertions of Coleridge's poetic superiority were tenable, he claimed to 'feel [him]self a little man by [Wordsworth's] side' (*CN* II, 3148) – a perception that was never retracted, even when he felt moved to revise evaluations of what the manliness of Wordsworth entailed. 'He is *all* man...a man of whom it might have been said, – "It is good for him to be alone"' (*TT* II, 391). On the other hand, the special ways that Coleridge conceded defeat kept open the question of Wordsworth's dominance, both as a questionable evaluation and as a question that kept generating writing – philosophical and imaginative. The most basic characterisation of the intellectual division of labour between Wordsworth and Coleridge, which Coleridge himself initiated and depicted as an inequality to which he submitted, challenged Wordsworth's dominance as man. Whatever else it did to one's generative powers, recourse to 'abstruse research', Coleridge's specialisation, rendered one a traditional man – autonomous, unfeeling, independent from others – as compared to the poet who felt, cared and talked about the everyday. Moreover, immersion in speculation shared with his acknowledged division of poetic labour an orientation towards the supra-natural and thereby challenged Wordsworth's manliness even from within their shared feminine sphere. Coleridge's criticisms of Wordsworth, especially in *Biographia Literaria*, further feminised him. They depicted Wordsworth's poetic genius as either ignorant of its actual operating procedures or unconscious of them. In other words, Wordsworth's genius left it to Coleridge's to bottom his fixed principles. This exchange fulfilled the logic of Coleridge's notion of poetry, whereby the part (composition) needs the whole (philosophy) of man. In addition, the philosophical sections of the *Biographia* culminated in a definition of imagination that presented it as the primary faculty of mind. Poetic creation was secondary.

One can play this gender power game indefinitely, in part because it remains conceived in terms of oppositions and their suitability for inversion. But what Coleridge's enactment of it contributed was some consciousness that categories of masculinity and femininity were constructed, mobile and thus subject to change. Even more fruitfully, when applied to men, femininity was seen as an incitement to poetry. As 'Dejection: An Ode' made clear, surrendering had its advantages. The process of conceding the loss of imagination eventually led to its recovery and a poetic masterpiece; in the meantime, the admission of its loss evoked compassion for a mind that declared itself alienated from others. Coleridge's private writing occasionally hinted at the desired outcome of such fantasies, whereby general sympathy turned into particular acts of erotic comfort.[17] His literary life sought to internalise surrender by making it constitutive of privileged minds: suspension of disbelief, absolute genius, remorse, wise passivity.

Gendering and engendering surrender was a major topic in 'Christabel', Coleridge's most remarkable statement on women, gender, a subject's coming-to-sexuality, and his or her formation by generic forms. The thematic treatment of gender alone set this poem apart from his other poems in the breadth and depth it ascribed to female characters and feminine character. No simple opposition between innocence and experience, Christabel, Geraldine and the wandering mother were all portrayed as desirous women differentiated in relation to their stages of desire – from pre-conscious to post-coital and post-mortal.[18] Each was depicted as circumventing a different regime and regimen of man (chivalric, tyrannic, Christian) and as cohering as a woman, and as women, around sex. Both the fact and the nature of this coming together in 'Christabel' represented an important departure for Coleridge. Radically non-phallic and anti-patriarchal, female reunion was neither harmonious nor paradisal. The balance of power clearly shifted after Christabel's surrender to Geraldine, but there were power plays from the start initiated by Christabel and her mother to ensure the encounter. On the other hand, this coming together of women did not occasion the usual idealisations or demonisations that attended hints of desirous women in other Coleridgean poems or plays. In 'Christabel', two out of the three were pagan, the third was hardly a lady, but none was simply evil.

With its unusual array of unusual women, Part 1 made a valuable beginning at reconfiguring family dynamics and their repression of female desire. Part 2 delineated just how far apart women were from men and analysed what kept them apart: the father's powers of separation and a form of chivalry that surpasses the love of women on all fronts – 'But never either found another / To free the hollow heart from pining.' The view of masculinity in 'Christabel' accords more with other of Coleridge's writings than its view of femininity, in part because Coleridge usually saw masculinity as complex – at times, as a hero-complex. For him, masculinity was generally troubled over the nature and duration of its power, the efficacy of its action, the fatality of sexualised women, especially their tragic ability to come between men. Part 2 did not resolve these troubles; in fact, it intensified them. It placed male friendship and heterosexual coupling at cross-purposes while exploring some secret purposes of intergenerational desire. Men's attraction to the daughters of their friends was as homosexual *and* incestuous as they could get.[19] At the same time, it deflated the self-sufficiency of man, designating the Baron's loss of his childhood friend as irreparable and the means of his recovery as juvenile: not just in being rejuvenated by the daughter but by a resumption of neighbourhood games. In turn, pride of place went to the bard, the only male equipped to read female interiority or tame the wilds.

The extent of the gender trouble in 'Christabel' disturbed its first readers and its fitful creator. Reviewers found it 'obscene', 'bewildering' and 'unmanly', except for the passage in which the Baron laments his boyhood friend, which virtually every reviewer cited with approval, including Hazlitt, who deemed it the only 'genuine burst of humanity' in the poem. Coleridge too considered them 'the best and sweetest Lines I ever wrote'.[20] Noteworthy here is the alliance among men over the passage that predicted their dissolutions, a convergence of peculiar irony for Coleridge, who was not only frequently devastated by male betrayals but whose publication of 'Christabel' gave Hazlitt the opportunity to publicly label its author a pervert: 'There is something disgusting at the bottom of his subject, which is but ill glossed over by a veil of Della Cruscan sentiment and fine writing' (*CL* IV, 686). Captivating women were hardly a match for the forms of castration suffered at the hands of men. But beyond the variety of femininities and masculinities displayed in the poem or its depictions of the incompatabilities between the sexes on the scores of chivalry, family and desire, the parts proved valuable in staging a more essential lesson. Two parts did not become one entity nor did they add up to a consistent identity.

'Christabel' did not say explicitly that desire threatened unity or rendered impossible a union between the sexes, nor did it assert directly that language was responsible for experiences of lack in either sex. But it made such interpretations possible by presenting interpretation as a process intimately related to gender. As Karen Swann has shown, this process is enacted in two ways, namely, by characterising hysteria (a standard interpretation of 'the wandering mother') as a condition that rendered subjects incapable of meaningful speech and by presenting even the poem's own narrators as hysterics unable to stabilise or authorise their stories.[21] Multiplicity of interpretation converged at Geraldine, the meaning of whom was never resolved but the construction of whom was shown to depend on which of various genres different narrators employed to 'read' and thus construe her character: romance, Gothic fiction, sentimental fiction, allegory. The effect of this reading was to relate gender to genre, to present both as permeable and undecidable, and, most important for feminist aims, to suggest that the attribution of hysteria to feminine forms was itself 'a hysterical response to a more general condition' of lack.[22] Authority figures within the poem (Baron and narrators) are joined by generations of literary authorities outside of it in finding themselves both silenced and enthralled by this woman, poem and author.

Coleridge's best writing apprehended that meaning-making is essential to living but a reduction of it too. Frequently he was too caught up in his own undecidability to apply the observation to gender, but his insight into the necessity and partiality of interpretation is available for better configurations of women and men.

NOTES

1 See Susan Wolfson, *Romantic Women Writers: Voices and Countervoices*, ed. Paula R. Feldman and Theresa M. Kelley (Hanover and London: University Press of New England, 1995), 33–68.

2 See H. J. Jackson, 'Coleridge's Women, or Girls, Girls, Girls Are Made to Love', *Studies in Romanticism*, 32, 4 (Winter 1993), 577–600, esp. 593–600. For a more positive assessment, see Jean Watson, 'Coleridge's Androgynous Ideal', *Prose Studies*, 6 (1983), 36–56.

3 Coleridge commented favourably on Wollstonecraft in the *Watchman* (p. 90). But he was not concerned with extending political rights to women, or improving women's economic opportunities, or envisaging options outside of marriage. Also in this period he planned to write to Wollstonecraft in order to encourage her to turn to religion (*CN* I, 261). But see Anya Taylor, 'Coleridge, Wollstonecraft, and the Rights of Woman', *Coleridge's Visionary Languages*, ed. Tim Fulford and Morton D. Paley (Cambridge: D. S. Brewer, 1993), 83–99; and Tim Fulford, *Romanticism and Masculinity: Gender, Politics and Poetics in the Writings of Burke, Coleridge, Cobbett, Wordsworth, De Quincey and Hazlitt* (Houndmills and London: Macmillan Press, 1999), 112–24.

4 See Molly Lefebure, *The Bondage of Love: A Life of Mrs Samuel Taylor Coleridge* (New York: Paragon House, 1989).

5 In the case of Pantisocracy, husbands in fact assumed the lion's share of the work. See *CL* I, 114–15.

6 Coleridge's metaphysical views on love were more complex than his usual comments on love between the sexes; see Anthony Harding, *Coleridge and the Idea of Love: Aspects of Relationship in Coleridge's Thought and Writing* (Cambridge

University Press, 1974), and J. Robert Barth, *Coleridge and the Power of Love* (Columbia: University of Missouri Press, 1988).

7 Coleridge also admitted to Southey, in announcing her birth, 'I had never thought of a Girl as a possible event,... however I bore the sex with great Fortitude' (*CL* II, 902).

8 On the erotic implications of form and the intertextual dialogue that culminated in 'Dejection', see Gene W. Ruoff, *Wordsworth and Coleridge: The Making of the Major Lyrics, 1802–4* (New Brunswick: Rutgers University Press, 1989), 75–103.

9 See Julie Carlson, *In the Theatre of Romanticism: Coleridge, Nationalism, Women* (Cambridge University Press, 1994).

10 See *ibid.*, 126–33.

11 Legitimate complaint would focus on the onesidedness of the 'three things... indispensable' for a good marriage outlined in his 'Advice on Marriage' in *Shorter Works and Fragments* (*SWF* II, 914). See also *CL* III, 92; IV, 93–8; V, 152; VI, 793–6, 878–9.

12 For a comparison in Joanna Baillie, see Julie Carlson, 'Baillie's *Orra*: Shrinking in Fear', forthcoming in *Joanna Baillie, Romantic Dramatist: Critical Essays*, ed. Thomas Crochunis (The Netherlands: Gordon and Breach).

13 Coleridge made a similar comment about Sara Coleridge (*CN* I, 979).

14 Fulford explores the reconstructions of masculinity in the writings of several Romantic men in *Romanticism and Masculinity*.

15 See Sonia Hofkosh, 'A Woman's Profession: Sexual Difference and the Romance of Authorship', *Studies in Romanticism*, 32, 2 (Summer 1993), 245–72, and *Sexual Politics and the Romantic Author* (Cambridge University Press, 1998); Anne K. Mellor, *Romanticism and Gender* (New York and London: Routledge, 1993); Marlon Ross, *The Contours of Masculine Desire – Romanticism and the Rise of Women's Poetry* (New York: Oxford University Press, 1989); and Karen Swann, 'Literary Gentlemen and Lovely Ladies: The Debate on the Character of Christabel', *English Literary History*, 52, 2 (1985), 397–418. On the femininity of the poet, see Alan Richardson, 'Romanticism and the Colonization of the Feminine', *Romanticism and Feminism*, ed. Anne Mellor (Bloomington: Indiana University Press, 1988), 13–15.

16 For the sexual dimensions of this relation, see Wayne Koestenbaum, *Double Talk: The Erotics of Male Literary Collaboration* (New York and London: Routledge, 1989), 71–111.

17 See, e.g., *CN* II, 2495, 3148; also *SWF* I, 206–7.

18 On the wandering mother, see Charles J. Rzepka, 'Christabel's "Wandering Mother" and the Discourse of the Self: A Lacanian Reading of Repressed Narration', *Romanticism Past and Present*, 10, 1 (Winter 1986), 17–43.

19 On the latter point, see Fulford, *Romanticism and Masculinity*, 103.

20 On the contemporary reception of *Christabel*, see Karen Swann, '*Christabel*: The Wandering Mother and the Enigma of Form', *Studies in Romanticism*, 23, 4 (Winter 1984), 533–53 (citations from Hazlitt and Coleridge, p. 544); and 'Literary Gentlemen and Lovely Ladies'.

21 Karen Swann, '*Christabel*: The Wandering Mother and the Enigma of Form', 541–3.

22 *Ibid.*, 545.

14

JAMES C. MCKUSICK

Symbol

The concept of the symbol was vitally important to Coleridge throughout his career as a poet, critic and professional man of letters. Although his articulation of this concept varied in emphasis at different moments of his career, the underlying concept of symbol remained important as a fundamental principle throughout his intellectual development. During the last two centuries, the concept of the symbol has become one of Coleridge's most influential contributions to the discourse of literary criticism.

One persistent area of concern throughout Coleridge's career is the question of the relation between language and thought. Coleridge formulates this question as follows: 'Is Logic the *Essence* of Thinking? in other words – Is *thinking* impossible without arbitrary signs? & – how far is the word "arbitrary" a misnomer? Are not words &c parts & germinations of the Plant? And what is the Law of their Growth?' (*CL* 1, 625). Coleridge is here pondering whether the arbitrary signs that, according to such contemporary linguists as John Horne Tooke, determine thought can in some sense be described as 'natural'. This question is a central one for Coleridge; it recurs at several crucial moments in his intellectual career. The concept of symbol, as it evolved in his mature philosophy of language, was in large part an effort to overcome the arbitrariness of the linguistic sign, and to demonstrate that at least in the realm of poetry, language could become the actual embodiment of thought.[1]

In his *1795 Lectures on Politics and Religion*, Coleridge uses the term 'symbol' to express the connection between the beautiful appearances of nature and the divine presence they signify:

> To the philanthropic Physiognomist a Face is beautiful because its Features are the symbols and visible signs of the inward Benevolence or Wisdom — — to the pious man all Nature is thus beautiful because its every Feature is the Symbol and all its Parts the written Language of infinite Goodness and all powerful Intelligence. But to a Sensualist and to the Atheist that alone can be beautiful which promises a gratification to the appetite — — for of wisdom and

217

benevolence the Atheist denies the very existence. The Wine is beautiful to him, when it sparkles in the Cup — — and the Woman when she moves lasciviously in the Dance, but the Rose that bends on its stalk, the Clouds that imbibe the setting sun — — these are not beautiful. (*Lects. 1795*, 158)

In this lecture, Coleridge seeks to refute the mechanistic reduction of beauty to mere hedonism. Vaguely echoing Kant's doctrine of aesthetic disinterestedness, Coleridge asserts that true beauty has nothing to do with personal gratification, but depends on more elevated notions of wisdom and benevolence as they are manifested in the appearances of nature. The very disjunction of these appearances from any human utility serves to authenticate the sentiments they arouse. '[T]he Clouds that imbibe the setting sun' cannot possibly be useful to us, and this is a precondition of their beauty, since they intimate a purpose beyond any limited human capacity of understanding, and are thus 'sublime' in the Kantian sense. Coleridge does not use the term 'symbol' here merely as a descriptive category, but in a stronger, more normative sense that hints at his later use of it as a norm towards which all language and particularly poetic language aspires. For Coleridge, a symbol is a *motivated sign*, that is, one whose form is determined by its referent.[2] Just as facial features are the direct index of a person's character, so too, Coleridge asserts, are the appearances of Nature the immediate representations of divine attributes.

This understanding of the symbol as a motivated sign is apparent in 'Frost at Midnight', first published in *Fears in Solitude* (1798), where Coleridge makes prominent and effective use of the divine-language topos:

> For I was reared
> In the great city, pent 'mid cloisters dim,
> And saw nought lovely but the sky and stars.
> But *thou*, my babe! shalt wander like a breeze
> By lakes and sandy shores, beneath the crags
> Of ancient mountain, and beneath the clouds,
> Which image in their bulk both lakes and shores
> And mountain crags: so shalt thou see and hear
> The lovely shapes and sounds intelligible
> Of that eternal language, which thy God
> Utters, who from eternity doth teach
> Himself in all, and all things in himself. (51–62)

Coleridge here emphasises that the eternal language of nature is intelligible even to a 'babe'; its meanings are not merely the result of arbitrary social conventions. His paradigm case of signification is given in the clouds which 'image in their bulk both lakes and shores / And mountain crags'. This process of imaging is one of mimetic representation, wherein the form of the sign is determined by the form of its referent. So too, Coleridge implies, are the 'lovely shapes and sounds' of nature determined by their mimetic relation to the 'Great universal Teacher', who teaches 'Himself in all, and all things in himself'. Natural appearances, in this view, have a much more direct and immediate relation to God than any human artefact possibly could, even those 'cloisters dim' built expressly for the purpose of religion. The overwhelming import of this passage is that all signifiers are *not* created equal; some are more adequate than others for the purpose of expressing the divine attributes.[3]

A similar process of mimetic representation is evoked in a passage from 'Religious Musings', first published in 1796:

> Yet thou more bright than all that Angel Blaze,
>
> . . .
>
> Despised GALILAEAN! Man of Woes!
> For chiefly in the oppressed Good Man's face
> The Great Invisible (by symbols seen)
> Shines with peculiar and concentred light,
> When all of Self regardless the scourg'd Saint
> Mourns for th'oppressor.   (7–14)

Here Coleridge asserts that the face of Jesus (the oppressed Good Man) is a direct representation of the Great Invisible. As in 'Frost at Midnight', he uses the term 'image' (21) to designate the paradigm case of divine language. He bolsters this concept with a footnote quoting John 14:9, 'He that hath seen me hath seen the Father.' Once again, there is nothing arbitrary about this process of signification; Jesus is a wholly adequate symbol of God. Coleridge often connects the concept of the symbol with the figure of translucence; the underlying implication is that a symbol actually participates in the reality that it renders intelligible.

Coleridge employs the notion of symbol in another poem of this early period, *The Destiny of Nations*. His conception of natural phenomena in the following passage is clearly derived from the parable of the Cave in Plato's *Republic*:

> For all that meets the bodily sense I deem
> Symbolical, one mighty alphabet
> For infant minds; and we in this low world
> Placed with our backs to bright Reality,
> That we may learn with young unwounded ken
> The substance from its shadow.   (18–23)

Coleridge claims that the objects of bodily sense are symbolical of the reality that lies behind them. As shadows, these objects are mimetic representations of substances; the only difficulty arises in trying to tell the two apart. We may be mistaken in deciding which is the real substance, but we will never fall into the error of thinking that the shadow is a mere arbitrary sign of its referent. Once again, Coleridge chooses a paradigm case in which the signifying connection is a necessary one.

The idea of nature as the language of God will continue to be important to Coleridge throughout his career. Of particular interest is a passage from the *Philosophical Lectures* that bears directly upon the question of what constitutes a 'symbol'. Coleridge is describing what might happen to an African who learns to read the Bible:

> The words become transparent and he sees them as though he saw them not... Then will the other great Bible of God, the Book of Nature, become transparent to us, when we regard the forms of matter as words, as symbols, valuable only as being the expression, an unrolled but yet a glorious fragment, of the wisdom of the Supreme Being. (*Phil Lects*, 366)

Coleridge evidently regards natural phenomena as possessing an inherently linguistic structure. By learning to read the Book of Nature, the primitive African gains access to the 'wisdom of the Supreme Being'. Coleridge asserts that the forms of nature are 'transparent' with respect to the reality underlying them, implying that the paradigmatic relation of a sign to its referent is a necessary one, evident to any persistent inquirer, no matter how far removed from European culture. Earlier in the *Philosophical Lectures*, he attributes this doctrine of nature as a divine language to Plato: 'Plato, with Pythagoras before him, had conceived that the phenomenon or outward appearance, all that we call thing or matter, is but as it were a language by which the invisible (that which is not the object of our senses) communicates its existence to our finite beings' (*Phil Lects*, 187). Coleridge considers Plato to be the true progenitor of the view that the fundamental dualism of western culture – the distinction between reality and appearance – can be overcome, or at least mediated, by regarding outward appearances as linguistic signs. Only by positing the connection between percept and concept as a necessary one can we even conceive of its possibility, since there is no empirical method to determine what each phenomenon 'stands for'.

Coleridge's conception of Nature as a symbolic language should be taken together with a Notebook entry of 1801, which poses the query, 'Whether or no the too great definiteness of Terms in any language may not consume too much of the vital & idea-creating force in distinct, clear, full made Images & so prevent originality' (*CN* I, 1016). Coleridge elsewhere describes the poetic imagination as a 'vital & idea-creating force', a wholly inward activity of '*modifying* and *co-adunating*' the raw data of perception (*CL* II, 866). Indeed, in a subsequent Notebook entry, Coleridge speculates that all of Nature may be regarded as a 'symbolical language' for his own inner Nature. This notion of a 'symbolical language' emerges unexpectedly from a meditative moment during his sojourn on the island of Malta in 1805, a time when Coleridge felt lonely and isolated, a stranger in a strange land. One night, looking out the window of his apartment onto the harbour of Valletta, Coleridge saw the shape of the moon as it glistened upon the still water, and intuitively he felt the importance of this familiar image in a foreign land:

> In looking at objects of Nature while I am thinking, as at yonder moon dim-glimmering thro' the dewy window-pane, I seem rather to be seeking, as it were *asking*, a symbolical language for something within me that already and forever exists, than observing any thing new. Even when that latter is the case, yet still I have always an obscure feeling as if that new phaenomenon were the dim Awaking of a forgotten or hidden Truth of my inner Nature / It is still interesting as a Word, a Symbol! It is Logos, the Creator! and the Evolver!
>
> (*CN* II, 2546)

For Coleridge the image of the moon presents itself as the answer to an unformulated question, the response to a calling-forth of his lonely soul to the beckoning universe. In this context, nature is more than just a set of fixed, aloof objects; the moon offers itself as an oblique fulfilment of desire, a modality by which the hunger of our 'inner Nature' may find satisfaction in the external world. Coleridge here examines the way that nature may become a 'symbolical language' that offers a response to the seeking, or *asking*, of the human spirit.[4]

Coleridge's increasingly subjective, vitalistic theory of imagination is reflected in his practical criticism. During the difficult, wandering years of 1804–10, he moves away from his youthful view of poetic language as a direct simulacrum, or image, of the objects of nature, and towards a theory of analogy. He first broaches this theory in a Notebook entry of 1804: 'Hard to express that sense of the analogy or likeness of a Thing which enables a Symbol to represent it, so that we think of the Thing itself – & yet knowing that the Thing is not present to us' (*CN* II, 2274). This is Coleridge's first clear enunciation of the doctrine he will later call '*negative* faith' (*BL* II, 134). Poetic language, according to this doctrine, is constituted (as aesthetic) by its *difference* from the thing represented. The language of poetry, in other words, resists representational transparency to the extent that it succeeds in foregrounding its own verbal texture. Coleridge goes on to formulate another of his favourite distinctions, that of 'imitation' versus 'copy':

> Surely, on this universal fact of words & images depends by more or less mediations the *imitation* instead of *copy* which is illustrated in very nature *shakespearianized* / – that Proteus Essence that could assume the very form, but yet known & felt not to be the Thing by that difference of the Substance which made every atom of the Form another thing / – that likeness not identity – an exact web, every line of direction miraculously the same, but the one worsted, the other silk.
>
> (*CN* II, 2274)

Here Coleridge describes the poet's task as one of imitating, not copying, the forms of nature. The poet possesses a 'Proteus Essence' that reproduces the form of the external object down to the last detail; but there remains a radical difference in the substance of his discourse. We may infer that this substance is the poetic medium, language itself. Coleridge evidently regards Shakespeare as the epitome and culmination of the purely linguistic aspects of poetry; and in his criticism of Shakespeare, Coleridge comes closest to defining, in practical terms, the linguistic and psychological underpinnings of the literary symbol.

Coleridge's most seminal literary criticism is contained in his public lectures of 1808–19, which established his reputation as a profoundly learned and brilliantly insightful reader of English and European literature. He introduced new methods of close reading and textual analysis to the study of literature, emphasising the integral relation of each detail to the larger structure of the work. Coleridge insists 'that in all points from the most important to the most minute, the judgment of Shakespeare is commensurate with his genius', seeking to refute the prevailing eighteenth-century view of Shakespeare as a wild, untutored genius, 'fertile in beautiful Monsters' (*C. Lects* I, 495). He stresses the imaginative coherence of Shakespeare's plays, arguing that all aspects of their portrayal of character, theme and situation are generated by an organic process of growth and development. Coleridge's reliance on the metaphor of organic development in his Shakespearean criticism is largely indebted to August Wilhelm Schlegel, but his use of the concept in the critical analysis of particular plays is highly original, going far beyond Schlegel in elucidating the deep structure of Shakespeare's language and imagery in relation to the psychological development of specific characters. However, Coleridge makes only occasional use of the concept of symbol in his literary criticism; this concept is mainly developed in the context of his biblical criticism.

In December 1816 Coleridge published *The Statesman's Manual; or the Bible the Best Guide to Political Skill and Foresight*, a work that examines the use and relevance of biblical interpretation in the context of everyday life and political decision-making. Coleridge rejects the barren literalism and the moralising tendencies of many contemporary biblical commentators, arguing that the relevance of the Bible to daily life can emerge only through rigorous interpretation informed by the historical circumstances of its composition and sensitive to its variety of generic forms. In a famous passage, he makes a crucial distinction between symbol and allegory as modes of narrative discourse:

> It is among the miseries of the present age that it recognizes no medium between *Literal* and *Metaphorical*. Faith is either to be buried in the dead letter, or its name and honors usurped by a counterfeit product of the mechanical under-standing, which in the blindness of self-complacency confounds SYMBOLS with ALLEGORIES. Now an allegory is but a translation of abstract notions into a picture-language which is itself nothing but an abstraction from objects of the senses; the principal being more worthless even than its phantom proxy, both alike unsubstantial, and the former shapeless to boot. On the other hand a Symbol (σἔστινᾶειταυτηγόρικον)[5] is characterized by a translucence of the Special in the Individual or of the General in the Especial or of the Univer-sal in the General. Above all by the translucence of the Eternal through and in the Temporal. It always partakes of the reality which it renders intelligible; and while it enunciates the whole, abides itself as a living part in that Unity, of which it is the representative. (*SM*, 30–1)

The most essential and distinctive aspect of the symbol, according to this passage, is its *translucence*, an optical analogy which evidently signifies the potential of symbolic imagery to point beyond itself while still retaining its concreteness and opacity. Coleridge regards the symbol as a product of the human imagination that bears witness to the presence of the Eternal (or 'the infinite I AM') in the most humble images of everyday life. He stresses the tangible quality of symbolic language, its ineluctable grounding in the temporal world. Allegory, on the other hand, is inferior to symbol because it lacks concreteness, drowning the living image in a welter of abstract notions. In Coleridge's view only a symbolic reading of biblical texts can uncover their essential relevance to modern life; allegorical reading tends to reduce these texts to a series of implausible fables and dry moral maxims.[6]

Coleridge's controversial views on biblical hermeneutics were more fully explored in a manuscript published posthumously as *Confessions of An Inquiring Spirit* (1840), which argues forcefully for the critical interpretation of the Bible in light of the entire history of its composition and transmission. Interestingly enough, this work makes no significant use of the concept of symbol, relying instead on historical and philological modes of analysis. Coleridge's religious views were further developed in his most substantial theological work, *Aids to Reflection* (1825). Written as a commentary on the aphorisms of Archbishop Robert Leighton, a seventeenth-century Anglican divine, this work provided Coleridge with a framework for his own deepest meditations on spiritual growth and the role of religion in everyday life. *Aids to Reflection* makes sustained and effective use of the concept of symbol, arguing that the biblical text may be 'at once Symbol and History'. Coleridge goes on to explain that the 'FIRST MAN' (i.e. Adam) must 'of necessity . . . be a SYMBOL of Mankind, in the fullest force of the word, Symbol, rightly defined – viz. *A Symbol is a sign included in the Idea, which it represents*' (*AR*, 263). According to this view, the biblical figure of Adam is both historical (because he actually existed) and symbolic (because he embodies the entire future potential of humankind). Coleridge acknowledges the human complexity that underlies the theological concept of Original Sin, and he denounces the widespread tendency among biblical commentators to regard Adam as merely an abstract, allegorical figure. Throughout *Aids to Reflection*, Coleridge develops the distinction of symbol and allegory as a practical means of biblical interpretation.[7]

Like *The Statesman's Manual*, *Aids to Reflection* failed to arouse much interest among the general reading public at the time of its original publication; but it grew steadily in popularity, reaching a second edition in 1831. Indeed, in the later nineteenth century it proved to be Coleridge's most popular prose work, going through numerous editions in England and America.[8] The first American edition of *Aids to Reflection* (1829), with an eloquent introduction by James Marsh, was particularly influential among the New England Transcendentalists, who admired its reconciliation of German philosophy with traditional religious faith. Many of Coleridge's American disciples remembered his philosophical engagement with the concept of organic form and cherished his inspiring remarks on the essential knowledge revealed in the perception of everyday objects. Among these admirers of Coleridge was Ralph Waldo Emerson, who visited Coleridge at Highgate in 1832, and who developed an essentially Coleridgean theory of language in his seminal essay *Nature* (1836), especially in his assertion of a deep symbolic correspondence between words and natural objects. In the fourth chapter of *Nature*, entitled 'Language', Emerson develops the proposition that 'Nature is the symbol of spirit', arguing that the entire human repertoire of concepts is derived from our collective experience of concrete natural phenomena: 'Have mountains, and waves, and skies, no significance but what we consciously give them, when we employ them as emblems of our thoughts? The world is emblematic. Parts of speech are metaphors, because the whole of nature is a metaphor of the human mind' (*Nature*, 24). Emerson does not merely assert that nature provides handy images for pre-existent mental concepts; rather, he suggests that there exists a precise correspondence between natural phenomena (mountains, waves and skies) and the cognitive repertoire that is mapped out in human language. In this sense, 'the whole of nature is a metaphor of the human mind'.

Henry David Thoreau is less explicit than Emerson in his acknowledgement of Coleridge's influence, but his description of Walden Pond nevertheless owes a great deal to Coleridge's concept of the symbol. For Thoreau, the correspondence between the pellucid waters of Walden Pond and the depth of his own intellect is not merely metaphorical or analogical. Rather, such a correspondence has substantial reality; it is *symbolic* in the strong Coleridgean sense. Thoreau affirms, 'I am thankful that this pond was made deep and pure for a symbol' (*Walden*, 551). The pond is indeed a symbol, since it concretely embodies the qualities of depth and purity; Thoreau would agree with Coleridge that a symbol 'always partakes of the reality which it renders intelligible' (*SM*, 30). But he would disagree with Coleridge's subsequent assertion that a 'material symbol' serves to represent 'the pure untroubled brightness of an IDEA' (*SM*, 50). Thoreau elsewhere expresses scepticism towards any such assertion of a purely transcendent realm: 'Here or nowhere is our heaven'.[9] In Thoreau's view, the symbolic attributes of Walden Pond do not arise from its participation in a transcendental Idea, but are inherent in its very existence as a material object. Thus the melting of the pond in springtime unleashes the immanent 'joy' of its watery being: 'It is glorious to behold this ribbon of water sparkling in the sun, the bare face of the pond full of glee and youth, as if it spoke the joy of the fishes within it, and of the sands on its shore' (570). Both Walden Pond and its human beholder are ineluctably grounded in the material world, and their acts of signification arise from a speaking-forth of their temporal existence.

Thoreau's response to Coleridge exemplifies the ineluctable tendency of modern American culture towards the secular, the material and the pragmatic. Coleridge would certainly have denounced such tendencies. Yet Coleridge's concept of symbol has proven remarkably resilient in the midst of such a profoundly secular culture. Indeed, the New Critical approach to literary interpretation is largely indebted to Coleridge, not only for its trademark method of 'practical criticism' (a term that I. A. Richards borrowed from Coleridge), but also for its frequent reliance upon the concept of symbol as a preferred mode of literary signification. Perhaps the single most important essay in the history of Coleridge criticism, and one of the most memorable exercises in close reading, is Robert Penn Warren's 'A Poem of Pure Imagination' (1946).[10] Warren's detailed close reading of 'The Rime of the Ancient Mariner' relies heavily upon the concept of symbol; he argues that the sun represents 'the light of practical convenience' (372) while the moon represents 'the modifying colors of the imagination' (367). Warren develops a coherent and thoroughly plausible interpretation of the poem in terms of these symbolic images, although he is overtly resistant to the metaphysical and epistemological baggage that comes along with Coleridge's doctrine of symbol and allegory. After quoting Coleridge's famous distinction of these two terms from *The Statesman's Manual*, Warren disclaims responsibility for their larger implications, though he does acknowledge that 'these statements by Coleridge raise the most profound and vexing aesthetic and, for that matter, epistemological questions, questions which I do not have the temerity to profess to settle' (351). As a true-born American pragmatist, Warren does not concern himself with the larger philosophical contexts of Coleridge's ideas. But Warren's humble, self-deprecating, backwoods attitude may appear disingenuous to the alert reader who is trained to recognise Socratic irony. Warren's refusal to consider epistemology is itself an unacknowledged 'common-sense' epistemology, and his disavowal of aesthetics entails a dogmatic know-nothing approach to aesthetics.[11]

William York Tindall, in *The Literary Symbol* (1955), provides a more fully articulated response to Coleridge's concept of symbol from a twentieth-century perspective. He cites Coleridge's famous passage on symbol and allegory from *The Statesman's Manual*, and unlike Warren he fully acknowledges the metaphysical context from which the distinction emerges: 'It is plain that Coleridge valued the symbol for helping him pass from matter to spirit or giving him the feeling of that passage' (39). Like Thoreau, however, Tindall is reluctant to follow Coleridge along that passageway of the spirit, and his book is devoted mainly to French Symbolist and Anglo-American Modernist examples of symbolic discourse that have become untethered from the transcendental ideas where Coleridge had sought to anchor his own conception of the symbol. To be sure, there is no reason why an idea should remain moored to its original context, and Tindall's book is particularly insightful because it does acknowledge the different philosophical orientations of the modern poetic practitioners of symbolic imagery, rather than presuming that there is only one 'common-sense' perspective available. Nevertheless, it is clear that Tindall himself is mainly concerned with the gloomy agnostic outlook of the Modernist writers, and his most incisively developed example of symbolism in literature is the giant billboard depicting the desolate image of Dr T. J. Eckleburg's gigantic blue irises, from the opening of *The Great Gatsby* by F. Scott Fitzgerald. The symbolic implications of this billboard are vast and depressing, but it is not exactly the sort of image that Coleridge would have chosen to exemplify his concept of literary symbolism.

Paul de Man, in a seminal essay entitled 'The Rhetoric of Temporality' (1969), takes the demystification of Coleridge's symbol to its greatest extreme. Going beyond the jovial, efficient, common-sense American outlook of Warren, Tindall and their progeny in the school of New Criticism, Paul de Man brings the sceptical, corrosive Old-World perspective of deconstruction to bear upon Coleridge's doctrine of symbol and its metaphysical postulates. Not surprisingly, De Man finds much to criticise in Coleridge's doctrine of the literary symbol, arguing that 'whereas the symbol postulates the possibility of an identity or an identification, allegory postulates primarily a distance in relation to its own origin' (190). In de Man's view, 'distance' is a correlative of authenticity, although it remains unclear in his analysis why *distance* should be any more authentic than *identity* as a mode of relation. Moreover, it would be ludicrous to assert that Coleridge was somehow unaware of the metaphysical premises of his own outlook. Despite the protestations of Paul de Man, Coleridge's doctrine of the symbol was not 'mystified'; it was merely different from that which the twentieth century regarded as 'common-sense'. A more truly disinterested historical perspective – an authentic 'rhetoric of temporality' – would seek to comprehend the philosophical tradition of transcendental Idealism that gave shape to Coleridge's ideas.[12]

A more rewarding approach to Coleridge's concept of the symbol is articulated by Susanne K. Langer in two provocative books, *Philosophy in a New Key: A Study in the Symbolism of Reason, Rite and Art* (1942) and *Feeling and Form: A Theory of Art* (1953). In both of these books, Langer gives the neo-Kantian aesthetic doctrines of Ernst Cassirer a more pragmatic turn, and in the writings of Coleridge (particularly the *Biographia Literaria* and 'The Rime of the Ancient Mariner') she finds a firm point of reference upon which to ground her discussion of symbolism as a new key for philosophy. Langer defines man as the 'symbolific animal' and she carefully distinguishes between *signs* (the arbitrary units of signification that constitute human language) and *symbols* (the open, presentational forms that pervade fine art, music and literature). Langer states this distinction most clearly in *Feeling and Form*: 'The artistic symbol, *qua* artistic, negotiates insight, not reference; it does not rest upon convention, but motivates and dictates conventions. It is deeper than any semantic of accepted signs and their referents, more essential than any schema that may be heuristically read' (22). Langer cites Coleridge's famous definition of Primary Imagination from *Biographia Literaria* (chapter 13) in support of her contention that the art symbol is an 'imaginal form' (54), and she examines the variation of past and present tense in 'The Rime of the Ancient Mariner' to suggest that in fiction 'there is nothing but virtual memory; the illusion of life must be experiential through and through' (265). Her conception of imaginative fiction as 'virtual memory' is clearly consistent with, and possibly derived from, Coleridge's theory of the 'willing suspension of disbelief for the moment, which constitutes poetic faith' (*BL* II, 6). For Langer, as for Coleridge, the literary symbol does not merely *describe* the world of ordinary experience; rather, it *re-presents* that world through rich sensory images that (at least momentarily) create an imaginary realm of 'virtual space' and 'virtual time' (as Langer terms the illusive dimensions of an alternative reality).

Langer is remarkably innovative in her use of the phrases 'virtual memory' (265), 'virtual space' (69) and 'virtual time' (109) to designate an alternative reality that is evoked in the mind of the reader by means of symbolic discourse. Langer's coinage of these three phrases in 1953 significantly antedates their use in the field of computer science. The *Oxford English Dictionary* attests the phrase 'virtual memory' as a computer term from 1959, but it fails to notice Langer's previous use of this phrase in the field of aesthetic theory.[13] In an even more prescient use of language, Coleridge uses the phrase 'virtually contained in the Present' to designate the way that symbolic discourse evokes (or foreshadows) an alternative reality. In *The Statesman's Manual*, Coleridge writes:

> The truths [of the Bible] and the symbols that represent them move in conjunction and form the living chariot that bears up (for *us*) the throne of the Divine Humanity...Hence too, its contents present to us the stream of time continuous as Life and a symbol of eternity, inasmuch as the Past and Future are *virtually* contained in the Present. (*SM*, 29; emphasis added)

Evidently, for Coleridge, the symbolic narratives presented in the Bible have a threefold significance: they offer a factual account of historical events, while they also look forward and backward in time, either recalling events that are prefigured in earlier books of the Bible (i.e. typological symbolism) or foretelling events that have not yet transpired (i.e. prophetic symbolism). By offering a glimpse of past and future events through the unfolding of an ostensibly factual narrative, the Bible becomes (in Coleridge's view) a normative model for other forms of symbolic discourse, since it offers the reader a 'virtual reality' whose relevance to the actual world gradually becomes apparent over the course of historical time.

Although Coleridge develops his basic concept of symbolic discourse mainly within the context of biblical interpretation, his description of the symbol as a temporal unfolding of the significance '*virtually* contained in the Present' is entirely consistent with Susanne Langer's analysis of the literary symbol as a repository of 'virtual memory'. For both Coleridge and Langer, the literary symbol contains more meaning than can ever be adequately expressed in a prose paraphrase; for this reason a symbolic narrative poem (such as 'The Rime of the Ancient Mariner') must be approached experientially, with a 'willing suspension of disbelief', so that its meanings may be unfolded through the temporal process of storytelling. The act of reading, as it occurs in the mind of a reader at a certain geographical and historical distance from the site of the poem's original creation, offers an arena for the discovery of meaning in 'virtual space' and 'virtual time'. The Ancient Mariner's strange tale of exploration and adventure carries no symbolic resonance until it is reconstituted in the reluctant, yet hypnotically vivid awareness of the Wedding-Guest, who serves (in this respect) as an avatar for the reader. Evidently, for Coleridge, the making of symbols is a two-part process: poetic *images* emerge fully formed from the crucible of the creative imagination, but they do not become *symbols*, laden with historical and cultural meaning, until they are appropriated and reconstituted by the awareness of a reader.

Perhaps this dynamic quality is the most distinctive characteristic of symbolic discourse as Coleridge conceives it. Rather than offering a static, purely abstract meaning (as allegory does), the literary symbol continuously evolves over historical time, and unfolds inexhaustible layers of significance through successive acts of interpretation by active, inquiring readers.

NOTES

1 The intellectual contexts of Coleridge's linguistic theory are more fully examined in James C. McKusick, *Coleridge's Philosophy of Language* (New Haven: Yale University Press, 1986).

2 Coleridge's concept of the symbol as a motivated sign is more fully examined by Robert N. Essick, 'Coleridge and the Language of Adam', *Coleridge's* Biographia Literaria: *Text and Meaning*, ed. Frederick Burwick (Columbus: Ohio State University Press, 1989), 62–74.

3 Further analysis of the symbol in relation to the natural world is provided by Douglas B. Wilson, 'Two Modes of Apprehending Nature: A Gloss on the Coleridgean Symbol', *Publication of the Modern Language Association of America*, 87 (1972), 42–52.

4 The inward, psychological dimension of symbolic discourse is analysed by Anca Vlasopolos, *The Symbolic Method of Coleridge, Baudelaire, and Yeats* (Detroit: Wayne State University Press, 1983).

5 'Which is always tautegorical' (Greek). According to the *Oxford English Dictionary*, Coleridge coined the word 'tautegorical'. He further elucidates this term in *CN* IV, 4711, and *AR*, 206.

6 For the theological context of Coleridge's concept of symbol, see J. Robert Barth, SJ, *The Symbolic Imagination: Coleridge and the Romantic Tradition* (Princeton University Press, 1977). For a contrasting view, see Nicholas Halmi, 'How Christian Is the Coleridgean Symbol?' *Wordsworth Circle*, 26 (1995), 26–30.

7 For further discussion of the role of symbol in Coleridge's biblical interpretation, see David Aram Kaiser, 'The Incarnated Symbol: Coleridge, Hegel, Strauss, and the Higher Biblical Criticism', *European Romantic Review*, 4 (1994), 133–50. See also Jon Whitman, 'From the Textual to the Temporal: Early Christian "Allegory" and Early Romantic "Symbol"', *New Literary History*, 22 (1991), 161–76.

8 The concept of symbol among Coleridge's intellectual progeny in Victorian England is investigated by Anthony John Harding, 'Development and Symbol in the Thought of S. T. Coleridge, J. C. Hare, and John Sterling', *Studies in Romanticism*, 18 (1979), 29–48. The logical underpinnings of the Coleridgean symbol are incisively examined by M. Jadwiga Swiatecka, *The Idea of the Symbol: Some Nineteenth-Century Comparisons with Coleridge* (Cambridge University Press, 1980).

9 Henry David Thoreau, *A Week on the Concord and Merrimack Rivers*, ed. Robert F. Sayre (New York: Library of America, 1985), 308.

10 A survey of the various critical responses to Warren's essay is provided by Max Schultz, 'Samuel Taylor Coleridge', *The English Romantic Poets: A Review of Research and Criticism*, ed. Frank Jordon (New York: Modern Language Association, 1985), 386–8.

11 Coleridge points out that 'common sense . . . differs in different ages. What was born and christened in the schools passes by degrees into the world at large, and becomes the property of the market and the tea-table' (*BL* I, 86–7n.).

12 A more detailed analysis of De Man's critique is provided by David Dawson, 'Against the Divine Ventriloquist: Coleridge and De Man on Symbol, Allegory, and Scripture', *Literature and Theology: An International Journal of Theory, Criticism and Culture*, 4 (1990), 293–310.

13 *Oxford English Dictionary* (2nd edn, 1989) defines 'virtual memory' only as a function of computer software (s.v. 'virtual' 4.g). The phrase 'virtual reality' is not defined in *OED*.

15

JOHN BEER

Coleridge's afterlife

After Coleridge's death it was hard to know how to come to terms with him. Those who had known him personally might be left with a sense of resonating marvel, as expressed in Wordsworth's tribute that he was 'the most *wonderful* man he had ever known'.[1] Even Thomas Arnold, who as a neighbour in the Lake District would have heard about the troubles of Coleridge's domestic life in some detail, wrote, 'I think with all his faults old Sam was more of a great man than anyone who has lived within the four seas in my memory.'[2] Hazlitt, among his many adverse criticisms, had described him as 'the only person I ever knew that answered to the idea of a man of genius' (Howe v, 167). De Quincey, in an access of enthusiasm, now termed him 'the largest and most spacious intellect . . . the subtlest and most comprehensive, that has yet existed among men'.[3] This last was written in the immediate aftermath of his death, however, and omitted from the account in subsequent years, reflecting contemporary uneasiness and a tendency to look warily at heroes of the previous age.

There was corresponding enthusiasm elsewhere, notably in London, where J. A. Heraud championed his reputation. Since the early 1820s it had been in Cambridge, however, that his standing was strongest. Julius Hare, tutor at Trinity College, was to recall how under the influence of his conversation one felt one's soul teeming and bursting 'as beneath the breath of spring';[4] Hare, in turn, influenced a number of students, including John Sterling and Frederic Denison Maurice, both members of the Cambridge club which came to be known as the Apostles and which continued to meet regularly in London. Writing to him in 1836, Sterling said: 'To Coleridge I owe education. He taught me to believe that an empirical philosophy is none, that Faith is the highest Reason, that all criticism, whether of literature, laws, or manners, is blind, without the power of discerning the organic unity of the object.'[5] Arthur Henry Hallam, another Apostle who had met him, called him 'the good old man, most eloquent'.[6]

The sense of a magic in the man would be rearoused when readers returned to the poetry and recognised its continuing power to haunt the consciousness. Resonances from his poems of the supernatural can be traced, for example, in Dickens's *A Christmas Carol*, in Mrs Gaskell's *Mary Barton* and in George Eliot's *Adam Bede*.[7] Coleridge's appeal, in all his writings, to the workings of heart and imagination promised the intervention of a mediating power that might assuage the oppressive effects of the contentions between science and religion. Readers who found themselves in that territory of doubt knew that Coleridge had been there before them by more than his discussions of similar problems: the account of the ills induced by over-developed habits of analysis in the 'Dejection' ode rendered with unexpected exactitude a drabness of feeling they could recognise.

In the first generation of Coleridge's readers it was the moral and religious elements in his thought that provoked most interest, nevertheless, even if those who said how much they owed to his doctrines were often unfortunately imprecise about the exact nature of their debt and confused about his moral example. The availability of texts for study at least simplified the position for some religious thinkers, since it became possible to discuss what Coleridge was saying on its merits, without reference to the failings of the man himself. On this basis Coleridge's writings enjoyed a long afterlife of their own in the world of English and American theology. There were also, however, subtler and more diffuse influences from Coleridge on writers of the Victorian age who recognised in his often fragmentary and divided thinking self-contradictions of their own.

People such as these found him a figure at once intriguing and bewildering. There were rumours of further depths to his thinking, associated among other things with his project of creating a revolutionary metaphysical system, of which, it was believed, only hints survived in his published writings.[8] The report that he had after all left in manuscript a long unpublished metaphysical work added to these rumours: some cherished the belief that when it eventually emerged it would prove to be the great work of intellectual reconciliation the age was longing for. Meanwhile Joseph Henry Green, charged with publishing such papers and making Coleridge's philosophy accessible to succeeding generations, produced instead his *Spiritual Philosophy: Founded on the Teaching of S. T. Coleridge* (1865), a volume which, whatever its qualities, did not provide a large-scale detailed systematisation.

The difficulty of seizing the nature of his achievement in more serious terms was exacerbated by the fact that, while in some important respects his thought had remained consistent over the years, in others it had also undergone changes, the records of which lay largely hidden in unpublished letters and manuscripts. Nevertheless it is possible to discern certain features that appealed to the age. The first was that, in a period when victory in the Napoleonic Wars had left many willing to carry on as if the previous quarter of a century had made no difference to human thought, Coleridge had recognised the impatience of thinking people, particularly among the young, who were disturbed by the failure to acknowledge the power of the ideas of the revolutionary period – particularly when idealistic thinking about humanity was being swept aside. Meanwhile readers were not lacking to welcome Coleridge's insistence on the need for noble ideals of conduct, as expressed in the title of his *Aids to Reflection in the Formation of a Manly Character*. The arguments in which he urged the reader to adopt an empirical approach to Christianity on the grounds that only if one did so would the truth of the doctrines be revealed had a strong appeal for minds that wished to move from questioning to action. And although, as its reception showed, his attempt to introduce into England critical modes of reading the Bible that had become familiar in Germany proved premature, the concessive title *Confessions of an Inquiring Spirit* under which it was published in 1840 made a similar appeal to such minds, as did his exhortation to look for the truths in the Bible that '*find*' the reader (*SWF* II, 1120–4).

The other major feature of *Aids to Reflection* was its stress on the nature of the spiritual, which Coleridge attempted to rescue from dismissive eighteenth-century attitudes that could see in a religion of the heart only 'enthusiasm' and inadmissible pretensions to inspiration. While acknowledging the force of arguments against an undue respect for 'mysticism' he contended for the existence of a core of truth at the heart of such experiences. At a time when people were turning against the dryness of current Anglicanism, his careful arguments in favour of a properly defined spirituality won admiration and support. To an age that was increasingly looking less for questioning minds than for voices to offer a note of assurance in difficult times, this Coleridge, who appeared to have distilled a message for his times from his own restless thought and experience, had a particularly strong appeal. Young men who were becoming conscious of the difficulty of holding Christian beliefs within the emergent intellectual climate found accents that they could understand. Some, such as Julius Hare, who had learned what was going on in Germany, appreciated his achievement still more.

Among these John Sterling was prominent: expressing his doubts concerning Shelley's ideas, he wrote:

> I scarcely hold fast by anything but Shakespeare, Milton, and Coleridge and I have nothing serious to say to any one but to read the 'Aids to Reflection in the formation of a *Manly* character' – a book the more necessary now to us all because except in England I do not see that there is a chance of any *men* being produced any where.[9]

While Sterling and others played an important part in founding the Broad Church movement, it is sometimes suggested that Coleridge's influence was as profound on the High Church movement (just as political reverberations of his thought have been traced both in nineteenth-century conservatism and in Christian socialism). There is an element of truth in this: some of the Oxford philosophy tutors were instilling a reverence for Coleridge in their young men and the Oxford Movement itself began in the Hadleigh Rectory home of Hugh J. Rose, an admirer of Coleridge's thought. But it would be equally true to say that it arose as an answer to views such as Coleridge's. Newman's remark 'I never did read Coleridge', sometimes quoted to establish a lack of influence on him, proves to have referred specifically to the period preceding the initiation of the Oxford Movement. In the 1830s, by contrast, he was anxiously engaged with some of Coleridge's ideas – particularly his views on Church and State and his stress on Christianity as a great religion of symbols. To Newman's logical mind religion must be 'real'; symbolic statements were not to the purpose. Yet the sensitivity of his mind meant that if he could not agree with Coleridge's religious position he could discern in him a kindred spirit.[10] When in old age he was approached in connection with the plan to place a bust of Coleridge in Westminster Abbey he replied that he could not support the proposal – but went on to declare that that was 'from no want of reverence for the genius of Mr Coleridge as poet and philosopher'.[11]

In 1840 there appeared one of the most balanced accounts of Coleridge in John Stuart Mill's review of his *Church and State*,[12] which included the well-known comparison with Jeremy Bentham: 'By Bentham, beyond all others, men have been led to ask themselves, in regard to any ancient or received opinion, Is it true? And by Coleridge, What is the meaning of it?'[13] Coleridge's position he expounded as follows: 'With Coleridge . . . the very fact that any doctrine had been believed by thoughtful men, and received by whole nations or generations of mankind, was a part of the problem to be solved, was one of the phenomena to be accounted for.'[14] Mill's characterisation of Coleridge's as one of the 'two great seminal minds of England in their age',[15] along with his further assertion that 'as a philosopher, the class of thinkers has scarcely yet arisen, by whom he is to be judged',[16] were tributes that would resonate.

Sterling's later career, meanwhile, was exhibiting with clarity a pattern of reaction not uncommon in admirers of Coleridge: an initial enthusiasm followed by disenchantment as awareness of his weaknesses induced a suspicion that one might after all have been fooled by an impressive demeanour and plausible rhetoric. A very severe critique of his, made privately,[17] no doubt partly reflects discussions of Coleridge's borrowings that had intervened since his death; between 1865 and 1870 such negative views were to be further reinforced by accusations of plagiarism from J. H. Stirling and C. M. Ingleby in which the note of moral reprobation was sounded still more clearly.[18]

The uneasiness which Sterling came to feel was no doubt connected with the injunction – so attractive to many when they first came across it – that one should act on doctrines about which one might not feel fully sure in the expectation that the acting out would reveal their truth. When, after Sterling's death, Julius Hare produced a biographical account which praised him chiefly for the qualities he had demonstrated as a clergyman, Carlyle was stirred to write a version of his own, dwelling on the intellectual features that he had found most important and which he believed to have been impeded by Sterling's decision to enter the Church – a decision to which, in Carlyle's view, he had been misled by the influence of Coleridge.

At the centre of his biography of Sterling, a chapter on Coleridge[19] disparaged the latter's reputation as a sage. Not only was the advocate of a 'manly character' depicted as himself a broken-down figure, 'flabby and irresolute', but his religious thought was blamed by Carlyle for the propagation of 'strange Centaurs, spectral Puseyisms, monstrous illusory Hybrids, and ecclesiastical Chimeras, – which now roam the Earth in a very lamentable manner!' While he endeavoured to be even-handed, commenting that in Coleridge 'a ray of heavenly inspiration struggled, in a tragically ineffectual degree, with the weakness of flesh and blood', the acerbity of other comments was too powerful to make this seem more than a chivalrous gesture. Readers who had learned from Carlyle's writings as a whole to respect the forceful will could not be expected to summon up more than a pitying sympathy. At the same time his presentation is not as fair or as accurate as its aura of candour would suggest.[20]

The divided response that can be discerned even within Carlyle's scathing account was displayed also by Matthew Arnold, whose attitude no doubt owed something to his father's favourable opinion. In his essay on Joubert, having praised Coleridge for the 'stimulus of his continual effort', he inserts the astonishing parenthesis ' – not a moral effort, for he had no morals –' before continuing with further praise for 'his continual instinctive effort, crowned often with rich success, to get at and to lay bare the real truth of his matter in hand'.[21] While continuing to disparage Coleridge's moral weaknesses he believed his view of Christianity as identical with the highest philosophy to be one of the crucial ideas for his time: 'it is true, it is deeply important, and by virtue of it Coleridge takes rank, so far as English thought is concerned, as an initiator and founder'. It was, indeed, 'henceforth the key to the whole defence of Christianity'.[22]

While this could be seen as a development of ideas that Arnold had im-
bibed from his father, contemporaries such as Arthur Hugh Clough, Thomas
Arnold's star pupil and a close friend of Matthew's, were less happy with
Coleridge's defence. Clough's first acquaintance with the works had been
either in the upper class at Rugby, where Thomas Arnold sometimes read them
aloud, or during his subsequent career at Oxford. In November 1840, when
he was in his last year, a contemporary described a wine-party at Balliol where
'The conversation soon became general, and turned shortly to Wordsworth
and from him to S. T. Coleridge and the *Aids to Reflection*.'[23] Whether or
not he joined in, Clough, who was noted among his contemporaries for his
strong sense of the actual, wrote, in the following February: 'I should like
much to have heard Carlyle's complaints against Coleridge. I keep wavering
between admiration of his exceedingly great perceptive and analytical power
and other wonderful points and inclination to turn away altogether from
a man who has so great a lack of all reality and actuality.'[24] Whatever the
'complaints' of Carlyle, and however they had come to Clough's attention, it
became possible for him and other contemporaries to read them at length and
in polished form in 1850, when the *Life of Sterling* appeared. By the time that
George Eliot reviewed the book, the criticisms of Coleridge had already been
widely extracted and quoted; her own insistence that 'the emphasis of quotation [could] not be too often given' to the 'pregnant paragraph', asserting
that it was lack of courage which had restrained Coleridge from pressing res-
olutely across 'the howling deserts of infidelity', reflected current concerns.[25]

The establishment of such attitudes was assisted a few years later by the
wave of thought initiated in 1859 by Darwin's *The Origin of Species*, which
demanded a new intellectual and moral stringency as the forcefulness of
earlier arguments concerning religion and morality declined. The possibility
of defending Christianity by retreating to permanent elements that would
survive the assaults currently being mounted – a hope which Coleridge's
work had seemed to support – faded; instead, the need for honesty in dealing with Darwin's theories introduced an unprecedented scepticism into the
examination of arguments and evidences. In the new climate Coleridge's argument that Christianity conformed to individual religious experience might
appear less a persuasive set of arguments than an encouragement of wish-
ful thinking, while Mill's identification of him as one who taught people
not to dismiss, as being meaningless, phenomena that had persisted through
time seemed less relevant as significance drained from the post-Darwinian
universe. Positive mentions by leading intellectuals became extremely rare;
yet Coleridge's thought could still appeal to a more general level of readers. When new editions of his prose works ceased to appear they were still
reprinted in the popular format of Bohn's Library.

Even those who were most inclined to dismiss Coleridge's thinking in the context of the new scientific positivism found reasons for hesitation. When the leading agnostic Leslie Stephen addressed the Royal Institution in 1888, for example, he took Coleridge for his subject as 'certainly one of the most fascinating and most perplexing figures in our literary history'. His choice was no doubt prompted partly by the fact that in writing an account of him for the *Dictionary of National Biography* he had recently been drawn to examine hitherto unpublished documents that might prompt further reflections on Coleridge's contradictory nature.[26]

The conditions of Leslie Stephen's time made it particularly difficult for such a writer to come to terms with Coleridge. One could not read him as an early protagonist of aestheticism without being brought up short by his frequent moral reflections, which might seem to challenge the conception of art for art's sake. Further publication of Coleridge's writings, meanwhile, drew added attention to the contradictions of his personality. The year 1895, an important one for his posthumous reputation, saw the appearance of his grandson's collection of extracts from the Notebooks, entitled *Anima Poetae*, in which some of his finest prose appeared for the first time. Although these passages were often touched up by the editor to make them more acceptable as belles-lettres, the qualities of Coleridge as a sensitive observer of nature and of his own sensations and mental processes came through very clearly. Meanwhile the passages of moral self-examination which were also interspersed through the volume were complemented by further revelations of his weaknesses when the first fully extended collection of the *Letters* appeared in the same year. Reviews extolling Coleridge's literary powers alternated with others lamenting or chastising his shortcomings. A simple way to deal with the situation was to revive the division between Coleridge the poet and Coleridge the thinker, praising the former at the expense of the latter.

During these years Coleridge had not been without champions of his thought. One of Stephen's friends, Shadworth Hodgson, firmly upheld the importance of his ideas from a philosophical point of view. In his book *The Philosophy of Reflection*, which was dedicated to Coleridge, he described how he had learned from him two great principles: the principle of reflection, and the principle of distinction of inseparables. He had been even more impressed by the possibility of producing an intimate union between the intellectual and emotional elements in human nature.[27] And, however much Carlyle might have mocked Coleridge for having found 'the sublime secret of believing by "the reason" what "the understanding" had been obliged to fling out as incredible', his work continued to find an audience. His insistence that if one followed truth one would find oneself led into a position where one could still keep faith with the past struck a note that was to become more acceptable with the loss of former certitudes. One of the more striking passages in *Aids to Reflection*, for example, had been the one in which he traced a line of nobility through the animal creation, looking for those elements – such as the faithfulness of swallows to their mates or the self-sacrificing orders among ant-colonies – which might be thought to prophesy and foreshadow the fuller development of such virtues in human beings. He had also believed that, while a pattern of striving ascent could be discerned in nature, it had not taken the form of an actual process of evolution through time but had formed a part of the original creation. It was a solution that appealed to some by its subtlety, rescuing human nobility without sacrificing the sense of developing form that was everywhere more and more evident. This kind of argument was, however, undermined by the recent evidences that such natural ascent had not only indeed taken place through time but by way of a process involving 'the survival of the fittest'. At the same time a more general and pervasive sense of 'flux', fostered by such things as the formulation of the Laws of Thermodynamics, rendered the relationship between the human mind and nature even more debatable. There might indeed be a match between the wavelike working of impressions in the mind and the unchannelled ocean of events in nature, but if so what significance could it have?

Although Coleridge's decreasing prominence as a religious thinker in the latter part of the century was no doubt particularly due to the fact that some of his most attractive arguments for a previous generation had thus lost cogency, all was not ruin. To some of the new generation (paradoxically, in twentieth-century eyes) the plangent note in his writings sounded a truly 'modern' note. This chimed with new modes of thought. In 1825, when writing the 'Conclusion' to his *Aids to Reflection*, he had brooded on one of the mysteries revealed by scientific investigations into the nature of matter:

> The characters, which I am now shaping on this paper, abide. Not only the forms remain the same, but the particles of the coloring stuff are fixed, and, for an indefinite period at least, remain the same. But the particles that constitute the size, the visibility of an organic structure...are in perpetual flux. They are to the combining and constitutive Power as the pulses of air to the Voice of a Discourser; or of one who sings a roundelay. The same words may be repeated; but in each second of time the articulated air hath passed away, and each act of articulation appropriates and gives momentary form to a new and other portion. As the column of blue smoke from a cottage chimney in the breathless Summer Noon, or the stedfast-seeming Cloud on the edge-point of a Hill in the driving air-current, which momently condensed and recomposed is the common phantom of a thousand successors; – such is the flesh, which our *bodily* eyes transmit to us; which our *Palates* taste; which our Hands touch.
>
> (*AR*, 397–8)

Coleridge's sense of this mysterious impalpability and transience in organic matter (which he saw as providing powerful evidence against a 'materialist' interpretation) was prophetic of the impressionism that dominated later nineteenth-century aesthetics. An important milestone in establishing new views came in 1866 with the publication of an article entitled 'Coleridge's Writings'[28] by Walter Pater, which stands interestingly against the earlier Victorian evaluations, showing how an intelligent young man was responding to the new challenge of *The Origin of Species*. Pater's attitude to the implications of such recent work was not only perceptive but cleverly adapted to the changing view of development – he wrote of 'the reserve of the older generation exquisitely refined by the antagonism of the new' and the consequent strength of the results: 'Communicating in this to the passing stage of culture the charm of what is chastened, high-strung, athletic, they yet detach the highest minds from the past by pressing home its difficulties and finally proving it impossible.'

Coleridge he included, rather surprisingly, among those who had 'the charm of what is chastened, high-strung, athletic', though he found his insistence on seeking the establishment of fixed principles, involving as it did the presupposition that one could reach an Absolute, disturbingly out of date. If one conclusion had emerged from recent thought, he believed, it was the necessity of thinking always in relative terms. In contrast to Wordsworth's conviction that there were 'certain latent affinities between nature and the human mind, which reciprocally gild the mind and nature with a kind of "heavenly alchemy"', sustained by the vibrancy of his 'blithe *élan*', Coleridge had proved unable to remain absorbed by his own power: 'What in Wordsworth is a sentiment or instinct, is in Coleridge a philosophical idea.' Wordsworth's notions had had the virtue of being held in solution; when adopted by Coleridge they stiffened into formulae. His mistake, in Pater's eyes, had been to try to fix into a final mode a soul which could never be experienced as other than a shaping influence.

In cultivating process, yet seeking to indicate a stability within that process, Pater was at once acknowledging, and resisting, the increasing tendency of scientific thought to impose a material interpretation on the workings of human life. The life of the soul was now set up as an alternative mode of existence, in which if one were prepared to question the limits of the palpable and quantifiable one would find oneself supported by other traditions and antecedents. Although Pater might decry Coleridge's striving after the Absolute he could recognise in him the force of an equally powerful yearning, summed up in his adaptation of Lamb's characterisation of him as one who had 'a hunger for eternity'.[29] And while he was criticising his movement towards an absolute, he was seeking a stability within the flux of process, a cultivation of 'soul-truth', which actually followed another strand of Coleridge's thinking, inherent in the title and subject-matter of *Aids to Reflection*. Enlightenment thinkers had found in the power to reflect one of the factors distinguishing human beings from the animal creation: an earnest of the human sense of responsibility. Rousseau on the other hand had declared in his *Discourse of Inequality* that 'a state of reflection is a state against nature and a man who meditates is a depraved animal'.[30] Pater was at one with Coleridge in his championship of the meditative mode; more importantly, his constant dwelling on the links between impressions through time necessarily involved these modes as an essential part in what he was doing, aligning him with that long movement in Romantic art which worked to establish a correspondence between the human mind and nature in a manner that would enhance the significance of both.

Coleridge's ultimate gift to human thinking lay in his capacity for double perception, for thinking at more than one level, an appreciation of which is necessary if one is to grasp the full nature of his continuing influence. At its best his mind positively recoiled from watertight formulations. The establishing of a system that would have been enough to make the reputation of another man was not for him, even though he could examine acutely such systems when formulated by others and even claim to reconcile them within a more comprehensive pattern (*TT* 1, 248–9). He was particularly subtle when paying attention to the larger workings of his own psyche. While endorsing contemporary respect for the human will, he knew from personal experience how unreliable a resource it could be. Systems that relied upon a sharp categorisation of the powers in the human mind, similarly, were probed by a man who knew how imperceptibly one mental power might blend into another. A chief contribution to the development of philosophy, which, as Thomas McFarland has shown, lay in his long exploration of the distinction between the philosophy of 'It is' and that of 'I am',[31] involved a distinguishing less between comparable rational systems than between two ways of dealing with the world that differed profoundly in their very terms. This made him most at home not in professional philosophy as commonly understood, but in the more difficult terrain where different *kinds* of discourse met one another, often in mutual incomprehension.

In the twentieth century the possibilities of thinking in this way were explored further; but Coleridge's contribution has been undervalued, partly because the psychological speculations of his early years which provide the key to a fuller understanding still lay, like his scientific ones, buried in unpublished notebooks and uncollected letters. Such manuscripts were to be explored by scholars such as I. A. Richards and Kathleen Coburn for their more straightforward relevance to modern psychological thought, but their full significance may still be missed. Virginia Woolf, who wrote perceptively about Coleridge, developed a view of the novel which rested on a similar kind of dual perception and a sense of what it might mean for writing. In her celebrated statement about the nature of the 'life' that novelists attempt to convey, she wrote: 'Life is not a series of gig lamps symmetrically arranged; life is a luminous halo, a semi-transparent envelope surrounding us from the beginning of consciousness to the end.'[32] D. H. Lawrence had a similar feeling for the complex nature of life, dismissing Wordsworth, Keats, Shelley and the Brontës as all 'post-mortem poets'.[33] The fact that Coleridge's name (like Blake's) was omitted may well be significant, since, while Lawrence always distrusted moralising, he could hardly have failed to pick up the note in Coleridge's early writings which brought him closer than any other Romantic poet to Lawrence's own feeling for the universal spirit of life. The serpent-imagery of 'Christabel' has thematic links with the 'serpent of secret shame' that Lawrence looks to redeem by bringing it to the light,[34] while the theme of the 'one Life' that is present in a number of the meditative poems and openly manifest in 'The Ancient Mariner' has very obvious connections with Lawrence's pervasive vitalism. In one of his most famous poems about sensitivity for life, remorse for his mean-mindedness in attacking a snake that came to drink at his water-trough is summed up in the words 'And I thought of the albatross, / And I wished he would come back, my snake.'[35] It is not surprising, then, to find him writing to Amy Lowell, 'I'd like to know Coleridge, when Charon has rowed me over.'[36]

Among writers of the later twentieth century Ted Hughes's strong admiration for Lawrence was shared by Sylvia Plath, who valued Virginia Woolf equally. While Plath hardly mentions Coleridge, Hughes, particularly in his later career, was fascinated. (Indeed, it may be suggested that his admiration for Plath bore strong resemblances to Wordsworth's for the equally mercurial Coleridge.) Hughes also believed that every poet had his own 'fountain', which he or she needed to discover in order to release what he had to give.[37]

Accordingly, he traced two selves in Coleridge: one was the Christian self who had been brought up as son to the Vicar of Ottery St Mary and was for ever afterwards trying to find his way back to fulfilment of his earliest religious identity; the other, the primitive self suppressed from earliest childhood when his mother ceased to give him proper attention. Hughes's Coleridge was always in flight from his deepest feelings; and, after his ill-fated marriage – contracted under pressure to a young woman from an orthodoxly religious family – only discovered his primitive self briefly, during walks with the wild young woman Dorothy Wordsworth on the Quantock hills in 1797 and 1798 – which was when he also wrote his three great visionary poems, 'Kubla Khan', 'The Ancient Mariner' and Part One of 'Christabel'. During this period, Hughes maintains, he was coming closer to acknowledgement of the other and truer side of his identity, figured as 'the snake in the oak'.

Hughes's eye being firmly fixed on the images of nature in the visionary poems, he draws attention, justly, to Coleridge's unusual amount of interest in wilder natural imagery during the Quantock period. He is sufficiently stimulated by them to create them into a poetic vision of his own, the starting-point being his division between Coleridge's Christian self and his 'unleavened' self of instinctive behaviour and paganism. That there was a division of some such kind within Coleridge's personality is undeniable: many pieces of evidence can be brought together to show how his Christian, preaching self was constantly undermined by the work of an imagination that attracted him into other paths of discourse – only to retreat unceremoniously when their fuller implications loomed. And Hughes's own imaginative powers give him an unusually privileged entrée to this sphere. They are most fruitfully at work when he can enter the dance of Coleridge's imagery and create his own pattern, but they also encourage him to concentrate on little-regarded aspects of the other poetry – such as the contributions to Southey's 'Joan of Arc' later used for the unfinished 'Destiny of Nations', which displayed his interest in myths, notably those of the northern nations – and on mythological images such as that of the birch. It may well be, as Hughes suggests, that Coleridge would have been a much better poet if he had given more rein to that side of himself. He is also constrained to make an admission, however: 'what I have to say here may be of use only to me. The only value of these remarks to some other reader may be – to prompt them to fill the vessel up themselves, from their own sources. Like the variety of potential readers the variety of potential interpretation is infinite.'[38] This is not strictly true, of course, at least to the discriminating, for whom the variety of valid potential interpretations is finite, constrained by various factors of language and the legitimacy of evidence. But Hughes is right to find the value of Coleridge's legacy in his power to rouse in others a dance of imagination similar to his own. It is, after all, the most valuable respect in which he lives on for his readers.

NOTES

Some of the material in this chapter appears also in John Beer, *Romantic Influences: Contemporary – Victorian – Modern* (London: Macmillan, 1995).

1 *The Prose Works of William Wordsworth*, ed. A. B. Grosart, 3 vols. (London: E. Moxon, 1876), III, 469.

2 A. P. Stanley, *Life and Correspondence of Thomas Arnold*, 2 vols. (London: B. Fellowes, 1844), II, 56.

3 Thomas de Quincey, 'Samuel Taylor Coleridge', *Tait's Edinburgh Magazine*, n.s. 1 (1834), 509.

4 Augustus J. C. Hare, *Memorials of a Quiet Life*, 2 vols. (London: Strahan and Co., 1873), II, 87.

5 John Sterling, *Essays and Tales*, 2 vols. (London: John W. Parker, 1848), I, xv.

6 See Henry Hallam, *Writings*, ed. T. H. Vail Motter (London: Oxford University Press, 1943), 42–3 and 160–71. The phrase derives partly from Milton's Sonnet x.

7 See John Beer, *Coleridge's Poetic Intelligence* (London: Macmillan, 1977), 284–5.

8 De Quincey had heard of this plan in 1803: see his *Diary of 1803*, ed. Horace A. Eaton (London: Noel Douglas, 1927), 191–2.

9 John Sterling, letter to J. W. Blakesley, 25 Nov. [1829], quoted in Peter Allen, *The Cambridge Apostles, The Early Years* (Cambridge University Press, 1978), 90–1.

10 For detailed discussion of his debts, see Beer, *Romantic Influences*, 167–8.

11 Letter of 5 Dec. 1884: Newman, *Letters and Diaries* (London: Thomas Nelson and Sons, 1973–7), XXX, 442–3.

12 *London and Westminster Review*, 33 (March 1840), 257–302; see also F. R. Leavis's edition, *Mill on Bentham and Coleridge* (London: Chatto and Windus, 1950).

13 *Mill on Bentham and Coleridge*, 99.

14 *Ibid.*, 100.

15 *Ibid.*, 40.

16 *Ibid.*, 103.

17 See also Beer, *Romantic Influences*, 152–3.

18 J. H. Stirling, 'De Quincey and Coleridge upon Kant', *Fortnightly Review*, 7 (1867), 377–97; C. M. Ingleby, 'On some Points concerned with the Philosophy of Coleridge', *Transactions of the Royal Society of Literature*, 2nd series, 9 (1870), 396–433.

19 Carlyle, *Life of John Sterling* (London: Chapman and Hall, 1851), Part I, ch. 8, 69–80.

20 See also Beer, *Romantic Influences*, 155, 163–4.

21 Matthew Arnold, 'Joubert', *Complete Prose Works*, ed. R. H. Super, 11 vols. (Ann Arbor: University of Michigan Press, 1960–77), III, 187.

22 Matthew Arnold, 'A Comment on Christmas' (1885), *Complete Prose Works*, ed. R. H. Super, 11 vols. (Ann Arbor: University of Michigan Press, 1960–77), X, 226–7.

23 G. G. Bradley, quoted by K. Chorley, *Arthur Hugh Clough, The Uncommitted Mind* (Oxford: Clarendon Press, 1962), 60.

24 A. H. Clough, Letter to J. N. Simpkinson, 18 Feb. 1841: *Correspondence*, ed. F. L. Mulhauser, 2 vols. (Oxford: Clarendon Press, 1957), I, 106.

25 *Westminster Review*, n.s. 1 (Jan. 1852), 249–50.

26 See also Beer, *Romantic Influences*, 158–60.

27 See also *ibid.*, 164–5.

28 *Westminster Review*, n.s. 29 (1866), 106–32.

29 John Forster, 'Charles Lamb', *New Monthly Magazine*, 1 (1835), 198.

30 1754 (trans. London: R. and J. Dodsley, 1761), 27.

31 Thomas McFarland, *Coleridge and the Pantheist Tradition* (Oxford: Clarendon Press, 1969).

32 V. Woolf, 'Modern Fiction', *The Common Reader* (London: L. and V. Woolf, 1925), 189.

33 D. H. Lawrence, *Phoenix*, ed. E. D. McDonald (London: William Heinemann, 1936), 552; cf. D. H. Lawrence, *Letters*, ed. G. J. Zytaruk and J. Boulton, 7 vols. (Cambridge University Press, 1979–93), II, 115.

34 D. H. Lawrence, 'The Reality of Peace' (1917), *Reflections on the Death of a Porcupine*, ed. Michael Herbert (Cambridge University Press, 1988), 35. See also John Beer, *Coleridge the Visionary* (London: Chatto and Windus, 1959), 196.

35 D. H. Lawrence, *Complete Poems*, ed. V. de Sola Pinto and Warren Roberts, 2 vols. (London: Heinemann, 1964), I, 351.

36 Lawrence, *Letters*, II, 223.

37 Ted Hughes, *Winter Pollen* (London: Faber and Faber, 1995), 374.

38 *Ibid.*, 394.

GUIDE TO FURTHER READING

Primary works by Coleridge are listed at the beginning of the book, in the table of abbreviations. Suggestions for further secondary reading are made below, chapter by chapter. For ease of reference, some books are mentioned under more than one heading.

Introduction

Adair, Patricia, *The Waking Dream: A Study of Coleridge's Poetry* (London: Edward Arnold, 1967).

Barfield, Owen, *What Coleridge Thought* (Middletown, CT: Wesleyan University Press, 1971).

Beer, John, ed., *Coleridge's Variety: Bicentenary Studies* (London and Basingstoke: Macmillan, 1974).

Brett, R. L., *S. T. Coleridge*, Writers and their Background Series (London: Bell, 1971).

Butler, Marilyn, *Romantics, Rebels and Reactionaries: English Literature and its Background, 1760–1830* (Oxford University Press, 1981).

Coburn, Kathleen, ed., *Coleridge: A Collection of Critical Essays* (Englewood Cliffs, NJ: Prentice-Hall, 1967).

Cookson, Katharine, *Coleridge* (London: Routledge, 1979).

Curran, Stuart, ed., *The Cambridge Companion to British Romanticism* (Cambridge University Press, 1993).

Davidson, Graham, *Coleridge's Career* (Basingstoke: Macmillan, 1990).

Empson, William, 'Introduction' to Samuel Taylor Coleridge, *Selected Poems*, ed. William Empson and David Pirie (Manchester: Fyfield, 1989), 13–100.

Everest, Kelvin, *Coleridge's Secret Ministry* (Harvester, 1979).

Grant, Allan, *A Preface to Coleridge* (London: Longman, 1972).

Gravil, Richard, and Molly Lefebure, eds., *The Coleridge Connection: Essays for Thomas McFarland* (Basingstoke: Macmillan, 1990).

Gravil, Richard, with Lucy Newlyn and Nicholas Roe, eds., *Coleridge's Imagination: Essays in Memory of Pete Laver* (Cambridge University Press, 1985).

Hamilton, Paul, 'Coleridge' in David P. Pirie, ed., *The Penguin History of Literature: The Romantic Period* (Harmondsworth, Middx: Penguin, 1994).

Hartman, Geoffrey, ed., *New Perspectives on Wordsworth and Coleridge* (New York: Columbia University Press, 1972).

Hayter, Alethea, *Opium and the Romantic Imagination* (London: Faber and Faber, 1968).

ed., *A Coleridge Companion* (London and Basingstoke: Macmillan, 1983).

Hill, John Spencer, ed., *Imagination in Coleridge* (London and Basingstoke: Macmillan, 1978).

House, Humphry, *Coleridge, The Clark Lectures 1951–2* (London: Rupert Hart-Davis, 1953).

Jackson, J. R. de J., ed., *Coleridge: The Critical Heritage*, 2 vols. (London: Routledge and Kegan Paul, 1970–1).

Lockridge, Laurence S., *Coleridge the Moralist* (Ithaca, NY: Cornell University Press, 1977).

Matlak, Richard, ed., *Approaches to Teaching Coleridge's Poetry and Prose* (New York: Modern Language Association, 1991).

McCalman, Iain, ed., *An Oxford Companion to the Romantic Age: British Culture 1776–1832* (Oxford University Press, 1999).

Paulin, Tom, *Minotaur: Poetry and the Nation State* (London: Faber, 1992).

Reiman, Donald H., ed., *The Romantics Reviewed: Contemporary Reviews of British Romantic Writers* (New York and London: 1972), Part A. i.

Richards, I. A., *Coleridge on Imagination* (London: Kegan Paul, 1934).

The Portable Coleridge (London and New York: Viking, 1971).

Stephen, Leslie, 'Coleridge' *Hours in a Library*, 3 (1888).

Sultana, Donald, ed., *New Approaches to Coleridge: Biographical and Critical Essays* (London: Vision Press, 1981).

Walsh, William, *Coleridge: The Work and the Relevance* (London: Chatto and Windus, 1967).

Wellek, René, 'Coleridge's Philosophy and Criticism' in *The English Romantic Poets: A Review of Research and Criticism* (New York: Modern Language Association, 1972), 209–58.

Willey, Basil, *Samuel Taylor Coleridge* (London: Chatto and Windus, 1972).

Woolf, Virginia, 'The Man at the Gate' and 'Sara Coleridge' in *The Death of the Moth and Other Essays* (London: Hogarth Press, 1942).

1 Coleridge's life

Allsop, Thomas, ed., *Letters, Conversation and Recollections of S. T. Coleridge*, 2 vols. (New York: Harper and Brothers, 1836).

Armour, Richard W., and Raymond F. Howes, eds., *Coleridge the Talker* (1940; rev. edn London: Johnson Reprints, 1969).

Ashton, Rosemary, *The Life of Samuel Taylor Coleridge: A Critical Biography* (Oxford: Basil Blackwell, 1997).

Bate, Walter Jackson, *Coleridge* (Toronto: Macmillan, 1968).

Campbell, James Dyke, *Coleridge: A Narrative of the Events of his Life* (London: Macmillan, 1894).

Chambers, E. K., *Samuel Taylor Coleridge: A Biographical Study* (Oxford: Clarendon Press, 1938).

Cornwell, John, *Coleridge: Poet and Revolutionary, 1772–1804* (London: Allen Lane, 1973).

Doughty, Oswald, *Perturbed Spirit: The Life and Personality of Samuel Taylor Coleridge* (Toronto, Ontario: Associated University Presses, 1981).

Gillman, James, *The Life of Samuel Taylor Coleridge* (1838).

Holmes, Richard, *Coleridge: Early Visions* (London: Hodder and Stoughton, 1989). *Coleridge: Darker Reflections* (London: Harper Collins, 1998).

Jackson, J. R. de J., ed., *Coleridge: The Critical Heritage* (London: Routledge and Kegan Paul, 1970).
Coleridge: The Critical Heritage, Volume 2: 1834–1900 (London: Routledge and Kegan Paul, 1971).

Lefebure, Molly, *The Bondage of Love: A Life of Mrs Samuel Taylor Coleridge* (London: Gollancz, 1986).
Samuel Taylor Coleridge: A Bondage of Opium (London: Gollancz, 1974).

Paley, Morton D., *Portraits of Coleridge* (Oxford: Clarendon Press, 1999).

Perry, Seamus, ed., *S. T. Coleridge Interviews and Recollections* (Houndmills, Basingstoke: Palgrave, 2000).

Pite, Ralph, ed., *Coleridge*, Lives of the Great Romantics (London: Pickering and Chatto, 1997).

Sultana, Donald, *Samuel Taylor Coleridge in Malta and Italy* (Oxford: Basil Blackwell, 1969).

2 The 'Conversation' poems

Abrams, M. H., *The Mirror and the Lamp: Romantic Theory and the Critical Tradition* (New York: Oxford University Press, 1953).
'Structure and Style in the Greater Romantic Lyric' in Frederick W. Hilles and Harold Bloom, eds., *From Sensibility to Romanticism* (Oxford University Press, 1965).

Beer, John, *Coleridge's Poetic Intelligence* (London: Macmillan, 1977).
ed., *Coleridge's Variety: Bicentenary Studies* (London and Basingstoke: Macmillan, 1974).

Boulger, J. D., 'Imagination and Speculation in Coleridge's Conversation Poems' *Journal of English and German Philology*, 64 (October 1965), 691–711.

Dekker, George, *Coleridge and the Literature of Sensibility* (London: Vision Press, 1978).

Everest, Kelvin, *Coleridge's Secret Ministry: The Context of the Conversation Poems, 1795–1798* (Hassocks, Sussex: Harvester, 1979).

Fruman, Norman, *The Damaged Archangel* (New York and London: Allen and Unwin, 1971).

Fulford, Tim, *Coleridge's Figurative Language* (London and Basingstoke: Macmillan, 1991).

Gerard, Albert, 'The Systolic Rhythm: The Structure of Coleridge's Conversation Poems' in K. Coburn, ed., *Coleridge: A Collection of Critical Essays* (Englewood Cliffs, NJ: Prentice-Hall, 1967), 78–88.

Gravil, Richard, with Lucy Newlyn and Nicholas Roe, eds., *Coleridge's Imagination: Essays in Memory of Pete Laver* (Cambridge University Press, 1985).

Heath, William, *Wordsworth and Coleridge: A Study of their Literary Relations in 1801–1802* (Oxford University Press, 1970).

Magnuson, Paul, *Coleridge and Wordsworth: A Lyrical Dialogue* (Princeton University Press, 1987).

Matlak, Richard, *The Poetry of Relationship: The Wordsworths and Coleridge, 1797–1800* (Basingstoke: Macmillan, 1997).

McFarland, Thomas, *Originality and Imagination* (Baltimore and London: Johns Hopkins University Press, 1985).
  Romanticism and the Forms of Ruin: Wordsworth, Coleridge, and Modalities of Fragmentation (Princeton University Press, 1981).

Newlyn, Lucy, *Coleridge, Wordsworth and the Language of Allusion* (Oxford: Clarendon Press, 1986; repr. 2000).
  Reading, Writing, and Romanticism: The Anxiety of Reception (Oxford University Press, 2000).

Parker, Reeve, *Coleridge's Meditative Art* (Ithaca, NY: Cornell University Press, 1975).

Perry, Seamus, *Coleridge and the Uses of Division* (Oxford: Oxford University Press, 1999).

Prickett, Stephen, *Coleridge and Wordsworth: The Poetry of Growth* (Cambridge University Press, 1970).

Roe, Nicholas, *Wordsworth and Coleridge: The Radical Years* (Oxford: Clarendon Press, 1988).

Ruoff, Gene, *Wordsworth and Coleridge: The Making of the Major Lyrics, 1802–1804* (New Brunswick, NJ: Harvester Wheatsheaf, 1989).

3 Slavery and superstition in the poems

Beer, John, *Coleridge the Visionary* (London: Chatto and Windus, 1959).
  'The Languages of *Kubla Khan*' in Richard Gravil with Lucy Newlyn and Nicholas Roe, eds., *Coleridge's Imagination: Essays in Memory of Pete Laver* (Cambridge University Press, 1985), 218–63.

Bostetter, E. E., 'The Nightmare World of "The Ancient Mariner"' *Studies in Romanticism*, 1 (1961–2), 241–54.

Coburn, Kathleen, 'Coleridge and Wordsworth and "the Supernatural"' *University of Toronto Quarterly*, 25 (1956).

Drew, John, '"Kubla Khan" and Orientalism' in Tim Fulford and Morton D. Paley, eds., *Coleridge's Visionary Languages: Essays in Memory of J. B. Beer* (Cambridge University Press, 1993), 41–9.

Eilenberg, Susan, *Strange Power of Speech: Wordsworth, Coleridge, and Literary Possession* (Oxford: Clarendon Press, 1992).

Harding, Anthony John, 'Mythopoesis: The Unity of *Christabel*' in Richard Gravil, with Lucy Newlyn and Nicholas Roe, eds., *Coleridge's Imagination: Essays in Memory of Pete Laver* (Cambridge University Press, 1985), 207–17.
  The Reception of Myth in English Romanticism (Columbia and London: University of Missouri Press, 1995), Chs. 1 and 5.

Kaczvinsky, Donald P., 'Coleridge's Polar Spirit: A Source' *English Language Notes*, 24 (1987), 25–8.

Kitson, Peter, 'Coleridge, the French Revolution and *The Ancient Mariner*: A Reassessment' *Coleridge Bulletin*, n.s. 7 (Spring 1996), 30–48.

Lee, Debbie, 'Poetic Voodoo in Keats's *Lamia*' *Times Literary Supplement*, 27 October 1995, 13–14.

Levinson, Marjorie, *The Romantic Fragment Poem* (Chapel Hill, NC, and London: University of North Carolina Press, 1986).

Lowes, John Livingston, *The Road to Xanadu* (London: Picador, 1978).

Magnuson, Paul, *Coleridge's Nightmare Poetry* (Charlottesville: University Press of Virginia, 1974).

McGann, Jerome J., 'The Meaning of "The Ancient Mariner"' *Critical Inquiry*, 8 (1981), 35–66.

Miall, David S., 'Guilt and Death: The Predicament of the Ancient Mariner' *Studies in English Literature 1500–1900*, 24 (1984), 633–53.

Nelson, Jane A., 'Entelechy and Structure in "Christabel"' *Studies in Romanticism*, 19 (1980), 375–93.

Newlyn, Lucy, *Paradise Lost and the Romantic Reader* (Oxford: Clarendon Press, 1993), Chs. 4 and 5.

Peterfreund, Stuart, 'The Way of Immanence, Coleridge, and the Problem of Evil' *English Literary History*, 55 (1988), 125–8.

Piper, H. W., 'The Disunity of *Christabel* and the Fall of Nature' *Essays in Criticism*, 28 (1978), 216–17.

Rajan, Tilottama, *Dark Interpreter: The Discourse of Romanticism* (Ithaca, NY: Cornell University Press, 1980).

Richardson, Alan, 'Romantic Voodoo: Obeah and British Culture, 1797–1807' *Studies in Romanticism*, 32 (1993), 3–28.

Rubenstein, Chris, 'A New Identity for the Mariner' *Coleridge Bulletin*, n.s. 3 (Winter 1990), 16–29.

Schneider, Elisabeth, *Coleridge, Opium, and 'Kubla Khan'* (University of Chicago Press, 1953).

Schwartz, Robert, 'Speaking the Unspeakable: The Meaning of Form in *Christabel*' *University of South Florida Language Quarterly*, 19, 1–2 (1980), 31–4.

Shaffer, Elinor, *'Kubla Khan' and the Fall of Jerusalem: The Mythological School of Biblical Criticism and Secular Literature, 1770–1880* (Cambridge University Press, 1975).

Ware, Malcolm, 'Coleridge's "Spectre Bark": A Slave Ship?' *Philological Quarterly*, 40 (1961), 589–93.

Watkins, Daniel P., 'History as Demon in Coleridge's "The Rime of the Ancient Mariner"' *Papers on Language and Literature*, 24 (1988), 23–33.

Wheeler, Kathleen M., *The Creative Mind in Coleridge's Poetry* (Cambridge, MA, and London: Heinemann, 1981).

Yarlott, Geoffrey, *Coleridge and the Abyssinian Maid* (London: Methuen, 1967).

4 *Biographia Literaria*

Abrams, M. H., 'Coleridge and the Romantic Vision of the World' in John Beer, ed., *Coleridge's Variety* (London: Macmillan, 1974), 103–15.

Bialostosky, Don H., 'Truth and Pleasure in Wordsworth's Preface and Coleridge's *Biographia Literaria*' in Richard E. Matlak, ed., *Approaches to Teaching Coleridge's Poetry and Prose* (New York: Modern Language Association, 1991), 57–62.

Buell, Lawrence, 'The Question of Form in Coleridge's *Biographia Literaria*' *English Literary History*, 46 (1979), 399–417.

Burwick, Frederick, ed., *Coleridge's* Biographia Literaria: *Text and Meaning* (Columbus: Ohio State University Press, 1989).

Bygrave, Stephen, 'Land of the Giants: Gaps, Limits and Audiences in Coleridge's *Biographia Literaria*' in Stephen Copley and John Whale, eds., *Beyond Romanticism: New Approaches to Texts and Contexts* (London: Routledge, 1992), 32–52.

Chandler, David, 'Coleridge: An Early Claim that the "Law of Association" came from Aristotle' *Notes and Queries*, n.s. 41, 3 (September 1994), 338–9.

Christensen, Jerome C., 'The Genius in the *Biographia Literaria*' *Studies in Romanticism*, 17, 2 (Spring 1978), 215–31.

Coleridge, Sara, and H. N. Coleridge, eds., *Biographia Literaria*, 2 vols. (London: 1847).

Cooke, M. G., '*Quisque Sui Faber*: Coleridge in the *Biographia Literaria*' *Philological Quarterly*, 50, 2 (April 1971), 208–29.

Corrigan, Timothy J., '*Biographia Literaria* and the Language of Science' *Journal of the History of Ideas*, 41, 3 (July–September 1980), 399–419.

Engell, James, and W. J. Bate, 'Introduction' to *Biographia Literaria*, 2 vols. (Princeton, NJ, and London: Princeton University Press and Routledge and Kegan Paul, 1983), I, xli–cxxxvi.

Fischer, Michael, 'Coleridge on Wordsworth: The Authority of Ordinary Language' *Soundings*, 74, 4 (Winter 1992), 555–69.

Fogel, Daniel Mark, 'A Compositional History of the *Biographia Literaria*', *Studies in Bibliography*, 30, ed. Fredson Bowers (Charlottesville: University Press of Virginia, 1977), 219–34.

Grow, Lynn M., 'The Consistency of the *Biographia Literaria*' *Wichita State University Bulletin*, 49, 2 (May 1973), 3–14.

Jackson, H. J., 'Coleridge's *Biographia*: When is an Autobiography Not an Autobiography?' *Biography*, 20, 1 (Winter 1997), 54–71.

Kearns, Sheila M., *Coleridge, Wordsworth, and Romantic Autobiography: Reading Strategies of Self-Representation* (Teaneck, NJ: Fairleigh Dickinson University Press, 1995).

Mallette, Richard, 'Narrative Technique in the "Biographia Literaria"' *Modern Language Review*, 70, 1 (January 1975), 32–41.

Marks, Emerson, *Coleridge and the Language of Verse* (Princeton University Press, 1981).

McFarland, Thomas, 'So Immethodical a Miscellany: Coleridge's Literary Life' *Modern Philology*, 83, 4 (May 1986), 405–13.

Moffat, Douglas, 'Coleridge's Ten Theses: The Plotinian Alternative' *Wordsworth Circle*, 13, 1 (Winter 1982), 27–31.

Perry, Seamus, 'The Rhetoric of Reconciliation: Wordsworth in *Biographia*' in *Coleridge and the Uses of Division* (Oxford University Press, 1999), 246–74.

Prickett, Stephen, '*Biographia Literaria*: Chapter Thirteen' in Deidre Coleman and Peter Otto, eds., *Imagining Romanticism: Essays on English and Australian Romanticisms* (West Cornwall, CT: Locust Hill Press, 1992), 3–23.

Princeton Encyclopedia of Poetry and Poetics (2nd edn), 'Fancy' and 'Imagination'.

Reiman, Donald H., 'Coleridge and the Art of Equivocation' *Studies in Romanticism*, 25, 3 (Fall 1986), 325–50.

Ruf, Frederick J., 'Coleridge's *Biographia Literaria*: Extravagantly Mixed Genres and the Construction of a "Harmonized Chaos"' *Soundings*, 74, 4 (Winter 1992), 537–53.

Shaffer, Elinor, 'The "Postulates in Philosophy" in the *Biographia Literaria*' *Comparative Literature Studies*, 7, 3 (1970), 297–313.

Shawcross, John, 'Introduction' to *Biographia Literaria*, 2 vols. (Oxford University Press, 1907), I, xi–lxxxix.

Walker, Eric, '*Biographia Literaria* and Wordsworth's Revisions' *Studies in English Literature*, 28, 4 (Autumn 1988), 569–88.

Wallace, Catherine Miles, *The Design of* Biographia Literaria (London: Allen and Unwin, 1983).

Whalley, George, 'The Integrity of the *Biographia Literaria*' *Essays and Studies*, n.s. 6 (1953), 85–101.

Wheeler, Kathleen M., *Sources, Processes and Methods in Coleridge's* Biographia Literaria (Cambridge University Press, 1980).

Wilson, Paul Scott, 'Coherence in *Biographia Literaria*: God, Self and Coleridge's "Seminal Principle"' *Philological Quarterly*, 72, 4 (Fall 1993), 451–69.

5 The Notebooks

Bygrave, Stephen, *Coleridge and the Self: Romantic Egotism* (Basingstoke and London: Macmillan, 1986).

Christensen, Jerome, *Coleridge's Blessed Machine of Language* (Ithaca, NY, and London: Cornell University Press, 1981).

Clark, Timothy, *The Theory of Inspiration: Composition as a Crisis of Subjectivity in Romantic and Post-Romantic Writing* (Manchester and New York: Manchester University Press, 1997).

Coburn, Kathleen, *Experience into Thought: Perspectives in the Coleridge Notebooks* (Toronto University Press, 1979).

The Self-Conscious Imagination: A Study of the Coleridge Notebooks in Celebration of his Birth 21 October 1772 (London: Oxford University Press, 1974).

Ford, Jennifer, *Coleridge on Dreaming: Romanticism, Dreams and the Medical Imagination* (Cambridge University Press, 1998).

Haven, Richard, *Patterns of Consciousness: An Essay on Coleridge* (Amherst: University of Massachusetts Press, 1969).

Mileur, Jean-Pierre, *Vision and Revision: Coleridge's Art of Immanence* (Berkeley, Los Angeles and London: University of California Press, 1982).

Modiano, Raimonda, *Coleridge and the Concept of Nature* (London and Basingstoke: Macmillan, 1985).

Rajan, Ballachandra, *The Form of the Unfinished* (Princeton University Press, 1985).

Rzepka, Charles, *The Self as Mind: Vision and Identity in Wordsworth, Coleridge, and Keats* (Cambridge, MA, and London: Harvard University Press, 1986).

6 The later poetry

Berkoben, Lawrence David, *Coleridge's Decline as a Poet* (The Hague: Mouton, 1975).

Brown, Lee Rust, 'Coleridge and the Prospect of the Whole', *Studies in Romanticism*, 30, 2 (1991), 235–53.

Burwick, Frederick, 'Coleridge's "Limbo" and "Ne Plus Ultra": The Multeity of Intertextuality', *Romanticism Past and Present*, 9 (1985), 73–95.

Coburn, Kathleen, 'Reflections in a Coleridge Mirror: Some Images in His Poems' in Frederick W. Hilles and Harold Bloom, eds., *From Sensibility to Romanticism* (Oxford University Press, 1965), 415–37.

Dorencamp, Angela G., 'Hope at Highgate: The Late Poetry of Coleridge', *Barat Review*, 6 (1971), 59–66.

Fulford, Tim, 'Paradise Rewritten? Coleridge's "The Blossoming of the Solitary Date-Tree"', *Wordsworth Circle*, 24 (1993), 83–5.

  Romanticism and Masculinity: Gender, Politics and Poetics in the Writings of Burke, Coleridge, Cobbett, Wordsworth, De Quincey and Hazlitt (London: Macmillan, 1999), ch. 5.

Greenberg, Martin, *The Hamlet Vocation of Coleridge and Wordsworth* (University of Iowa Press, 1986).

Mays, J. C. C., 'Coleridge's New Poetry', *Proceedings of the British Academy*, 95 (1997), 127–56.

McGann, Jerome J., *The Romantic Ideology: A Critical Investigation* (University of Chicago Press, 1983).

  The Poetics of Sensibility: A Revolution in Style (Oxford: Clarendon Press, 1996).

Paley, Morton D., *Coleridge's Later Poetry* (Oxford: Clarendon Press, 1996).

Schulz, Max, *The Poetic Voices of Coleridge* (Detroit: Wayne State University Press, 1963).

Stillinger, Jack, *Coleridge and Textual Stability: The Multiple Versions of the Major Poems* (New York: Oxford University Press, 1994).

Suther, Marshall, *Visions of Xanadu* (New York: Columbia University Press, 1965).

Watson, Jeanie, *Risking Enchantment: Coleridge's Symbolic World of Faery* (Lincoln: Nebraska University Press, 1990).

Watson, Lucy E. (née Gillman), *Coleridge at Highgate* (London: Longman, 1925).

Whalley, George, "'Autumn's Amaranth": Coleridge's Late Poems', *Transactions of the Royal Society of Canada*, 4th series, 2 (1964), 159–79.

  Coleridge and Sara Hutchinson and the Asra Poems (London: Routledge and Kegan Paul, 1955).

  'Coleridge's Poetic Canon: Selection and Arrangement', *A Review of English Literature*, 7 (1966), 9–23.

  'The Harvest on the Ground', *University of Toronto Quarterly*, 38 (1969), 248–76.

7 The talker

Bateson, F. W., *A Guide to English Literature*, 2nd edn (London: Longman, 1967; rev. repr., 1970).

Beer, John, 'Coleridge and Wordsworth: Influence and Confluence' in Donald Sultana, ed., *New Approaches to Coleridge: Biographical and Critical Essays* (London: Vision, 1981), 192–211.

Berlin, Isaiah, 'The Apotheosis of the Romantic Will' in his *The Crooked Timber of Humanity: Chapters in the History of Ideas*, ed. Henry Hardy (London: Murray, 1990), 207–37.

Burke, Peter, *The Art of Conversation* (Cambridge: Polity Press, 1993).

Bygrave, Stephen, *Coleridge and the Self: Romantic Egotism* (Basingstoke and London: Macmillan, 1986).

Coates, Jennifer, 'The Construction of a Collaborative Floor in Women's Friendly Talk' in T. Givón, ed., *Conversation: Cognitive, Communicative and Social Perspectives* (Amsterdam/Philadelphia: Benjamins, 1997), 55–89.

Coburn, Kathleen, ed., *Inquiring Spirit: A New Presentation of Coleridge from his Published and Unpublished Prose Writings* (London: Routledge and Kegan Paul, 1951).

Goodson, A. C., ed., *Coleridge's Writings. Vol. III: On Language* (Basingstoke: Macmillan, 1998).

Hill, Geoffrey, *The Lords of Limit: Essays on Literature and Ideas* (London: Deutsch, 1984).

Lovejoy, A. O., 'Optimism and Romanticism', *Publication of the Modern Language Association of America*, 42 (1927), 921–45.

Lucas, E. V., *The Life of Charles Lamb*, 2 vols. (London: Methuen, 1905).

McFarland, Thomas, *Romanticism and the Forms of Ruin: Wordsworth, Coleridge, and Modalities of Fragmentation* (Princeton University Press, 1981).

Paley, Morton D., *Portraits of Coleridge* (Oxford University Press, 1999).

Perry, Seamus, *Coleridge and the Uses of Division* (Oxford University Press, 1999).

Rorty, Richard, *Philosophy and the Mirror of Nature* (Oxford: Basil Blackwell, 1980).

Wheeler, Kathleen M., *Romanticism, Pragmatism and Deconstruction* (Oxford: Basil Blackwell, 1993).

8 The journalist

Aspinall, A., *Politics and the Press, c. 1780–1850* (London: Home and Van Thal, 1949).

Bishop, James, and Oliver Woods, *The Story of* The Times (London: Michael Joseph, 1983).

Bourne, H. R. Fox, *English Newspapers: Chapters in the History of Journalism*, 2 vols. (London: Chatto and Windus, 1887).

Christie, William, 'Going Public: Print Lords Byron and Brougham', *Studies in Romanticism*, 38, 3 (Fall 1999), 443–75.

Coleman, Deirdre, *Coleridge and the* Friend *(1809–1810)* (Oxford: Clarendon Press, 1988).

'Conspicuous Consumption: White Abolitionism and English Women's Protest Writing in the 1790s', *English Literary History*, 61 (Summer 1994), 341–62.

Gilmartin, Kevin, 'Radical Print Culture in Periodical Form' in T. Rajan and J. Wright, eds., *Romanticism, History, and the Possibilities of Genre: Re-forming Literature, 1789–1837* (Cambridge University Press, 1998).

Hindle, Wilfrid, *The Morning Post, 1772–1937* (London: Routledge, 1937).

Kitson, Peter, 'The Whore of Babylon and the Woman in White: Coleridge's Radical Unitarian Language' in T. Fulford and M. D. Paley, eds., *Coleridge's Visionary Languages: Essays in Honour of John Beer* (Cambridge: D. S. Brewer, 1993).

Klancher, Jon, *The Making of English Reading Audiences, 1790–1832* (Madison and London: The University of Wisconsin Press, 1987).

Koss, Stephen E., *The Rise and Fall of the Political Press in Britain*, 2 vols. (Chapel Hill: University of North Carolina Press, 1981–4).

Liu, Alan, *Wordsworth: The Sense of History* (California: Stanford University Press, 1989).

McCalman, Iain, ed., *An Oxford Companion to the Romantic Age: British Culture 1776–1832* (Oxford University Press, 1999).

McKusick, James C., ' "Wisely forgetful": Coleridge and the Politics of Pantisocracy', *Romanticism and Colonialism: Writing and Empire, 1780–1830* (Cambridge University Press, 1988).

Thomas, Donald, 'Press Prosecutions of the Eighteenth and Nineteenth Centuries', *Library* 5th series, 32, 4 (December 1977), 315–32.

Thompson, E. P., 'A Compendium of Cliché: The Poet as Essayist', in *The Romantics: England in a Revolutionary Age* (New York: The New Press, 1997).

Wells, Roger, *Wretched Faces: Famine in Wartime England, 1763–1803* (Gloucester: Alan Sutton Publishing, 1988).

Werkmeister, Lucy, *The London Daily Press, 1772–1792* (Lincoln: University of Nebraska Press, 1963).

9 The critic

Appleyard, J. A., *Coleridge's Philosophy of Literature: The Development of a Concept of Poetry 1791–1819* (Cambridge, MA: Harvard University Press, 1965).

Badawi, M. M., *Coleridge: Critic of Shakespeare* (Cambridge University Press, 1973).

Baker, J. V., *The Sacred River: Coleridge's Theory of Imagination* (Baton Rouge, LA: Louisiana State University Press, 1957).

Beer, John, 'Coleridge as Critic' in Peter J. Kitson and Thomas N. Corns, eds., *Coleridge and the Armoury of the Human Mind: Essays on His Prose Writings* (London: Frank Cass, 1991), 4–17.

Burwick, Frederick, 'Coleridge and Schelling on Mimesis' in Richard Gravil and Molly Lefebure, eds., *The Coleridge Connection: Essays for Thomas McFarland* (Basingstoke and London: Macmillan, 1990), 178–99.

Christensen, Jerome, 'The Genius in *Biographia Literaria*', *Studies in Romanticism*, 17 (1978), 215–31.

' "The Symbol's Errant Allegory": Coleridge and his Critics', *English Literary History*, 45 (1978), 640–59.

Corrigan, Timothy J., *Coleridge, Language, and Criticism* (Athens: University of Georgia Press, 1982).

Eagleton, Terry, *The Function of Criticism: From 'The Spectator' to Post-Structuralism* (London: Verso, 1984).

The Ideology of the Aesthetic (Oxford: Basil Blackwell, 1990).

Engell, James, *The Creative Imagination: Enlightenment to Romanticism* (Cambridge, MA: Harvard University Press, 1981).

Framing the Critical Mind: Dryden to Coleridge (Cambridge, MA: Harvard University Press, 1989).

Fogle, Richard Harter, *The Idea of Coleridge's Criticism* (Berkeley: University of California Press, 1962).

Goodson, A. C., *Verbal Imagination: Coleridge and the Language of Modern Criticism* (Oxford University Press, 1988).

Hamilton, Paul, *Coleridge's Poetics* (Oxford: Basil Blackwell, 1983).

Hayden, John O., *The Romantic Reviewers, 1802–1824* (London: Routledge and Kegan Paul, 1969).

Jackson, J. R. de J., 'Coleridge on Dramatic Illusion and Spectacle in the Performance of Shakespeare's Plays', *Modern Philology*, 62 (1964–5), 13–21.

Method and Imagination in Coleridge's Criticism (London: Routledge and Kegan Paul, 1969).

Marks, Emerson R., 'Means and Ends in Coleridge's Critical Method', *English Literary History*, 26 (1959), 387–401.

Morgan, Peter F., *Literary Critics and Reviewers in Early 19th-Century Britain* (London and Canberra: Croom Helm, 1983).

Murray, Penelope, *Genius: The History of an Idea* (Oxford: Basil Blackwell, 1989).

Shaffer, Elinor, 'Coleridge's Theory of Aesthetic Interest', *Journal of Aesthetics and Arts Criticism*, 27 (1968–9), 399–408.

Simpson, David, ed., *The Origins of Modern Critical Thought: German Aesthetic and Literary Criticism from Lessing to Hegel* (Cambridge University Press, 1988).

Vickers, Brian, 'The Emergence of Character Criticism, 1774–1800', *Shakespeare Survey*, 34, 11–21.

Wellek, René, *A History of Modern Criticism: 1750–1950: The Romantic Age* (1955; repr. 1970).

'Coleridge's Philosophy and Criticism' in *The English Romantic Poets: A Review of Research and Criticism* (3rd edn New York: Modern Language Association of America, 1972), 209–58.

10 Political thinker

Barrell, John, *Poetry, Language and Politics* (Manchester University Press, 1988).

Colmer, John, *Coleridge, Critic of Society* (Oxford: Clarendon Press, 1959).

Cornwell, John, *Coleridge: Poet and Revolutionary, 1772–1804* (London: Allen Lane, 1973).

Fulford, Tim, '"Living Words": Coleridge, Christianity and National Renewal', *Prose Studies*, 15, 2 (August 1992), 187–207.

Fulford, Tim, with Morton D. Paley, eds., *Coleridge's Visionary Languages* (Cambridge: Boydell and Brewer, 1993).

Kitson, Peter J., 'Coleridge, Milton and the Millennium', *Wordsworth Circle*, 18, 2 (1987).

'"The Electric fluid of truth"' in Kitson and Corns, eds., *Coleridge and the Armoury of the Human Mind*, 36–62.

'"Sages and patriots that being dead do yet speak to us": Readings of the English Revolution in the Late Eighteenth Century', in James Holstun, ed., *Pamphlet Wars: Prose in the English Revolution* (London: Frank Cass, 1992), 205–30.

'"Our Prophetic Harrington"', *Wordsworth Circle*, 24 (1993), 97–102.

'Coleridge, the French Revolution and *The Ancient Mariner*: A Reassessment', *Coleridge Bulletin*, n.s. 7 (Spring 1997), 30–48.

Kitson, Peter J., with Thomas N. Corns, eds., *Coleridge and the Armoury of the Human Mind: Essays on his Prose Writings* (London: Frank Cass, 1991).

Leask, Nigel, *The Politics of Imagination in Coleridge's Critical Thought* (Basingstoke: Macmillan, 1988).

Morrow, John, *Coleridge's Political Thought: Property, Morality and the Limits of Traditional Discourse* (Basingstoke: Macmillan, 1990).

Piper, H. W., *The Active Universe. Pantheism and the Concept of the Imagination in the English Romantic Poets* (London: Athlone Press, 1962).

Pollin, B. R. 'John Thelwall's Marginalia in a Copy of Coleridge's *Biographia Literaria*', *Bulletin of the New York Public Library*, 74 (1970), 73–94.

Roe, Nicholas, *Wordsworth and Coleridge: The Radical Years* (Oxford: Clarendon Press, 1988).

'Coleridge and John Thelwall: The Road to Nether Stowey', in Richard Gravil and Molly Lefebure, eds., *The Coleridge Connection: Essays for Thomas McFarland* (Basingstoke: Macmillan, 1990), 60–82.

Smith, Olivia, *The Politics of Language, 1791–1819* (Oxford University Press, 1984).

Storch, R. F., 'The Politics of Imagination', *Studies in Romanticism*, 21 (1982), 448–56.

Thompson, E. P., 'Disenchantment or Default: A Lay Sermon' in C. C. O'Brien and D. Vanech, eds., *Power and Consciousness* (London and New York: University of London Press, 1969), 149–81.

Woodring, Carl, *Politics in the Poetry of Coleridge* (Madison: University of Wisconsin Press, 1961).

Wylie, Ian, *Young Coleridge and the Philosophers of Nature* (Oxford: Clarendon Press, 1989).

11 The philosopher

Bowie, Andrew, *Aesthetics and Subjectivity: From Kant to Nietzsche* (Manchester University Press, 1990).

Schelling and Modern European Philosophy – An Introduction (London: Routledge, 1993).

Burwick, Fred, 'Coleridge and Schelling on Mimesis', in Richard Gravil and Molly Lefebure, eds., *The Coleridge Connection: Essays for Thomas McFarland* (Basingstoke and London: Macmillan, 1990), 178–199.

Christensen, Jerome, *Coleridge's Blessed Machine of Language* (Ithaca, NY, and London: Cornell University Press, 1981).

Coulson, J., *Newman and the Common Tradition* (Oxford: Clarendon Press, 1970).

Deleuze, Gilles, *Difference and Repetition*, trans. Paul Patton (London: Athlone Press, 1997).

Dews, Peter, 'Deconstruction and German Idealism', in *The Limits of Disenchantment* (London: Verso, 1995), 115–48.

Emmet, Dorothy, 'Coleridge as Philosopher' in R. L. Brett, ed., *S. T. Coleridge*, Writers and their Background Series (London: Bell, 1971), 195–220.

Foucault, M., *Language, Counter-Memory, Practice: Selected Essays and Interviews*, ed., with intro., D. Bouchard (Oxford: Basil Blackwell, 1977).

McFarland, Thomas, *Coleridge and the Pantheist Tradition* (Oxford: Clarendon Press, 1969).

Mill, John Stuart, *Essays on Bentham and Coleridge*, ed. F. R. Leavis (London: Chatto and Windus, 1950).

Muirhead, J. H., *Coleridge as Philosopher* (London: George Allen and Unwin, 1930).

Orsini, G. N. G., *Coleridge and German Idealism* (Carbondale: Southern Illinois University Press, 1969).

Pater, Walter, *Appreciations, With an Essay on Style* (London: Macmillan, 1910).

Perkins, Mary Anne, *Coleridge's Philosophy: The Logos as Unifying Principle* (Oxford: Clarendon Press, 1994).

Perry, Seamus, *Coleridge and the Uses of Division* (Oxford University Press, 1999).

Pym, David, *The Religious Thought of Samuel Taylor Coleridge* (New York: Barnes and Noble, 1978).

Richards, I. A., *Coleridge on Imagination* (London: Kegan Paul, 1934).

Ryle, Gilbert, *The Concept of Mind* (London: Hutchinson, 1949).

Schmitt, Carl, *Political Romanticism*, trans. Gary Oakes (Cambridge, MA: MIT Press, 1986).

Shaffer, Elinor, 'Coleridge and Natural Philosophy: A Review of Recent Literary and Historical Research', *History of Science*, 12 (1974), 284–98.

'Coleridge and Schleiermacher' in Richard Gravil and Molly Lefebure, eds., *The Coleridge Connection: Essays for Thomas McFarland* (London: Macmillan, 1990), 200–9.

'Kubla Khan' and The Fall of Jerusalem (Cambridge University Press, 1975).

'The "Postulates in Philosophy" in the *Biographia Literaria*', *Comparative Literary Studies*, 7, 3 (1970), 297–313.

Vallins, David, 'Production and Existence: Coleridge's Unification of Nature', *Journal of the History of Ideas*, 56 (1995), 107–24.

Wellek, Rene, *Immanuel Kant in England 1793–1838* (Princeton University Press, 1931).

Wheeler, Kathleen, *Sources, Processes and Methods in Coleridge's* Biographia Literaria (Cambridge University Press, 1980).

Zizek, Slavoj, *The Indivisible Remainder: An Essay on Schelling and Related Matters* (London: Verso, 1996).

12 Religious Thinker

Abrams, M. H., *Natural Supernaturalism: Tradition and Revolution in Romantic Literature* (New York: Norton, 1971).

Barth, J. Robert, SJ, *Coleridge and Christian Doctrine* (New York: Fordham University Press, revised reprint, 1987).

J. D. Boulger, *Coleridge as Religious Thinker* (New Haven: Yale University Press, 1961).

Cantor, Paul, *Creature and Creator: Myth-making and English Romanticism* (Cambridge University Press, 1984).

Harding, A. J., *Coleridge and the Inspired Word* (Kingston and Montreal: McGill-Queen's University Press, 1985).

D. Jasper, ed., *The Interpretation of Belief: Coleridge, Schleiermacher and Romanticism* (London: Macmillan, 1986).

Levere, Trevor H., *Poetry Realized in Nature: Samuel Taylor Coleridge and Early Nineteenth-Century Science* (Cambridge University Press, 1981).

McFarland, Thomas, *Coleridge and the Pantheist Tradition* (Oxford: Clarendon Press, 1969).

Perkins, Mary Anne, *Coleridge's Philosophy. The Logos as Unifying Principle* (Oxford: Clarendon Press, 1994).

Prickett, Stephen, *Romanticism and Religion: The Tradition of Coleridge and Wordsworth in the Victorian Church* (Cambridge University Press, 1976).

Reardon, Bernard M. G., *From Coleridge to Gore: A Century of Religious Thought in Britain* (London: Longman, 1971).

Religion in the Age of Romanticism (Cambridge University Press, 1985).

Ruoff, Gene W., 'Romantic Literature and the Problem of Belief' in Karl Kroeber and Gene W. Ruoff, eds., *Romantic Poetry: Recent Revisionary Criticism* (New Brunswick, NJ: Rutgers University Press, 1993), 240–50.

Wendling, Ronald C., *Coleridge's Progress to Christianity: Experience and Authority in Religious Faith* (Lewisberg, PA: Buckland University Press, 1995).

Wylie, Ian, *Young Coleridge and the Philosophers of Nature* (Oxford: Clarendon Press, 1989).

13 Gender

Barth, J. Robert, SJ, *Coleridge and the Power of Love* (Columbia: University of Missouri Press, 1988).

Carlson, Julie, *In the Theatre of Romanticism: Coleridge, Nationalism, Women* (Cambridge University Press, 1994).

Ellison, Julie, *Delicate Subjects: Romanticism, Gender, and the Ethics of Understanding* (Ithaca, NY: Cornell University Press, 1990).

Fulford, Tim, *Romanticism and Masculinity: Gender, Politics and Poetics in the Writings of Burke, Coleridge, Cobbett, Wordsworth, De Quincey and Hazlitt* (London: Macmillan Press, 1999).

Harding, Anthony, *Coleridge and the Idea of Love: Aspects of Relationship in Coleridge's Thought and Writing* (Cambridge University Press, 1974).

Hofkosh, Sonia, 'A Woman's Profession: Sexual Difference and the Romance of Authorship', *Studies in Romanticism*, 32, 2 (Summer 1993), 245–72.

Sexual Politics and the Romantic Author (Cambridge University Press, 1998).

Jackson, H. J., 'Coleridge's Women, or Girls, Girls, Girls Are Made to Love', *Studies in Romanticism*, 32, 4 (Winter 1993), 577–600.

Jacobus, Mary, *Romanticism, Writing and Sexual Difference* (Oxford: Clarendon Press, 1989).

Koestenbaum, Wayne, *Double Talk: The Erotics of Male Literary Collaboration* (New York, London: Routledge, 1989).

Lefebure, Molly, *The Bondage of Love: A Life of Mrs Samuel Taylor Coleridge* (New York: Paragon House, 1989).

Mellor, Anne K., *Romanticism and Gender* (New York and London: Routledge, 1993).

Richardson, Alan, 'Romanticism and the Colonization of the Feminine' in Anne Mellor, ed., *Romanticism and Feminism* (Bloomington: Indiana University Press, 1988), 13–15.

Ross, Marlon, *The Contours of Masculine Desire – Romanticism and the Rise of Women's Poetry* (New York: Oxford University Press, 1989).

Rzepka, Charles J., 'Christabel's "Wandering Mother" and the Discourse of the Self: A Lacanian Reading of Repressed Narration', *Romanticism Past and Present*, 10, 1 (Winter 1986), 17–43.

Swann, Karen, '*Christabel*: The Wandering Mother and the Enigma of Form', *Studies in Romanticism*, 23, 4 (Winter 1984), 533–53.

'Literary Gentlemen and Lovely Ladies: The Debate on the Character of Christabel', *English Literary History*, 52, 2 (1985), 397–418.

Taylor, Anya, 'Coleridge, Wollstonecraft, and the Rights of Woman', in Tim Fulford and Morton D. Paley, eds., *Coleridge's Visionary Languages* (Cambridge: D. S. Brewer, 1993), 83–99.

Watson, Jean, 'Coleridge's Androgynous Ideal', *Prose Studies*, 6 (1983), 36–56.

Wolfson, Susan, *Romantic Women Writers: Voices and Countervoices*, ed. Paula R. Feldman and Theresa M. Kelley (Hanover and London: University Press of New England, 1995), 33–68.

14 Symbol

Barth, J. Robert, SJ, *The Symbolic Imagination: Coleridge and the Romantic Tradition* (Princeton University Press, 1977).

Dawson, David, 'Against the Divine Ventriloquist: Coleridge and De Man on Symbol, Allegory, and Scripture', *Literature & Theology: An International Journal of Theory, Criticism and Culture*, 4 (1990), 293–310.

De Man, Paul, 'The Rhetoric of Temporality', in Charles Singleton, ed., *Interpretation: Theory and Practice* (Baltimore: Johns Hopkins University Press, 1969), 173–209.

Emerson, Ralph Waldo, 'Nature', in Joel Porte, ed., *Essays & Lectures* (New York: Library of America, 1983).

Essick, Robert N., 'Coleridge and the Language of Adam', in Frederick Burwick, ed., *Coleridge's Biographia Literaria: Text and Meaning* (Columbus: Ohio State University Press, 1989), 62–74.

Halmi, Nicholas, 'From Hierarchy to Opposition: Allegory and the Sublime', *Comparative Literature*, 4 (Fall 1992).

'How Christian Is the Coleridgean Symbol?' *The Wordsworth Circle*, 26 (1995), 26–30.

Harding, Anthony John, 'Development and Symbol in the Thought of S. T. Coleridge, J. C. Hare, and John Sterling', *Studies in Romanticism*, 18 (1979), 29–48.

Coleridge and the Inspired Word (Montreal and Kingston: McGill-Queen's University Press, 1985).

Kaiser, David Aram, 'The Incarnated Symbol: Coleridge, Hegel, Strauss, and the Higher Biblical Criticism', *European Romantic Review*, 4 (1994), 133–50.

Knights, L. C., 'Idea and Symbol: Some Hints from Coleridge', in K. Coburn, ed., *Coleridge: A Collection of Critical Essays* (Englewood Cliffs, NJ: Prentice-Hall, 1967).

Langer, Susanne K. *Philosophy in a New Key: A Study in the Symbolism of Reason, Rite and Art* (Cambridge, MA: Harvard University Press, 1942).
  Feeling and Form: A Theory of Art (New York: Charles Scribner and Sons, 1953).

McKusick, James C., *Coleridge's Philosophy of Language* (New Haven: Yale University Press, 1986).

Piper, H. W., *The Singing of Mount Abora: Coleridge's Use of Biblical Imagery and Natural Symbolism in Poetry and Philosophy* (Rutherford, NJ: Fairleigh Dickinson Press, 1987).

Prickett, Stephen, *Words and the Word: Language, Poetics, and Biblical Interpretation* (Cambridge University Press, 1986).

Richards, I. A., *Practical Criticism: A Study of Literary Judgment* (London and New York: Harcourt, Brace, 1929).

Schulz, Max, 'Samuel Taylor Coleridge', in Frank Jordan, ed., *The English Romantic Poets: A Review of Research and Criticism* (New York: Modern Language Association, 1985), 341–463.

Swiatecka, M. Jadwiga, *The Idea of the Symbol: Some Nineteenth-Century Comparisons with Coleridge* (Cambridge University Press, 1980).

Thoreau, Henry David, *A Week on the Concord and Merrimack Rivers; Walden; or, Life in the Woods; The Maine Woods; Cape Cod*, ed. Robert F. Sayre (New York: Library of America, 1985).

Tindall, William York, *The Literary Symbol* (Bloomington: Indiana University Press, 1955).

Vlasopolos, Anca, *The Symbolic Method of Coleridge, Baudelaire, and Yeats* (Detroit: Wayne State University Press, 1983).

Warren, Robert Penn, 'A Poem of Pure Imagination: An Experiment in Reading', in *New and Selected Essays* (New York: Random House, 1989), 335–423.

Whitman, Jon, 'From the Textual to the Temporal: Early Christian "Allegory" and Early Romantic "Symbol"' *New Literary History*, 22 (1991), 161–76.

Wilson, Douglas B. 'Two Modes of Apprehending Nature: A Gloss on the Coleridgean Symbol', *Publication of the Modern Language Association of America*, 87 (1972), 42–52.

15 Coleridge's afterlife

Allen, Peter, *The Cambridge Apostles, The Early Years* (Cambridge University Press, 1978).

Arnold, Matthew, 'Joubert', in R. H. Super, ed., *Complete Prose Works*, 11 vols. (Ann Arbor: University of Michigan Press, 1960–77), III, 183–211.
  'A Comment on Christmas' (1885), in R. H. Super, ed., *Complete Prose Works*, 11 vols. (Ann Arbor: University of Michigan Press, 1960–77), X, 218–38.

Beer, John, *Coleridge's Poetic Intelligence* (London: Macmillan, 1977).
  Romantic Influences: Contemporary – Victorian – Modern (London: Macmillan, 1995).

Carlyle, Thomas, *Life of John Sterling* (London: Chapman and Hall, 1851), Pt 1, ch. 8, 69–80.

De Quincey, Thomas, 'Samuel Taylor Coleridge', *Tait's Edinburgh Magazine*, n.s. 1 (1834), 509–20, 588–96, 685–90: n.s. 2 (1835), 2–10.

Eliot, George, *Westminster Review*, n.s. 1 (Jan. 1852), 249–50.

Hallam, Arthur Henry, *Writings*, ed. T. H. Vail Motter (London: Oxford University Press, 1943).

Hare, Augustus J. C., *Memorials of a Quiet Life*, 2 vols. (London: Strahan and Co., 1873).

Hughes, Ted, *Winter Pollen* (London: Faber and Faber, 1995).

Hodgson, Shadworth, *The Philosophy of Reflection*, 2 vols. (London: 1878).

Ingleby, C. M., 'On some Points concerned with the Philosophy of Coleridge', *Transactions of the Royal Society of Literature*, 2nd series 9 (1870), 396–433.

Lawrence, D. H., *Phoenix*, ed. E. D. McDonald (London: William Heinemann, 1936). 'The Reality of Peace' (1917), in Michael Herbert, ed., *Reflections on the Death of a Porcupine* (Cambridge University Press, 1988), 25–52.

McFarland, Thomas, *Coleridge and the Pantheist Tradition* (Oxford: Clarendon Press, 1969), chs. 3 and 4.

Mill, John Stuart, 'Coleridge', *London and Westminster Review* (March 1840), 33, 257–302.

  Mill on Bentham and Coleridge, ed. F. R. Leavis (London: Chatto and Windus, 1950).

Pater, Walter, *Westminster Review*, n.s. 29 (1866), 106–32.

Stanley, A. P., *Life and Correspondence of Thomas Arnold*, 2 vols. (London: B. Fellowes, 1844).

Sterling, John, *Essays and Tales*, 2 vols. (London: John W. Parker, 1848).

Woolf, Virginia, 'Modern Fiction', *The Common Reader* (London: L. and V. Woolf, 1925).

INDEX